SOURCES OF LAW

Second Edition

AUSTRALIA

LBC Information Services
Sydney

CANADA AND the USA

Carswell

NEW ZEALAND

Brooker's
Wellington

SINGAPORE AND MALAYSIA

Thomson Information (S.E. Asia)
Singapore

Sources of Law

AN INTRODUCTION TO LEGAL RESEARCH AND WRITING

Second Edition

THOMAS O'MALLEY, MA, LLM, BL

Faculty of Law, NUI, Galway

DUBLIN
ROUND HALL SWEET & MAXWELL
2001

Published in 2001 by
Round Hall Ltd
43 Fitzwilliam Place
Dublin 2

Typeset by
Gough Typesetting Services
Dublin

Printed by
ColourBooks, Dublin

ISBN 1-85800-185-4

A catalogue record for this book
is available from the British Library.

Preface

This second edition of *Sources of Law* has the same objective as the first: to introduce students to the primary and secondary sources of law, and to equip them with basic research skills. The main focus is on Irish, British, European and international law, although there are also chapters on American and Commonwealth law much of which is now easily accessible on the Internet. The book was originally developed as a student text, but because practitioners have occasionally found it useful as well, some new material has been added for their benefit. For example, the practitioner's guide to the sources of European Human Rights Law in Appendix 7 has been included to facilitate those lawyers who will have to become familiar with that branch of law once the European Convention on Human Rights is incorporated into Irish law.

When Sir Robert Megarry first published his *Manual of the Law of Real Property*, his stated aim was to help "the examination candidate whose main anxiety is not whether he will head the list but whether he will appear in it at all". The present book cannot even guarantee an appearance in the list. But it will hopefully eliminate some of the confusion understandably felt by students as they as they try to become familiar with legal sources, something they must generally do quite quickly once they embark on the study of law. Today's law students, of course, must be able to use the so-called virtual libraries as well as real libraries. However, familiarity with conventional paper sources is still essential, both for their own intrinsic value and in order to make sense of the various electronic databases.

I would like to reiterate my thanks to those who helped with the first edition. The research for the present edition was carried out in the libraries of NUI, Galway, the Honorable Society of King's Inns (Dublin) and the University of Oxford. I am much indebted to the staff of all three libraries. As always, I am indebted to Thèrése Carrick and her colleagues at Round Hall Sweet and Maxwel, for their patience and assistance.

Tom O'Malley
Galway.

June 2001

Table of contents

CHAPTER 1

Legal Documentation

1.01 The resurgence in Irish legal publishing during the past twenty years or so is routinely, indeed ritualistically, acknowledged and welcomed by book reviewers and other writers. Certainly, the number of law books and periodicals now being published is phenomenal, especially when compared with the remarkably low output during the first 50 years or so after the foundation of the State in 1922. But, as a study of certain superior court judgments delivered during that period will reveal, it would be a serious mistake to assume that the dearth of published work reflected a want of scholarship. Take, for example, the judgments delivered in *O'Byrne v. The Minister for Finance* [1959] I.R. 1 which dealt with the constitutionality of subjecting judicial salaries to income tax. These judgments delve deep into historical and comparative legal sources ranging from the Commonwealth of Australia Act 1900 to the *Federalist Papers*, and firmly belie any suggestion that the dearth of native legal publishing at the time automatically impoverished the quality of jurisprudence. The problem, of course, was that this learning was shared and transmitted largely on an oral level and was seldom committed to writing except in reserved judgments such as those in *O'Byrne*. Another drawback was that this and many other significant judgments dating from the same period were subjected to little or no contemporaneous analysis. Part of the problem was there were few full-time academic lawyers. Until the mid-1970s when full-time law professorships and lectureships were established in the various universities, law faculties were staffed mainly by part-time lecturers who combined teaching with practice. The appointment of full-time academic lawyers created a new intellectual environment that facilitated legal research and publication. Academic lawyers cannot, of course, take all the credit for the upsurge in publishing. Many leading texts have been produced, especially in recent years, by judges and practitioners, a trend that will hopefully continue.

PRIMARY SOURCES OF LAW

1.02 Aside from the Constitution, the primary sources of domestic law are legislation, which includes statutes and statutory instruments, and law reports. Irish lawyers and law students generally need access not only to those statutes enacted by the Oireachtas since 1922, but also to statutes made at Westminster and applied to Ireland between 1801, when the Act of Union came into force, and 1922. Indeed, there are also some pre-1800 statutes still in force, of which the Statute of Frauds (Ireland) 1695 would be a prime example. Recent law reform has resulted in the repeal of several pre-1922 statutes, but many others, in amended form at least, remain part of our law. Access to the law can sometimes be problematic as a result. Take, for example, the Larceny Act 1916 which, at the time of writing is still in force, although due for repeal in the near future. The Irish government publications service does not stock this Act because it predates the foundation of the State. Neither can it be had from any of the British or Northern Ireland government publications agencies, because it was repealed in its entirety in the U.K. in 1968. One must therefore rely on library copies or on a reproduction of the Act in a collection of legislation.[1]

1.03 All Acts of the Oireachtas are reasonably accessible, both in hard copy and electronic form (see 4.18 and 4.30 below). Paper-based services for investigating and updating legislation have been less than satisfactory, particularly during the past twenty years or so. Legal researchers must be able to discover the statute law on a particular topic and, having identified the primary statute, must be able to trace any subsequent repeals or amendments. They must also be able to identify any reported or unreported cases in which relevant sections of a statute have been interpreted or discussed. Up until the mid-1980s, comprehensive indexes to the Acts of the Oireachtas were periodically produced, with subject indexes as well as tables of repeals and amendments. However, the most recent bound volume, covering the years 1922 to 1995 has no subject index, although it is otherwise very valuable for its annual lists of statutes, tables of amendments and so forth (see 4.31 below). The CD and Internet versions of the Statutes for 1922 to 1998, by virtue of being searchable, compensate partly, but not entirely, for this deficiency. But there is much to be said for a professionally compiled subject index, especially one that takes account of repeals and amendments. The electronic versions of the statutes are unrevised which renders research rather cumbersome to say the least.

1.04 The Oireachtas web site now contains the texts of statutes enacted since 1997 including very recent ones (4.30, below). These can be printed off in "pdf" format, which means that they can be reproduced more or less exactly as they were originally printed. The relevant Oireachtas debates can be conveniently accessed through the same web site. Another commendable feature of this site is that it provides both the Irish and English texts of some statutes. This is a distinct improvement on the situation that has prevailed since the early 1980s when the Government, in clear disregard of Article 25.4.4 of the Constitution, simply stopped producing bilingual versions of the statutes. Article 25 provides

---

[1] Thankfully, McCutcheon's *Larceny Act 1916* (Dublin: The Round Hall Press, 1988) includes a revised text of the Act with a detailed commentary. Amendments since 1988 are easily traced.

that when a Bill is signed by the President in one official language, an official translation shall be issued in the other. Indeed, the Supreme Court has recently reiterated the Government's obligation under this constitutional provision. The situation with statutory instruments is, of course, a great deal worse; they have been produced in one language only, almost invariably English, since 1974. Users have sometimes had to resort to litigation to force the Government to provide Irish versions of relevant instruments and associated standard forms. The cost of providing official translations of all legislation is, of course, significant, but without them it is difficult to see how citizens can exercise their right to conduct litigation and other official business through the medium of Irish.

1.05 Modern statutory instruments pose the same research difficulties as statutes. The absence of a current subject index makes research difficult, although again compensated for to some extent by the electronic versions of the instruments from 1922 to 1998 and 2000. Humphreys' *Index to Irish Statutory Instruments* (Dublin, Butterworths, 1988) in three volumes is an excellent reference service for statutory instruments up until the end of 1986. Since then, one must rely on a variety of sources, including the various indexes published by the Government, but none of them really compensate for a consolidated index such as Humphreys'.

Law reporting

1.06 Accuracy, currency and comprehensiveness are the hallmarks of good law reporting. Irish law reports have a good reputation for accuracy, but the same cannot be said of their currency, less still of their comprehensiveness. As will be outlined in more detail in Chapter 4, published law reports contain no more than a small proportion of the decisions handed down by the courts in any one year. The general law report series[2] are devoted almost exclusively to reserved judgments of the superior courts namely, the High Court, Court of Criminal Appeal and Supreme Court. Many reserved judgments and, of course, many *ex tempore* judgments such as those of the Court of Criminal Appeal, are never formally reported. Law report editors usually select those judgments which develop or deal with an important point of law, or illustrate the application of a particular rule, or arise from an unusual set of facts. Other reserved judgments remain unreported in typescript form. LEXIS carries Irish unreported judgments since 1985, although it is not as comprehensive in this respect as it might be. Most are now becoming available on the Internet (www.bailii.org), although only for very recent years.

1.07 The *Irish Reports* now appear in four volumes a year, compared with one volume until 1989. They are well edited and well produced, and often contain

---

[2] On the classification of law reports, see 4.51 *et seq.* below.

a summary of the arguments of counsel as well as the usual headnotes, lists of authorities cited and so forth. Unfortunately, they tend to appear a year or more in arrears, although the pace of production appears to have improved considerably in recent years. The *Irish Law Reports Monthly* appear in 14 parts and two annual volumes a year, and so are usually the first to carry recent judgments. They, too, are well edited, but do not include summaries of the arguments of counsel. The *Employment Law Reports* are also reasonably current, although confined entirely to tribunal and judicial decisions on labour law matters.

1.08   District Court decisions are very seldom reported. It is, after all, a court of summary jurisdiction, so reserved judgments are rare. The situation with the Circuit Court is rather more serious, in view of its extensive jurisdiction in many core areas of law including contract, tort, family law, landlord and tenant law, and criminal law. Few reserved judgments emerge from this court, and fewer still are formally reported. This is unfortunate, particularly as, in former times, Circuit Court judgments were routinely reported in the *Irish Law Times Reports* and the *Irish Jurist Reports* (4.52 and 4.53 below). It must be recorded, however, that, after a lull of many years, written Circuit Court judgments are now appearing again, and some are being reported. The *Irish Law Times*, since it adopted its present format some years ago, usually carries one or more Circuit Court judgments in each issue. The *Irish Law Reports Monthly* series is also willing to publish Circuit Court judgments. For example, it recently published the judgment of McMahon J in *Curran v. Cadbury (Ireland) Ltd* [2000] 2 I.L.R.M. 343.

1.09   The Court of Criminal Appeal is generally badly served by all the law reports series. Historically, of course, it has been very well served by the three volumes of Frewen (4.57 below), but they end with the year 1989. Any further volumes are likely to be many years in arrears. The Court of Criminal Appeal is ordinarily the highest appeal court in criminal matters. In the recent past, it has issued many important judgments in relation to sentencing, and will hopefully continue to do so, but most of them remain largely unknown because of the absence of a regular reporting system. Unfortunately, some of the electronic sources are as deficient as their print counterparts in this respect. There is a case to be made for a specialist series of criminal appeal reports, possibly sponsored by the Courts Service or other official agency in light of the limited commercial demand for such a series in a small jurisdiction. Demand should not be the sole consideration when it comes to assessing the need for a law reporting service.

FINDING THE LAW

1.10   Irish case law is considerably more difficult than English case law to research. There is no Irish equivalent of *The Digest* or, for that matter, of the *Red Index* (which indexes English law reports since 1951; see 6.40 below). Instead we must rely on a variety of sources no one of which is entirely satisfactory. It is most unfortunate that there has never been either a case index or subject index to the *Irish Reports*, though it is worth noting that the *Irish Law Reports Monthly* series includes various cumulative and annual indexes. There are, admittedly, some services which compensate to a degree for the absence of comprehensive case law indexes. The various *Irish Digests* (described at 4.69 *et seq.* below) which appear periodically cover the main published law reports including the *Northern Ireland Law Reports*. They do not, however, digest the many judgments that remain unreported. The so-called Red, Green and Blue Indexes (4.73 below) list cases reported from 1966 to 1989. The *Irish Current Law* service, begun in 1995, includes both a monthly digest and a yearbook (4.79 below). However, it is not as comprehensive as its English counterpart. Its coverage of Court of Criminal Appeal judgments is generally rather patchy, and it seldom, if ever, picks up significant newspaper reports of cases. The *Annual Review of Irish Law*, which began with the year 1987 and now appears a year or 15 months in arrears (a good record for an annual review), is remarkably comprehensive and covers most written and many *ex tempore* judgments for the year under review. Overall, it is an excellent service, both for the breadth of coverage and depth of analysis. Finally, some of the electronic services, expensive though they may be, are very useful for research purposes. This is particularly true of LEXIS (2.15 *et seq.* below) for case law since 1950 and the recently-released CD version of the *Irish Reports* from 1919 onwards.

1.11   It is easy, of course, to be critical about the state of our indexing and digesting systems. The problem is not uncommon in a small jurisdiction such as Ireland where the demand for such services was historically quite limited and the production of which would scarcely have been viable without state subvention. But, as we embark on a new century in a state of unprecedented economic prosperity, the idea of producing a centennial digest in either print or electronic form, drawing together the case law of the twentieth century is worthy of serious consideration. With the advanced technology and the resources now available, it should be possible to draw up a cumulative edition of the various digests and indexes published from 1900 to 2000, including as much unreported case law as possible from all available resources. One need not dwell on the advantages of such a service for everyone engaged in legal research, whether for practical or academic purposes.

ELECTRONIC SOURCES

1.12   There is a story told of the eighteenth-century Irish lawyer, John Philpot Curran, who rose from a humble background to become one of the great advocates of his time and, later, Master of the Rolls in Ireland. Once as a young barrister, he found himself arguing a case before Judge Robinson who was not, by all accounts, the most patient or tactful of judges. Curran claimed that having consulted all his law books, he could find no authority to support the propositions advanced by the other side. "I expect", said Judge Robinson, "that your law library is rather contracted", in an apparent reference to Curran's straightened circumstances. Curran's reply, though spontaneous, was, as ever, a model of eloquence. Having acknowledged his lack of wealth, he said: "I have prepared myself for this high profession rather by the study of a few good books than by the composition of a great many bad ones". He then made some pointed remarks about wealth and poverty, which probably had a chastening effect on the judge. (The full story is told by James Comyn in *Irish at Law* (London, 1983) p.27). Today, a lawyer responding to a similar judicial remark, might say, "I have hardly any books, My Lord, but I do have access to the Internet". The advent of the World Wide Web, one of the main services offered by the Internet, has resulted in hundreds of millions of people, lawyers included, having access to vast amounts of primary and secondary legal literature. In this sense, the Internet has begun to democratise the law, a process that looks set to continue, as more and more legal literature becomes freely available on the Web. Yet, even in this electronic age, Curran's remark about a few good books being preferable to a multitude of bad ones remains valid, and all the more so when applied to electronic materials. The World Wide Web is still in its infancy and its future direction is difficult to predict. Right now it is a valuable resource, although marred by the lack of any central quality control. First-time users are faced with a bewildering array of web sites, many of them offering the same information, and many others offering information of little practical use. But, barring a catastrophe, it is here to stay, and all the indications are that the lawyers and law students of the future will look first to the Internet for modern law and, in time perhaps, for older law as well. The Web, in that well-worn phrase, brings opportunities as well as challenges. It will provide unrivalled opportunities to receive and transmit information and documentation, as it becomes available. Those with limited access to conventional sources such as books, journals and law reports, will no longer be at a major disadvantage compared with those of their colleagues who enjoy access to well-stocked libraries. The challenges will be to bring order to the Web, an exercise that has already begun with indexed search engines, and to devise conventions and strategies for the prudent and effective use of material extracted from it.

1.13   As noted earlier, the political branches of government have reacted well to the opportunities afforded by the Internet, especially in terms of providing access to legislation, parliamentary debates, policy documents and other material. The years ahead will hopefully witness similar moves from the courts system. Indeed, the establishment of the new Courts Service has provided the administrative framework for the systematic electronic publication of judgments.

Already some judgments are published on the Bailii web site (2.14 below). Ideally, every reserved judgment, since it is likely to be produced on a word processor in the first place, should be placed on the Internet, using a neutral citation system (3.30 *et seq.* below). The practice of reading out judgments may be a hallowed tradition, but is scarcely necessary any more. As in some other jurisdictions, judgments could as easily be posted on the courts' web site, with hard copies, if needed, made available to the parties. Modern technology allows for many other reforms as well. It would be surprising, for example, if, in the years ahead, civil procedure were not reformed and simplified by allowing for the electronic transfer of documents, both between parties and between the parties and the courts.

RESEARCH TOOLS: A BRIEF SUMMARY

Statutes

1.14 To make effective use of statutory material, one must be able (a) to locate the texts of statutes; (b) to find statutes relevant to a particular topic; (c) to discover if a statute is in force; and (d) to discover if a statutory provision has been repealed, amended or judicially interpreted.

Texts

1.15 In most jurisdictions, including Ireland, Government agencies publish statutes individually and in bound annual volumes. Bills, whether or not eventually enacted, are published individually. The texts of statutes may also be published commercially with or without annotations. Such series include the *Irish Current Law Statutes Annotated* and, in England, *Halsbury's Statutes.* Annotated statutes are most helpful, but when drawing on a statutory text for any official purpose, it is always advisable to consult the official version just in case there has been a transcription error.

Indexes

1.16 An index will usually list statutes in two or three ways, e.g. in chronological order, by title in alphabetical order and, perhaps, by subject matter in alphabetical order. The subject index usually directs the reader to the statutory material on a particular topic. A chronological index is particularly helpful in a jurisdiction in which statutes are cited primarily by year and number. In the United Kingdom, for example, statutes used to be cited by regnal year and number, a system explained at 3.38 below.

Operational dates

1.17 Some jurisdictions are better served than others in terms of the availability of information services in regard to the dates on which statutes, or sections of them, have come into force. The services available in Britain are described in Chapter 5. In Ireland, one should first consult the statute itself to discover the arrangements for bringing it into force. This information is usually contained in the first or last section. Since 1984, the *Irish Current Law Statutes Annotated* have provided information on commencement dates as a standard feature of the annotations. However, the annotations are usually completed within a short time of the passage of the Act. Therefore, if a statute is expressed to come into force on a date or dates to be decided by the relevant Minister, one must check through the statutory instruments or the indexes to them for the relevant information. The citator service in *Irish Current Law Statutes Annotated* is also useful for this purpose.

Statute citators

1.18 The purpose of a statute or legislation citator is to indicate the manner in which statutes (and statutory instruments in the case of legislation citators) have been amended, repealed and judicially interpreted. They are generally arranged chronologically in accordance with the dates of the statutes affected. As already noted, there is now a citator service included with the *Irish Current Law Statutes Annotated*, but it has existed only since 1984. However, it describes amendments to all earlier statutes effected since the beginning of 1993. This must be used in conjunction with the Index to the Statutes (see 4.31 below).

Case law

1.19 The skills required for effective use of case law are very similar to those governing the use of statutes. One must be able to find (a) the texts of law reports; (b) reports relevant to a particular topic; (c) the sources of reports for which one has the names of the parties, but not the year or citation; and (d) the manner in which a judicial decision or interpretation has been treated by later courts.

Texts

1.20 As in the case of statutes, law reports are usually available in official or quasi-official series (such as the *Irish Reports*) and in commercially-produced series (such as the *Irish Law Reports Monthly*). Those published in official series are to be preferred. Courts usually demand than an official series be cited in preference to an unofficial one. Moreover, the judgments appearing in official series are sometimes checked in advance of publication by the courts in which they were handed down. Commercially-published series are often quicker to appear and may have helpful references to other publications. The *All England Law Reports*, for example, have cross-references to *Halsbury's Laws of England* and to *The Digest*. There are also many series of specialist law reports, more often than not commercially produced, in areas such as labour law and family law, which are convenient for practitioners and students specialising in a particular area and which often include judgments and decisions not published elsewhere.

Digests

1.21   The function of a digest is to provide a short summary of cases arranged by subject matter. The subject headings are usually broad, although there are usually sub-divisions as well. The various Irish digests are described at 4.70 below. When using a digest it is important to check the sources from which it is derived. Some digests, including the Irish ones, deal only with reported cases, and even then cases reported in certain report series. This makes them less reliable in a jurisdiction, such as Ireland, in which many cases remain unreported.

Indexes

1.22   To find the citation of case (meaning the report series, the year or volume number, and initial page number), one must consult a general index that lists cases in alphabetical order. Many law report series have their own indexes covering several years or decades. For English cases one can consult the most recent case index of *The Digest* (see 6.43 below) or, if that is not available, the case index to *Halsbury's Laws of England* is often a good substitute. If the case is an English one which has been decided within the past 50 years or so, consult the *Red Index* to the *Law Reports* (see 6.40 below). Unfortunately, there is no one index to Irish cases since 1922. One must consult the various *Irish Digests* for the period since then, and more recently, the *Annual Review of Irish Law* since 1987 or *Irish Current Law* since 1995. For pre-1922 cases, consult the older *Irish Digests* or *The Digest*, preferably an older edition when it was known as *The English and Empire Digest*.

Citators

1.23   A case citator describes how a case has been treated in later decisions and judgments, e.g. if it has been applied, distinguished, approved or overruled. It may also indicate journal articles written about a case. The English citator system is described at 6.48 below. Unfortunately, there is no Irish case citator, but the various *Irish Digests* can be used to serve this purpose indirectly, though only, of course, in respect of those reported cases which they contain.

CHAPTER 2

Electronic Sources Of Law

2.01 Recent developments in information technology have been compared with the industrial revolution in terms of their social and economic impact, and all the indications are that this comparison is justified. Right now it is difficult to predict how completely electronic sources of information will eventually replace paper sources, but already few lawyers or law students can afford to ignore the various electronic services available. The main Internet, compact disk (CD) and online subscription services will be described in some detail in later chapters of this book. The purpose of this chapter is to provide a general map of these services and, in particular, to introduce the reader to the Internet, assuming that any such introduction is still necessary. The costs of these services vary enormously. At one extreme, the Internet provides masses of information largely free of charge, apart from the rather modest start-up and connection charges. At the other, there are several subscription services such as LEXIS, Westlaw and various CD-based sources, which tend to be quite expensive, although they are generally more comprehensive and reliable than the Internet web sites. For the individual office-based user, web-based or online services have the advantage of being continuously updated without any effort from the user. CDs, on the other hand, usually have to be replaced, sometimes quite frequently, if the user is to remain up to date. Universities and similar institutions are usually licensed to place CDs on central servers under the supervision of professional library staff, so users can generally be confident of having access to the most recent version. Most of the web sites described here are freely available. There are also however, several subscription services available. Among the leading subscription databases are those in the JUSTIS series published by Context Ltd, London. See their site at www.justis.com. Their electronic version of the *Irish Reports* is described at 3.28 below.

THE INTERNET

2.02 Although the Internet rarely impinged on most of our lives before the mid-1990s, the concept on which it is based was developed over 30 years ago when an American scientist linked two computers together so as to enable data to be transferred between them. The Internet as it exists today is really no more than a massive extension of that original experiment. The data now accessible through the Internet is not stored on any one computer. It is stored on a large number of computers located in different parts of the world but linked together in such a way that a subscriber to an Internet service can be connected, sometimes within seconds, to whichever computer holds the data being sought. For example, when a subscriber in Ireland gains access to a web site containing judgments of the United States Supreme Court, the chances are that he or she has been connected to a computer at Cornell University in New York State. The World Wide Web was developed in 1990 by Tim Berners-Lee, a computer scientist at CERN, the European Centre for Particle Physics.

The World Wide Web (WWW)

2.03   The Internet consists of several different services including electronic mail (e-mail), the World Wide Web, newsgroups of various kinds and Telnet. Here we shall concentrate on the World Wide Web, the Web for short, which is the main source of primary and secondary legal materials on the Internet. At the outset, however, it bears saying that while the Web has greatly facilitated access to certain legal materials, it has not yet brought about any significant changes in the structure and content of the materials themselves. Statutes are still being drafted and judgments written as they always were (though as we shall see in Chapter 3, some changes are being introduced in relation to citation conventions). It is just that instead of having to track them down in the printed volumes of statutes and law reports, we can read them on our computer screens. Most of us, if we are to be honest, usually print them off as well, which puts paid to the idea of technology producing paperless offices. Richard Susskind, a leading expert on legal information technology, has drawn a distinction between automation and innovation in the structure and transmission on legal information.[1] Until now, as he says, the emphasis has been on automation – making conventional legal sources available electronically. More innovative systems may be developed in the future, possibly through the adoption of problem-centred approaches. For example, a subscriber may be able to enter a question such as, "how do I make a will?", and receive advice and instructions as well as the relevant legislation, case law and precedents. This will not necessarily render lawyers redundant. In fact, it has often been said that the lay testator, because of his propensity to make mistakes, is the lawyer's best friend![2]

2.04   It should also be remembered that the Internet is free in more ways than one. From a user's point of view the main financial advantage is that once the connection fee, if any, is paid, vast amounts of information can be obtained for the cost of local phone call. But the Internet is also free in the sense that anyone

---

[1]   Susskind, *The Future of Law: Facing the Challenges of Information Technology* (Oxford: Clarendon Press, 1998).
[2]   See Mongey, *The Weird and Wonderful World of Wills* (Dublin: Fort Publications, 1997), p. 38 for an amusing piece of doggerel on the topic.

can construct their own web site, at little or no cost, and make it available to all and sundry. In such an environment, quality control is extremely difficult. As a result, browsing through the Internet, unless being done as a leisure activity, can be a monumental waste of time. The vast majority of web sites are of little interest to anyone other than their creators. Those using the Web for research purposes, therefore, are well advised to spend some time investigating and bookmarking (see 2.11 below) the most useful legal information sites. This, admittedly, will involve a certain amount of browsing at the outset, but it will be time well spent.

2.05 Finally, it should be noted that in contrast to LEXIS and Westlaw, the legal resources available on the Internet are currently quite limited. Statutes and law reports from several countries are now available on the Web, but seldom go back further than the mid- to late 1990s, though improvements are being made all the time. In Britain, for example, all the statutes since 1988 are available on the web, as are judgments of the superior courts for the past four years or so (see Chapter 6 below). One American web site provides all U.S. Supreme Court judgments since 1893, but that is the exception rather the rule. However, if present tends continue, many jurisdictions are likely to backdate the amount of legal material available on the Web. Ireland, in fact, has set a good example by placing all the statutes and statutory instruments from 1922 to 1998 on the Attorney General's web site, as well as producing them on CD-ROM. Hopefully, they will be updated regularly from now on.

Locating material on the Web: (1) URLs.

2.06 Someone who visits a law library seeking information on a particular topic may have a citation for a specific source such as an article. He may know, for example, that there is an article on international sales in volume 105 of the *Law Quarterly Review*, beginning at page 201. Alternatively, he may know that there is article on the topic in some volume of that journal, or he may be hoping to find one or more articles in some available journal. In that case, he will have to consult a subject index to the *Law Quarterly Review* or a general index to legal periodicals, as the case may be. Likewise, when searching for material on the Web, one may have a specific address, which is much the same as having the exact citation for a law review article. Alternatively, one may have to search for relevant material using one of the search engines on the Internet, which is roughly equivalent to searching through an index of legal periodicals. Obviously, the quickest way of finding material is to enter the exact address if it is to hand.

2.07 Every Web page has its own address, known as a URL (uniform resource locator). The URL is entered in the window near the top of the screen. As a rule, any existing URL will automatically delete itself as soon as the user begins typing a new one. If it does not, it can simply be blocked and deleted. A typical URL (that for *The Irish Times,* as it happens) would be: http:// www.ireland.com. The first part of the address, "http", stands for hypertext transfer protocol, which is the main system through which information is transferred over the Web. Nowadays it is seldom necessary to include this in a URL as it will automatically be presumed. The second element, "www" obviously stands for World Wide Web, while the remainder leads to the particular site. The last element usually indicates a country, such as "ie" (for Ireland) or "uk". Sometimes, it indicates some kind of organisation such as "co" or "com" for company, "org" for organisation, "edu" or "ac" for an educational institution, or "net" for network. Non-geographical codes are particularly prominent in the United States to which the Internet, at one time, was largely confined. For instance, the U.S. address of Amazon, the leading online bookseller is www.amazon.com/ while its U.K. address is www.amazon.co.uk/. The middle part of the URL is the name of the host server, usually an organisation or service of some description. For example, www.irlgov.ie is the Irish Government web site, just as www.findlaw.com is for Findlaw, the leading US legal web site. A host name may have more than one component, and there may also be a file name at the end. Take the following URL:

www.lib.ed.ac.uk/lib/howto/bhi.shtml

The primary host server is "ed.ac.uk/" which stands for the University of Edinburgh. However, it also identifies a particular section within the University, namely the library, "lib". The part after "uk/" identifies a particular file, "lib/ howto/bhi" which happens to be a library document giving advice on how to use the *British Humanities Index* (see 7.46 below). The very last element of such addresses, "shtml" in this case, simply indicates the language in which the file is formatted, a matter that need not worry us here.

Locating material on the Web: (2) search engines

2.08　One problem with using URLs, assuming one can find and remember them, is that they must be entered with absolute accurately. One letter, stop or dash out of place, and the URL, which will be incorrect as a result, will fail to locate the desired document. For this reason, it is often necessary to resort to the other main research strategy, the search engine. The leading search engines are Google (www.google.com), Alta Vista (www.altavista.com), Lycos (www.lycos.com), Excite (www.excite.com) and Yahoo! (www.yahoo.com). Typically a search engine will have a query function, a blank window in which a query, in the form of a word or phrase, can be typed, e.g. "jury" or "fair trial". One then presses the return key on the keyboard or clicks on "Go" on the screen. With luck, the engine will retrieve several relevant documents that can be viewed by clicking on the titles that appear on the screen in hypertext (see 2.10 below). None of the search engines can claim to be fully comprehensive. There are millions of pages on the Internet and only a small fraction of them are tracked by any one engine. Of the general search engines just mentioned, Google is particularly good, even if the name is unfortunate! Like some other engines, it uses Boolean notation very effectively. This simply means joining search terms using plus and minus signs. Thus, if one wanted to find web sites on, say, judicial independence (on which there are many excellent sites, as it happens), one would type in the search box "judicial + independence". This will retrieve documents in which both words appear. Otherwise, by entering just "judicial independence", one would probably retrieve many irrelevant documents containing the words "judicial" or "independence", but not both. It also allows for search by specified domain, e.g., uk, ie, int or ac.

Yahoo

2.09   For legal research, the best engine by far is Yahoo which is essentially an indexing facility. Its law pages are simply superb, as they provide legal sources from all over the common law world and elsewhere. When you enter the Yahoo homepage, click first on "Government", then on "Law". This, in turn, will retrieve a list of topics reproduced in figure 2 below. Many of the sites deal exclusively, or almost so, with United States law. Thus "Supreme Court and Judiciary" is about the U.S. Supreme Court (see 11.10 below). However, by clicking on "Countries", one will retrieve a long list of countries including Ireland, the United Kingdom, Canada, Australia and New Zealand which, in addition to the United States, are likely to be of most interest to Irish and British researchers. Australia is particularly worthy of investigation because of the outstanding Australian Legal Institute service (www.austlii.edu.au), widely acknowledged as one of the best legal sites in the world. It was on this that the recently developed British and Irish legal web site (www.bailii.org) was modelled. Every law student would therefore be well advised to spend some time browsing through the law pages of Yahoo in order to become acquainted with the wide range of law materials on offer.

Hypertext and navigation

2.10   Hypertext is a facility that allows the user to go from one document to another by means of a link built into the first document. The reader of a Web document will notice that often certain words or titles are printed in bold text or in a different colour or underlined. By clicking on that word or title, one is automatically brought to another title. Take, for example, the following (fictitious) passage:

> Further protection for the spouses and children of deceased property owners was provided by the *Succession Act, 1965* which introduced a legal right share for surviving spouses and …..

The text of the Succession Act 1965 is available on the Web (on the Attorney General's web site). By clicking on the underlined words in the above passage, one would be brought automatically to the text of that Act. To use this effectively, one must be able to navigate the Web, which is a fairly simple matter. For instance, in the above example, if one went to the Succession Act and then wished to return to the original document, one would simply click on the "back" button, usually a backward-looking arrow on the tool bar. Beside it is a forward-looking arrow which is the "forward" button. One can navigate backwards and forward through a series of documents by clicking repeatedly on these buttons.

Bookmarking (or "favourites")

2.11   Bookmarks or favourites are another great facility on the Web. Both words refer to the same facility, except that Microsoft uses "favourites" while Netscape uses "bookmarks". Essentially, this facility allows individual users to build up their own personal collection of favourite web sites. Once you enter a particular site as a favourite, you need never remember the URL or rely on a search engine again. Suppose, for example, you have accessed Findlaw (www.findlaw.com), using the URL. This site can be bookmarked by going through the following procedure. While Findlaw is on the screen, click on "Bookmark" or "Favourite" at the very top of the screen over the toolbar. A window will drop down which will include the command "Add to favourites" or "Add to bookmarks" as the case may be. By simply clicking on these words (and answering any further questions that may appear as a result), you automatically save Findlaw as a favourite. The next time you need to consult this site, just click on "Bookmark" or "Favourites", and Findlaw will be there on the list. You then highlight it by scrolling down to it, press the return key on the keyboard, and it will appear on the screen.

Keeping up to date with legal web sites

2.12   Because the Web is still comparatively new, and because new sites are added by the day, it is difficult to keep abreast of new sites in any area or discipline, law included. No doubt, something equivalent to the *Index to Legal Periodicals and Books* will eventually appear giving a detailed index of available material. For the present, one must rely primarily on the Web itself for information about its contents, and a good search engine such as Google is usually the best way of retrieving material by subject. Certain portals, such as those mentioned in para. 2.14 are also a useful way of discovering relevant material. Sites such as JURIST (www.jurist.law.pitt.edu/) are also useful sources of information about law sites, as is Irish Law. A more extensive list of such sites is given in Appendix 7 of this book. Each Tuesday, *The Times* (London) carries a law supplement which often includes a column by Richard Susskind or other expert on information technology describing recent developments.

Books describing the Internet

2.13   As a visit to any reasonably large bookshop will reveal, there are dozens
of guides to the Internet, most of them claiming to be the "ultimate" or, better
still, the "idiot's" guide. Angus J Kennedy's *The Internet and World Wide Web,*
in the Rough Guide series, must rank as one of the best. It describes Internet
services clearly and gives a good list of useful or popular sites. New editions
now seem to be published annually. The best book aimed specifically at lawyers
is McGuinness and Short, *Research on the Net* (London: Old Bailey Press,
1998). The chapter devoted to law sites on the Web is particularly good, and
there are also chapters on accountancy, business, health and science, humanities and world politics. Gross's *Pocket Tour of Law on the Internet* (San Fran-
cisco: Sybex, 1995) is useful, though it should be remembered that the Web is
developing all the time, and URLs change. Holmes and Venables' *Researching
the Legal Web* 2nd edn (London: Butterworths, 1999) is excellent but, at £45 for
a paperback, is overpriced. We may forgive them that, however, because their
web sites must rank among the best in the world, and are available free to all.
Nick Holmes's site is at www.infolaw.co.uk, while Delia Venables's is at
www.venables.co.uk.

A selection of useful Web sites

2.14   Those beginning to use the Web for legal research are well advised to
select and bookmark a few good general sites providing access by way of
hypertext to more specific sources. The term "portal" is often used to describe a
site that directs the user to other sites. The homepages of many university law
faculties and professional bodies serve this purpose admirably. Ideally, a portal
will enable a law student to gain access to the main sources of Irish, British,
European, American, Canadian, Australian and New Zealand law. European
law, of course, includes both the Council of Europe and the European Union. It
is also a good idea to have easy access to a selection of sites providing library
catalogues, law journals (some of which are now published either fully or partially online), dictionaries and reference books, and current affairs. Depending
on one's area of study, it may also be useful to have access to a selection of
social science, historical or policy-oriented sites as well. In later chapters of
this book, many of the sites relevant to the various jurisdictions covered will be
mentioned. The following sites, however, should prove useful, whatever one's
area of study might be. As will become clear as soon as one starts using them,
there is a significant degree of overlap; many portals and homepages lead to
other useful ones.

Portals.   For the main sources of Irish and British law on the Web, the
                         best site is www.bailii.org. Here one will find all Irish and
                         British judgments currently available on the Web as well as

the Irish statutes and statutory instruments from 1922 to 1998 (at the time of writing), U.K. statutes since 1996 and statutory instruments since 1997. One advantage of this portal is that it has a small number of good sites which means that it is easily navigated. The Law Society of Ireland has an excellent portal available at www.lawsociety.ie/links.htm/ . It provides links to the main Irish sites, as well as to the Australian Legal Information Institute, Europa (which includes the Web pages of the European Court of Justice, the European Commission, European Parliament and other European agencies), the Labour Relations Commission, U.K. Government sources and many others. For American law, the best portal is Findlaw (www.findlaw.com). Particularly useful sites on this portal are "Laws: Cases and Codes" which leads to federal constitutional materials, "US State Resources" which deals with the laws of individual states, and "Law Schools" which provides access to a wide range of law journals and reviews. Finally, of course, there is the Australian Legal Institute (www.austlii.edu.au)which provides a magnificent selection of materials from Australia, New Zealand and many other jurisdictions. Delia Venables's web site at 2.13 above includes all of these and more, and should certainly be bookmarked.

Law libraries. As will be mentioned in Chapter 7 below, the online catalogues of leading law libraries are a convenient way of checking out the books available on any given subject. It is advisable, therefore, to bookmark the Bodleian law library at Oxford as well as the libraries at Harvard, Yale and Trinity College Dublin, Oxford and Cambridge, the respective addresses of which are:

http://hollisweb.harvard.edu
http://ringding.law.yale.edu
www.tcd.ie/Library/online.htm
http://library.ox.ac.uk/
www.lib.cam.ac.uk/

Current affairs. One of the most interesting sites on the Internet is "Arts and Letters Daily" (www.aldaily.com). This site gives direct access every day to all the major English language newspapers and periodicals published around the world, including the *New York Times, Boston Globe, Washington Post, Prospect, Lingua Franca* and many others. In addition, each day a selection of leading articles from the various journals and newspapers is put up on the site and they remain there throughout most of the year. It is a veritable treasure house of material on politics, current affairs, philosophy, literature and, sometimes, law-related issues.

WESTLAW

2.14a   Westlaw (www.westlaw.com) is the leading online legal information service in the US, and its owner, the Thomson Corporation, is using the Westlaw platform to make legal materials published by Thomson companies in all jurisdictions available online. Westlaw UK (accessible at www.westlaw.co.uk) connects the authority of Sweet & Maxwell with the technical expertise of Westlaw and covers UK, EU and Scots law. In addition to UK users, most Irish university law faculties and some of the larger law offices subscribe to it.

2.14b   Westlaw UK is organised in a series of intersearcheable databases, covering current awareness, case reports, legislation, journal articles, news and business information. The following is a small sample of the materials included (the full list may be obtained by logging into www.westlaw.co.uk, clicking on "User Guides" and clicking on "Database Identifier List"):

Legislation
- United Kingdom statutes from 1267 to date (including Acts of the Scottish Parliament), and statutory instruments from 1948 to date, consolidated to show their current status. Time travel is available from 1992 to date, so you can see how an Act or S.I. looked, e.g. in 1998.
- EU legislation from 1952 to date and EU treaties from 1951 to date.

Case reports
- The Law Reports from 1891 to date.
- Common Market Law Reports from 1963 to date.
- Scots Law Times reports from 1930 to date.
- European Human Rights reports.

Analytical commentary
- Articles from journals, such as *European Human Rights Law Review* and *International Company and Commercial Law Review*.
- *The White Book*.
- Woodfall on *Landlord and Tenant*.

Indexes

- *Legal Journals Index*, indexing articles published from 1986 to date in a large range of journals.
- *Financial Journals Index*, from 1992.
- *Derwent World Patents* index, from 1963 to date.

Directories

- *Simons European Law Directory*.
- *Havers Companion to the Bar*.

2.14c   Westlaw IE will be launched by Round Hall in November 2001 and will be accessible at www.westlaw.ie. The service will be limited to current awareness coverage at launch, but will be added to over time until it offers the same level of comprehensiveness as Westlaw UK.

LEXIS

2.15   LEXIS is an online information retrieval system containing vast amounts of primary and some secondary legal material from several jurisdictions. Most university law faculties and many law offices subscribe to it. Because it is a rather expensive service, users should be trained to use it economically, unless the terms of the licence allow for unlimited use. Training sessions, handbooks and directories are available as part of the service. Two fundamental points about LEXIS should be noted at the outset. First, it is a full text service, and this is its great advantage. One get retrieve the full text of any case, statute or other document stored in its memory. Secondly, however, it is not an "expert" service. It is not there to provide the answer to specific problems, but simply to provide the text of the raw materials.

2.16   LEXIS itself is divided first and foremost into libraries. Generally, there is a library for each jurisdiction covered, although there are also separate libraries for many specific aspects of American law. When one first logs on to LEXIS, the first screen to appear is the list of libraries. Thus, IRLAW is for Irish law, ENGGEN for English law, EURCOM for European Union material, and so forth. One can usually guess the content from the name of the library. Libraries, in turn, are divided into files. As it happens, the Irish library, IRLAW, has only one file, entitled "Cases" which provides the text of reported cases from 1950 and unreported cases from 1985. Other libraries such as ENGGEN and NZ (New Zealand) have several files devoted to cases, statutes and other materials. After one has chosen a library, by typing its name in the address box near the top of the screen, a list of files will appear. One must then type in the name of the file to be searched, even if there is only one file. Thus, after entering the IRLAW library, one must type CASES, even though that is the only file currently on offer. Then one can type in a search term, using the various protocols available. What follows is a short account of the various protocols. Obviously, to become efficient, a user should either attend a training session or study one of the manuals.

Using truncated words

2.17   Lexis will search literally for whatever word or words one enters. Thus, if one enters "tenant", it will retrieve documents with that word, but not with related words such as "tenants" or "tenancy". One way around this problem is to use what may be termed the exclamation mark approach. In other words, if one types "tenan!", LEXIS will retrieve words beginning with those five letters, e.g. "tenant", "tenants", "tenancy", "tenancies". Likewise, "contrac!" should retrieve documents containing words such as "contract", "contracts", "contractual", "contracted".

Using connectors

2.18   Because of the enormous number of documents on LEXIS, especially in large files such as the CASES file of ENGGEN, any ordinary word will retrieve a huge, and unmanageable, number of documents. A very useful command is available, however, to deal with this problem. Say one wanted to retrieve cases dealing with sentencing for manslaughter. Words like "sentencing" or "manslaughter" on their own would retrieve hundreds of files, if not more, most of them irrelevant. What we need are cases with both words in close proximity. This can be done by entering a search phrase such as "sentencing w/5 manslaughter". This will retrieve documents in which "sentencing" and "manslaughter" occur within five words of each other. One can obviously vary the distance between the words, e.g. "w/3" or "w/10". Needless to say, in the example just given, the search strategy being pursued is not very sensible. Many relevant documents may exist with words such as "sentence" or "sentenced" and "manslaughter" in close proximity. Again, the truncated or exclamation mark approach should be used, e.g. "sentenc! w/5 manslaughter". Before starting such a search, therefore, it is worthwhile jotting down the possible variables; one can save a good deal of time, and possibly money, by having searches well planned in advance.

Statutory material

2.19   IRLAW does not contain the texts of Irish statutes (they are available on the Web, 4.30 below). However, one can retrieve cases dealing with statutes simply by entering the short titles of statutes. Again, however, it is wise to use connectors between the title and the year. For example, the search term "Unfair Dismissals Act 1977" might miss an important case in which the judge referred to "the Unfair Dismissals Act passed in 1977". One can get around this problem by entering "unfair dismissals w/5 1977". This should retrieve cases referring the Unfair Dismissals Act 1977 and the Unfair Dismissals Acts 1977 to 1993 (as a collective title). The STAT file of the ENGGEN library contains the texts of the statutes in force, although there is usually an interval before very recent ones are added.

Viewing the results

2.20   When the search has been processed, LEXIS will tell the user that their search has yielded a certain number of documents, say 20. One can then view them in a variety of ways. First one can get a list of them using the various icons on the toolbar. These are CITE, KWIC, and FULL VIEW. By clicking on CITE, the full list of documents will appear on the screen. Most searches by lawyers and students are for cases, so the list will give the names and citations for the cases. To investigate any of these cases further, type the number into the address box. This will probably provide a KWIC view of the case, which is a short excerpt containing the original search words. This should be enough to give an idea if the case is of value for the research being pursued. To retrieve the full text, click on FULL. Not all subscriptions to LEXIS allow users to print entire documents. The more restricted subscriptions may only allow the screen to be printed. This can be a tedious way of printing a lengthy document, but the great value of LEXIS for case research is the list of cases it produces. One can then read them in the usual printed sources.

Changing libraries, files and searches

2.21   Once connected to LEXIS, one should be able to use it as economically as possible without constantly exiting and signing on again. Become familiar therefore with those icons on the toolbar which allow one to begin a new search. To begin a new search in the same file, say Irish cases, click on "New Search". To change to another file within the same library, say in the ENGGEN library, click on "Change File", and to change to a new library, say from IRLAW to ENGGEN, click on "Change Library".

A short selection of LEXIS libraries

2.22   Irish lawyers will probably find the following libraries most useful;

IRLAW   Irish law (cases)
ENGGEN   English law
AUST   Australian law

SCOT   Scottish law
NILAW   Northern Ireland law
COMCAS   Commonwealth law
NZ   New Zealand law
EURCOM   European Community law and policy

There are many American libraries, but the more useful ones for comparative research are:

FEDSEC
STATES

FEDSEC provides all federal cases including those of the U.S. Supreme Court. STATES has cases from all the States. This is particularly useful as it is difficult to get access to the paper editions of these reports on this side of the Atlantic, and for most core areas of law such as contract, tort and criminal law, decisions of state courts are often more valuable for comparative purposes than federal cases.

COMPACT DISKS (CDs)

2.23   An ever-increasing amount of legal material is becoming available on compact disks (CDs). The value of a CD is that it can accommodate a vast amount of written material, often thousands of pages, on a disk the same size as an ordinary music disk. Such disks generally have 'read only memory' (ROM), meaning that the text cannot be erased or changed by an individual user. Many libraries now have CD-ROMS loaded on a central server thereby allowing several users to consult them at the same time at different computer terminals. The publishers of certain major texts and reference works such as Archbold's *Criminal Pleading, Evidence and Practice* now provide a CD version of the text as an optional extra to purchasers and subscribers at a modest additional cost. Right now prices vary enormously. There can scarcely be better value than the CD-ROM containing all the Acts of the Oireachtas and Statutory Instruments since 1922. This costs IR£20. At the other end of the spectrum, a CD-ROM called *Crime Desktop* produced in England by Sweet and Maxwell costs almost £1,000, excluding VAT. Whatever the cost, which will hopefully decrease over time, CD-ROMs are tremendously convenient. Most laptop computers nowadays have a CD-ROM drive. Lawyers therefore can carry entire libraries of statutes and law reports with them on a few compact disks and consult them at any time.

Current legal information

2.24   This is one of the most extensive reference services available on CD, and is also available as a subscription service on the Web at http:// 193.118.187.160/cli.htm . Most universities subscribe to this service in one or other format, so it should be available to students, often through the home page of their own university library. It contains several distinct services notably, the *Legal Journals Index, Current Law Monthly Digest, Current Law Case Citator, Current Law Legislation Citator* and the *Badger Grey Paper Index* which lists official publications, newspaper articles dealing with law, and similar material. The *Legal Journals Index* is now available exclusively in electronic form, and the electronic version contains all issues since the *Index* began in 1986. Material from over 400 legal journals is included. The great advantage of this *Index* is that it is an abstracting service as well as an indexing service. In other words, it provides a short description of the content of each article indexed. To find very recent articles, just click on the heading *"What's New this Month?"* which provides titles and one-line summaries of recent articles.

2.25   The *Current Law* file of *Current Legal Information* provides in effect the same information as the *Current Law Monthly Digest*, but only since 1986. The advantage of this electronic version is that one can check all the entries since that time in the one search rather than going through the paper version of the *Year Book* and *Monthly Digest* volume by volume. Remember, however, that it goes back only as far as 1986, whereas the paper service began in 1947 One must check the paper version for the earlier years.

2.26   Other services on *Current Legal Information* include the *Daily Law Reports Index* since 1988. This is an index of law reports appearing in newspapers such as *The Times* and *Financial Times*. Also included are the *Current Law Case Citator* and the *Current Law Legislation Citator* from 1989 onwards. Another interesting component of this service provides the library catalogues of the London Inns of Court. The Gray's Inn Catalogue contains all new titles acquired since 1991 whereas the catalogues of the Inner Temple, Middle Temple and Lincoln's Inn are far more extensive and include a good deal of historical material. This is another useful way of checking out material on English law, in particular, though all of these libraries would have reasonably large Commonwealth holdings also.

Other British material on CD

2.27   A good deal of other British law is becoming available on CD-ROM. *Crime Desktop*, mentioned earlier, includes the complete text of Archbold with updates, the *Criminal Law Review* since 1967 and the *Criminal Appeal Reports* since 1967. Certain series of law reports including the *Weekly Law Re-*

ports and *All England Law Reports* are available in this format. Students should check with their own libraries to see what is available.

Irish law on CD

2.28   The most valuable Irish CD-ROM is the *Irish Statute Book* mentioned above. The most recent version at the time of writing contains the texts of the Acts of the Oireachtas 1922-1998, the Statutory Instruments and chronological tables. Also included are the texts of constitutional amendments. It is proposed to publish this CD annually, so it will always be reasonably up to date. The CD is accompanied by a helpful explanatory booklet and there is a help desk for users which may be contacted by phone, fax or e-mail. This CD is very easy to use and has excellent search facilities. This compensates for the lamentable absence of a printed subject-index to the statutes which has persisted for many years. The *Irish Statute Book* is also available on the Internet at the Attorney General's web site, www.irlgov.ie/ag, although the web site is somewhat more cumbersome to use than the CD-ROM. There are apparently many errors in texts of the statutes on this CD, so the original stationery office versions should always be consulted before quoting any section in a piece of written work or in legal proceedings.

2.29   The other major Irish legal resource on CD is the JUSTIS version of the *Irish Reports*. Context Ltd, which owns the JUSTIS databases, have published an electronic version of the *Irish Reports* since 1919. Also included on the CD are the *Irish Digests*. The service is updated quarterly on CD-ROM. The ISSN number is 1470-8280. The service is excellent but remarkably expensive. Some of the JUSTIS databases are also available as subscription services on the Internet, but this one is currently available on CD only. As noted in Chapter 1, there is no general subject index to the *Irish Reports*, and no case citator. This CD compensates substantially for the absence of a subject index. Other CD services include Butterworth's *Irish Property Law Service* and the CD version of *Murdoch's Dictionary of Irish Law*.

2.29a   Round Hall offers a number of its looseleaf services on CD (e.g. *Irish Employment Legislation*, *Family Legislation Service*, *Family Law Practitioner*, *Consolidated Circuit Court Rules*, *The Licensing Acts* (2nd edition)). The frequency of updates varies by title but is at the minimum annually.

2.30   As in the case of the Internet and on-line srevices, CD-ROMs may or may not eventually replace hard copy publications. But, so long as they are current, they provide excellent reference sources. Those of us who find reading computer screens less congenial than reading books can use CD-ROMs and other electronic sources to find the relevant references and then consult the material itself in its usual printed format.

CHAPTER 3

Citing Legal Materials

3.01 There is no universal standard governing the citation of legal materials. Certain citation conventions, especially in relation to case law, are widely observed, but much depends on the house style of the publication in which the work appears. The consistency associated with law report citations is due partly to the instructions contained in the reports themselves and partly to certain general conventions such as the use of square brackets or parentheses when indicating the year of a report (see 3.25 below). In the United States where virtually every law school publishes at least one law review or journal, the *Uniform System of Citation*, better known as the Blue Book, published by the Harvard Law Review Association, contains detailed rules for citing legal sources and is regularly updated. The American citation system set out in the Blue Book differs in many respects from ours. For example, in American legal writing, book titles, rather than being italicised as they are here, are placed in small capitals. Titles of journal articles, on the other hand, are italicised whereas here they are placed in inverted commas. There is nothing inherently right or wrong about any of these systems. Citation conventions are the product of tradition as much as anything else. The important thing is to be familiar with the system prevailing in whichever jurisdiction one happens to be writing. Irish and British citation systems are largely identical, although Scotland adopts a more economical approach to case citation. The citation methods employed by the main reporting systems in the jurisdictions covered in this book will be described in later chapters. Here we shall concentrate on some general citation issues with particular reference to Irish and U.K. cases and statutes. As mentioned earlier, many cases are never formally reported. Our concern, therefore, is almost exclusively with High Court and appellate judgments. We shall begin with a few general issues and then move on to criminal cases, which are the simplest to deal with. Civil cases are slightly more complicated. The citation of secondary materials is also dealt with in some detail in Chapter 14.

CITING CASES

3.02 The citation of a case may be regarded as its address. It points users to the location where the case can be found. The name of the case is clearly essential, but it must be accompanied by other information indicating the report series, volume and initial page number. Thus, the citation

The State (Healy) v. Donoghue [1976] I.R. 325

tells us that the case will be found in the 1976 volume of the *Irish Reports*, beginning at page 325. This is a fairly common citation convention, although it omits one important piece of information - the court that decided the case. On the other hand, the jurisdiction in which a case was decided will generally be deducible from the name of the report series, Ireland in this particular case. Experienced users of the *Irish Reports* will know that *The State (Healy) v. Donoghue* must have been decided by the High Court, Supreme Court or both, but this is not apparent from the citation itself. There are some law report series devoted solely to one court, such as the various series reporting the decisions of the U.S. Supreme Court (11.10, below). Most series, however, including those devoted to a particular branch of law, include reports from several courts or tribunals. The movement for neutral case citations (3.30 below) is attempting to replace references to law report series with references to the courts and juris-dictions in which the cases were decided. However, conventional citations will continue to be used, for the foreseeable future at least, alongside the neutral citations. And, in any event, older cases will still be cited in the traditional way.

Use of italics

3.03   The name of a case is always placed in italics; that is a convention al-most universally observed in these islands, but not in the United States.[1] The remainder of the citation is in ordinary type, as illustrated by the citation for *The State (Healy) v. Donoghue* above. If, for some reason, one were using the full title, as opposed to the abbreviated form, of a law report series, it would be placed in italics as well. However, that will seldom arise in a case citation as virtually all law reports have recognised abbreviations. Thus, the law report element of *The State (Healy) v. Donoghue* citation is: [1976] I.R. 325. On the other hand one would write: "the *Irish Reports* are published in four volumes a year". In the days when scripts were submitted to typesetters in hand-written or typewritten form, words or phrases intended to appear in italics when printed were underlined. Nowadays, with word processors, italics can easily be in-serted at the outset. But it is still acceptable when producing a typescript to underline the name of a case, a book or a journal, that would appear in italics if printed. What one must not do is both; in a typed document, the name of a case should appear in italics if possible; otherwise it may be underlined, but not both. Occasionally, an article about a case will simply bear the case name as its title, in which event it should be placed in italics because it is a case name, but within inverted commas to indicate that it is an article rather than a law report, e.g. Wright, "*Sinclair v. Brougham*" (1938) 6 C.L.J. 305.

---

[1]   In the U.S., case names are placed in ordinary type.

CRIMINAL CASES

3.04   Article 30 the Constitution of Ireland provides that all offences pros-ecuted in any court constituted under Article 34 of the Constitution, other than the District Court, shall be prosecuted in the name of the People at the suit of the Attorney General "or some other person authorised in accordance with law to act for that purpose". The Prosecution of Offences Act 1974 established the office of the Director of Public Prosecutions (D.P.P.) which, as permitted by Article 30, took over virtually all of the prosecuting functions of the Attorney General. Consequently, offences prosecuted on indictment (meaning that they are triable in the Circuit Court, the Central Criminal Court or the Special Criminal Court) are prosecuted in the name of the People at the suit of the D.P.P. since early 1975, or at the suit of the Attorney General before that. Typical citations for criminal cases would therefore be:

The People (Director of Public Prosecutions) v. Tiernan [1988] I.R. 250

The People (Attorney General) v. O'Callaghan [1966] I.R. 501.

It is generally acceptable to use the abbreviations "D.P.P." and, perhaps to a lesser extent, "A.G." in such citations. In speech, these cases are referred to as "The People against Tiernan" and "The People against O'Callaghan". At this point, a student familiar with the facts of *The State (Healy) v. Donoghue*, men-tioned above, may well ask if this was not a criminal case and, if so, why is it cited thus. Certainly, it began as a criminal prosecution and resulted in a con-viction and sentence. But it came before the High Court by means of what we now call judicial review, which is a form of civil proceeding, even when used to challenge the legality of a criminal conviction. Judicial review applications are dealt with at 3.14 below.

3.05   Ireland does not apply the convention followed in certain other jurisdic-tions of reversing the names of the parties on appeal. Take, for example, the case of *The People (Director of Public Prosecutions) v. O'Shea* [1996] 1 I.R. 556. This was an appeal by Mr O'Shea to the Court of Criminal Appeal against the sentence imposed upon him in the Central Criminal Court. But it continues to bear the name it assumed at trial level. Logically, perhaps, the name of the applicant, Mr O'Shea, should come first as it is he who is taking the appeal. It would not, of course, be very logical to list the People or the D.P.P. as the respondent or defendant, as the application is being taken against a court deci-sion. Overall, therefore, the present system is quite acceptable.

3.06   Virtually all reported criminal cases are appellate decisions of the Court of Criminal Appeal, the Supreme Court or the High Court (by way of case stated). Reserved judgments or reported *ex tempore* judgments of the Central Criminal Court are quite rare, though generally very valuable. A writer may sometimes need to refer to a criminal case dealt with by the Circuit Court, Special Criminal Court or District Court. Offences in the first two courts will have been prosecuted on indictment, so they can be cited in the same way as the *Tiernan* case above. The District Court deals mainly with summary offences, although it is also empowered to deal with certain indictable offences that are adjudged to be minor in nature. Most summary offences are prosecuted by members of the Gardaí or by regulatory agencies acting as common informers or, indeed, by private individuals acting in the same capacity. A member of the Gardaí may prosecute a summary offence in the name of the D.P.P. without first obtaining the D.P.P.'s consent.[2] There does not appear to be any settled way of referring to District Court criminal cases, largely because they are seldom, if ever, cited in written judgments or in textbooks. It is probably acceptable to refer to them solely by the names of the defendants, so long as the nature of the case is clear from the context. Sometimes, the identity of a non-police prosecutor will be known, in which case the names of both the prosecutor and defendant can be included, e.g. *Shannon Regional Fisheries Board v. Cavan County Council*, followed by the name of the District Court and the date of the relevant hearing. It will generally be helpful, however, to indicate the name, date and, if possible, page number of the newspaper in which the report appeared – as that is the most likely source of the writer's information.

3.07   In England and Wales, most criminal cases are prosecuted in the name of the Crown. A typical citation will therefore be *R v. Smith*, referred to in speech as "The Crown against Smith". ("*R*" stands for *Rex* (King) or *Regina* (Queen), depending on the gender of the reigning monarch). Many textbooks and law report series dealing exclusively with criminal law omit the reference to the Crown entirely, and refer simply to the name of the defendant or appellant as the case may be, e.g. *Smith*. This system may also be used in Ireland, though it is suitable only for works dealing mainly or exclusively with criminal law. Otherwise, for the sake of consistency, it is preferable to use the full title. Some English criminal cases bear the name of the D.P.P. as prosecutor. They are therefore cited as *Director of Public Prosecutions v. Morgan* [1975] 2 All E.R. 347.

CIVIL CASES: IRELAND

3.08   The vast majority of reported civil cases will either have begun in the High Court or else have arrived there from a lower court or tribunal by means of an established procedure such as appeal or judicial review. Civil proceedings are generally begun in the High Court by way of a summons, a petition or an originating notice of motion. Those who are beginning the study of law need not

[2]   *People (D.P.P.) v. Roddy* [1977] I.R. 177.

concern themselves unduly with these procedural details, apart from noting that the manner in which a case begins determines the way in which it is eventually cited. Let us start with that group of cases which occupy the greater part of the High Court's list, and certainly the most sought-after by lawyers, personal injury actions. At the time of writing, a person who is seeking £30,000 or more in compensation from someone who has injured her must take her case in the High Court. The person taking the case is the *plaintiff* and the person against whom it is being taken is the *defendant*. To get the action under way, the plaintiff (or, in reality, her lawyers) must issue what is known as a plenary summons. This is a short document summoning the defendant to appear in the High Court and answer the plaintiff's claim. It is called a plenary summons because it allows for a full hearing to take place, with witnesses and so forth. It is obviously essential that this summons should clearly identify both the plaintiff and the defendant. There will seldom be any difficulty about this: Jane Murphy is suing John Kelly. But several variations are possible. The plaintiff may be a minor (under 18 years of age) and minors cannot sue in their own right. There may be several defendants, or one or more of the parties may be a limited company or some other kind of organisation. Various conventions, which are strictly observed in practice, have been adopted to deal with these situations. Thus, if Jane Murphy is a five-year old child who has been injured by a car driven negligently by John Kelly, the summons will bear a title along the following lines:

Jane Murphy (suing by her father and next friend Peter Murphy) v John Kelly.

Titles, such as Mr, Ms, Dr, are never used in summonses.[3] If this case eventually results in a reported judgment of the High Court or Supreme Court, it will continue to bear the same title. For citation purposes, however, it will be sufficient to refer to the surnames of the plaintiff and defendant, e.g.

Murphy v. Kelly [2005] 3 I.R. 300

3.09   The rules for citing cases may be summarised as follows. A law report usually begins with the full, formal title of the case as it appeared in the plenary summons or other originating document. The reader can therefore immediately identify who the parties are, and there may be many of them. However, when citing the case, it is not necessary to use the full title. In a typical case involving two private individuals, it will be sufficient to mention their surnames, as in *Murphy v. Kelly* above. If there are two or more plaintiffs or defendants, it will be sufficient to mention the surnames of the first plaintiff and first defendant. Thus, *Jane Murphy and Simon Black v. Tom Jones and John Smith* may be

---

[3]   Strangely enough, even in Ireland, titles of nobility do appear to be used. See for example, *Lord Henry Mountcharles, the Earl of Mountcharles v. Meath County Council* abbreviated to *Earl of Mountcharles v. Meath County Council* [1997] 1 I.L.R.M. 446.

cited simply as *Murphy v. Jones*. The general rule, therefore, is that a case is cited by reference to the surname or corporate names of the first plaintiff and first defendant. What follows is merely an elaboration on this rule to take account of cases involving commercial organisations and public authorities of various kinds.

3.10   When a party to a case is a commercial company, the name is given in full and should include "Ltd" or "plc" as the case may be. Thus, the case of *Lascomme Ltd, trading as Ballyglass House Hotel v. United Dominions Trust (Ireland) Ltd.* is cited as:

  Lascomme Ltd. v. United Dominions Trust (Ireland) Ltd. [1993] 3 I.R. 412.

Needless to say, if the first plaintiff or defendant listed in the case title is a natural as opposed to a legal person, all that need be given is the surname of that natural person. Thus, *Raymond Jackson and Allied Irish Banks Capital Markets Plc v. Lombard and Ulster Banking Ltd* is cited as:

  Jackson v. Lombard and Ulster Banking Ltd. [1992] 1 I.R. 94.

In many commercial cases, the full case title, as in *Lascomme* above, will indicate the trading name of a person or company. ("Trading as" is often abbreviated to "t/a"). This need not be included in a citation. For example, *Masterfoods Ltd. t/a Mars Ireland v. H.B. Ice Cream Ltd. and H.B. Ice Cream Ltd. v. Masterfoods Ltd. t/a Mars Ireland* is cited as

  Masterfoods Ltd. v. H.B. Ice Cream Ltd. [1993] I.L.R.M. 145.

As the full title of this case indicates, there were two actions joined together. Essentially, Mars were suing H.B. and H.B. were suing Mars. It is sufficient for citation purposes to give the names of the first plaintiff and first defendant in the first-mentioned action.

3.11   The defendants in many cases, especially in the area of planning and development, are local authorities (e.g. county councils or borough councils). When citing such a case it will be sufficient to use the relevant local authority's abbreviated title. For example, *Glencar Explorations plc and Andaman Resources plc v. The County Council of the County of Mayo* is cited as:

  Glencar Explorations plc v. Mayo County Council [19993] 2 I.R. 237.

In this case, however, the first plaintiff is a public limited company and must therefore be given its full name. When the defendant is a corporation or borough council, the full title of the case will be more elaborate but, again, it may be cited in an abbreviated form. Thus, *Mark Keogh and Others v. The Mayor, Aldermen and Burgesses of the County Borough of Galway (Nos 1 & 2)* is cited as:

> *Keogh v. Galway Corporation (Nos 1 and 2)* [1995] 3 I.R. 457.

3.12 This last-mentioned case illustrates another aspect of case citation, namely the use of numbers. Sometimes, the same proceedings will result in more than one reported decision. For example, a plaintiff might first issue proceedings seeking damages for breach of contract but, before the hearing of the case, seek an injunction to prevent the defendant from reducing the assets held by him within the jurisdiction (known as a Mareva injunction). Each of these actions might result in a reserved judgment of the High Court or Supreme Court, or both. The first judgment to issue would carry "(No.1)" as part of the title as above, and the second "(No.2)". In fact, the *Keogh* citation just given is rather unusual, as both judgments are reported together, hence "(Nos. 1 and 2)". More commonly, they would appear in different years or in different law report volume for the same year. However, it is only when two or more decisions are issued in respect of the same proceedings that numbers are used. If, for example, another person called Keogh had instituted legal proceedings against Galway Corporation in a totally unrelated matter, and that also resulted in a reported judgment in 1995, it would simply be cited as *Keogh v Galway Corporation.*

3.13 In many constitutional and public law cases, the defendant or respondent is the State, the Attorney General or a Government Minister. Often, in fact, two or more of these will be listed as defendants. When citing the case, simply follow the general rule of including the first defendant listed in the formal title, e.g. *Joseph Kavanagh v The Government of Ireland, the Director of Public Prosecutions, the Attorney General and the Special Criminal Court* is cited as *Kavanagh v. The Government of Ireland* [1996] 1 I.R. 321.

Judicial review applications

3.14 Thus far, we have been considering civil cases governed by private law rules, principally the rules of tort and contract. However, many disputes to which the State is a party are governed by the rules of public law which are applied by the High Court and Supreme Court in judicial review proceedings. Although the number of cases coming before the superior courts by way of judicial review has increased greatly during the past twenty years or so, the purpose of this procedure is quite limited, and may briefly be described as follows. Decisions affecting the rights and liabilities of individuals are made by a wide variety of public bodies including courts, tribunals, local authorities, professional bodies and government departments. The general policy of the superior courts (meaning, for this purpose, the High Court and Supreme Court) is not to interfere with or attempt to second guess the decisions of these bodies many of which, after all, will have a highly specialised knowledge of the areas with which they deal. In other words, the Adoption Board and An Bord Pleanála (the planning appeals board), to give but two examples, can reasonably be expected to possess more detailed knowledge of adoption and planning, respectively, than the High Court itself. However, there is always the possibility that any of these bodies may fall into legal error by, for example, acting outside of its jurisdiction, failing to apply the rules of natural justice or abusing the discretion conferred upon it by law. All of these matters are governed by public law rules. The purpose of judicial review, therefore, is to allow the High Court and, on appeal, the Supreme Court, to exercise a supervisory jurisdiction over the lower courts and other public bodies so as to ensure that they behave legally. Judicial review should not be confused with an appeal. The purpose of an appeal is to challenge the *merits* of a decision, e.g. to contend that a sentence imposed was unduly severe or that damages awarded for a personal injury were too low. Judicial review, on the other hand, is primarily concerned with *procedural propriety*. It is concerned, not with the merits of a decision, but with whether proper procedures were followed in reaching it. For example, a decision of a local authority to make a material alteration to its development plan without first fulfilling certain requirements prescribed by statute, such as notifying the public about the proposed alteration, would be liable to be quashed by the High Court on review. The High Court will quash the decision, not because it disagrees with the local authority's proposal (that matter is outside the Court's jurisdiction), but because proper procedures have not been followed. The procedural rules governing judicial review itself have changed over the years and the methods of citing cases begun by way of judicial review have changed in the process.

3.15 Students beginning the study of law may be puzzled by case citations such as: *R v. Panel on Take-overs and Mergers, ex parte Datafin plc* [1987] Q.B. 815, *R (Kane) v. Tyrone Justices* (1906) 40 I.L.T.R. 181, *R (Martin) v. Mahoney* [1910] 2 I.R. 695, or *The State (Holland) v Kennedy* [1977] I.R. 193. All of them are what are now called judicial review cases. Before the foundation of the State, public law remedies were known as prerogative writs. The Crown *(R)* was nominally acting on behalf as the prosecutor (such as Kane in the second of the examples just given) to have a decision of a respondent (such as the Tyrone Justices) brought up for quashing by the High Court. After the foundation of the State, these writs became known as state-side orders. Thereafter, it was the State, rather than the Crown, that nominally acted on behalf of the prosecutor, as in *The State (Holland) v. Kennedy*. This system was further changed and simplified by the Rules of the Superior Courts 1986 (Order 84). The term "state-side order" has been abandoned and replaced with "judicial review". Since these rules came into force, judicial review cases are now entitled and cited in much the same way as an ordinary civil case. If *The State (Healy) v. Donoghue* were decided today, it would be cited simply as *Healy v Donoghue*. The following are post-1986 judicial review cases:

Blackhall v. Grehan [1995] 3 I.R. 208.
McNeill v. Commissioner of An Garda Síochána [1997] 1 I.R. 469
Eogan v. University College Dublin [1996] 1 I.R. 390.

3.16   The description of the parties also changed with the introduction of the 1986 Rules. Before that the person seeking the remedy was known as the prosecutor (or prosecutrix in the case of a woman). Now the parties are known simply as the applicant and the respondent. It should also be remembered that judicial review proceedings involve a two-stage process. One must first apply to the High Court for leave to apply for judicial review, and to succeed one must satisfy the criteria set out in *G v. D.P.P.* [1994] 1 I.R. 374. If denied such leave, the applicant may appeal against that refusal to the Supreme Court (as occurred in *G* itself). This first application is *ex parte* (meaning that only one side, the applicant, is represented at this point) unless there is a statutory provision, as there is in relation to judicial review of certain planning decisions, requiring that the application be made on notice to the other side. Once leave to proceed is given, there will be a full hearing of the application at which point, of course, both applicant and respondent will be represented.

Relator actions

3.17   A relator action is one in which the Attorney General, as guardian of the public interest with responsibility for asserting public rights, is brought into a case at the instance of a private individual who might otherwise lack the necessary standing. Such cases are cited as *Attorney General (McGarry) v. Sligo County Council* [1991] 1 I.R. 99.

Cases begun by petition

3.18   Certain high court proceedings, particularly in the area of company law, are begun by way of petition. For example, an examiner appointed under the Companies (Amendment) Act 1990 may be applying to the High Court for directions on certain matters, or there may be a petition to wind up a company on various grounds. The format customarily used in citing such cases is: *"In re..."* which means "in the matter of...". Examples include *In re Atlantic Magnetics Ltd.* [1993] 2 I.R. 561, and *In re Yorkshire Woolcombers Association Ltd.* [1903] 2 Ch. 284. The same practice is followed in citing probate cases dealing, for example, with the validity or interpretation of wills, e.g. *In re Borough* [19938] 1 All E.R. 375. Sometimes, this is followed by the names of the actual parties who are in dispute over the estate (if there is a dispute) e.g. *In re Abbott, Peacock v Frigout* [1893] 1 Ch. 54.

Article 26 references

3.19   Under Article 26 of the Constitution, the President may, before signing a Bill into law, refer it to the Supreme Court for a decision on whether the Bill or any of its provisions are repugnant to the Constitution. The Court, which for this purpose must consist of at least five members, must give its decision within 60 days of the reference. Only one judgment may be delivered, and the existence of any other opinion, assenting or dissenting, must not be disclosed. The judgment delivered in respect of such a reference is formally entitled (to take a fairly recent example): *In the matter of Article 26 of the Constitution and in the matter of the Matrimonial Home Bill 1993.* However, it may be cited simply as *In re The Matrimonial Home Bill 1993* [1994] 1 I.R. 305. A list of Article 26 references, up until early 2000, is given in Casey, *Constitutional Law in Ireland* 3rd edn, (Round Hall, Dublin, 2000) at p. 89. To these must now be added the references in respect of the Planning and Development Bill 1999 and the Illegal Immigrants (Trafficking) Bill 1999. Both bills were upheld by the Supreme Court in judgments delivered on 28 August 2000, and available on the Internet at www.bailii.org/ie/cases/.

Admiralty cases

3.20   Admiralty cases usually involve disputes concerning shipping vessels, and are generally known by the name of the vessel at the centre of the dispute. The full title of the case will include the names of the parties, e.g. *The M.V. "Turquoise Bleu": Medscope Marine Ltd. v. MTM Metal Trading and Manufacturing Ltd.* [1995] 3 I.R. 437. As a rule, however, it is sufficient to cite the case by reference to the name of the vessel involved, e.g. *Re M.V. "Turquoise Bleu"* [1995] 3 I.R. 437. "M.V." stands for motor vessel, while "S.S." stands for steamship.

Preserving anonymity

3.21   By virtue of Article 34.1 of the Constitution, cases should ordinarily be heard and judgments ordinarily delivered in public. However, certain cases, notably in the areas of family law and criminal law, are heard in camera or otherwise than in public. Judgments delivered in such cases may, of course, be published or otherwise circulated but they must avoid identifying the parties involved. In family law, the usual convention is to identify the case by the initials of the parties, e.g. *R.C. v. E.B.* [1997] 1 I.R. 305. As it happens, the full title of this case in the *Irish Reports* is *R.C. v E.B. (Nullity)* while the one immediately succeeding it is *R.C. v. C.C. (Divorce).* The inclusion of the words in parentheses is not strictly necessary, although they are a useful way of remembering the case, as any student preparing for a family law examination will testify. Sometimes, a case may be cited as *N (orse K.) v. K.* [1985] I.R. 733.

"Orse" stands for "otherwise" referring, as a rule, to another name by which the female party to matrimonial proceedings is or has been known. Under the law on sexual offences, certain defendants in criminal cases must remain anonymous. Such a case may be cited as: *G. v. Director of Public Prosecutions* [1994] 1 I.R. 374. A case of this kind reported in a newspaper but for which there is no written judgment (and consequently no indication of the name or initials of the defendant), may be referred to as *The People (DPP) v. X*, followed by the date of the newspaper report or the date of the court decision and the name of the court. In *Roe v. Blood Transfusion Service* [1996] 1 I.L.R.M. 555, the High Court (Laffoy J.) held that, in view of the specific and mandatory terms of Article 34.1 of the Constitution, requiring that justice be administered in public, the Court had no jurisdiction to allow a plaintiff to prosecute the proceedings under a fictitious name.

Identifying the judge

3.22   When several different judgments have been delivered in the same case, as will often occur in cases decided by, say, the Irish Supreme Court or the House of Lords in the U.K., the member of the court being quoted is usually indicated by the use of the word *"per"*. One would write therefore that "the Supreme Court (*per* Walsh J.) held that this statutory provision was unconstitutional".

CIVIL CASES: ENGLAND AND WALES

3.23   English civil cases are cited in essentially the same way as Irish civil cases, e.g. *Donoghue v. Stevenson* [1932] A.C. 562. Judicial review cases, however, are still cited in the old-fashioned way described earlier, e.g.

R v. Secretary of State for the Home Department, ex p. Brind [1991] 1 A.C. 696.

In this case, the applicants, Brind and others (a group of journalists), sought judicial review of a decision of the Home Secretary to prohibit the broadcasting of words spoken by members of certain organisations. Yet, on first impression, the case title would lead one to believe that the case was being taken by the Crown. As noted earlier (3.15 above) this is actually the theory; the Crown, on behalf of Brind and others, is commanding the respondent Home Secretary to bring the case before the High Court for quashing unless it can be upheld under rules of public law. *"ex p. "* in the case title stands for *"ex parte"* meaning in this context, "on behalf of".

3.24   British law report citations, for both civil and criminal cases, often include, immediately after the citation, an indication of the court that decided the case. This is because, as noted earlier, the citation itself rarely indicates the court. For example, Privy Council cases as well as House of Lords cases are reported in the *Appeal Cases* (6.19 below). A case citation may therefore read:

Pepper v. Hart [1993] A.C. 593, HL

R v. Jockey Club, ex parte RAM Racecourses Ltd [1993] 3 All E.R. 225, DC

Associated Picture Houses v. Wednesbury Corporation [1948] 1 K.B. 223, CA

In these instances, "HL" stands for House of Lords, "DC" for Divisional Court, and "CA" for Court of Appeal, just as "PC" stands for Privy Council, and "QBD" for Queen's Bench Division. Likewise in Ireland, it may be helpful to include either "HC" for High Court or "SC" for Supreme Court, after a citation to indicate the court in which the judgment was delivered.

Law reports

3.25   So far, we have been dealing with case names. The name of is only part of the citation; the address is equally important. The Irish and British law re-porting systems are described in detail in Chapters 4 and 6 below. In the present context, it should be noted that all law report series have standard abbrevia-tions, e.g. "I.R." for *Irish Reports*, "All E.R" for *All England Law Reports*, "C.M.L.R." for *Common Market Law Reports* and so forth. Lists of such ab-breviations will be found in the sources listed in 6.35 above/below and (selec-tively) in Appendix 2 of this book. Most law report series are published in one or more annual volumes and the more popular ones appear frequently through-out the year in individual parts. The *Irish Reports*, for example, are now pub-lished in eight parts each year and these are eventually collected into four volumes with two parts in each. Some law report series are numbered sequentially by volume. In other words, the first volume to appear will have been number 1 while the most recent may be number 356. This is the system adopted, for ex-ample, by the *United States Supreme Court Reports* (U.S.), e.g. *Standard Oil v. U.S.* (1911) 221 U.S.1. More commonly, in these islands at least, reports are identified by year, e.g. *McNamee v. Buncrana U.D.C.* [1983] I.R. 213, *Glencar Explorations plc v. Mayo County Council* [1993] 2 I.R. 237 or All E.R. These examples are instructive in various ways. In the first place, all of the citations include a date, even in the case of the U.S. reports which are cited primarily by volume number. Obviously the date is crucial in the case of the *Irish Reports* and *All England Reports*. In these report series, the year is enclosed in square brackets. This is to indicate that the series is identified primarily by year. If there were two or more volumes for the year in question, the volume number is included *after* the date. If there was only one volume for the year, there is no need to include the number, as it is self-evident. Note, therefore, the difference between the citations for *McNamee* and *Glencar* in the examples just given. In contrast with these, it would be quite easy to find the American case *Standard*

Oil v. U.S. even if no date were given. One would simply track down volume 221 of the U.S. Supreme Court Reports and find the case at page 1. The date given in this case is merely additional information to inform the reader as when the judgment was handed down. That is the reason why it is included in parentheses or round brackets; it is additional as opposed to essential information for finding the case.

3.26   As already mentioned, most Irish and British reports are identified primarily by year. In fact, two English series which until recently were identified by volume number have now begun to adopt the year approach. These are the *Criminal Appeal Reports* and the *Criminal Appeal Reports (Sentencing),* both published commercially by Sweet and Maxwell. Until the end of 1994, the *Criminal Appeal Reports* were cited primarily by volume, e.g. *R v. Williams* (1994) 99 Cr. App.R. 163. Since then, they have been cited primarily by year, e.g. *R v. Sharkey* [2000] 1 Cr. App. R. 409, meaning the first volume for the year 2000. Likewise the first 16 volumes of the *Criminal Appeal (Sentencing) Reports* were cited primarily by volume number up until the end of 1995. Since then, they have been cited primarily by year, as in the case of the *Criminal Appeal Reports.*

3.27   The Scottish system of citing cases is slightly different. Its report series are all identified by year, but without any square brackets, e.g. *Murray v. Rogers* 1992 STL 221. The sources of Scots Law are described in para 6.56 *et seq.* below. The main law report series in Northern Ireland, on the other hand, follows the conventional approach, e.g. *Carroll v. Routledge* [1925] N.I. 1.

3.28   In report series identified by date, the year given in square brackets is that in which the volume in question was published but not necessarily the year in which all the judgments contained in it were delivered. The 1999 volumes of the *Irish Reports* contain several cases decided in 1998. In report series identified by volume number, on the other hand, the year mentioned in parentheses is that in which the case was decided and may or may not be the same as the year in which the volume was published. Generally speaking, the cases included in law reports, irrespective of how they are cited, will be quite recent. Occasionally, however, a case may be included which was decided many years earlier, but despite its legal importance, had remained unreported. The last part of the second volume of the *Irish Law Reports Monthly* for 1995, for example, was devoted entirely to significant but hitherto unreported judgments from earlier years, some dating back as far as 1979. Occasionally, an earlier judgment may be reported as an addendum or supplement to a recent one which relied upon or referred to it. Examples include *The State (McCarthy) v. Governor of Mountjoy Prison,* in which judgment was delivered in 1967 but which was reported at [1997] 2 I.L.R.M. 361, as an appendix to *Healy v. Governor of Cork Prison* [1997] 2 I.L.R.M. 357. These cases may be cited in the usual way by reference to year of the law reports in which they are published. But it may be helpful, depending on the context, to indicate the date of judgment, e.g. *The People (D.P.P.) v Aylmer* [1995] 2 I.L.R.M. 624 (judgments delivered by Supreme Court on 18 December, 1986), or more economically, *The People (D.P.P.) v. Aylmer* [1995] 2 I.L.R.M. 624, SC (judgments delivered December 18, 1986).

Parallel citations

3.29   Some cases are reported in more than one series. Many Irish judgments are reported in both the *Irish Reports* and *Irish Law Reports Monthly*. An important English case may be reported in several different law report series. In certain contexts, it may be helpful to give parallel citations, in other words to mention all or most of the series in which the case is reported. This will help a reader who has access to, say, the *All England Law Reports* but not to the *Law Reports* (see 6.19 below). Some book publishers follow the practice of including just one citation in the text or footnotes but giving full parallel citations in the table of cases. As a rule, the official or semi-official series is mentioned first, followed by the others, e.g.

Taylor v. Smith [1991] 1 I.R. 142; [1990] I.L.R.M. 377
Associated Provincial Picture Houses Ltd. v. Wednesbury Corporation
[1948] 1 K.B. 223; [1947] 2 All E.R. 680.

Sometimes, the same case is reported under different names in different series. This is true of two leading British cases, *Donoghue v. Stevenson* and *R v. Morgan*.

Neutral citations

3.30   The Internet has opened up many new possibilities for law reporting, possibilities that commercial publishers view with some alarm. If Internet users can gain access to the full texts of judgments immediately after delivery and virtually free of charge, they will have less need of the various print series which tend to be expensive as well as selective in the cases they report. Furthermore, there is often a long delay before a judgment appears in one of these series. Traditional law reports do, of course, have advantages over the Internet, at least as it now operates. The main advantage consists of "added value" in the form of catch words, headnotes and, in some instances, the arguments of counsel in summary form. Copyright of this added value material, including page numbers, remains with the publisher. Designers of web sites must find their own way of citing judgments without infringing on the copyright of other publishers. The main strategy they have adopted is to develop neutral case citations which indicate the jurisdiction and court rather than a particular law report series. Australia has been very much to the fore in this process. Traditionally, for example, judgments of Australia's High Court were reported in the *Com-*

monwealth Law Reports, and they still are. There they are cited as *Crimmins v. Stevedoring Committee* (1999) 200 C.L.R. 1. The neutral citation for this case on web site of the Australian High Court is [1999] H.C.A. 59, H.C.A. standing for High Court of Australia. In Canada likewise, judgments of the Supreme Court are cited before publication as *R v. Latimer* 2001 SCC 1 (the neutral citation). Once formally reported in the Canadian *Supreme Court Reports,* the neutral citation may be used as a parallel citation, e.g. *R v. Latimer* [2001] 1 S.C.R. xxx, 2001 SCC 1.

3.31   Similar developments have taken place in Ireland and in England and Wales. The judgments of the Irish High Court and Supreme Court now appearing on the Internet bear neutral citation systems. Examples include *Ryan v. Minister for Justice* [2000] I.E.S.C. 33, presumably meaning the 33rd case in which the Supreme Court delivered judgment in 2000, and *Carey v. Hussey* [1999] I.E.H.C. 71, the 71st case in which the High Court delivered judgment in the year 1999.

3.32   In England and Wales, there is a Practice Direction (Judgments: Form and Citation) [2001] 1 W.L.R. 194 setting out the arrangements for the neutral citation of judgments, with effect from January 11, 2001. It applies to both divisions (civil and criminal) of the Court of Appeal and to the Administrative Court of the High Court. A unique number will be given to each approved judgment issued out of these courts and the abbreviations for the courts will be as follows:

Court of Appeal (Civil Division)   [2001] E.W.C.A. Civ. 1, 2, 3, etc.
Court of Appeal (Criminal Division) [2001] E.W.C.A. Crim. 1,2,3, etc
High Court (Administrative Court)   [2001] E.W.H.C. Admin. 1, 2, 3, etc

Furthermore, judgments of the Court of Appeal and all divisions of the High Court will be in numbered paragraphs. Where more than one judgment is delivered in the same case, the paragraph numbering will continue in an unbroken sequence throughout out. Thus, the first paragraph of the second judgment might be number 127, the final paragraph of the first judgment having been 126. To avoid confusion, paragraph numbers, when cited, will be placed in square brackets. The following fictitious examples illustrate the new system:

R v. Smith [2001] E.W.C.A. Crim. 32 at [64]

This is the 32nd judgment delivered by the Court of Appeal, Criminal Division, in the year 2001 at paragraph 64.

Lyes v. Phibbs [2001] E.W.C.A. Civ. 98 at [65]-[72]

This is the 98th judgment delivered by the Court of Appeal, Civil Division, in the year 2001 at paragraphs 65 to 72.

> *Black v White* [2001] E.W.H.C. Admin. 32 at [12], [33]

The 32nd judgment delivered by the High Court (Administrative Court) in 2001 at paragraphs 12 and 33. Once the judgment is reported in the ordinary law reports, the neutral citation will be given first, e.g.

> *Lyes v. Phibbs* [2001] E.W.C.A. Civ. 98, [2001] 3 W.L.R. 2456, [2001] 3 Q.B. 1234.

A similar system is likely to be applied to all courts before long. In fact, there is already such a system for House of Lords judgements on the Web where they are cited as:

> *Johnson (A.P.) v. Unisys Ltd.* [2001] U.K.H.L. 13

STATUTES

Modern Irish and British statutes

3.33   The citation conventions for modern statutes are fairly straightforward. An Irish Act, in the sense an Act made by the Oireachtas since the foundation of the State, is cited by its short title, e.g. Succession Act, 1965. In such Acts, there is always a comma after the word "Act", to separate it from the date. Since 1963, British statutes are cited in much the same way. Up until that time, as we shall see, there was a more cumbersome method of statutory citation based on regnal years. However, by virtue of the Parliamentary Numbering and Citation Act 1962, acts are now numbered in chronological order, starting with number 1 at the beginning of each calendar year, as in Ireland. However, unlike Ireland, the number known, for reasons we shall come to, as the "chapter", is often inserted after the title of a British statute. Thus, the Human Rights Act passed in by the U.K. Parliament in 1998 may be cited as

> Human Rights Act 1998, c. 42

More commonly, however, it will be cited simply by the short title set out in the final section, in this case the Human Rights Act 1998. Note that there is no comma separating the word "Act" and the date in British legislation.

Statute numbering in Ireland

3.34   In Ireland, all our statutes are numbered chronologically starting with number 1 at the beginning of each calendar year, but the number does not form part of the short title. If, however, for some reason, one wanted to refer to it, one would simply write, e.g. "the Age of Majority Act, 1985 (No 2)". Tables of statutes in textbooks and elsewhere often include the number so as to guide the reader more easily to the text of the statute itself, as the Acts are arranged in chronological order in the bound volumes of statutes. Care must taken, though, to distinguish between this practice and the situation that arises when two or more Acts with identical titles are passed in the same year. For example, three Courts Acts were enacted in 1986. The second and third of these are cited as: the Courts (No. 2) Act, 1986 and the Courts (No. 3) Act, 1986. When the number is part of the title, as in these instances, it must, of course, be included in any citation. Just remember that the function of the number in such a title is to indicate that this was the second or third Act, as the case may be, with the same name enacted that year. The chronological numbers of these Acts are a different matter.

Scotland and Northern Ireland

3.35 The Scottish Parliament (6.59 below) and the Northern Ireland Assembly (Chapter 5 below) have been enacting their own statutes since 1999 and 2000 respectively. Scottish Acts are cited by their short titles, but with the addition "asp" (short for "Act of the Scottish Parliament") followed by the chronological number. Thus, the first Act passed by the Parliament in 1999 was the

Mental Health (Public Safety and Appeals) (Scotland) Act 1999 asp 1

Acts passed during the year 2000 included:

Budget (Scotland) Act 2000 asp 2
Adults with Incapacity (Scotland) Act 2000 asp 4

Two things will be noted about the citation system. First, the word "Scotland" in parentheses occurs in the title itself and *before* the word "Act". Secondly, as mentioned, the main part of the title is followed by the chronological number. Therefore, "asp" in Scotland serves the same role as "c" in Westminster statutes.

3.36 Northern Ireland's citation system, on the other hand, is closer to Westminster's. An Act passed by the Northern Ireland Assembly is cited as:

Appropriation Act (Northern Ireland) 2000 c 2.

It will be noted that "Northern Ireland" appears in parentheses *after* the word Act and before the date. This is quite important, and it reflects a convention that existed long before the establishment of the present Northern Ireland Assembly. When the words "Northern Ireland" appear after the word "Act", they indicate that the Act as made in Northern Ireland itself. If, on the other hand, they appear before the word "Act", they indicate that it is an Act made at Westminster but applicable only to Northern Ireland as opposed to other parts of the U.K., e.g. the Judicature (Northern Ireland) Act 1978. The same convention applies to statutory instruments.

Older statutes

3.37   The first Act of Parliament passed in England was the Statute of Merton in 1235. It took its name from the Surrey village in which Parliament met to enact it. This became the convention for a century or more afterwards. Thus, we have the Statute of Marlborough (1267), the Statute of Westminster (1275) and the Statute of Gloucester (1278). More commonly, however, titles of early statutes were determined by their principal subject matter, as in the Statute of Mortmain (1279), the Statute of Uses (1535) or the Statute of Frauds (1677). However, from the 16th century onwards, statutes began to be cited by their short titles in much the same as they are now, e.g. the Relief of Irish Protestants Act, 1688. However, their official citation was by regnal year (see immediately below). A few important statutes have short titles which do not include the year, e.g. the Act of Settlement (1700), the Statute of Frauds (1677). When citing them, it is as well to place the year in parentheses after the title, as in the two examples just given.

Citation by regnal year

3.38   Students are often puzzled when they encounter an Act cited solely by regnal year. They may read in a footnote, for example, that the larceny of a dog is an offence by virtue of 6 & 7 Geo. 5, c. 50, s. 5. The last two elements of this citation should be easy to decipher. They clearly refer to section 5 of the fiftieth statute enacted in a certain year. But, which year? That is to be found in the first element, 6 & 7 Geo. 5. We might guess that "Geo. 5" refers to King George the Fifth, and that is indeed the case. This leaves us with "6 & 7" which refers in fact to the sixth and seventh years of the reign of King George V. The statute in question is the Larceny Act, 1916.

3.39   Up until 1963, U.K statutes were cited by regnal year (as, indeed, were pre-1800 Irish statutes). A regnal year runs from the date on which the monarch ascends to the throne. In the case of the present Queen Elizabeth II, it runs from February to February. A parliamentary session, on the other hand, runs from autumn to autumn and will therefore, in all probability, straddle two regnal years. That is why the Larceny Act, 1916 is cited as 6 & 7 Geo 5. It was enacted during the parliamentary session that straddled the sixth and seventh years of the reign of King George V. Likewise, the Offences Against the Person Act, 1861 is cited as 24 & 25 Vic. c.100. It was the 100th statute passed in the parliamentary session extending over the 24th and 25th years of the reign of Queen Victoria.

3.40   While it is useful to be aware of the regnal year mode of citation, one rarely encounters many difficulties as a result of it. Modern tables and indexes of statutes almost invariably give the short titles and dates of all statutes, included those enacted before 1963. But familiarity with the system can be helpful when consulting older volumes of statutes, some of which have the regnal years rather than the calendar years on their spines. Full lists of regnal years are given in Appendix 1 of Walker's *Oxford Companion to Law* (Oxford, 1980), in French, *How to Cite Legal Authorities* (London, 1996), and in Raistrick's *Lawyers' Law Books* 3rd edn (London, 1997) at p. 599.

Chapter numbers

3.41   The practice of numbering statutes by chapter may also seem peculiar. In fact, it simply derives from the idea that only one statute was passed in each parliamentary session, but that this annual statute was divided into chapters. This was largely fictitious because each chapter was in fact a separate statute. However, as noted earlier, the convention is still followed today in both Westminster and Northern Ireland Assembly legislation.

Local and personal Acts

3.42   Local and Personal Acts are cited in much the same way as Public General Acts, e.g. United Reformed Church Act 2000. The only difference is that the chapter numbers of such Acts are given in Roman numerals. Therefore, the full citation for the Act just mentioned would read:

United Reformed Church Act 2000, c. ii.

SECONDARY MATERIAL

3.43   This topic is also considered in Chapter 14 below, but will be briefly summarised here. Essentially, the title of a book or a journal (when given in full) is placed in italics, and all other information is given in ordinary type. The other important rule to remember is that the title of an article is always placed in inverted commas. When citing a book, one must give the name(s) of the author or authors, the title of the book, the edition if there is more than one, the place and date of publication. The name of the publisher is often included as well, but that depends on the house style of the publication for which one is writing. The rule about putting the titles of books in italics also applies to titles of reports, reference works and encyclopaedias. One feature of law books is that they tend to be published in new editions fairly frequently to reflect changes in the law itself. Consequently, it is always important to indicate the edition to which one is referring when more than one edition has been published. When referring to the author's name, it is usually sufficient to include the surname, although some publishers insist on having the initials as well. If a book consists of an edited collection of articles or essays, the name(s) of the editor or editors are given instead of the author's. The following examples illustrate these rules.

Book by one author

3.44   A book by one author may be cited as:

Smith, Criminal Evidence (London, 1995)

Alternatively: J. Smith, *Criminal Evidence* (London, 1995); Smith, *Criminal Evidence* (London: Sweet and Maxwell, 1995); or J. Smith, *Criminal Evidence* (London: Sweet and Maxwell, 1995), depending on whether the author's initials and/or publisher are required as part of the publisher's style sheet or student essay instructions.

Book by more than one author

3.45   A book by more than one author may be cited as:

Byrne and Binchy, *Annual Review of Irish Law 1989* (Dublin, 1990).

Note here that the year under review, 1989, is part of the title, and must be included. The names of the authors should be given as they appear on the title page, and not in alphabetical order. Again, the writer may be required to insert authors' initials and/or publisher as in the immediately preceding example.

Titles and sub-titles of books

3.46   Many books have a sub-title as well as a main title. Generally, it is preferable to include the entire title, as it may provide a better indication to the reader as to what the book is about. The sub-title may be separated from the main title by a colon, e.g.

Sunstein, After the Rights Revolution: Reconceiving the Regulatory State (Cambridge, MA., 1990).

Edited books

3.47   The name of the editor is given in the same way as an author, but followed by "ed.", usually in parentheses, e.g.

O'Dell (ed.), *Leading Cases of the Twentieth Century* (Dublin, 2000).

Again, the editor's initials and/or publisher may be required, depending on instructions.

Translated books

3.48   When a book has been translated from one language to another, the name of the translator is usually included after the title, e.g.

> Foucault, *Discipline and Punish: the Birth of the Prison*, trans. by A. Sheridan (London, 1977).

Edition number

3.49   The edition number is usually included immediately after the title, e.g.

> Craig, *Administrative Law* 3rd edn (London, 1994).

The abbreviation for "edition" varies. Some prefer "ed.', others "edn", the latter being the one recommended by the *Oxford Dictionary for Writers and Editors* (Oxford: Clarendon Press, 1991).

Identity of publisher

3.50   When the publisher's name is given, it is usually inserted after the place of publication from which it is separated by a colon, e.g.

> Kennedy, *Treat Me Right: Essays in Medical Law and Ethics* (Oxford: Clarendon Press, 1988).

The place of publication should always be given, even in the case of university presses such as Harvard, Yale, Oxford or Cambridge. Some of these have publishing houses in different locations, e.g. Harvard University Press has offices at both Cambridge, Massachusetts and London. When both are given on the title page or the reverse of the title page, it is generally sufficient to mention one.

Journal articles

3.51   This matter is dealt with more specifically in Chapter 14, but a typical citation would be:

> Bollinger, "Free Speech and Intellectual Values" (1983) 92 Yale L.J. 438.

Where a journal is cited primarily by volume number, as most of them are, the year is included in parentheses before the volume number. In certain journals which are identified primarily by year, as in the case of the *Criminal Law Review,* the year is placed in square brackets as in the case of a law report, e.g.

> Spencer, "The Case for a Code of Criminal Procedure" [2000] Crim .L.R. 519.

Abbreviated journal titles

3.52   Most journals have abbreviated titles, as in the two examples just given. The general convention appears to be that a journal title is placed in italics only if the full title is given, e.g. *Yale Law Journal* or *Criminal Law Review*. If any part of it, as in "Yale L.J." above, is abbreviated, it is placed in ordinary type.

Indicating particular pages

3.53   Often in a footnote, one will need to refer to a particular page of a book or an article. This is done simply by writing " at p. 123". In the case of a journal article, the initial page number is given first, e.g.

>   Spencer, "The Case for a Code of Criminal Procedure" [2000] Crim. L.R.
>   519 at 528.

Sometimes, "at" is replaced by a comma, e.g. "519, 528". When referring to the page of a book, one can just write:

>   Smith, *Criminal Evidence* (London, 1995), 27 (or p. 27).

When referring to a sequence of pages, one can write,

>   Smith, *Criminal Evidence* (London, 1995), 27-32 (or pp. 27-32).

Official reports and publications of law reform bodies

3.54   These publications will rarely have an identified author. The body or government department that produced the report is generally treated as the author. For example, the cover of the Law Reform Commission's report on dishonesty reads: *The Law Reform Commission Report on Dishonesty.* The title page, however, is a better guide as it reads: The Law Reform Commission; LRC43 – 1992; *Report on the Law Relating to Dishonesty.* The best way of citing this is to treat the Commission as the author, e.g.

>   Law Reform Commission, *Report on the Law Relating to Dishonesty*,
>   LRC43-1992 (Dublin, 1992).

The number of a report or consultation paper is usually included after the title. There is seldom any need to mention the publisher in such a case as it will almost invariably be the law reform body itself.

3.55   A publication of a government department is usually cited in the same way, e.g.

>   Department of Justice, *The Management of Offenders: A Five-Year Plan* Pn.
>   0789 (Dublin, 1994).

Government departments often change names with the formation of new governments. For example, the Department of Justice is now the Department of Justice, Equality and Law Reform. When citing publications, use whatever name the department had at the date of publication.

3.56 Some official publications are produced by specially appointed commissions or groups, and their reports may not have any particular titles. Again, the group is treated as the author and the publication referred to generally as "report", "interim report" or whatever. Thus, the *Final Report of the Expert Working Group on the Probation and Welfare Service* is cited as:

> Expert Working Group on Probation and Welfare Service, *Final Report*, Pn. 7234 (Dublin, 1999).

> Royal Commission on Criminal Justice, *Report*, Cm. 2263 (London: HMSO, 1993).

Official publications, unlike Irish Law Reform Commission Reports, are generally published by the state stationery office, HMSO in the U.K, the Stationery Office in Ireland. This can be included after the place of publication, as in the case of the Royal Commission Report above. The publication details for the report on probation could read: (Dublin: Stationery Office, 1999).

CHAPTER 4

Primary Sources of Irish Law

CONSTITUTIONAL LAW

4.01   The Constitution of Ireland, *Bunreacht na hÉireann*, was enacted by the People in a referendum held in July 1937 and entered into force on December 29, 1937. It superseded the Constitution of the Irish Free State which had been in force since 1922 and which had been amended many times (see 4.14 below). The present Constitution may be amended, whether by way of variation, addition or repeal, in accordance with the provisions of Articles 46 and 47. A proposed amendment must be processed through the Houses of the Oireachtas as a Bill in the same way as an ordinary piece of legislation. However, instead of entering into law by receiving the President's signature, it must be submitted to the People in a referendum. For the amendment to be adopted, it must be supported by a majority of those voting in the referendum. Once passed by referendum, the Bill incorporating the amendment must be signed and promulgated as law by the President. There is no right of popular initiative, though such a right did exist in the early days of the 1922 constitution.[1] As a matter of practical politics, therefore, any amendment proposed nowadays must have the support of the Government. Otherwise, it would stand little chance of securing the necessary support in the Dáil and Seanad. Once a proposal is submitted to the People, all it requires is the support of a majority of those voting, even if the turnout is very low. This arrangement has some drawbacks, but it also has advantages. Certain amendments, such as those adopted in 1979 in relation to university representation in the Seanad and child adoption,[2] while undoubtedly of public importance, are of limited public interest. They might stand little chance of being adopted if a qualified voting majority were required.

4.02   When the Constitution was first enacted in 1937, it contained a Preamble and 63 Articles. However, Articles 51 to 63 were transitory and all of them have now lapsed. Their main purpose was to validate certain existing arrangements and institutions, such as the courts, pending the enactment of legislation to give effect to the precise terms of the new Constitution. The document now

---

[1]   Article 48. The initiative was abolished by the Constitution (Amendment No 10) Act, 1928.
[2]   Now Articles 18.4.2 and 37.2 respectively.

consists of a Preamble and 50 Articles in both Irish and English texts. Article 25.5.4 provides that in the case of conflict, the Irish text shall prevail. This is a somewhat illogical arrangement, given that the English text alone was debated in the Dáil in 1937 (there was no Seanad at the time). There are a few obvious textual conflicts. For example, the English text of Article 12.4 provides that every citizen who has reached his 35th year is eligible for election as President, whereas the Irish text requires the citizen to have completed his 35th year. Attached to the Constitution are two comprehensive indexes, one in Irish and one in English, with some interesting differences between the two. The entry for "women" in the English index, for example, says, "See family; sex". The entry for "mná" in the Irish Index, on the other hand, includes references to Dáil Éireann, nationality, citizenship and livelihood, all of which are categorised under "Sex" in the English index!

4.03   The text of the present Constitution is published in book form and available from the Government Publications Sale Office and from other booksellers. Article 25 authorises the Taoiseach to cause to be prepared under his supervision a text of the Constitution in both Irish and English incorporating all amendments up to that point. The most recent text dates from December 1999 and is certainly more handsomely produced than its predecessors. A complete text will also be found in Kelly, Hogan and Whyte, *The Irish Constitution*, which is currently in its third edition published in 1994. This edition does not, naturally enough, include the more recent amendments, but it is about the only accessible source of the transitory articles (formerly Articles 51 to 63) which are printed at the end of the book.

The Irish Text of the Constitution

4.04   As noted earlier, the Constitution is enrolled in both Irish and English texts, and in the case of conflict, the Irish text prevails. Traditionally, Irish was written in Gaelic script with its own distinctive lettering and with lenition designated by a dot or stop sign over the relevant consonant. Since the early 1960s, Gaelic script has ceded to Roman script, with lenition designated by a 'h' immediately after the relevant consonant. There has also been a long-running debate over the standardisation of the Irish language. Considerable variations continue to exist in matters of spelling and grammar. Throughout the first fifty years or so of the 20th century, there was a good deal of controversy over whether Roman script should replace Gaelic script. Ever since the foundation of the State, Oireachtas publications, including the Irish version of statutes, showed a clear preference for the Roman script with modernised spelling. In the late 1920s, the Gaelic League mounted a strong campaign against the abandonment of the Gaelic script and, as Professor Ó Cúiv has written, so powerful was this point of view that in 1937, the Government decided to publish the new Constitution in Gaelic type and outmoded spelling.[3] Later published editions adopted the Roman script and more modern spelling, and each published edition now states on the reverse of the title page that the spelling used is in accordance with the standards of the Translation Section of the Houses of the Oireachtas. There have been two important scholarly analyses of the Irish text of the Constitution and the problems associated with the orthographical changes it has undergone. The first is a lengthy article by Richard Humphreys in the *Irish Jurist*[4] and the other a study commissioned by the All-Party Oireachtas Committee on the Constitution. The latter study, entitled *Bunreacht na hÉireann: A Study of the Irish Text*, by Micheal Ó Cearúil, is a major work, running to 760 pages, providing a detailed linguistic analysis of virtually every word and phrase in the entire Irish text. It will doubtless be of great interest to students and scholars of the language, but would also be very helpful to a court called upon to interpret the Irish text or to any person or body commissioned to re-draft it. The introductory chapter contains a particularly fine survey of the problems associated with the Irish text.

Parliamentary history

4.05   The draft Constitution of 1937 was considered by the Dáil alone, the Senate having been abolished in 1936. On March 3, 1937, the President of the Executive Council, Mr de Valera, was given leave to introduce the draft Constitution. The text appears to have been circulated to members of the Dáil on April 30. The second stage began on May 11, 1937, and the debate on the various stages continued until the text was approved on June 14, 1937. The entire exercise was completed in 14 days or so, and many other unrelated bills and topics were considered in the meantime. For example, on June 3, after a Committee Stage debate on the Constitution, the Dáil moved on to consider destitution in Tipperary. The references for the Dáil debates on the draft Constitution are as follows:

1st Stage   65 *Dáil Debates* cols. 1438-9 (March 10, 1937)

2nd stage   67 *Dáil Debates* cols. 29-163, 190-322, 325-470 (May 11, 12, 13, 1937)

Committee   67 *Dáil Debates* cols. 941-999, 1003-1080, 1084-1142, 1160-1234, 1237-1310, 1321-1378, 1394-1472, 1483-1664, 1650-1793, 1847-1925 (May 25 to June 4, 1937).

Report etc   68 *Dáil Debates* cols. 114-248, 258-306, 332-345, 345-434 (June 9 to June 14, 1937).

---

[3]   "The Changing Form of the Irish Language" in Ó Cúiv (ed.), *A View of the Irish Language* (Dublin, 1969) p. 22 at p. 30.
[4]   "The Constitution of Ireland: The Forgotten Textual Quagmire" (1987) 22 Ir Jur (n.s.) p. 169.

Referendum materials

4.06 As noted earlier, a proposed constitutional amendment is unlikely to be put to a referendum unless it has the support or, at least, the consent of the Government of the day. Until recently, the Government was free to campaign actively in support of a proposed amendment and to use public funds for that purpose. Opposition parties, pressure groups and private individuals were, of course, free to oppose it so long they had the necessary resources. All of this changed radically with the Supreme Court's decision in *McKenna v. An Taoiseach* [1995] 2 I.R. 10. A majority of the Court held that it was unconstitutional for the Government to spend public money to promote a particular result in a referendum. This called for a new strategy to ensure that members of the public were informed in a balanced way of the issues involved in proposed amendments.

4.07 The conduct of referenda is now governed primarily by the Referendum Acts of 1994 and 1998. The Act of 1994 deals comprehensively with procedural matters including the organisation of ballots, voting, appeals and so forth. The Act of 1998 is the more germane to our present purposes, as it was intended to deal with the problems caused by the *McKenna* judgment. This Act provides that when a constitutional referendum is due to be held, the Minister for the Environment and Local Government may establish a referendum commission[5] chaired by a retired superior court judge or a serving judge of the High Court and consisting of four other members who serve *ex officio*.[6] The functions of this Commission, as set out in section 3 of the Act, include the preparation of statements explaining the subject matter of the proposed amendment as well as statements setting out arguments for and against the proposal. The statements must be fair to all interests concerned. They must be published and distributed using the various media, and should endeavour to promote and facilitate a fair discussion of the proposal. Within a specified period after the holding of the referendum, the Commission must prepare a report for the Minister in relation to the performance of its functions in respect of the referendum in question. These reports are published by the Referendum Commission (www.refcom.ie) and are available in university libraries, possibly in some public libraries, and in the Ombudsman's Office. When two or more referenda are held on the same day, the reports are likely to be incorporated in the same document. This is true of the Commission's Report on the Amsterdam Treaty 1998 and the constitutional changes made in response to the Good Friday Agreement 1998 which were the subject matter of the 18th and 19th Amendments, respectively, signed into law on 3 June 1998. A book entitled *Referendums in Ireland 1937–1999*,

---

[5] The actual appointment is made by statutory instrument. See, for example, S.I. No 53 of 1998 appointing a commission in respect of the referendum on the Amsterdam Treaty.

[6] These are the Comptroller and Auditor General, the Ombudsman, the Clerk of the Dáil and the Clerk of the Seanad. The details are set out in s. 2 of the Act.

available for £5 from The Government Publications Sales Office, is a mine of information about all referendums up to 1999 with detailed accounts of the results in each case.

Primary constitutional materials

4.08   The Constitution itself is quite a short document. It makes fairly detailed provisions in relation to the political institutions of the State, but deals with personal and fundamental rights in much broader terms. The study of constitutional law, therefore, must embrace not only of the text itself, but also the statutes that have been enacted to give effect to its provisions and, of course, the many judgments issued by the High Court and Supreme Court interpreting particular provisions. Like most common-law countries, but unlike many civil law jurisdictions, Ireland does not have a special constitutional court. Instead, the High Court and Supreme Court, in addition to all their other functions, deal with constitutional cases. Judgments delivered in these cases will be found in the two general law report series, the *Irish Reports* and *Irish Law Reports Monthly* (4.51 below). It is reasonably safe to assume that all major constitutional cases will appear in one or both of these series, but such is the volume of unreported cases that one can never be confident that every case raising a constitutional issue will be formally reported. For example, *McGrath and Ó Ruairc v. Trustees of Maynooth College* [1979] I.L.R.M. 166, which raised some important constitutional issues remained unreported for over 10 years. The 1976 to 1980 volumes of *Irish Law Reports Monthly* were not published until the late 1980s and early 1990s. (They were back issues, the series itself began in 1981). One must always have regard therefore to unreported as well as reported cases (discussed further at 4.46 below). Constitutional law is constantly being developed by the courts, so textbooks will seldom be completely up to date. Byrne and Binchy's *Annual Review of Irish Law*, which usually appears within 12 months of the end of the year with which it deals, is a good source of information on recent constitutional developments. Summaries of very recent cases will, of course, be found in *Irish Current Law* (4.79 below).

Constitutional review

4.09   The Constitution may be amended at any time as the need arises, in accordance with the terms of Articles 46 and 47, but there have also been some general reviews of the entire document in order to identify any provisions that might benefit from amendment or re-wording. A detailed account of the reviews to date is given in the *First Progress Report of the All-Party Oireachtas Committee on the Constitution* Dublin, 1997) pp. 105-110. The first major review was carried out in 1967, presumably to coincide with the 30th anniversary of the Constitution, by a committee of the Oireachtas. *The Report of the Committee on the Constitution* (Pr 9817) contains the conclusions of this review. Another review was begun in 1982 by a committee chaired by the Attorney General of the day, in conjunction with the so-called constitutional crusade initiated by the then Taoiseach, Dr Garrett Fitzgerald. This never led to a formal report, although some documents produced in conjunction with it seem to be extant. The most significant and far-reaching review was begun in 1995 and is on-going at the time of writing. The first stage of this review, the expert stage, was concluded with the publication of the *Report of the Constitution Review Group* (Pr 2632) in 1996. This group, chaired by Dr T.K. Whitaker, consisted of academic experts from a number of disciplines, practising lawyers and others. Its *Report* is a major document, running to over 700 pages, reviewing the entire Constitution in detail and making many recommendations for reform. It also includes appendices on possible reforms in the electoral system and other matters. The second stage, which may be termed the political stage, is ongoing and is in the hands of the All-Party Oireachtas Committee on the Constitution. Already this Committee has produced a number of progress reports (five at the time of writing). The third progress report, for example, dealt with the Presidency while the fourth dealt with the courts and the judiciary. These reports contain valuable analyses of their respective topics and often include interesting comparative material from other jurisdictions. Irrespective therefore of the shape and content of the Committee's final report, the progress reports will remain valuable to future researchers as indications of political thinking on a variety of constitutional matters and as sources of comparative information. Incidentally, the Review Group produced a large number of working documents on various aspects of the Constitution which are also valuable sources of information. Hopefully, they will eventually be found in most university libraries. Finally, although not an official document, there exists a proposed new Constitution, called *Constitution for a New Republic*, drafted in 1988 by a political party, the Progressive Democrats, shortly after its foundation. This was referred to extensively by the Review Group and seems to have influenced some of its recommendations.

Secondary constitutional materials

4.10   Secondary materials consist of books, reports and periodical literature. The sources of these materials are described in Chapter 4 below. The bibliography in Appendix 4 of this book (hopefully) includes every book on modern Irish constitutional law. There are three major treatises on the Constitution: those by Casey, Forde and Kelly, Hogan and Whyte. At the time of writing, the most up-to-date is Casey's *Constitutional Law in Ireland* the third edition of which was published in 2000. A new edition of Kelly, Hogan and Whyte, *The Irish Constitution* is in preparation. The latter text, which was originated by Professor John Kelly, consists of a detailed article-by-article analysis of the entire Constitution similar to a critical commentary on a classical text. After Professor Kelly's death in 1991, the third edition was prepared by Dr Gerard Hogan and Mr Gerry Whyte who had earlier collaborated with Professor Kelly on a Supplement to the second edition. The article-by-article commentary has been retained and this, combined with detailed analysis and extensive reference to secondary materials, makes it a particularly valuable resource for anyone working in public law generally but especially, of course, in constitutional law. The other textbooks mentioned are organised thematically, although in terms of subject matter, they generally follow the sequence of the Constitution itself.

4.11   There is no journal devoted exclusively to Irish constitutional law. Articles on the topic will be found in a range of journals, especially the *Irish Jurist* and the *Dublin University Law Journal*. So wide, however, is the influence of the Constitution that relevant articles and case notes will be found in a wide variety of journals such as those dealing with criminal law, labour law and family law. Valuable articles on the Irish Constitution will occasionally be found in foreign journals as well. In 1987, for example, a colloquium on Irish and US constitutional law was held at the University of St Louis, Missouri. Papers delivered at that colloquium were later published in (1998) 7:2 *St Louis University Public Law Review* (Papers presented in conjunction with the Smurfit Bicentennial Lectures).[7] Other noteworthy contributions to foreign law journals include Hogan's "Law and Religion: Church-State Relations in Ireland from Independence to the Present Day" (1987) 35 *American Journal of Comparative Law* 47-96, and Casey's "Judicial Power under Irish Constitutional Law" (1975) 24 *International and Comparative Law Quarterly* 305-324.

4.12   Unfortunately, there is no bibliography of Irish constitutional law; this is a gap waiting to be filled, possibly by an Internet enthusiast. Nor, surprisingly, is there an up-to-date book of cases and materials on the Constitution. There is, of course, a very fine collection of cases and materials by O'Reilly and Redmond but it was published in 1980 and, while still valuable, is long out of date. This is another task awaiting an enterprising scholar.

Constitutional history

4.13   The present Constitution is sometimes said to be the third constitution adopted or enacted in Ireland during the twentieth century. This is not strictly true; it is the second, the first having been the Constitution of the Irish Free State 1922. The other document to which people are usually referring is the Constitution of the first Dáil, adopted on January 21, 1919. This was not intended as a constitution for the State, which did not in any event exist at the time. Rather it was intended to govern the Dáil itself and was one of a number of documents adopted at its first meeting which must rank as one of the most

---

[7]   1987 happened to be both the 50th anniversary of the enactment of the Irish Constitution and the 200th anniversary of the drafting of the United States Constitution.

productive in Irish history. The texts of these documents will be found in Mitchell and Ó Snodaigh, *Irish Political Documents 1916-1949* (Dublin, 1985).[8] Broadly viewed, the Irish constitutional tradition extends back much further than 1919. A concise account of the salient developments is provided by Casey in *Constitutional Law in Ireland*, 3rd ed. (Dublin: Round Hall Sweet and Maxwell, 2000), Chapter 1, and a more detailed account by Ward, *The Irish Constitutional Tradition: Responsible Government and Modern Ireland 1782–1992* (Dublin: Irish Academic Press, 1994)

4.14 The Constitution of the Irish Free State 1922 attracted a good deal of scholarly attention during the first decade or so of its existence. The best known and most comprehensive study is Leo Kohn's *The Constitution of the Irish Free State* (London, 1932). Other book-length studies, such as those by Mansergh and McNeill, are listed under "Constitutional Law" in Appendix 4 of the present book.[9] The 1922 Constitution is contained in a schedule to Act No 1 of 1922 and will therefore be found in the first volume of the Acts of the Oireachtas, available in all law libraries. A copy of this Constitution was reprinted in a separate booklet some years ago and is (or was) available from the Government Publications Sale Office. Bear in mind, however, that this Constitution, which could be amended by ordinary legislation throughout its entire existence, underwent many changes between 1922 and 1937. Kohn indicates the various amendments and deletions that had been effected by the time his book was completed in 1932. Subsequent constitutional amendments can be identified by consulting the alphabetical lists in *Achtanna an Oireachtais* (4.18 below) for the years 1932 to 1937, or indeed the *Chronological Tables of the Statutes* (4.31 below) for the same years. For more detailed research on Irish constitutional history, the National Archives are an obvious source of primary material.

LEGISLATION

4.15 As a legal source, legislation may be divided into two categories. Primary legislation consists of the statutes enacted by the Oireachtas and those carried over into Irish law in accordance with Article 50 the Constitution. Secondary legislation consists of statutory instruments, bye-laws and similar rules made under the authority of a parent statute. An example of the distinction between these two categories of legislation has already been encountered in the

---

[8] For further information on the first Dáil, see Macardle, *The Irish Republic* (Dublin, 1951), Farrell, *The Founding of Dáil Éireann* (Dublin, 1972) and Farrell, "The Legislation of a 'Revolutionary' Assembly: Dáil Decrees 1919-1922" (1975) 10 Ir Jur (n.s.) 112.

[9] There are also some useful articles on the topic, e.g. Towey, "Hugh Kennedy and the Constitutional Development of the Irish Free State" (1977) 12 Ir Jur (n.s.) 355.

earlier part of the Chapter dealing with the Constitution. The Referendum Act 1998 is a piece of primary legislation, enacted by the Oireachtas. This Act, as noted, authorises, but does not require, the Minister for the Environment and Local Government to establish a commission to provide public information on the subject matter of a referendum. When the Minister decides to appoint such a commission, he or she does so by way of statutory instrument.

4.16 Each year, the Oireachtas (which consists of the Dáil, the Seanad and the President[10]) enacts 30 to 40 statutes. They vary in length and complexity and owe their origins to a variety of factors. In an era of coalition or partnership governments, it has become customary for the participating political parties to draw up a programme for government as part of the agreement to form an administration. This programme will usually include commitments to introduce a reasonably wide range of legislation reflecting the collective policies of the parties involved. Many other statutes are introduced to give effect to international obligations including, of course, those imposed by membership of the European Community. Pressure groups also exercise considerable influence over the introduction and content of legislation in certain areas. Statutes are occasionally enacted in response to some particular emergency or event. The Offences Against the State (Amendment) Act 1998, for example, was introduced and passed within weeks of the Omagh bombing.

Statutes in force (1): Pre-1922 Statutes

4.17 The statutes currently in force in Ireland have been enacted by several different parliaments over many centuries.[11] The most convenient way of tracking down pre-1800 statutes nowadays is through collected editions. One such collection is Grierson's *Statutes at Large Passed by the Parliaments held in Ireland from 1310 to 1786* and continued to 1800. This was first published in 20 volumes with a later edition in 12 volumes. A revised edition of the Irish statutes from 1310 to 1800 was published by HMSO in 1885, and is a more manageable collection than Grierson's. More recently, a single volume entitled *The Irish Statutes, Revised Edition AD 1310–1800*, with an introductory essay by Professor W.N. Osborough, was published by Round Hall Press (Dublin, 1995). Some pre-1800 statutes are still relevant, although with recent law reform, they are becoming fewer in number. The most convenient source of such statutes will often be collected legislation (4.28 below). Many of the older statutes still in force have to do with land law and conveyancing, and all of them will be found, with annotations, in Wylie's *Conveyancing Law* (Dublin: Butterworths, 1999). The texts of older criminal statutes, in so far as they are

---

[10] The President, although above politics, is part of the Oireachtas (legislature), as she must sign each Bill which has been passed by the Oireachtas before it becomes law.
[11] See Newark, *Notes on Irish Legal History* (Belfast, 1964) 27.

still relevant, will be found in the various *Justices of the Peace*.[12] From the entry into force of the Act of Union of Great Britain and Ireland in 1801 until the foundation of Irish Free State in 1922, legislation for all of Ireland was made in London. This legislation will be found in the volumes of the *Public General Acts and Measures* for the 19th and early 20th centuries, which are to be found in most law libraries in the British legislation section and which are further described at 6.06 below. Researchers may sometimes have reason to consult an older private Act dating from the 19th century. During the 19th century, especially with the spread of the railway system, many such Acts were passed to deal with local issues in Ireland, e.g. the Athenry and Limerick Junction Act, 1863. Bound volumes of the older Local and Personal Acts are found in some libraries. The mode of citing these Acts has been described at 3.42 above. A six-volume index to the Private Acts made between 1797 and 1995 was recently published by HMSO, the final volume appearing in 1999. It is a tremendous help to anyone trying to identify relevant private legislation.

Statutes in force (2): Acts of the Oireachtas

4.18   Since the foundation of the State in 1922, the sole and exclusive power to enact legislation has been vested in the Oireachtas, which consists of the Dáil, the Seanad and the President. Virtually all Acts passed by the Oireachtas are public Acts, meaning that they are of general application. Occasionally, local or private Acts are passed, but they are few and far between. Immediately, after an Act is signed into law by the President in accordance with the terms of the Constitution, a printed version of it is issued and it remains available for purchase from the Government Publications Sales Office as long as it is in force. Until the end of 1981, all the Acts were later published in bound annual volumes known as *Achtanna an Oireachtais (The Acts of the Oireachtas)*. These contained the texts of the Acts in the language in which they were passed (almost invariably English) together with a facing translation in the other official language, Irish or English as the case may be. Since the foundation of the State only a few Acts have been passed in Irish alone or in both Irish and English. Under the Constitution, the authoritative text of the Act is in the language in which it was enacted. If it was enacted in both official languages, the Irish version prevails in the case of conflict between the two texts. For some unknown reason, is the publication of *Achtanna an Oireachtais* seemed to come to an abrupt end in 1981, although in 2000 a volume suddenly appeared for 1982. Since1981, the statutes have been produced in bound annual A4-size

---

[12] These were reference works, many of which were published throughout the 19th and early 20th centuries for the guidance of magistrates and Justices of the Peace. They typically included texts of all statutes relevant to or applicable by courts of summary jurisdiction. A leading Irish example would be O'Connor's *The Irish Justice of the Peace* 2 vols. (1915). They also listed and summarised relevant cases.

volumes entitled *Acts of the Oireachtas as Promulgated*. The full texts of the Statutes for 1922 to 1998 are now available on both the Internet and CD-ROM (see 2.28 above). Nowadays, there are often two, three or four annual volumes of *Acts of the Oireachtas as Promulgated* for each year, depending in the volume of legislation passed. An alphabetical and chronological index for the Public General Acts appears at the beginning of each volume. If, as seldom happens, a Private Act has been passed during the year, it is included at the very end of the volume. There is a separate entry for Private Acts at the end of the chronological index as such Acts are numbered separately. Thus, the Altamont (Amendment of Deed of Trust) Act, 1993 is Number 1 (Private Act) of 1993.

Citation and division of statutes

4.19   Each statute has a long title and a short title. The long title is recited in capital letters at the very beginning of the Act just before the enactment formula. The short title is given in a section towards the end of the Act, sometimes towards the beginning. Take, for example, the Companies Act, 1963 which has the following long title:

> AN ACT TO CONSOLIDATE WITH AMENDMENTS CERTAIN ENACTMENTS RELATING TO COMPANIES AND FOR PURPOSES CONNECTRED WITH THAT MATTER. [*23rd December 1963*].

The date is not part of the long title. It is the date on which the Act was signed into law. The short title in this case is given in section 1(1) which states:

> This Act may be cited as the Companies Act, 1963.

Nowadays, the short title is more commonly found in the last section.

Collective titles and joint construction

4.20   The last section of a statute may also provide for a collective citation. This occurs when a later statute supplements or amends an earlier one dealing with the same topic. Section 17 of the Unfair Dismissals (Amendment) Act, 1993, for example, provides:

> (1) .....
> (2) The Unfair Dismissals Acts, 1977 and 1991, and this Act may be cited together as the Unfair Dismissals Acts, 1977 to 1993.
> (3) The Unfair Dismissals Acts, 1977 and1991 and this Act shall be construed together as one.

---

[13] Bennion, *Statutory Interpretation*, 3rd ed. (London: Butterworths, 1997) 590.

A collective citation provision, as in subsection (2), has, according to Bennion, "a like effect from the point of view of interpretation as a provision equipping an Act with a short title".[13] This is of little practical importance unless one is referring to the relevant Acts in a general way, e.g. "the Unfair Dismissals Acts 1977 to 1993 provide redress for employees claiming to have been unfairly dismissed". Normally, however, it will be necessary to refer to specific sections of legislation, e.g. " s. 2(i)(j) the Unfair Dismissals Act, 1977 as amended by s. 3 of the Unfair Dismissals (Amendment) Act, 1993". As for the joint construction provision, as in subsection (3) above, Bennion says that where "two or more Acts are required by a provision in the later Act to be construed as one, every enactment in the two Acts is to be construed as if contained in a single Act, except in so far as the content indicates that the later Act was intended to modify the earlier Act".[14]

Division of statutes

4.21 Statutes are divided into sections, sub-sections, paragraphs and sub-paragraphs. Sections and sub-sections are denoted by Arabic numerals, paragraphs by letters in alphabetical order and sub-paragraphs in Roman numerals. Some publications insist on spelling out the word "section" in every case. However, it is quite acceptable to abbreviate it to "s" or "s.", with or without the stop, depending on house style. Likewise, "subsection" is usually abbreviated to "subs.", and "paragraph" to "para". Generally, in fact, there is no need to refer to subsections, paragraphs and sub-paragraphs. A reference to:

$$s.6(1)(b)(ii)$$

means sub-paragraph (ii) of paragraph (b) of subsection (1) of section 6.

4.22 Statutes, particularly longer ones, are often divided into Parts. This is true, for example, of the Companies Act 1963. The courts generally "will not read a section in one part or division as relating to a subject matter that is dealt with in another part or division of the Act unless it is clear from the wording of the section that it must be read in that way and that the section has therefore been placed in the wrong part or division."[15]

4.23 Many Acts have one or more schedules, placed at the end, which can serve a variety of purposes. One common purpose is to list earlier statues being repealed or amended by the present one. Or, a schedule may provide a list of one kind of another, such as the list of proscribed drugs at the end of the Misuse of Drugs Act, 1977, or the list of indictable offences triable summarily under the Criminal Justice Act, 1951. A schedule is usually tied to some substantive

---

[14] *Ibid.*, 588.
[15] Gifford and Salter, *How to Understand an Act of Parliament* (London: Cavendish Publishing, 1996) 42.

provision of the Act. A section may provide that "the enactments set out in Schedule 2 are repealed or amended". Thus, section 5 of the Children Act, 2001 provides that "[t]he enactments specified in Schedule 2 are repealed to the extent specified in *column* (3) of that Schedule . . ." Schedule 2 then lists 13 earlier statutes which are either fully or partly repealed.

Draft statutes

4.24 A draft statute proceeding through the Houses of the Oireachtas is known as a Bill, and bears the date of the year in which it was introduced. When it becomes an Act it bears the date of the year in which it was enacted. Thus, the Criminal Justice Bill (No.2) 1997 has now become the Criminal Justice Act 1999. Any member of the Oireachtas may introduce a Bill. However, the vast majority of those passed into law will have begun as Government Bills which means that they are reasonably sure of the securing the necessary support in both Houses of the Oireachtas. All Bills introduced in the Dáil are published on green paper, while Bills introduced in the Seanad are published on yellow paper. A Bill passes through five stages in the House in which it is introduced. The first stage is largely formal, simply noting the Bill. The second and third stages are the more important; this is when members of the House get the opportunity to discuss the Bill in detail. The second stage is generally known as the second reading while the third is the committee stage. The fourth and final stages proceed more expeditiously. When a Bill has been through all five stages in the first House (usually the Dáil), it proceeds automatically to the second stage in the other. When all stages have been completed, the Bill is presented to the President for signature. The President must sign the Bill unless it contains a proposal to amend the Constitution or unless she proposes to refer it to the Supreme Court under Article 26 of the Constitution. The purpose of such a reference is to obtain the Court's decision as to whether the Bill or any part of it is repugnant to the Constitution. Neither a Money Bill nor a Bill for which time has been abridged under Article 24 of the Constitution may be referred to the Supreme Court under Article 26.

4.25 Generally speaking, once an Act becomes law, the draft Bills leading to it are of little interest. Sometimes, however, it may be useful to refer to them in order to trace the history of government or parliamentary thinking on a particular provision that was amended between introduction and enactment. University libraries usually maintain archives of all Bills whether or not they have become law. Lawyers and law students are more likely to need access to Bills in progress. Care should be taken, however, to distinguish between government Bills and Private Members' Bills, as the latter will probably never get beyond the second reading. There will be nothing on the face of the Bill to indicate the category to which it belongs. Towards the end of the last page, however, will be the name of the person who introduced it. If it has been introduced by a Minister in the Dáil or by the Leader of the Seanad, it is a government Bill. But if it has been introduced by an opposition deputy or senator, it is clearly a Private Member's Bill. Acts and Bills may be purchased in the Government Publications Sale Office (see Appendix 7).

Private member's bills and private bills

4.26 Any member of the Dáil or Seanad can introduce a bill, and when a bill is introduced other than on behalf of the Government, it is known as a Private Members Bill. The main limitation on Private Members Bills is that they cannot impose a charge on the Exchequer. A few such Bills have become law. For example, the Judicial Separation Act 1989 originated in a Private Member's Bill introduced by Deputy Alan Shatter. More often than not, Private Members Bills are introduced by Opposition spokespersons in order to promote party policy and, perhaps, to goad the Government of the day into introducing similar legislation.

4.27 A Private Bill is something quite different. It deals with a matter relating solely to a particular person, property or locality. They are few and far between. A complete list of Private Acts passed from 1922 to 1995 is given in the *Index to the Statutes* (4.31 below). A recent example would be The Altamont (Amendment of Deed of Trust) Act, 1993 which was enacted to allow for the Altamont estate at Westport, Co, Mayo to descend to the daughters of the present holder. The deed of trust had provided that the estate could only descend down the male line.

Collected legislation

4.28 There are several publications either in standard book form or in looseleaf form which conveniently collect together the main statutory provisions governing a particular branch of law. In the latter half of the 19th century, for example, several *Justices of the Peace* was published by various authors. These were usually substantial volumes that included, among other things, the main statutes applicable to the work of lay justices and resident magistrates. Indeed, they are still valuable as a source of some older criminal legislation. In recent years, several modern collections of legislation have been published dealing with conveyancing law, planning law, family law, competition law, commercial law, labour law and other areas. They vary in format and purpose. Some of them are intended merely as handy compendia of legislation for use in court or in the classroom. Others are extensively and expertly annotated. Wylie's *Conveyancing Law* (Dublin: Butterworths, 1999), for example, includes annotated versions of all the main conveyancing statutes, many of them dating from the 19th century and earlier. Another good example is O'Donnell's *Planning Law* (Dublin: Butterworths, 1999). Likewise, the statutes included in the loose-leaf work,

Irish Employment Legislation by Kerr, are very well annotated. All of these collections indicate provisions that have been repealed or amended. To update them, one need only check for repeals or amendments since the collection in question was published. All of the modern collections are listed under the appropriate subject headings, as well as under "Legislation, collected" in Appendix 4 of this book.

Annotated legislation

4.29   In 1984, Sweet and Maxwell introduced a very valuable service, the *Irish Current Law Statutes Annotated*. This is a publication, now running to many volumes, in loose-leaf format in which the text of each statute is given together with an introduction and detailed commentary by an expert in the relevant area of law. Other added value dimensions of the annotations include the date(s) of entry into force and the references for the Oireachtas debates. Unlike their English counterparts, all the volumes from 1984 onwards remain in loose-leaf form which means that older statutes can be updated to reflect new developments. There is now a separate loose-leaf volume with tables of statutes, statutory instruments and (a welcome development) a statute citator, described further at 4.33 below. Butterworths have recently introduced their own series of Irish Annotated Statutes consisting of separate volumes dedicated to a particular branch of law. The volumes by Wylie and O'Donnell mentioned in the previous paragraph are part of this series.

Electronic sources of legislation

4.30   A great leap forward in the accessibility of Irish legislation took place with the publication of the CD entitled *The Irish Statute Book 1922-1998* which contains the Acts of the Oireachtas, the statutory instruments, with chronological tables, from the foundation of the State up until 1998. The CD is easily searchable both by free search and also by reference to year and number of statute, or statutory instrument, as the case may be. Scrolling through the chronological table is, however, rather wearisome. To engage the search facility, just click on "search" which will produce a drop-down menu, which is fairly self-explanatory. The CD available from the Government Publications Sales Office for about £20 which means that users can carry it with them and use on lap top computers with a CD drive. The CD is accompanied by an explanatory booklet and there is help desk that can be contacted for further assistance. The entire contents of the CD are also available on the Attorney General's web site (www.irlgov.ie/ag) which can also be contacted through Delia Venables' web site (www.venables.co.uk/ireland.htm). This site has recently been revamped and is much easier to use now than it was at first. It is anticipated that both the CD and the web site will be updated annually. Remember, however, that the statutes on both the CD and the web site are the statutes as originally passed; they are *not* revised statutes. One could use the search facility to update the statutes, but the most reliable updating method is to use the *Chronological Table of the Statutes 1922-1995* (4.31 below) and the statute citators in the *Irish Current Law Statutes Annotated* (4.29 above) since then. The *Chronological Table*, updated to 1998, is now available on the Attorney General's web site (above). The persistent failure of the Government to produce regular and prompt tables to the Statutes in paperform is incomprehensible and a cause of great inconvenience to lawyers and researchers. As stated earlier, the electronic versions are not, as yet, entirely reliable for use for official purposes (see 2.28 above).

Indexes to the statutes since 1922

4.31 The Stationery Office has published various indexes to the statutes. There are fairly comprehensive indexes available for years 1922 to 1989. They are available in a single volume, *Index to the Statutes*, for years 1922 to 1985, although even within this volume the indexes for the years 1983 to 1985 are included as a supplement. The indexes for the years 1986 to 1989 are available in individual pamphlets. Now, there is also a general *Chronological Table of the Statutes 1922 to 1995* available as a single volume, but it does not include a subject index. We shall deal first with the *Chronological Table of the Statutes 1922-1995*. This is divided into six parts, the most important of which, for practical research purposes, are Parts I and V. Before using this volume read the foreword and table of contents carefully, as they explain very clearly the kind of information that can be obtained.

Part I is a chronological table of the Public Acts since 1922 indicating any repeals or amendments made by subsequent legislation, e.g.

Year & Number	Short Title	How Affected	Affecting Provision
1959			
31	Transport Act, 1959	s. 2 am.	24/1963 s. 34
32	Funds of Suitors Act, 1959	not affected	
33	*Electoral Amendment Act, 1959*	r.	19/1961 s. 9(3)

Titles of repealed statutes are shown in italics. This Part also lists in alphabetical order Acts brought into force by statutory instrument. Part I serves two useful purposes. If one has a reference to a statute by number, e.g. 31/1959, one can find the full title. It also indicates how the Acts have been affected by later Acts. Thus, in the above examples, s. 2 of the Transport Act was amended by s. 34 of Act No. 24 of 1963, while the Electoral Amendment Act, 1959 has been repealed in its entirety. One will have to consult the chronological list for 1963 to find out what Act No. 24 of the year was, and likewise with Act No. 19 of 1961. To find out the subsequent history of these Acts, consult the legislation update in *Current Irish*

Law Statutes Annotated (the Prelims and Tables volume). For very recent Acts, there may be no option but to check through the schedule of repeals and amendments at the end of each to see if there have been any relevant changes.

Part II consists of an alphabetical list of Orders made under Section 6(1) of the Ministers and Secretaries (Amendment) Act, 1939.

Part III consists of a Chronological List of Regulations made under Section 3 of the European Communities Act, 1972.

Part IV consists of a chronological table of the Private Acts 1922-1995

Part V consists of pre-1922 statutes indicating how they were affected. The most important part of this Part is Table 4 which shows how Public Statutes made during the lifetime of the Act of Union have been affected by Acts of the Oireachtas since 1922. The following extract serves as an example:

Session & Chapter	Short Title	How Affected	Affecting Provision
33 & 34 Vic.			
c. 57	*Gun Licence Act, 1870*	r.	28/1925, s. 49, sched. 3
c. 70	Gas and Waterworks Facilities Act, 1870	Trans of functions under.	S.I. No. 125 of 1959 S.I. No. 295 of 1977 S.I. No. 9 of 1980
c. 71	National Debt Act, 1870	Rstrct.	16/1989, ss 2, 18(1)
		Ss. 17, 73 (in pt) r	27/1965, ss.8, 9, sch.2, pt. 3

It will be noted that these statutes are listed primarily by regnal year and chapter number (3.38 above). However, the short titles in the second column always give the date as well, so one can go on that. Secondly, it will be noted that not all statutes are listed. There is no reference, for example, to statutes 58 to 69 for the session 33 & 34 Vic. It may be assumed these are unaffected or perhaps they did not apply to Ireland. It will also be noted that some of the changes, e.g. in the case of the Gas and Waterworks Facilities Act are made by statutory instrument rather than by statute. Some statutes are entirely repealed such as the Gun Licence Act. In other cases, entire sections are repealed such as s. 17 of the National Debt Act whereas in other cases, sections are only partly repealed, such as s. 73 of that Act. Obviously, to find out which statute is 16/1989, one goes back to the table in Part I.

Part VI is an alphabetical list of expressions used in British or Saorstát Éireann statutes which have been adapted by orders made under the Adaptation of Enactments Act, 1922 or the Constitution (Consequential Provisions) Act, 1937. For example, for "Bank of England" has been adapted to "Bank of Ireland".

4.32   The only thing missing from the *Chronological Table* is a subject index. This is to be found in the Indexes to the Statutes mentioned above, but unfortunately only up to 1989. However, one will find a general subject guide to the Statutes, though not a remarkably helpful one, in the Prelims and Tables Volume of *Irish Current Law Statutes Annotated.* The commencement dates for the statutes from 1993 to 1999 are also provided in this volume, immediately after the citators described in the next paragraph. There is also a list of legislation not yet in force. For more recent updates, consult the *Irish Current Law Monthly Digest* under both the main subject headings and the lists of statutory instruments.

Statute citator

4.33   Ireland did not have a proper statute citator until 1993 when it was introduced as part of the *Irish Current Law Statutes Annotated*, again in the Prelims and Tables volume. This is another excellent service provided by the *Statutes Annotated.* At present, there is a cumulative citator for the years 1993 to 1998, and a separate one for 1999. They are included under the indent entitled "Legislation Update". Every statute in force which has been in any way affected, whether by later statutory amendment or statutory instrument, or which has been the subject of a judicial decision since 1993 is listed in chronological order, with the appropriate changes or decisions mentioned. The earliest statute listed at present is the Fraudulent Conveyance Act, 1634. The citator is arranged in the same way as its English equivalent which is illustrated at 6.52 below.

Cases on statutes

4.34   It is often necessary to discover if there have been any judicial decisions on statutory provisions. Again, from 1993 onwards, the statute citator mentioned in the previous paragraph provides this information. To find out if, for example, there have been any cases dealing with section 2 of the Larceny Act, 1916, just track down the title of that Act in the 1993-1998 citator (it happens to be on page 18) where one will find the following entry;

6 & 7 Geo. 5 (1916)

50. Larceny Act

....

s.2, see *O'Shea v. Assistant Commissioner Conroy* [1995] 8 I.C.L.M.D

40; *D.P.P. v. O'Neill* [1998] 1 I.L.R.M. 221; *Killeen v. D.P.P.* [1997] 3
I.R. 218, S.C.

I.C.L.M.D. stands for *Irish Current Law Monthly Digest*, and the above reference tells us that the *O'Shea* case is digested at paragraph 40 of issue 8 for
1995. We must then turn to the citator for years after 1998 to see if there have
been further cases.

4.35   For the years before 1993, one must rely on the various *Digests* (4.70
below) which provide lists of statutes considered in reported cases, and these as
it happens brings one up to 1993. The Indexes to the *Irish Law Reports Monthly*
have tables of statutes judicially considered by cases reported in that series.
Each volume of the *Irish Reports* has, at the beginning, a chronological table of
statutes considered in the cases reported in that volume, with are reference to
the relevant page numbers of the volume. Once more, one can only remark on
the unfortunate absence of a set of cumulative tables to the *Irish Reports*, The
Green Index (4.74 below) which lists unreported cases from 1966 to 1975 has
a statutory index as well. Those with access to LEXIS can use the search facility to discover references to any Act in reported cases since 1950 and unreported cases since 1985. Anyone with access to the CD version of the *Irish
Reports* can use the search facility for the same purpose.

STATUTORY INSTRUMENTS (S.I.s)

4.36   The Statutory Instruments Act, 1947 defines a statutory instrument (S.I.)
as every "order, regulation, rule, scheme or bye-law" made in the exercise of a
statutory power. A copy of each S.I. must be sent to each of 10 designated
libraries and published by the Stationery Office. The Attorney General, however, is entitled to exempt a particular instrument from the provisions of the Act
of 1947, including the publication requirement, if satisfied that it is of purely
local or personal application, or for any other reason. Notice of the exemption
must be published in *Iris Oifigiúil*. Certain instruments relating to the defence
forces, for example, are not available to the public as a result of the application
of this exemption.

4.37   Hundreds of S.I.s are made every year. Shortly after being made, each
S.I., unless exempted, becomes available in typescript form in the language in
which it was made, almost invariably English. Later, they are published in bound,
blue-covered volumes of which there may be several for each year, and are
available since 1948 in this form. Sometimes, in between original publication
and their appearance in bound form, they may become available individually in
printed pamphlet form. Up until the end of 1973, all the published statutory
instruments appeared in the bound volumes in both Irish and English. Since

1974, however, they have been published solely in the language in which they were made, almost invariably English. Before the Act of 1947 came into force, S.I.s were known as Statutory Rules and Orders (S.R. & O.) which were published in volumes 1 to 39, between 1922 and 1947 with both Irish and English texts.

Citation and division of S.I.s

4.38 Nowadays, S.I.s are generally cited as:

Local Government (Planning and Development) Regulation (S.I. No 89 of 1990).

A pre-1948 Statutory Rule or Order is cited as:

Aliens Order (S.R. & O. No 395 of 1946).

An example of modern S.I. is given in Appendix 1 of this book. S.I.s are divided in more or less the same way as a statute, with a short explanatory note indicating its purpose at the end. Some S.I.s are very short, running to no more than a page or two. Others are very lengthy indeed. The various Rules of Court (below) would be prime examples of the latter category.

Rules of Court

4.39 Rules of Court are usually made by a Rules Committee, as permitted by statute. There are three sets of rules with which lawyers have frequent contact. First, there are the *Rules of the Superior Courts* (S.I. No. 15 of 1986) which is available in hardback book form running to more than 1,000 pages in all. These rules apply to the Supreme Court, the High Court and the Court of Criminal Appeal. An annotated version of these *Rules* under the title *Practice and Procedure in the Superior Court*, by O Floinn and Gannon has been published by Butterworths (Dublin, 1996). When using either of these volumes, bear in mind that the Rules are updated fairly often and one should therefore check the recent statutory instruments (or the lists of the them published in *Irish Current Law* (4.79 below) to see if there have been any amendments. The titles of any new instruments will generally begin with the words "Rules of the Superior Courts ....", so they are easy to identify. The *Rules of the Superior Courts*, abbreviated as R.S.C., are divided first of all into Orders, and each Order is further divided into Rules. Thus, the procedures governing applications for judicial review are set out in Order 84, while the time limits to be observed when making such an application are set out in Order 84, rule 21(1), which would usually be abbreviated to O. 84, r. 21(1).

4.40 The *Rules of the Circuit Court* are also in the form of a statutory instrument (No 179 of 1950), although they have been amended many times in the interim. For example, Circuit Court Rules (No 1) 1997 (S.I. No 84 of 1997) deals with proceedings under the Family Law (Divorce) Act, 1996 and related legislation. The CD of the Statutes and Statutory Instruments, and the Attorney General's web site (4.30 above) are useful sources of identifying new rules made for the Circuit Court since up until 1998. For later rules, check out the lists of statutory instruments in *Irish Current Law* (4.79 below). They are cited in the same way as the *Rules of the Superior Courts.*

4.41 The *Rules of the District Court* of 1948 were available in a slender volume. However, they had been amended many times and so, in 1997, they were reissued in a large A4 loose-leaf volume (S.I. No. 93 of 1997). They are divided and cited in the same way as the *Rules of the Superior Courts,* and sometime abbreviated to D.C.R. A detailed account of the practice and procedure of the District Court is provided by Woods in his various books, which are listed in the Bibliography in Appendix 4 of this book under the heading "Practice and Procedure".

Indexes of S.I.s

4.42 There are two indexes of S.I.s, one published by the Stationery Office, and the other published commercially by Butterworths. The Stationery Office *Index* is in several volumes covering the periods 1922-1938, 1938-1945, 1946-1947, 1948-60, 1961-1963, 1964-1970, 1971-1974, 1975-1979, 1980-1986, 1987-1995. Each is divided into two main parts, the first giving an alphabetical list of statutes and subsidiary legislation and showing the instruments made thereunder, together with the year and number of each instrument. The second part gives an alphabetical list of instruments with the year and number of each, or the volume of *Iris Oifigiúil* in which it is recorded as well as the statutory authority under which it was made.

4.43 Humphreys' *Index to Irish Statutory Instruments* (Dublin: Butterworths, 1998) is in three volumes. The first consists of an alphabetical list of all instruments, rules and orders made between December 1922 and December 1986. Those printed in bold type were still in force at the time of going to press, those in italics had been repealed. The second volume consists of an alphabetical list of enabling Acts as well as the instruments made under them. The third volume is a subject index. This remains a very useful reference work, and it would be good to see it updated.

4.44 The Prelims and Tables volume of *Irish Current Law Statutes Annotated* has both alphabetical and numerical tables of S.I.s from 1985 to 2000. Each year is listed separately in both tables. One distinct limitation of this service is that it does not indicate which are still in force and which are repealed. Current S.I.s are briefly digested in *Irish Current Law Monthly Digest*, with a cumulative list for the year in each issue and in the *Year Book* in both alphabetical and numerical order.

CASE LAW [16]

4.45   Case law consists essentially of judgments and decisions handed down by the law courts, although nowadays it may be extended to include the decisions of certain tribunals such the Employment Appeals Tribunal (EAT). For reasons explored in Chapter 1, the case law of most significance in Ireland consists of the reserved judgments of the High Court, Supreme Court and Court of Criminal Appeal (collectively known as the superior courts). However, *ex tempore* judgments of the Court of Criminal Appeal as well as published Circuit Court judgments are also becoming important.

4.46   The first distinction to note is that between a reported and an unreported judgment. A reported judgment is one that is published in an established law report series such as the *Irish Reports* or the *Irish Law Reports Monthly*. An unreported judgment is one that is approved and made available for circulation in typescript form. Law libraries generally hold unreported judgments in bound volumes or else keep them on desk reserve to prevent them being lost. All judgments are unreported to begin with, but some of them later become reported. Law report editors select judgments for publication primarily on the basis of legal significance. Cases dealing with constitutional or statutory interpretation, or which address novel points of law or which provide a good illustration of an existing legal principle are generally given priority. The fact that a judgment remains unreported does not, of course, mean that it is devoid of legal value. Even today, many important Irish judgments remain unreported although, as we shall see, efforts have been made in recent years to produce printed collections of some of the older ones.

4.47   As noted earlier, formal law reports, such as the *Irish Reports*, contain a good deal of "added value" for the information and convenience of the user. These elements, which are inserted by the editors, include the catchwords, a summary of the case and the decision, the names of the lawyers representing the parties and, sometimes, a summary of the arguments of counsel. Obviously the most important element is the text of the judgment itself, or the judgments when there is more than one. The reader who is relying on an unreported judgment, on the other hand, must use her own skill and expertise to extract the relevant principles from the report and to assess its value as a precedent for a later case.

---

[16] The rules and conventions governing the citation of cases are described in Chapter 3 above.

Reading a law report

4.48   Learning to read a law report is a fairly simple matter, which is often more than can be said about the law it seeks to expound. Apart from the judgment itself, the reader should be alert to the other information contained in a law report. The status of the Court in which judgment was given is clearly important: was it the High Court, the Court of Criminal Appeal or the Supreme Court? If either of the first two, its decision could, of course, be reversed by the Supreme Court. If the judgment is recent, one should check if it is under appeal (the reporter will often indicate if it is) or if in fact the appeal has since been dealt with. The date of delivery of judgment should be noted as well; law reports occasionally include judgments delivered some years earlier but which remained unreported. In the case of multiple judgments delivered by the Supreme Court or a divisional High Court (typically consisting of three High Court Judges and reserved for important cases), one must obviously be careful to identify the majority decision. Which members of the court were in agreement as to the outcome and which members dissented? Of course, the headnote usually conveys this information accurately, but for more detailed research or analysis, one must read the judgments in their entirely to discover the opinions expressed by the individuals judges on specific legal points. The earlier cases listed in the report will often provide useful pointers for further research, as will the arguments of counsel if they are recorded in summary form (and they sometimes are in the *Irish Reports*). It is often interesting to note who argued the case, and how they argued it, as they may later become judges themselves. For example, of the six barristers involved in the leading constitutional case, *East Donegal Co-operative v. Attorney General* [1970] I.R. 317, five later became judges.

Irish law reporting until 1866

4.49   There is a long tradition of law reporting in Ireland although some of the older reports can be difficult to find.[17] The oldest reports appear to be Sir John Davies' *Irish Equity Cases* covering the period 1604 to 1612, and published in Norman French in 1615. From the late 18th to the late 19th century, several series of nominate reports were published. They were nominate in the sense that they were known by the name of the reporter, e.g. Ridgeway. (English nominate reports are described at 6.16 below). Most of them lasted for only short periods. There does not appear to be any comprehensive list of such reports. As it happens, however, the library of the High Court of Australia (www.hcourt.gov.au/library) lists a very large number of Irish nominate reports on its web site. From 1827 to 1867, several series of law reports of continuing importance were published

---

[17] See "History of Law Reporting in Ireland" (1869) 3 I.L.T.S.J. 659-660; 673-674; G. Bing, "Law Reporting in the Irish Context" (Society of Young Solicitors, Lecture 82, April 1964).

commercially, and are still to be found in many law libraries. They include:[18]

	CITED AS
The Law Recorder (4 vols.) 1827-31	*Lawless v. Blake* 4 Law Rec. (O.S.) 185
The Law Recorder, New Series (6 vols.) 1833-1838	*Bradley v. Grattan* 1 Law Rec. (N.S.) 33
Irish Law Reports (13 vols.) 1838-50	*Keogh v. Walker* 2 Ir. Law Rep. 210
	CITED AS
Irish Equity Reports (13 vols.) 1838-50	*Boyd v. Burke* 8 Ir. Eq. Rep. 660
Irish Common Law Reports (17 vols.) 1849-66	*Montgomery v. Montgomery* 6 I.C.L.R. 522
Irish Chancery Reports (17 vols.) 1850-66.	*Browne v. Maunsell* 5 Ir. Ch. R. 351.

Law reporting since 1866

4.50 In 1866, the Incorporated Council of Law Reporting for Ireland was established and the following year it inaugurated a series of law reports. At first, it published two series, the *Irish Reports Common Law Series* and the *Irish Reports Equity Series*. They are cited as follows:

> *Maquis of Donegal v. Werner* (1872) I.R. 6 C.L. 504.
> *Byrne v. Rorke* (1869) I.R. 3 Eq. 642.

Note that they are cited primarily by volume number. e.g. volume 6 of the *Common Law Series* and volume 4 of the *Equity Series* in the examples given. With the passage of the Judicature (Ireland) Act, 1877, which caused the fusion of the courts of law and equity, the reports were reduced to a single series called the *Law Reports (Ireland)*. A report in this series was cited as

> *Twaddle v. Murphy* (1881) 8 L.R. Ir. 123.

Finally, in 1894, these reports became known as the *Irish Reports*, the title they still bear today. From then on, they have been cited primarily by year, and not by volume.

---

[18] This list, together with the sample citations, are taken from *A Guide to the Law Collections at University College Galway* by the kind permission of the author, Ms Maeve Doyle. As she points out, the abbreviations of these early reports vary in form.

Current law report series (general)

4.51   At present, two general series of Irish law reports are published, the *Irish Reports* and the *Irish Law Reports Monthly*. The *Irish Reports*, as noted, are published by the Incorporated Council of Law Reporting for Ireland and began in 1894. They are cited primarily by year, but the number of volumes published each year has fluctuated over time. In the late 19th and early 20th centuries, they generally appeared in two volumes a year, Throughout most of the 20th century, they appeared in one volume a year. However, in the 1990s, they increased gradually to two, three and four annual volumes. Right now, they appear in eight parts a year which are later cumulated into four volumes. A case appearing in this series is cited as: *O'Donoghue v. Minister for Education* [1996] 2 I.R. 20. (The citation of law reports is treated in more detail in Chapter 3 above). Each part clearly indicates the volume to which it belongs. For example, a reader consulting the case of *Horgan v. Murray* which appears in the fifth part for 1997, will note that it bears the citation [1997] 3 I.R. 23, as it appears in the third volume for that year.

4.52   The *Irish Law Reports Monthly*, which are published commercially by Round Hall Ltd, began in 1981. They appear in about 14 parts a year which are later cumulated into two annual volumes. There was only one annual volume until the end of 1993. A case reported in this series is cited as: *Doran v. Delaney* [1998] 2 I.L.R.M. 1. In the early 1990s, the publishers of this series decided to publish some back issues containing judgments that had hitherto remained unreported. Volumes were published for the years 1976/77, 1978, 1979 and 1980. Any case reported in these volumes may be cited in the usual way, e.g. *White v. McCooey* [1976-77] I.L.R.M. 72. As with the *Irish Reports*, each part in the *Irish Law Reports Monthly* indicates the volume to which it belongs. Some Circuit Court judgments are now being reported, usually in the *Irish Law Times* (7.16 below), which publishes them either in whole or in summary form.

Discontinued series: (1) *Irish Law Times Reports*

4.52a   This series deserves special mention here because, although no longer published, it is still frequently cited. The *Irish Law Times and Solicitor's Journal* was published more or less weekly between 1867 and 1980. It included short articles, news of interest to the legal profession and formally reported judgments. When cumulated in annual volumes, the law reports were brought together towards the end of each volume and paginated separately, a point to remember when searching for a report in this series. It was cited primarily by volume number. A typical citation would therefore be: *O'Haran v. Divine* (1964) 100 I.L.T.R. 53. The series includes some important judgments that have never been reported elsewhere, e.g. *The State (Killian) v. Attorney General* (1958) 92 I.L.T.R. 182. Circuit Court judgments were also occasionally reported in this series and, famously, it contains the judgment of District Justice O Floinn in *Attorney General v. Simpson* (1959) 93 I.L.T.R. 33, the so-called *Rose Tatoo* case.. It should be noted that the report section of this series was known as *Irish Law Times Reports* (I.L.T.R.) while the journal element was known as the *Irish Law Times and Solicitor's Journal* (I.L.T.S.J.). Therefore, an article appearing in the latter would be cited as Anon, "The Education of a Solicitor" (1968) 102 I.L.T.S.J. 131.

Discontinued series: (2) *Irish Jurist Reports*

4.53   The *Irish Jurist* (7.14 Below) regularly published reports, including Circuit Court reports, from 1935 to 1965. It seemed to specialise mainly in short reports. A case reported in this series is cited as: *Foyle Fisheries Commission v. Gallen* [1960] Ir. Jur. Rep. 35.

Specialist law reports and collected judgments

4.54   Like many other jurisdictions, Ireland now has a number of report series devoted to specific branches of law. There are also some volumes of collected judgments in particular areas like planning law and company law. There is now an increasing amount of material on the Internet. What follows is a description of some of the main specialist sources. There are also, of course, several casebooks on various branches of law. A casebook, however, is intended to provide a handy compendium of relevant extracts from leading cases, mainly for the benefit of students and will usually consist of a mixture of reported and unreported cases. It therefore serves a different function from the collected judgments being described here, although some casebooks provide the texts of judgments that might otherwise be difficult to track down. When reading the following sections, bear in mind that the *Annual Review of Irish Law* (4.83 below) covers recent developments in all of these and other areas, sometimes in great depth.

Company law

4.55   Ireland does not have an equivalent of *Butterworths Company Law Cases*, although many cases reported in that series are relevant to Ireland because of the similarity between Irish and English company law. The *Irish Reports* and *Irish Law Reports Monthly* carry many company law cases. Daly's *Irish Company Law Reports 1963-1983* (Dublin: Round Hall Sweet and Maxwell, 1996) provides the text of hitherto unreported judgments for the 20-year period in question. The *Commercial Law Practitioner* (7.19 below) provides summaries and expert analysis of recent company and commercial law cases.

Competition law

4.56   Competition law is governed by the Competition Act, 1991 and Competition (Amendment) Act, 1996 as well as by Articles 81 and 82 (ex Articles 85 and 86) of the EC Treaty. Court judgments on competition matters are occasionally reported in the general law reports. However, the Competition Authority, established under the Act of 1991, issue many decisions which are an important source of competition law. All of its decisions from 1991 onwards are available on its web site (www.tca.ie) which may also be accessed through Bailii (www.bailii.org). The best paper source of Irish competition law is Cregan's *Competition Law in Ireland* (Dublin: Gill and Macmillan, loose-leaf). O'Connor's two-volume *Competition Law Sourcebook* (Dublin,1995) is also excellent. There is also a series, *Competition Law Cases*, published by Baikonur.

Criminal law

4.57   The *Judgments of the Court of Criminal Appeal* is a three-volume work containing otherwise unreported judgments of the Court from 1924 to 1989. It is popularly known as *Frewen*, after the late Gerard Frewen, who was responsible for the first two volumes, and indeed it is so cited. A case appearing in this series is cited as: *The People (D.P.P.) v. Capaldi* (1949) 1 Frewen 95. In addition to the full texts of judgments, the three volumes include the headnotes and summaries of judgments of the Court from 1924 to 1989 which are reported elsewhere, mainly in the *Irish Reports*. A fourth volume is in preparation. The *Irish Criminal Law Journal* (7.19 below), now published four times a year, provides summaries of recent cases, together with comment. Unfortunately, however, many Irish criminal cases, and especially Court of Criminal Appeal judgments, remain unreported.

Employment law

4.58   The *Employment Law Reports* (E.L.R.) have been published since 1989 by Round Hall Sweet and Maxwell in four parts a year, later cumulating in a single annual volume. They contain judgments of the law courts in employment law cases, decisions and judgments of the Labour Court as well as determinations of the Employment Appeals Tribunal (EAT) and recommendations of Equality Officers. A case reported in this series is cited as: *Coote v. Ashmore Hotels Ltd.* [1992] E.L.R.1. The Employment Equality Act, 1998 established the Equality Authority, in place of the former Employment Equality Agency. The Authority has a useful web site at: www.equality.ie/index.html .The Office of the Director of Equality Investigations also has an excellent web site which contains, among other things, a detailed guide to investigation procedures and equality case law. The address is: www.odei.ie/. A fine collection of decisions on unfair dismissals will be found in Kerr and Madden, *Unfair Dismissals: Cases and Commentary* 2nd edn (Dublin: IBEC, 1996). Most decisions of the Labour Court and EAT are made available in mimeographed form and only a selection of them are ever published. Redmond's *Unfair Dismissal Law in Ireland* (Dublin:

Butterworths, 1999), and Bolger and Kimber, *Sex Discrimination Law* (Dublin: Round Hall Sweet and Maxwell, 2000) are the best sources for the topics with which they deal. Certain codes are used to identify decisions of industrial tribunals, and the main ones being:

DEE   Labour Court determination under Employment Equality Acts
EE   Equality Officer's recommendation
I   EAT determination under Protection of Employees (Employers' Insolvency) Act, 1984.
M   EAT determination under the Minimum Notice and Terms of Employment Act 1973
P.   EAT determination under Maternity Protection Acts
UD   EAT determination under Unfair Dismissals Acts 1977 to 1993.

The code and number are generally inserted after the name of the case, e.g. *Gleeson v. Rotunda Hospital and Mater Misericordiae Hospital* DEE003/2000. When the case is reported, as this one is, at [2000] E.L.R. 206, there may be no need to include the code if the nature of the case is evident from the context. There is a cumulative index to the Employment Law Reports for ther period 1990–1999.

Environmental and planning law

4.59   *Irish Planning Law and Practice* is a two-volume loose-leaf work, edited by Michael O'Donnell and Mr Justice Philip O'Sullivan, which amounts, in effect, to an encyclopaedia of planning law. It includes the relevant statutory provisions and extensive extracts from cases arranged under broad subject headings. As of January 2001, A&L Goodbody, Solicitors, Planning and Environment Law Unit have been engaged to undertake the annual update. The *Irish Planning and Environmental Law Journal* (7.19 below) has a regular Case and Comment section, dealing with recent cases.

Family law

4.60   The *Irish Family Law Journal* (7.19 below) regularly carries family law judgments. The *Irish Journal of Family Law* (7.19) has a Cases and Comment section which includes summaries of recent cases together with commentary. A series entitled *Irish Family Law Reports* was established by Baikonur publishers, beginning in the late 1990s.

Freedom of Information Act, 1997

4.61   The Office of the Information Commissioner, established under the Freedom of Information Act, 1997 publishes its decisions taken under section 34 of the Act. The first volume, for example, deals with the period April 21, 1998 to December 31, 1998. Decisions are also available on a web site: www.bailii.org/ ie/cases/ieic.

Human rights

4.62   The Human Rights Commission Act, 2000 established a Human Rights Commission composed of a President and eight other members. The Act is due to be amended in 2001 in order to increase the number of other members from eight to 14. The first President is Mr Justice Barrington, a retired Judge of the Supreme Court. The Commission's functions, as set out in section 5 of the Act, include keeping under review the adequacy of laws and state practice relating to human rights, conducting enquiries and so forth. It may also apply to the High Court or Supreme Court to be joined as *amicus curiae* in proceedings involving human rights issues. At the time of writing, the Commission is just being established, but it is likely to be producing documentation before long. Hopefully, it will follow the example of the Competition Authority and the Equality Authority and place all its documents on a web site. After all, access to information should be an important concern of any human rights body. The Government has also committed itself to introducing legislation to incorporate the European Convention on Human Rights into Irish law. It remains to be seen if this will generate anything like the law reporting, seminar and guidebook industry that attended the incorporation of the Convention into U.K. law. But it is fair to predict that this development will increase rather than diminish the volume of Irish legal documentation.

Tax law

4.63   The *Irish Tax Reports* are now published by Butterworths, and currently consist of 5 hardback and two soft-cover volumes which cover the law from 1922 to 1997. The first volume covers the period from 1922 to 1945. Recent issues include cumulative tables, which are very convenient. For example, the 1999-2000 volume has cumulative tables and an index covering the period 1922 to 2000. It also includes determinations of Appeals Commissioners. A case in this series is cited as: *Hibernian Insurance Co. Ltd v. MacUimis (Inspector of Taxes)* [1999-2000] I.T.R. 113. Both Butterworths and the Institute of Taxation have very active tax publishing programmes, and their main tax law publications are listed in Appendix 4 of this book under "Tax Law". Certain annual volumes, such as *Judge's Irish Income Tax* by Professor Alan Ward, are reliable guides to recent case law and legislation.

Tort law

4.64   Leading tort cases are well covered in the general law reports. However, in the field of professional negligence, there is a valuable collection of hitherto unreported cases edited by Bart Daly, *Professional Negligence Reports* (Dublin: Brehon Publishing, 1995), covering the years 1968 to 1993. A third edition of the standard textbook on the topic, *Law of Torts* by Judge Brian McMahon and Professor William Binchy, has just been published (Dublin, Butterworths, 2000), and covers all cases of any significance up until very recently. Levels of damages awarded by the Superior Courts, a topic dear to the hearts of most personal injuries lawyers, are regularly reported in the *Irish Law Times* (7.16 below).

Judgments available in electronic format

4.65 LEXIS (Chapter 3) has Irish reported judgments since 1950 and unreported judgments since 1985. Apart from that, Irish courts and law report publishers have been slow to go "on-line", but a beginning is now being made. The first publisher to take the initiative is the appropriately named FirstLaw, based in Dublin. It began recently by making available on CD-ROM a selection of 163 judgments by the superior courts dating from 1998 and 1999. [19] One of the great strengths of this service is that it will include all the judgments circulated by the Courts Service. The distinction between reported and unreported judgments will therefore become rather meaningless as the judgments circulated by the Service include those of the High Court, Supreme Court, Court of Criminal Appeal, Special Criminal Court, Court-Martial Appeals Court and, hopefully to an increasing extent, the Circuit Court. Subscribers to the service, which currently costs £250 annually, will receive four CDs a year, each superseding the other, which means that they can always be certain of having reasonably up-to-date judgments.

4.66 The other major, and welcome, development has been the establishment of a case law site as part of Bailii (2.14 above). Right now, it is developing fast, with almost 900 High Court and over 100 Supreme Court judgments mainly since 1999. Hopefully, this will develop to a point where all Superior Court judgments and decisions (including those of the Court of Criminal Appeal) will be posted as soon as they are delivered. The neutral citation system employed on this site has already been described (3.30 above). The URL is: www.bailii.org/ie/cases/.

Current awareness services

4.67 Current awareness services do not, as a rule, provide the texts of judgments, but they do provide abstracts or short accounts of the substance of judgments. There are now several such services in Ireland, although some of them

---

[19] See review by Jennifer Aston in (2000) 5:8 *Bar Review* 453.

are confined to particular branches of law. *Irish Current Law*, described in more detail at 4.79 below, has been published in monthly parts with an annual cumulated volume since 1996. It provides a short description of all reserved and some *ex tempore* judgments of the superior courts, usually within some months of delivery. Both the *Irish Law Times*, published about 20 times a year, and the *Gazette of the Law Society of Ireland*, published monthly, contain current awareness services including short abstracts of judgments. Some specialist journals have similar services. The *Commercial Law Practitioner*, a monthly publication, has an excellent service providing abstracts of, and commentary on, cases in the areas of commercial law, company law and banking law. The *Irish Criminal Law Journal*, now published four times a year, does the same for criminal cases.

FINDING IRISH CASE LAW

4.68   The traditional research tools for finding case law on a particular topic are digests, indexes, current awareness services and annual reviews. To these must now be added the research facilities available in the various electronic media. However, since electronic publishing in Ireland, as in many other countries, is still in its infancy, one must still have recourse to the traditional research tools to identify relevant cases. Even LEXIS database is confined to cases reported from 1950 onwards as well unreported cases from more recent years. The services available for tracking down Irish cases are, by any standards, quite fragmented. As noted earlier, it is distinctly unfortunate that a cumulative subject index has never been produced for either the *Irish Reports* or the *Irish Law Times Reports*. For older cases, the digests remain the most reliable source. For newer cases, they must be supplemented by a variety of other sources.

Irish digests

4.69   A digest is a compilation of case law from a particular era, classified by subject. It provides a synopsis of each case (or more frequently, each reported case) in the relevant area as well as indicating, through one or more law report citations, where the full text of the judgment will be found. By way of illustration, Figure 1 contains the entry from Ryan's *Irish Digest 1959-1970* in which *Macauley v. Minister for Posts and Telegraphs* [1966] I.R. 345 is digested. Where appropriate, earlier cases applied, considered, distinguished or overruled will be listed as well. Digests are usually divided into broad subject areas such as Constitutional Law, Criminal Law and Tort, with appropriate sub-headings in alphabetical order. At the end of each subject area will be found an alphabetical list of key words with cross-references to appropriate cases. This is illustrated by Figure 2, taken from the same digest, which gives some of the key cross-references under the heading "Constitutional Law". Thus, if seeking a case on English divorce decrees, one is referred to case number 5 in the chapter on "Conflict of Law".

4.70 The following is a list of the main Irish digests, beginning with the most recent. ("ICLRI" in the publication details stands for Incorporated Council of Law Reporting for Ireland).

Clancy,	*The Irish Digest 1994-1999* (Dublin: ICLRI, 2001) digests *Irish Reports* 1994-1999, *Irish Law Reports Monthly* 1994-1999, *Northern Ireland Law Reports* 1992-1999 and the *Irish Reports Special Reports* (through Irish) 1980-1998.
Clancy,	*The Irish Digest 1989-1993* (Dublin: ICLRI, XXX) digests *Irish Reports* 1989-1993, *Irish Law Reports Monthly* 1989-1993 and *Northern Ireland Law Reports* 1986-1991.
Clancy and Ryan,	*Irish Digest 1984-1988* (Dublin: ICLRI, 1991) digests *Irish Reports* 1984-1988, *Irish Law Reports Monthly* 1976-1979and 1984-1988, and *Northern Ireland Law Reports* 1984-1985.
De Blaghd*	*Irish Digest 1971-1983* (Dublin: ICLRI, nd)
Ryan*	*Irish Digest 1959-170* (Dublin: ICLRI, nd)
Harrison*	*Irish Digest 1949-1958* (Dublin: ICLRI, nd)
Harrison*	*Irish Digest 1939-1948* (Dublin: Falconer, 1952)
Ryland*	*Irish Digest 1929-1938* (Dublin: Falconer, 1941). This digests reports of the Irish Free State Section of the Law Journal 1931-1943 as well as the various Irish and Northern Ireland reports).
Ryland*	*Irish Digest 1919-1928* (Dublin: Falconer, 1930).
Maxwell*	*Irish Digest 1904-1911; 1894-1918* (Dublin, 1921). Includes *New Irish Jurist* reports.
Stubbs*	*Digest of Cases 1894-1903* (Dublin, 1905).
Murray & Dixon,	*Irish Reports Digest 1867-1893* (Dublin, 1899).
Green,	*Digest of Irish Reports 1867-1877* (1879)
Green,	*Digest of Cases in the Law Reports (Ireland), Vols. 1-XX (1878-88)* (1890).
Gamble & Barlow,	*Index to all Reported Cases in the Courts of Equity in*

Ireland 1838-1867 2 vols. (Dublin, 1868).

Millin,   *Digests of Reported Decisions of the Superior Courts relating to the Petty Sessions in Ireland 1875-1898* (1898).

Brunker,   *A Digest of Common Law in Ireland – " a Digest of all the Reported Cases decided in the Superior Courts and other Courts of Common Law in Ireland and the Court of Admiralty from Sir John Davies Reports to the present time"* (Dublin, 1865).

Blackham & Dundas,   *Digest of Cases Decided in the Courts of Equity in Ireland as Reported in the First Eleven Volumes of the Irish Equity Reports and the First and Second Volumes of the Irish Jurist* (Dublin, 1850).

O'Donnell & Brady,   *Digest of Cases, Statutes and General Orders on Equity 1766-1838, with addenda to 1846* (Dublin, 1846).

Finlay,   *A Digest and Index of All Irish Reported Cases in Law and Equity from the Earliest Period to the Present Time and also of the Reported Cases in Ecclesiastical and Criminal Law* (Dublin, 1830).

4.71   When using digests, two points should be borne in mind. The vast majority of them deal only with cases reported in the main law report series, a limitation that is scarcely defensible in this day and age. The three more recent digests by Clancy and Ryan, and Clancy, for example, deal only with cases reported in the *Irish Reports*, *Irish Law Reports Monthly* and the *Northern Ireland Law Reports*. It has nothing from the *Employment Law Reports*, the *Family Law Journal*, not to mention the many unreported judgements. Secondly, it should be noted that some of the older digests, especially those published before the Judicature Acts, are devoted exclusively to common law or equity cases.

Notes on cases

4.72   There is a useful series of mini-digests for the period 1949 to 1978 compiled by the late Professor Edward Ryan of University College Cork. They were intended as a stop-gap measure to provide information on recent cases in between the publication of the various *Digests* of which Professor Ryan himself edited one, and co-edited another. They are still useful to have to hand in the absence of the *Digests* for the periods covered. In fact, one often finds remaindered copies of these *Notes* being sold quite cheaply in bookshops. The publication details are as follows:

Notes of Irish Cases 1949-1958 (Cork University Press, 1960)
Notes of Irish Cases 1959-1968 (Cork University Press, 1970)
Notes of Irish Cases 1969-1978 (Cork University Press, 1982).

Indexes of written and unreported judgments

4.73   There are now several indexes of Irish judgments for specific periods, but unfortunately, there is no general index of written judgments from 1924 onwards, that being the date on which the Courts of Justice Act which established the present court system was passed. The three general indexes available are commonly known as the *Green Index*, the *Red Index,* and the *Blue Index*.

4.74   The *Index to Unreported Judgments of the Irish Superior Courts 1966-1975* (the *Green Index*) was published by the Irish Association of Law Teachers. It covers unreported judgments only; reported judgments are indexed in the *Digests* covering this period. The *Green Index* is divided into five parts. Part 1 consists of an alphabetical list of cases, with a brief indication of what each case is about, any statutes or rules with which it deals, and the Dublin libraries in which it may be found. Parts 2, 3 and 4 consist of tables of constitutional provisions, statutes and statutory instruments judicially considered. Part 5 is a subject index.

4.75   The *Index to Irish Superior Court Written Judgments 1976-1982* (the *Red Index*) was edited by Aston and Doyle, and published by the Irish Association of Law Teachers. It covers both reported and unreported judgments of the High Court, Supreme Court and Court of Criminal Appeal for the period 1976 to 1982. It is divided into two parts. Part 1 consists of an alphabetical list of cases with a brief indication of the subject matter, and with law report references where appropriate. Part 2 consists of a subject index, based on the "Pink Sheets" (see 4.81 below). Each entry is followed by the case title, the reference for which can be found by turning back to Part 1.

4.76   The *Index to Superior Court Written Judgments 1983-1989* (the *Blue Index*) was edited by Aston and published by the General Council of the Bar of Ireland. It covers the judgments of the High Court, Supreme Court and Court of Criminal Appeal for the period 1983 to 1989. It is laid out in the same way of the *Red Index*.

4.77   There are two bound indexes to the *Irish Law Reports Monthly Index*, both compiled by Clancy, one covering the period 1976-1990 and the other the period 1991-1995. These indexes deal only with cases reported in the I.L.R.M.. However, the tables of cases judicially considered are a useful way of tracking down references for other cases, and of identifying how those cases were dealt with by later courts. Each *Index* is divided into five parts: (1) alphabetical list of cases; (2) table of cases judicially considered; (iii) table of constitutional and legislative provisions considered; (iv) subject index; and (v) table of words and phrases judicially considered.

4.78 The *Irish Times Law Reports – Index for the Years 1989-1994*, compiled by Clancy, indexes the law reports published in Monday's *Irish Times* for the years indicated.

Current law services

4.79 The general digests and indexes just described cover Irish case law up until 1999 (always bearing in mind the caveat that the *Irish Digests* deal with reported cases only). For the period since 1999, the sources are more fragmented and generally less satisfactory. It is best perhaps to begin with the period from 1995 to the present, which is reasonably well served by *Irish Current Law*, which began its digesting service in 1995. This operates in much the same way as its English counterpart, on which it appears to be modelled, and which is described in more detail at 6.47 below. The Irish service is not however, as comprehensive as the English one. Essentially, the *Irish Current Law Monthly Digest* (I.C.L.M.D.) is published 11 times a year. It summarises the recent law under fairly detailed subject hearings, e.g. Insolvency, Licensing, Local Government, Taxation, and so forth. Most of the entries are short case summaries, and it is for these that the *Digest* is most valuable. There are also short summaries of statutes and statutory instruments, together with lists of any articles or books published in the various subject areas. The second part of the *Digest* is devoted to tables, including lists of recent Acts of the Oireachtas, dates of commencement, statutory instruments, European Union legislation implemented by statutory instruments, and a table of cases. When consulting the *Digest*, remember that many of the cases will have been unreported at the time at which they were digested. Many will subsequently be reported in the *Irish Reports,* the *Irish Law Reports Monthly* or, perhaps, the *Employment Law Reports*. At the end of each year, the *Monthly Digests* are cumulated in the *Irish Current Law Year Book* which is arranged in the same way as the monthly issues.

4.80 The *Irish Law Log* began in 1988 under the editorship of Neville Lloyd-Blood and was published in 10 issues a year, later collected in annual bound volumes. It lasted in this form until 1991. It summarised all written and some *ex tempore* judgments delivered during the period covered. Each issue and annual volume included a list of words and phrases legally defined. Each bound volume included tables of cases, statutes and constitutional provisions judicially considered, as well as lists of corrections and additions.

4.81 The *Index to High Court and Supreme Court Written Judgments* (better known as the *Pink Sheets*) was compiled by the Bar Council and the Law

Society, and made available to subscribers to the *Law Society Gazette*. It was arranged in the same way as the *Red Index* (4.75 above) which was, in fact, based on the *Pink Sheets*. This *Index* used to be circulated once a year, usually in June, with the *Gazette*. Shorter summaries, known as the *Green Sheets*, used to be published with the *Gazette* periodically throughout the year.

4.82   Both the *Irish Law Times* and the *Law Society Gazette* publish summaries of cases and other legal developments in each issue. However, *Irish Current Law Monthly Digest* is still probably the most reliable guide for research purposes.

Annual Review of Irish Law

4.83   The other major resource from 1987 onwards is the *Annual Review of Irish Law* by Byrne and Binchy. It appears in a single, though very substantial, annual volume divided in chapters dealing with broad subject areas, e.g. Company Law, Family Law, Practice and Procedure and so forth. It provides a complete account of all legal developments in each subject area for the year under review. Cases, statutes, statutory instruments, relevant European law, and Law Reform Commission reports are described and analysed. As one reviewer wrote of an early issue, if there was an equivalent to the Booker Prize available for Irish legal writing, it would have to go to the *Annual Review*.[20] This remains true today. The recent introduction of specialist contributors has added further value to the *Review*, although it has meant that some areas are treated in greater detail than others.

Summary of current awareness services

4.84   Users, and student users in particular, are apt to be confused by the array of digests, indexes and summaries available. Assuming, therefore, one wanted to find Irish case law on a topic from 1922 onwards, one would begin with the *Irish Digests* which, at present, cover all reported judgments of the Superior Courts down to 1999. For the period 1993 to 1995, one could use the *Irish Law Log*, the *Pink Sheets* or the *Annual Review of Irish Law*. From 1995 onwards, one can use the *Irish Current Law Year Books* and the *Irish Current Law Monthly Digests* and the *Annual Review of Irish Law*. For the period up until 1993, one would need to supplement this research with sources of unreported judgments in so far as they are available. However, the *Red Index, Green Index* and *Blue Index* list unreported judgments for the period 1966 to 1989. The *Annual Review of Irish Law*, which began in 1987, covers unreported judgments from then onwards.

---

[20] Hogan, (1989) 11 D.U.L.J. (n.s.) 247.

WORDS AND PHASES

4.85   The outcome of a case can often depend on how a particular word or phrase is interpreted by the court. Lawyers must, therefore, be in a position to discover how a given word or phrase has been judicially interpreted or defined by statute. There is no single compilation of words and phrases judicially defined in Ireland. Bound volumes of words and phrases legally defined in England are described at 6.55 below, and these will often be of assistance to Irish lawyers because of the links between the two jurisdictions. To find out how Irish courts have interpreted a word or phrase, one must consult a number of sources. The *Irish Digests* mentioned at 4.70 above list words and phrases, as do the bound volumes of the *Irish Law Log,* the *Irish Reports* and the *Irish Law Reports Monthly.* So, nowadays, does *Irish Current Law*, both in the monthly and annual issues. But the fact remains that finding definitions of words and phrases in Ireland is more laborious than in other common-law jurisdictions.

CHAPTER 5

Northern Ireland Law

CONSTITUTIONAL STATUS

5.01   Northern Ireland, which is constitutionally part of the United Kingdom, consists of the six counties of Antrim, Armagh, Derry (also known as Londonderry), Down, Fermanagh and Tyrone. Before the Act of Union of Great Britain and Ireland came into force in 1801, Ireland had its own parliament. From 1801 until the Government of Ireland Act 1920, legislation for all of Ireland was made in London. Under the Act of 1920, a parliament was established in what then became Northern Ireland, and was formally opened in June 1921. It was a bicameral legislature, consisting of a House of Commons and a Senate, and was empowered to make law on most domestic issues, though certain matters were reserved to the imperial parliament in London. From 1932 onwards, the Northern Ireland parliament met at Stormont, outside Belfast, and thus became known as the Stormont parliament. Following the outbreak of political violence in the late 1960s, the Stormont parliament was suspended in 1972 and replaced by direct rule from Westminster (the U.K. parliament). This direct rule lasted, in effect, until legislative powers were devolved to the new Northern Ireland Assembly in December 1999. There have been two other assemblies in the meantime, one in 1974 which had some legislative powers but which lasted only some months, and another from 1982 to 1986 which had no legislative powers. The present Assembly came into being following an agreement, popularly known as the Good Friday Agreement, which was signed at Belfast on April 10, 1998. It was legally established by the Northern Ireland Act 1998 (a U.K. statute) and consists of 108 members elected from the existing Westminster constituencies. The Act of 1998 also provides for an executive consisting of a First Minister, a Deputy First Minister and ten ministers, and for other institutions including cross-border bodies. It authorizes the Assembly to make primary legislation in several areas including health, education, social services and agriculture. The first Act passed by the Assembly was the Financial Assistance to Political Parties Act (Northern Ireland) 2000 c.1, perhaps as good a sign as any that Northern Ireland politics were, at last, returning to normal!

5.02   For those interested in the constitutional history of Northern Ireland, there is a useful volume available in many libraries entitled *The Statutes Relating to the Constitution of Northern Ireland* (London: Butterworths, 1957), which is in fact a reprint from the second edition of *Halsbury's Statutes of England*. It contains the texts, with annotations, of certain key statutes which had received Royal Assent before 31 December 1949. Included are the Government of Ireland Act 1920 and the Habeas Corpus Act (1871-2). There is, of course, an enormous secondary literature on this topic, though much of it is written from a political perspective. Leading legal works include Harry Calvert's *Constitutional Law in Northern Ireland* (London: Stevens, 1968), Brigid Hadfield's *The Constitution of Northern Ireland* (Belfast: SLS Legal Publications, 1989) and Claire Palley's monumental article on the Northern Ireland constitution in (1972) 1 *Anglo-American Law Review* 368-374. A short account of more recent developments is provided in a fact sheet published by the House of Commons, and available on the Internet at www.parliament.uk/commons/lib/fs15.pdf.

LEGISLATION

Statutes

5.03   As in the case of the Republic of Ireland, the statutes applicable in Northern Ireland derive from several different legislative eras (4.17 Above). The statutes made for Ireland, including what is now Northern Ireland, in London from 1801 to 1921 are to be found in the *Public General Acts and Measures* (6.06 above). The statutes passed by the Stormont Parliament were published in annual volumes, known from 1921 to 1966 as *Public General Acts: Northern Ireland* and from 1966 onwards as the *Northern Ireland Statutes*. With the introduction of direct rule in 1972, legislation on all matters which would have fallen within the remit of a legislative assembly had there been one in existence was made by way of Orders in Council which were laid before the Westminster Parliament under what was known as the affirmative procedure. Sometimes, an Act passed by that Parliament would apply to the whole of the U.K. including Northern Ireland, or perhaps to England and Wales, and Northern Ireland, but not to Scotland. When reading a statute made at Westminster, it is always important to check the last or second last section which will usually indicate, among other things, the area to which it applies. Thus, for example, section 22 of the Human Rights Act 1998 expressly states in subsection (6): "This Act extends to Northern Ireland". Certain other Acts extend to Northern Ireland only, in which case the name of that jurisdiction will appear in the title, e.g. The Statute Law Revision (Northern Ireland) Act 1980, section 22 of which states that "this Act extends to Northern Ireland only". Or, a statute may provide that only certain of its provisions are to apply to Northern Ireland. The texts of all Northern Ireland Orders in Council made since the beginning of 1997 are available on the Web: www.northernireland-legislation.hmso.gov./ .

5.04   Northern Ireland lawyers are more fortunate than their counterparts in the Republic in having access to revised statutes. In a revised statute, the original text is amended or in part deleted to take account of amendments effected in later statutes. If a statute has been completely repealed it will be omitted from the collection of revised statutes. Two editions of the *Statutes Revised Northern Ireland* have been published in paper form, one in 1950 and the other in 1982. The latter edition were published in 13 loose-leaf binders, the first four, A to D, having older statutes up to 1920, and the subsequent volumes 1 to 9 having the revised Northern Ireland statutes from 1921 to 1981. For each year thereafter, there is a loose-leaf volume a year of the *Northern Ireland Statutes,* meaning in effect Orders in Council. Even more impressively, there is now a web site, *Northern Ireland Legislation*, which contains the full text of the Revised Northern Ireland Statutes (2nd edition), 1350 of them in all. They can be searched by initial letter or by using the data base search. The URL is: www.bailii.org/nie/legis/num-act/ .

5.05 Virtually every document emanating from, or connected with, the new Northern Ireland Assembly is available on the Web. First, however, there is a very useful web page maintained by HMSO which provides links to all the legislation connected with the establishment of the Assembly, including the text of the Northern Ireland Act 1998. The URL for this site is: www.legislation.hmso.gov.uk/stat.htm. All Acts of the Assembly are generally placed on the Web within 24 hours of their publication in printed form. The URL is: www.northernireland-legislation.hmso.gov.uk/ . It has the texts of all the Acts to date. The same web site provides the texts of the Explanatory Notes for Acts of the Assembly. These documents are also available from the Stationery Office in Belfast.

Statutory instruments

5.06 The delegated legislation applicable in Northern Ireland is rather complex, especially since Orders in Council took the form of statutory instruments although, in substance, they were equivalent to statutes. The various forms of secondary legislation made by Northern Ireland authorities up until the end of 1973 were known as *Statutory Rules and Orders* (S.R. & O.). From then on, they have been known as *Statutory Rules* (S.R.). They are available in bound volumes, *Northern Ireland Statutory Rules and Orders*, published by the Stationery Office, Belfast which also publishes them individually. For more detailed account, see George Woodman, "Legislation in Northern Ireland" (1987) *The Law Librarian* 45-49, and *Dane and Thomas on How to Use a Law Library* (5.11 below) which has a chapter on Northern Ireland.

PARLIAMENTARY PROCEEDINGS

5.07 The official reports (Hansard) of the Northern Ireland assembly are available on the Internet at www.ni-assembly.gov.uk/hansard.htm. One can retrieve the report for any given day since 6 December 1999 by simply clicking on the date in question. The report for each day is posted on this site at 11.30 the following day. Reports of the Assembly for the period before the devolution of legislative power can be accessed through the same web site.

LAW REPORTS

5.08   The *Northern Ireland Law Reports* (N.I.) have been published by the Incorporated Council of Law Reporting for Northern Ireland since 1925. Reports for the years 1921 to 1924 were included in the *Irish Reports* and *Irish Law Times Reports* (see previous Chapter). The *Northern Ireland Law Reports* are published in two annual parts, later cumulated in a single volume. A case reported in this series is cited as: *R v Martin* [1985] N.I. 324. Since 1970, law reports are published more quickly in the *Northern Ireland Law Reports Judgments Bulletin*. This used to appear in several parts a year, but now appears in two substantial parts published by Butterworths in association with the Law Reporting Council for Northern Ireland. It is cited as: *R v Hassan* [1981] 9 N.I.J.B. 123. The NILAW library of LEXIS has all the cases reported in the *Northern Ireland Law Reports* since 1945 and all unreported cases since March 1984. There is a web site entitled Legal-Island (www.legal-island.com/) that provides access to more specific legal sites in both Northern Ireland and the Republic of Ireland. It has some Northern Ireland judgments, but so far only very few. Click on "Court Judgments". Northern Ireland Court of Appeal and High Court decisions can be accessed on Bailii (www.bailii.org).

5.09   Various indexes to the reported Northern Ireland cases have been produced over the years. However, there is now a cumulative index entitled *Index to the Northern Ireland Cases 1921-1997* published in 1998 by Butterworths in association with the Incorporated Council of Law Reporting for Northern Ireland. It contains the usual lists of cases reported, a subject index and tables of statutes, cases and rules judicially considered.

DIGEST

5.10   There is *Digest of Northern Ireland Law,* edited by Brice Dickson and Deborah McBride, consisting of 14 chapters, each of which provides an introduction to a particular branch of law. The second edition was published by SLS Legal Publications (Belfast) in 1996, and it is intended gradually to add further chapters to it. It indicates the relevant differences between English and Northern Ireland law are indicated, and provides an good account of certain important pieces of legislation such as the Wills and Administration Proceedings (NI) Order 1994, and the Sale and Supply of Goods Act 1994 .

CURRENT AWARENESS PUBICATIONS

5.11   The *Bulletin of Northern Ireland Law*, begun in 1981, is published in 10 parts a year by SLS Legal Publications, Belfast. It gives a short account of legal developments under subject headings arranged in alphabetical order, and deals with cases, statutes, statutory instruments, orders, statements and journal articles. It also includes English cases decided on the basis of law which is the same as that applicable in Northern Ireland. The *Bulletin* is an excellent source of up-to-date information on all aspects of Northern Ireland law. An index is published for each year. The various *Irish Digests* (4.70 above) include cases reported in the *Northern Ireland Law Reports*. The most recent digest, edited by Clancy, covering the years 1989 to 1993, brings the Northern Ireland cases up as far as 1991. The problem is that the Digests do not differentiate between the two jurisdictions. Therefore, the section on, say, criminal law, will include cases from both Northern Ireland and the Republic of Ireland, although it will of course be clear from the case citation at the end of each entry which jurisdiction is involved. The *Current Law Monthly Digest* also covers recent legal developments in Northern Ireland, for which it has a separate section, as does the annual *Year Book*. In short, therefore, if carrying out research on Northern Ireland case law, one would use the *Index of Northern Ireland Cases* for developments up to the end of 1997, and then consult the *Bulletin of Northern Ireland Law* and, perhaps, *Current Law Monthly* for the period since then. In any event, it will not take too long to browse through the recent issues of the *Northern Ireland Law Reports* and *Judgments Bulletin*.

SECONDARY LITERATURE

Periodicals

5.12   The *Northern Ireland Legal Quarterly* (N.I.L.Q.) is a long-established and much respected legal journal, published by the Queen's University of Belfast. Each issue contains several substantial articles on many aspects of law, and by no means confined to the law of Northern Ireland. For periodical literature on Northern Ireland up to 1983, consult O'Higgins's *Bibliography of Periodical Literature Relating to Irish Law* with supplements (7.22 Below). References to more recent literature will be found in the *Legal Journals Index*, the *Bulletin of Northern Ireland Law*, *Current Law Monthly Digest* and, to a lesser extent, in the *Index to Legal Periodicals and Books* (7.23 below).

Books

5.13   During the past 20 years or so, a large number of books have been published on Northern Ireland law, mainly under the auspices of S.L.S. Legal Publications established by the Council of Legal Education for Northern Ireland. One book particularly worthy of mention in the present context is Professor Brice Dickson's *The Legal System of Northern Ireland* 3rd edition (Belfast: SLS Legal Publications, 1993) which gives a fine account of the system as well as describing in detail the sources of Northern Ireland law. For more information on sources of Northern Ireland law, see the chapter by George Woodman in Winterton and Moys (eds.), *Information Sources in Law* 2nd edition (London: Bowker Sauer, 1997) and Cope and Thomas, *Dane and Thomas on How to Use a Law Library* 3rd edition (London: Sweet and Maxwell, 1995).

CHAPTER 6

Primary Sources of British Law

BRITISH CONSTITUTIONAL LAW

6.01   The term "British constitutional law" is often used in contexts where, strictly speaking, the reference should be United Kingdom constitutional law. England and Wales are treated as a single jurisdiction,[1] even though there is now a National Assembly for Wales established under the Government of Wales Act 1998. England and Wales together with Scotland (which is a separate jurisdiction) constitute Great Britain. Great Britain together with Northern Ireland make up the United Kingdom, while the United Kingdom together with the Isle of Man and the Channel Islands make up the British Isles. British or United Kingdom constitutional law has undergone considerable change since the Labour Government came to power following the general election of 1997. Irish readers are sometimes puzzled by reference to Britain's constitution because of the belief that it does not have one. It is true that Britain is one of the very few countries not to have a onstitution in the form of a single document, like Ireland's *Bunreacht na hÉireann*, setting out the fundamental law of the state. It does, however, have a Constitution that is partly written and partly unwritten. The written element consists of certain important statutes, leading judicial decisions, conventions, the law and custom of parliament and, nowadays, European Community law. Conventions and customs are the main unwritten sources. Many Conventions have to do with the role of the Crown and its relationship to Parliament, although strangely enough the Cabinet and Prime Minister also owe their existence to convention as opposed to legislation. For most practical purposes, the best guides to the content of the British constitution are the leading treatises and textbooks on the topic, some of which are listed at 6.04 below.

6.02   The devolution polices that were implemented during the last few years of the 20th century obviously constitute an important element of modern British constitutional law. The main statute involved was the Scotland Act 1998 which devolved powers to a new Parliament sitting at Edinburgh which enacts primary and secondary legislation on a wide range of issues, although Westminster retains the power to legislate for Scotland on trade and industry, national security and certain other matters. This represented a major constitutional de-

---

[1]   Under the Wales and Berwick Act 1746, mention of England in a statute was deemed to include Wales also. This was changed by the Welsh Language Act 1967.

velopment as the English and Scottish parliaments had been united under the Act of Union of 1707, although Scotland continued to retain its own legal system, educational system and local government. The powers granted to the National Assembly for Wales under the Government of Wales Act 1998 are more restricted. The Assembly has no power to make primary legislation, but is entitled to make secondary legislation which would previously have been a function of the Secretary of State for Wales whose functions, together with those of the Welsh Office, were taken over by the Assembly. The Northern Ireland Assembly was established by the Northern Ireland Act 1998, following the so-called Good Friday (or Belfast) Agreement. It is empowered to enact legislation in several areas that had previously been handled by various Northern Ireland government departments. It began work properly in December 1999, although it has had a rather troubled existence to date, having been suspended for some months by the Northern Ireland Act 2000. The Assembly has since been restored. Meanwhile in England itself, there is a growing trend in favour of regional government as reflected in the direct election of a Mayor of London in 2000. There are now some good web sites dealing with British constitutional law, one of the best being that maintained by School of Public Policy at University College London (www.ucl.ac.uk/constitution-unit/) which has, among other things, an excellent update on the devolution process.

6.03   The new assemblies in Scotland, Wales and Northern Ireland all took to the Internet with enthusiasm, and their proceedings and legislation are readily available on the Web. The main site of the Northern Ireland Assembly is www.northernireland-legislation.hmso.gov.uk/ . It provides links to primary and secondary legislation made by the Assembly, Explanatory Notes to the Acts and Northern Ireland Orders in Council. The text of the official reports (Hansard) of the Assembly are available, and searchable on a daily basis at www.ni-assembly.gov.uk/hansard.htm .The equivalent Welsh site is www.wales-legislation.hmso.gov.uk/ which contains all Welsh statutory instruments since 1999. The Scottish web site is particularly impressive. The URL for the main site is www.scottish.parliament.uk and it gives access to research papers, reports and many other documents. Acts of the Scottish Parliament will be found at www.scotland-legislation.hmso.gov.uk/.

Texts on British constitutional law

6.04   There are several modern textbooks on the British Constitution. They include de Smith and Brazier, *Constitutional and Administrative Law*, 8th edition (London: Penguin, 1998), Hood Philips and Jackson, *Constitutional Law and Administrative Law*, 8th edition (London: Sweet & Maxwell, 2001), Munro, *Studies in Constitutional Law* 2nd edition (London: Butterworths, 1999), Barendt, *Introduction to Constitutional Law* (Oxford: Clarendon Press, 1998), Brazier, *Constitutional Reform* 2nd edition (Oxford: Oxford UP, 1998), University of

Cambridge Centre for Public Law, *Constitutional Reform in the United Kingdom* (Oxford: Hart Publishing, 1998). There is a particularly good collection of cases and materials on the British constitution: Allen and Thompson, *Cases and Materials on Constitutional and Administrative Law* 6th edition (London: Blackstone Press, 2000). A new edition of Walter Bagehot's classic work, *The English Constitution*, edited by Miles Taylor was published by Oxford University Press in 2001. The other classic work, of course, is A.V. Dicey's *Introduction to the Study of the Law of the Constitution*, 10th edition (1959). A more extensive bibliography will be found in of the leading texts such as that by de Smith and Brazier (above).

LEGISLATION

6.05   The history of the publication of the Acts of Parliament is set out by Derek French in *How to Cite Legal Authorities* (London: Blackstone Press, 1996), Chapter 3. As he says, statutes began to be printed shortly after the introduction of printing to England in 1476, but the ways in which they have been produced and cited have changed a good deal in the meantime. Law students will seldom need to consult a pre-1800 statute. Some older statutes are, admittedly, still relevant. They include the Statute of Frauds (1677), the Bill of Rights (1689) and the Act of Settlement (1700). The most convenient sources of such statutes are collections of cases and materials on British land law or constitutional law as the case may be. Texts of some older constitutional documents such as the Magna Carta and the Bill of Rights are available on the Internet (www.constitutional-law.net/uk.html). In the early 19th century, as a result of the work of a royal commission, an 11-volume work entitled *The Statutes of the Realm* was published. This included all Acts up to 1713. Throughout the 19th century, various collections of statutes, arranged in chronological order, were published and are known as the *Statutes at Large* which came up as far as 1869.

Public general Acts and measures

6.06   Each statute that is enacted by Parliament and receives Royal Assent is published individually and remains available from the Stationery Office so long as there is a demand for it. Since 1831, statutes have also been published in the series *Public General Acts and Measures* in which the statutes are arranged chronologically. As a rule, there are now three or four red-covered volumes a year. They have been published in A4 format since 1987. At the beginning of each volume there are alphabetical and a chronological lists of the statutes for that year. This series is available in most law libraries, and is the most authoritative source of older statutes, so long as one remembers that any statute may have been repealed or amended in the meantime. The annual volumes also include a list of Local and Personal Acts for the year, but those Acts are published in a separate volume, and would seldom be of interest to Irish lawyers. A separate volume of tables and indexes is also published for each year. The most substantial part of this volume is entitled "Effects of Legislation" which lists in chronological order the earlier Acts and Measures repealed, amended or otherwise affected by the Acts passed in the year in question.

Other current series of British statutes

6.07   There are several commercially-published series of statutes. One of the more useful is the *Current Law Statutes Annotated*, published since 1948 by Sweet and Maxwell. It was on this series that its Irish counterpart (4.29 above) was modelled. The complete text of each Act is reproduced with annotations, some of which are very detailed. The individual annotated statutes for each year are later reissued in bound annual volumes. When using these statutes, therefore, one should consult one of the updating services (6.51 below) to see if there have been any appeals or amendments.

The Law Reports: Statutes are published by the Incorporated Council of Law Reporting. There are several parts issued throughout the year, each containing one or more recent Acts. They are later issued in bound annual volumes. This series contains the official versions of the statutes, known as the Queen's Printer Copy.

Halsbury's Statutes of England, now in its fourth edition, is published by Butterworths. The aim of the series is to provide the current texts of all *English* statutes in force, arranged according to subject matter. It contains several different components which can take some time to get used to, but it is worth the effort. They are as follows:

> *Main volumes.* There are about 50 main volumes containing the statutes that were in force when the present edition was completed in the late 1980s. Statutes are arranged alphabetically under broad subject headings. Occasionally, when there have been significant changes in the law, the relevant volume will be reissued and the word "reissue" stamped on the spine of the volume. It is always important therefore to note the date of publication of the volume being consulted.

> *Current Statutes Service.* This consists of several loose-leaf volumes containing statutes that have not as yet been incorporated into the bound volumes.

> *Cumulative Supplement.* Each year there is issued a single cumulative volume containing changes made to the statutes in both the bound volumes and the *Current Statutes Service*. The issue for each year contains all the relevant material in the previous year's supplement.

Noter-up Service. This is monthly publication indicating the changes made since the publication of the last cumulative supplement.

Table of Statutes and General Index. This includes both an alphabetical list of statutes and a subject index. It is issued annually, so it is generally up to date, but one still needs to consult the noter-up service for any very recent changes.

Is it in Force? This is an annual publication giving the commencement date of all Public General Acts for the previous 25 years.

Butterworths Annotated Legislation Service. This service reprints the texts of selected Acts with annotations. Statutes are selected for inclusion on the basis of their usefulness to practitioners.

6.08   *Textbooks.* Nowadays, some publishers, notably Blackstone Press, publish texts devoted entirely to recent Acts. Typically such a book will include the full text of the Act with schedules, and a lengthy introduction in several chapters written by one or more experts analyzing all the main provisions of the Act. It is worth checking the Blackstone Press catalogue for a list of recent publications. There are also several texts providing collected legislation in core subject areas, usually without annotation. Again, Blackstone Press has several such texts some of which are published annually in areas such as criminal law, family law, property law and many others.

British statutes on the Internet

6.09   The web site managed by HMSO on behalf of the Queen's Printer contains the text of all Public General Acts since the first such Act of 1988. The address for this site is: www.legislation.hmso.gov.uk/acts.htm. Simply click on the relevant year which appears in hypertext, say 1990, and a full list of Acts for that year will appear. To retrieve the text of the Act, just click on the title. All local Acts since the beginning of 1991 are available on the same site. Another welcome development is that since the beginning of 1999, almost all Public Acts from which result from Bills introduced into either House of Parliament by a Government Minister must be accompanied by Explanatory Notes, which are intended to explain the legislation and its purpose to the general reader. These are also available on the HMSO web site (www.legislation.hmso.gov.uk/legislation/uk-expa.htm) There are similar sites available for Scottish and Northern Ireland legislation (see 6.03 above). The texts of all statutory instruments made by the National Assembly for Wales can be found at www.wales-legislation.hmso.gov.uk/legislation/.

Westlaw UK

6.09a   The full texts of English, UK-wide and Scottish statutes in force are available on Westlaw UK. See Chapter 2 above.

                                    L E X I S

6.10   The full texts of English statutes in force are available on LEXIS in the ENGGEN library, STAT file. See Chapter 2 above.

Tables of statutes

6.11   The *Chronological Table of Statutes*, published annually provides a chronological list of all English and U.K. Statutes since 1235, and indicates the current status of each section. The *Index to the Statutes in Force* is a useful subject index. The *Statutes in Force* series itself provides the revised and consolidated texts of statutes, taking amendments and repeals into account.

Legislation citators

6.12   The Current Law Legislation Citator system will be described at 6.51 below in the context of the Sweet and Maxwell Current Law service.

Citing statutes

6.13   The rules governing the citation of British statutes have already been described in Chapter 3 above. Essentially nowadays, all statutes are cited by their short title, e.g. Human Rights Act 1998 (without any comma between the word "Act" and the date). In more formal writing, the chronological number of the statute is given as well, e.g. Human Rights Act 1998, c. 42.

Statutory instruments

6.14   Statutory Instruments (S.I.s) of general application are published by HMSO as they are made and later in bound annual volumes. *Halsbury's Statutory Instruments* is a consolidated collection of S.I.s in force arranged by subject matter in over 20 volumes, together with various loose-leaf supplements and indexes. Locating S.I.s is easy enough so long as one as access to basic sources such as *Halsbury's Statutory Instruments* which has a numerical index, in case one is searching by year and number. Volume 53 of the *Halsbury's Laws of England* has an alphabetical list of S.I.s. Obviously the user should check out the various supplements to Halsbury (7.26 below) to update this list. The *Current Law Year Book* and the *Current Law Monthly Digest* (below) also have regular numerical and alphabetical lists. Two publications are particularly useful for finding S.I.s by subject. They are the *Consolidated Index* of *Halsbury's Statutory Instruments* and the *Annual List of Statutory Instruments* published by HMSO. In any event, alphabetical lists are often reasonably good, though not infallible, guides to subject matter.

6.15   All U.K. statutory instruments made since the beginning of 1987 are available in full-text on the Internet at www.legislation.hmso.gov.uk/stat.htm . Draft statutory instruments for 1997 to the present are available on the same site. Once this web site has been entered, the user can just click on the relevant year and a list of statutory instruments for that year will appear. There is also a search engine that will help to retrieve particular instruments and search the texts of all documents on the site. All Welsh statutory instruments from 1999 onwards are on another site: www.wales-legislation.hmso.gov.uk/ . They are generally published here within 24 hours of appearing in paper form (see also www.bailii.org/databases).

CASE LAW

Older reports

6.16   The history of English law reporting may be divided into three periods. The first extends from about 1272 to 1535. During this period, some law reports, together with arguments of counsel and other court proceedings, were published in *Year Books.* Many of the recorded cases deal with disputes over land. Printed editions of some of the *Year Books* have been published by the Selden Society. They are valuable for historical research but are otherwise unlikely to be encountered by law students. The second era, which extended from about 1535 to 1865, belonged to the nominate law reports. These were reports compiled and published by private individuals, and were called "nominate" because they were known by the names of the reporters. There were hundreds of such reports, although some of the series lasted for only short periods of time. In terms of quality, they vary from the classic reports of Coke (1552-1643) which are a major source of our knowledge of the early common law, to those of the unfortunate Espinasse of whom it was said that he heard only half of what went on in court, and reported the other half. An interesting account of early English law reports and their discovery by legal historians is given by Professor J.H. Baker in his inaugural lecture, *Why the history of English Law has not been finished,* published by Cambridge University Press in pamphlet form in 1999.

The English reports

6.17   Many of the nominate or private reports are still relevant and useful, but are nowadays difficult to locate. Fortunately, an extensive selection of them has been reprinted in a 176-volume series called the *English Reports* (E.R.) which has a two volume index (volumes 177 and 178). It is important to know how to use this series because some of the older cases are still cited by reference to the nominate reports in which they originally appeared. One might find a reference, for example, to *Allison v. Hayden* 3 Car & P 246. To find this case in the *English Reports*, consult the case index in volumes 177 and 178. In fact, there are two cases bearing this name listed in the index, but that reported in 3 Car and p 246 is followed by the figures "172 406", meaning page 406 of volume 172 of the *English Reports*.

6.18   Sometimes, one will have the reference (e.g. 3 Car and P 246), but not the name, of a case reported in a nominate series. To track down the case in the *English Reports*, one must consult the index chart which was issued with them and which contains an alphabetical list of all the nominate reports and the volumes of the *English Reports* in which they are reprinted. Unfortunately, the index, being a slender document, has the habit of disappearing from libraries, so one may therefore have to engage in the more laborious task of checking the spines of the individual volumes of the *English Reports* to see which nominate reports they reproduce. Better still, just consult *Raistrick's Index to Legal Citations and Abbreviations*, the second edition of which was published by Bowker Sauer (London) in 1993. This is an indispensable reference work which gives the abbreviations for all known law report series and legal periodicals past and present from Britain, Ireland, the United States and elsewhere. Also, when dealing with the English nominate law reports, it indicates the volumes of the *English Reports* in which they are reprinted. Thus in relation to "Car. And P.", it tells us that this stands for *Carrington and Payne's Nisi Prius Reports* published between 1823 and 1841 and reprinted in volumes 171 to 173 of the *English Reports*.

The modern period: the *Law Reports*

6.19   In 1865, a more formal law reporting system was established under the auspices of what is now the Incorporated Council of Law Reporting for England and Wales. The reports published by the Council are known simply as the *Law Reports* and have a semi-official status. Judges are given the opportunity of revising the texts of those of their judgments to be published in this series, and a summary of the arguments of counsel is generally included as well. By convention, these are the reports, i.e.. A.C., Q.B., Ch., and Fam. cited by counsel in the English courts. A practice direction ([1991] 1 W.L.R. 1) issued by the Master of the Rolls provides that in the Court of Appeal, as in the House of Lords, the reports published by the Incorporated Council of Law Reporting should be cited in preference to other series when there is a choice. It is also the practice of some book publishers and journal editors to require that cases be cited by reference to the *Law Reports* alone, or that this series be cited first, e.g.

Christie v. Leachinsky [1947] A.C. 573, [1947] 1 All E.R. 567.

To understand the present organisation of the *Law Reports*, it is necessary to know something of the history of the courts in England and Wales since 1865. This information is given in most textbooks on the English legal system, but for our present purposes it is sufficient to know that the Judicature Act 1873 created a single Supreme Court consisting of a Court of Appeal and the High Court. At first, the High Court had five divisions, but now it has only three: the Chancery Division (dealing with trusts, mortgages, wills and similar matters), the Queen's Bench Division (dealing with actions in contract and tort, judicial review, commercial and admiralty matters), and the Family Division (dealing with matrimonial and family matters). The Court of Appeal has two divisions, civil and criminal, the latter being largely equivalent to the Irish Court of Criminal Appeal. The House of Lords is the highest court which hears appeals in from both divisions of the English Court of Appeal, appeals in civil cases from Scotland, appeals from the Northern Ireland Court of Appeal and certain appeals from the English and Northern Ireland High Courts. There are two lower courts of some importance. The Crown Court has exclusive jurisdiction over all trials on indictment (serious cases which carry the right to trial by jury) which means that it performs the functions exercised in Ireland by the Central Criminal Court, the Circuit Court and, indeed, the Special Criminal Court combined. Some of its judgments are occasionally reported. The County court is a court of civil jurisdiction that deals with smaller claims in contract, tort, property and related matters. The English equivalent of our district court is the magistrates' court which is a court of summary jurisdiction. In most cases, it consists of a bench of lay magistrates, although there are also some full-time stipendiary magistrates who are qualified lawyers. Finally, there is the Privy Council which has the same membership as the House of Lords and which deals with appeals from certain Commonwealth countries.

6.20 To return, then, to the organisation of the *Law Reports*, they were originally published in 11 sections or series reflecting the way in which the courts were organised in those pre-Judicature Act times. Now, they are published in four series:

> Appeal Cases (A.C.)
> Queen's Bench Division (Q.B.)
> Chancery Division (Ch.)
> Family Division (Fam.)

The *Appeal Cases* contain House of Lords and Privy Council cases only. So, as soon as one sees "A.C." in the citation, one knows that the case was decided by one or other of these courts. Judgments of the Court of Appeal are reported in the series relating to the High Court division in which the case originated. Thus, a judgment of the Court of Appeal (Civil Division) in a case that originated in the Queen's Bench Division will appear in the Queen's Bench Reports. The same arrangement holds for appeal cases originating in the Family and Chancery divisions. The reports of the Family and Chancery divisions are published together in 12 annual parts. Thus, Part 12 for December 2000 includes both [2000] Ch. 601- 701 and [2000] Fam. 153-197. However, when they appear in bound volumes, the two divisions are separated. The Appeal Cases and Queen's Bench reports also appear in 12 annual parts, later cumulated in one or two annual volumes. The Queen's Bench reports nowadays include cases from the European Court of Justice, as well as the Court of Appeal and the Queen's Bench itself. Judgments from some criminal appeals are also included. The indexing system of the *Law Reports* will be described at 6.40 below.

Citation of the *Law Reports*

6.21   The *Law Reports* have traditionally been cited by reference to year, volume number (if there is more than one volume for the year), court and initial page number, e.g.

> *Newbold v. The Queen* [1983] 2 A.C. 705.
>
> *Morris v. Murray* [1991] 2 Q.B. 6.

A recent practice direction has provided for neutral citation. See 3.32 above.

Criminal Appeals

6.22   The Court of Appeal (Criminal Division) is occupied mainly with appeals from the Crown Court (6.19 above). There is a commercially-published series, the *Criminal Appeal Reports* (Cr. App. R.), devoted in large part to reporting the judgments of this division of the Court of Appeal, although they also include judgements of the House of Lords, the Privy Council and the High Court in criminal matters. This series has been published since 1908, following the establishment of what was then the Court of Criminal Appeal. Since 1979, a separate, complementary series, the *Criminal Appeal Reports (Sentencing)* (Cr. App.R.(S)) has been published and, as the title suggests, is devoted exclusively to sentencing cases. Criminal appeal cases will also be found in the *Weekly Law Reports*, especially in volume 1 and some are also reported in the Queen's Bench reports. Needless to say, criminal appeals decided by the House of Lords and the Privy Council are reported in the *Appeal Cases*.

The Weekly Law Reports

6.23   The *Weekly Law Reports* (W.L.R.) have been published since 1953 by the Incorporated Council of Law Reporting Council for England and Wales.

Their purpose was to make superior court law reports available reasonably quickly, as there is usually a considerable delay in the publication of the *Law Reports* themselves. They are published in weekly parts later cumulated in three annual volumes. Those published in the second and third volumes will later appear in the *Law Reports*, while those in the first volume will not. This explains why each weekly part is likely to contain some cases from volume one and some from volumes two or three. The *Weekly Law Reports* superseded the *Weekly Notes* (W.N.) published in 87 volumes from 1866 to 1952. There is no separate general index for the *Weekly Law Reports*, but all cases published in this series are included in the indexes to the *Law Reports*, described at 6.40 below, which are always reasonably current.

The All England Law Reports

6.24   The *All England Law Reports* (All E.R.) have been published commercially by Butterworths since 1936. They are published in weekly parts and later cumulated in four annual volumes. They do not contain the arguments of counsel but have helpful cross-references to *Halsbury's Laws of England* and *The Digest* (see 7.26 and 6.43 below). There is a separate series, the *All England Law Reports Reprint*, published in 36 volumes by Butterworths between 1957 and 1968. It reprinted reports for the period 1558 to 1935 that still had some relevance or value, and most of them still have. A further 16-volume series was later published for the period 1861 to 1935, though this was mainly for the Australian market. The *All England Law Reports* series has an excellent indexing service that will be described at 6.41 below. The *All England Law Reports Annual Review* has been published in a single annual volume since 1982. It contains review essays by leading experts on developments in all the core areas of law for the year under review. More recently, the *All England Legal Opinion* has been introduced. This is a short document, circulated with the reports themselves, providing comments, usually by leading practitioners, on important cases. It includes short summaries of other recent cases in the "Case Alerter" section.

Lloyd's Law Reports

6.25   This series, formerly entitled *Lloyd's List Law Reports*, has been published since 1919, and is devoted to maritime and commercial cases. The old series, consisting of volumes 1 to 84, ran from 1919 to 1950. The present series has been published since 1950. One characteristic of this series is that it includes cases from foreign jurisdictions, some of which are not reported elsewhere. Recently, for example, it reported an Irish case, *The Von Rocks* [1998] 2 Lloyd's Rep. 198; both High Court and Supreme Court judgments are included. Many of the cases reported in this series deal with shipping vessels and are therefore known by the name of the ship. Reports of prize cases have always been included in this series. A prize case is one arising from the capture of a ship or an aircraft or other goods in a time of war. Lloyd's also published a 10-volume series of prize cases arising from the First World War, *Lloyd's Reports of Prize Cases* (I-X, Ll.Pr.Cas.), and one volume of cases arising from the Second World War, *Lloyd's Reports of Prize Cases* (Ll.Pr.Cas. N.S.). There is a comprehensive citator for the entire series, *Lloyd's Law Reports Citator 1919-1999* which includes (i) a table of cases reported, (ii) a table of prize cases, (iii) a table of cases judicially considered, and (iv) a table of statutes judicially considered. This citator covers not only *Lloyd's Law Reports*, but also its sister publications including the *Building Law Reports, Lloyd's Reinsurance Law Reports, Lloyd's Law Reports Professional Negligence* and others.

Tax Cases

6.26   There are two series of tax reports published in England and Wales. *Reports of Tax Cases* (T.C.) have been published since 1875, nowadays in a volume a year. However, the cases are first issued periodically throughout the year in leaflet form, and are cited in this form as, for example, *Rigby v. Samson* (1997) T.C. No. 3512. However, they are later cumulated in annual volumes, and once they are reported in this form, they are cited in the usual way, e.g. *Rignell v. Andrews* (1990) 63 T.C. 312. It will be noted that this series of reports still cited primarily by volume number rather than by year (see 3.25 above). The other series is *Simon's Tax Cases* (S.T.C.) which began in 1973 and is published by Butterworths. This series covers tax cases decided by the U.K. courts, the European Court of Justice and the European Court of Human Rights. Judgments are reported in full and issued to subscribers as soon as possible after delivery. They are issued weekly in the punched parts to be filed in *Simon's Tax Cases* binder. Early the following year, subscribers receive the bound volume. A volume of cumulative tables and indexes for the entire year is issued annually. It includes lists of cases reported and considered, statutes considered, words and phrases considered, and a subject index. There is also a useful web site maintained by Grey's Inn Tax Chambers (www.taxbar.com/case.htm) which includes the full texts of many tax cases.

Company Law

6.27   The leading specialist series is *Butterworth's Company Law Cases* (B.C.L.C.) which are published in several annual parts and later cumulated in two annual volumes. This series, which has been published since 1983, is edited by Professor D. Prentice of Oxford University. It covers cases dealing not only with company law, but also with financial services and related matters. Decisions from Commonwealth and other jurisdictions outside the U.K. are also included. Ten issues are published each year which are filed in a loose leaf binder. The bound volumes are issued later, each of which has a subject index as well as an index of cases reported and statutes considered.

Employment Law

6.28   Judgments of the law courts dealing with labour law, trade union and industrial relations issues will, of course, be found in the general law reports series, but there are two specialist series devoted to industrial relations cases. The *Industrial Relations Law Reports* (I.R.L.R.), which have been published monthly since 1972, include decisions of the Employment Appeal Tribunal as well as the law courts. A case reported in this series is cited as *Benyon v. Scadden* [1999] I.R.L.R. 700. Cumulative indexes are published periodically. The *Industrial Cases Reports* have been published by the Incorporated Council of Law Reporting since 1972 in 11 parts a year. Included are judgments of the law courts, the European Court of Justice and the Employment Appeal Tribunal. There is a cumulative index at the end of each year listing all cases reported since the series began in 1972. A case cited in this series is cited as *Alexander v. Home Office* [1988] I.C.R. 685.

Human rights

6.29   With the recent incorporation of the European Convention on Human Rights into U.K. law, decisions of both the domestic and European courts on human rights issues have assumed a new importance, and publishers have not been slow to take advantage of this new market. The *Law Reports* and the *Weekly Law Reports* have begun to report all important cases under the Human Rights Act 1998. With effect from January 2001, the "new look" Part 1 of the *Weekly Law Reports* has expanded its general coverage of cases, including human rights cases. However, there are also some specialist series. *Butterworths Human Rights Cases* is published in 10 issues a year with two bound annual volumes. This series is by no means confined to European or U.K. cases. It covers a wide range of jurisdictions, and covers developments in areas such as medical law, employment law, family law and media law.

Other current series

6.30   There are many other specialist law report series published in England and Wales. The *Criminal Appeal Reports* series published by Sweet and Maxwell have already been described (6.22 above). In the area of intellectual property, the *Reports of Patent, Design and Trade Mark Cases* (R.P.C.) are published by Sweet and Maxwell for the Patent Office in 25 issues a year. Like all Sweet and Maxwell report series, this one has now adopted a neutral citation system (see 6.21 above). This means that instead of giving a page number, the case number is provided instead. Thus, *Wheatley (Davina) v. Drillsafe Ltd.* [2001] R.P.C. 7 refers to the seventh case published in the 2001 volume, although it appears on page 133 (in the fourth part). Judgments are in numbered paragraphs, so would might refer to *Wheatley (Davina) v. Drillsafe Ltd.* [2001] R.P.C. 7 at [12], meaning paragraph 12 of that report. The *Property, Planning and Compensa-*

tion Reports (P.& C.R.) have been published since 1949, and were previously known as the *Planning and Compensation Reports*, the *Road Traffic Reports* (RTR) have been published since 1970 and appear 10 times a year while the *Fleet Street Reports* which deal with intellectual property, patents and related matters appear in several parts a year.

Discontinued series

6.31   Some English law report series which have been discontinued are still commonly referred to. They include the *Law Journal Reports* (1823–1949) issued weekly in nine volumes in the first series (1823–1831) and in 118 volumes in the second series (1832–1949). The *Law Times Reports* were published in 200 volumes from 1843 to 1947. The *Times Law Reports* were issued weekly between 1884 and 1952 in 71 volumes. *Cox's Criminal Cases* were published between 1843 and the early 1940s. Until the early 20th century, they included Irish cases and are therefore an important primary source of Irish criminal law.

Newspaper law reports

6.32   Some British newspapers publish semi-formal reports of recent cases. The most extensive reporting service is provided by *The Times,* although reports are also published by *The Guardian*, *The Independent* and *The Financial Times*. Generally, the reports are just summaries of the judgments actually delivered, but are still useful, if only as a current awareness service. *The Times* is available on the Internet (www.thetimes.co.uk) and the recent law reports can be found by clicking on "British News". There is also an archive of older reports going back a few months. (This, at least, is the arrangement at the time of writing). At the end of each year, the reports which appeared in *The Times* are collected together in a loose-leaf folder which has a detailed subject index at the back. When using this service, however, remember that by the time of your research, many of the cases will have been reported in full in the one or more of the standard series such as the *Weekly Law Reports* or the *All England Law Reports*. Each Tuesday, *The Times* publishes a law supplement, which includes some law reports as well as general news, articles and comments of legal interest.

Electronic sources of law reports

6.33   Judgments of the House of Lords since 14 November 1996 are on the Web at: www.parliamentary.the-stationery-office.co.uk/ . Click on "House of Lords" and then on "Judicial Work and Judgments". Judgments of the Judicial Committee of the Privy Council since 1999 are on the Web at www.privy-council.org.uk/judicial-committee/jindex.htm . An interesting feature of this web site is that it includes some key judgments before 1999 such as *Ibrahim v. The King* (1914) which deals with the voluntariness requirement for the admission of confessions in criminal trials. Decisions from all three divisions of the English High Court from early 1996 onwards (as well as some pre-1996 cases) are available at www.bailii.org. In fact, the Bailii web site gives access to all primary sources of British and Irish law. See Appendix 7 below.

Westlaw UK

6.33a   All U.K. statutory instruments made since the beginning of 1948 are available in full-text on www.westlaw.co.uk. Also available are judgments and the following series of reports:

- The *Law Reports* from 1891.
- *Entertainment and Media Law Reports* from 1992.
- *Fleet Street Reports* from 1966.
- *Human Rights Law Reports* from 1999.
- *Landlord and Tenant Reports* from 1998.
- *Lloyd's Law Reports* from 1919.
- *Personal Injuries and Quantum Reports* from 1992.
- *Reports of Patent Cases* from 1977.

6.34   LEXIS is a good source of English case law since 1945. It provides the full text of all reported judgments since that date in its ENGGEN library as well as tax cases since 1875 and unreported judgments since 1980. Judgments are to be found in the CASES library of the ENGGEN library.

Identifying law report citations

6.35   With the present proliferation of specialist law reports, it is not uncommon to encounter an abbreviated law report citation one does not recognise. The same, of course, will often happen with older, discontinued series of reports. The best source to consult in these circumstances is *Raistrick's Index to Legal Citations and Abbreviations* 2nd edition (London, 1993) which has a comprehensive list of abbreviations up until 1993. Other useful lists will be found in any volume of the *Current Law Year Book* or, indeed, any issue of the *Current Law Monthly Digest*. A list of abbreviations will be found at the beginning of the first volume of *Halsbury's Laws of England* or the first volume of *The Digest*. Shorter lists will be found in most law dictionaries (7.31 below) and in Appendix 2 of this book.

Notes on recent cases

6.36   The best way of finding articles and notes on recent English cases is to consult the case indexes of the *Legal Journals Index* and the *Index to Legal*

Periodicals and Books. The *Current Law Monthly Digest* usually provides a list of relevant articles recently published in the various areas of law digested, though not all of these will necessarily deal with recent cases. Generally speaking, all criminal cases of any significance are digested and expertly analyzed in the *Criminal Law Review* which is published monthly. Notes and comments on many other cases are regularly published in leading journals such as *The Law Quarterly Review*, the *Modern Law Review* and the *Cambridge Law Journal*.

FINDING ENGLISH CASE LAW

6.37   To be able to use English case law effectively, one must be familiar with a number of research tools such as indexes, digests, citators and current law digests. An index is a list of cases, arranged alphabetically or classified by subject matter or both, and including the appropriate law report citations. A digest classifies cases according to subject matter including a brief abstract of each case and indicating where to find it. A citator lists reported cases and states how they have subsequently been dealt with, i.e. if they have been over-ruled, applied, approved or distinguished. A current law update gives a short account of recent cases and other legal developments, usually classified by subject.

Indexes

6.38   Most law report series publish their own indexes and cumulative indexes periodically. Indexes serve several purposes. They generally provide the full citation for a case for which one has the name, but not the law report reference. The better indexes usually list cases by subject as well, but remember that there may be relevant cases reported in series other than the one you are consulting.

6.39   *The Digest* (6.43 below) is one of the most comprehensive case indexes available anywhere. It is, among other things, the only index to the English law reports for the period 1865 to 1950, although cases from many other jurisdictions, including Ireland, are also included. Needless to say, it covers all post-1950 cases which have been digested as well, but these can usually be found in the indexes to the *Law Reports* (below). Para. 6.44 below describes how to use the indexes to *The Digest*.

6.40   The *Law Reports* (6.19 above) have a particularly good index covering all cases reported since 1951. There are five bound volumes of what is popularly known as the Red Index or, now, the Red Book, each covering a ten-year period: 1951-1960, 1961-1970, 1971-80, 1981-1990 and 1991-1999. The Red Index includes all cases published in the *Law Reports*, the *Weekly Law Reports* and the *Industrial Cases Reports* and contains references to cases reported in several other series including the *All England Law Reports,* the *Criminal Appeal Reports*, *Lloyd's Law Reports* and the *Road Traffic Law Reports.* Each volume has a complete alphabetical list of cases for the 10-year period covered, an extensive subject index as well as tables of cases, statutes, statutory instruments, European Community legislation and international conventions judicially considered. A "Pink Index" is published three times a year, each issue superseding the other. Therefore, when researching a particular subject area, one must begin with the five volumes of the Red Index which at present will bring one up to the end of 1999, then proceed to the final pink index for 2000 and any pink indexes published to date for 2001. There is a weekly update in the *Weekly Law Reports.*

6.41   The *All England Law Reports* also has an excellent indexing service. There is a one-volume index for the *All England Law Reports Reprint* covering the period 1558 to 1935. Then, there is a three-volume *All England Law Reports Consolidated Tables and Index 1936-1998.* The first volume includes a full alphabetical list of cases reported and considered, statutes considered, and words and phrases considered. The second and third volumes consist of a subject index. There are annual indexes for the years since 1998 and each issue contains updates.

6.42   As noted earlier, several of the specialist series of law reports, such as *Lloyd's Law Reports,* have their own indexing and citator systems. The *Criminal Law Review* has a general index in each annual volume, with periodic cumulative indexes. There is a full index in a separate bound volume covering the period 1954 to 1989.

Digests

6.43   One of the major reference works in English law is *The Digest*, formerly known as the *English and Empire Digest.* This is very useful source of information on case law, so it is worth while becoming familiar with it. *The Digest* is now in its third edition. The first edition was published between 1919 and 1932 with annual cumulative supplements up until 1951. The second edition, published in 56 volumes between 1951 and 1970, was known as the Blue Band Edition because of a blue bind on the spine of each volume. The third edition, known as the Green Band Edition, was published between 1971 and 1987. While concerned mainly with English law, *The Digest*, especially the older editions, includes many Irish and Commonwealth cases which will be found towards the end of individual entries. At present, there are apparently 500,000 cases digested from more than 1000 series of law reports from around the world.

6.44   *The Digest* may appear confusing at first because it consists of the 95 main volumes, reissue volumes, a cumulative supplement, consolidated tables and index volumes, and a quarterly survey. The main work is divided into more than 160 broad subject areas, known as titles, which are listed on the spine of each volume, so at least one knows where to begin searching. When the relevant area of law has undergone important changes, a new volume may be published which is known as a "reissue" volume. For example, in 1999, there was a 3rd reissue of volumes 9 and 10 dealing with Company Law. It is always important, therefore, to check the date of publication of the volume being consulted. There will, of course, have been many legal developments that do not warrant the reissue of a volume. To find these developments, one must first of all check under the appropriate subject headings in the annual Cumulative Supplement which is now published in two volumes. The Supplement is in the same format as the main volumes with the subject areas arranged in the same sequence. The *Quarterly Survey* which will usually be found filed beside the main volumes records reported cases since the last Cumulative Supplement was issued. Again, it is arranged in the same way as the main volumes. There is a table of new cases are the beginning of each issue. Remember that the number given after each case is not the page number but the case number.

6.45 The subject headings in *The Digest* correspond closely to those in *Halsbury's Laws of England* for which it was designed as a companion volume. *The Digest* has an extensive indexing system. There is an consolidated subject index published annually in two volumes and a three-volume table of cases. The latter lists virtually almost all English cases as well as many from the Commonwealth jurisdictions, Ireland and the European courts. It is therefore valuable if one has the name but not the citation for a case. Suppose, for example, one were trying to track down the case of *Bradshaw v. Toulmin*. It appears in the consolidated table of cases as:

Bradshaw v. Toulmin (1784) 38 Real Prop.

Note that the law report reference is not given here. All we are told is the year in which it was decided and the volume of *The Digest* (Volume 38 dealing with Real Property) in which it is digested. We must now go the case index of Volume 38 which will direct us to Para. 5003 of that volume. This paragraph reads:

> 5003. effect of simultaneous death. If two persons perish by one blow, the estate will remain as it was. *Bradshaw v. Toulmin* (1784) 2 Dick. 633; 21 E.R. 417.
>
> See Law of Property Act 1925 (c. 20) s. 184; 27 *Halsbury's Statutes* (3rd ed.) 602.

We now know what the case is about, where it can be found in both the nominate reports and the *English Reports* and the (English) legislation that should be consulted to bring the law up to date. One should also check the continuation volumes and the cumulative supplement to see if there have been any recent developments.

The Current Law Service

6.46   The other main digest and citator service is provided by Sweet and Maxwell's *Current Law Service*. This service has several components: *Current Law Statutes* (see 6.07 above), *Current Law Monthly Digest, Current Law Year Book, Current Law Statute Citator, Current Law Statutory Instrument Citator* and *Current Law Case Citator.*

Current Law Monthly Digest and Year Book

6.47   The *Current Law Monthly Digest,* published 12 times a year, provides an account of legal developments in England and Wales, Scotland, Northern Ireland and the EU. Each of these jurisdictions has its own separate part in each issue. Legal developments, principally in the form of case summaries, are presented under broad subject headings, with a list of recent publications at the end of each section. The *Current Law Year Book* is an annual cumulation of the monthly digests, divided into the same subject areas with each paragraph assigned its own number. A case digested in the *Year Book* is cited as: *Thomas v. University of Bradford* [1987] C.L.Y. 1276 (i.e. at paragraph, *not* page, 1276 of the 1987 *Current Law Year Book*). Sometimes, in fact, the *Digest* and *Year Book* may be the only sources of information about cases that are not subsequently reported.

Current Law Case Citator

6.48   The *Current Law Case Citator* is the second major component of the Current Law Service. It provides the law report citation(s) for every case digested in *Current Law* since it began in 1947, and gives the following additional information in respect of each case: the volume of *Current Law* in which it is digested, its subsequent history (e.g. if it has been overruled, applied or relied upon) and any articles or notes published about it. Pre-1947 cases considered in any of the digested cases are also listed. The *Case Citator* has been published in bound volumes to date covering the periods 1947 to 1976, 1976 to 1988, 1989 to 1995, 1996 and 1997, 1988 and 1999. There is also a *Case Citator* covering the entire period 1977 to 1997 which can be used instead of those covering shorter periods during this 20-year era. This is the situation at the time of writing (early 2001). Generally speaking, one can expect to find case citators available in one format or another up until about a year before one's research date.

6.49   The use of the *Case Citator* can be illustrated by the following exercises. Suppose one wanted to find the case of *Slattery v. Mance*, for which one does not have any reference. Of course, there is no guarantee that it will be listed in the *Case Citator*, as it may not have been decided or considered by any English court since 1947. If it is not listed there, one should consult the case indexes to *The Digest, Halsbury's Laws of England,* the *English* Reports, the *All England Law Reports* and the *All England Law Reports Reprint.* One would have to be exceptionally unlucky if it was not listed in one of them. In fact, we will find it in the first *Case Citator*, that covering the years 1947 to 1976, and the entry reads:

> *Slattery v. Mance* [1962] 1 QB 676; [1962] 2 WLR 569; 106 SJ 113;
> [1962] 1 All ER 525; [1962] 1 Lloyd's Rep.
>
> *Digested 62/2870.*

This information gives us a list of the law reports in which the case was reported and tells us that it was digested in paragraph 2870 of the *Current Law Year Book* for 1962. This paragraph will tell us briefly what the case was about. However, we also wish to know the subsequent history of this case, so we must consult the later citators. The 1977 to 1988 Case Citator has the following entry:

> *Slattery v. Mance* (1962)
> *Applied 81/1442; Considered 88/3220*

By consulting paragraph 1142 of the 1981 *Current Law Year Book* and paragraph 3220 of the 1988 *Year Book*, we can discover the names of the cases in which it was applied and considered.

6.50   Let us now perform a similar exercise with *Solle v. Butcher* the entries for which have some additional elements. The entry in the Case Citator for 1947 to 1976 reads:

> *Solle v. Butcher* [1950] 1 KB 76; 66 TLR (Pt. 1) 448; [1949] 2 All ER
> 1107; [94 SJ 465, 482, 514; 209 LT 66, 167; 15 MLR 297; 66 LQR
> 169; 14 Conv 93]CA
>
> *Digested 4201 8914*
>
> *Applied 1785, 9247; 53/3290; 67/623; 69/1819; 71/6632.*
>
> *Considered ...... etc.*

There are some additional features in this entry. First, it will be noted that the law report references are followed by a series of other references enclosed in square brackets. These are references to law journals where articles or comments on the case will be found e.g. in volume 15 of the *Modern Law Review* at page 297. A list of abbreviations for law reports and journals will be found at the beginning of each volume of the *Year Book*. Secondly, we are told that the case is digested at 4201 and 8914. These are clearly paragraph numbers but for which volume we are not told. The reason is that the *Year Books* for 1947 to 1951 inclusive were in one volume, and references to this volume are by paragraph number only. To follow up on the subsequent history of *Solle v. Butcher*, consult the 1977 to 88 Case Citator which has the following entry:

> *Solle v. Butcher* [1949] [103 LQR 594]
> *Applied* 78/1515; 83/3888; *Disapproved* 88/449.

The two pieces of information in square brackets after the case title tell us that it was decided in 1949 and was the subject of an article or comment in Volume 103 of the *Law Quarterly Review*. There are no entries for this case in the *Case Citator* for 1989 to 1991, or in those for subsequent years.

Current Law Legislation Citator

6.51   The legislation citators have also appeared in several volumes covering various periods. First, there is a *Current Law Statute Citator* covering the period 1947 to 1971. Next, there is the *Current Law Legislation Citator* for the period 1972 to 1988 which covers both statutes and statutory instruments. The next *Legislation Citator* covers statutes for the years 1989 to 1995 and statutory instruments for the years 1993 to 1995. After that there have been separate volumes for statutes and statutory instruments: a *Current Law Statute Citator* for 1996 to 1999 and a *Current Law Statutory Instrument Citator* for 1996 to 1999. Taken together, the Statute Citators give the following information:

(a) a list of all Public General Acts since 1947;
(b) details of amendments and repeals since 1947 to statutes of any date, either before or after 1947;
(c) cases dealing with statutes or sections of them;
(d) details of statutory instruments issued under statutory provisions enacted since 1947;
(e) a table of legislation not yet in force.

Remember that the Statute Citators list many statutes enacted long before 1947 if they have been in any way affected by statutes enacted since then or if there have been cases dealing with them. Suppose, for example, one were looking for cases decided in the period 1989 to 1995 on sections 16 and 18 of the Offences

Against the Person Act 1861. One would turn to the Statute Citator for 1989 to 1995 where one would find, towards the beginning (as the statutes are listed in chronological order), the following entries:

24 & 25 Vic (1861)
100 Offences Against the Person Act 1861

s. 16, see *R. v. Tait* [1989] 3 WLR 891 CA

s. 18, see *R. v. Stubbs* (1988) 88 Cr App R 53; CA; *E. v.Morrison* (1989) 89 Cr App R 17, CA.

6.52   Table 1 illustrates in more detail how one would use the Statute Citators and *Current Law Statutes* to trace the statutory history and judicial interpretation of the Interception of Telecommunications Act 1985 (c.56).

Table 1: Using the Current Law Statute Citator

The Act was passed in 1985, so we begin with the Statute Citator for 1972–1988 where we find, at p. 577:

> **56. Interception of Communications Act 1985.**
> Royal Assent. July 25, 1985.
> Commencement order: 86/384.
> s. 12, order 86/384.

The Statute Citator for 1989 to 1995 has the following entry at p. 278:

> **56. Interception of Communications Act 1985.**
> ss. 1–5, 7, 9, see *R. v.Uxbridge Justices, ex p. Offomah* [1992] C.O.D. 155, D.C.
> ss. 1, 9, see *R. v. Effik (Goodwin Eno)*; *R. v. Mitchell (Graham Martin)* [1994] 3 W.L.R. 583; H.L.
> ss. 1, 9, 10, see *R. v. Governor of Belmarsh Prison, ex p. Martin* [1985] 1 W.L.R. 412, D.C.
> ss. 2, 6, 9, see *R. v. Preston (Stephen)*; *R. v. Clarke (Nicholas Henry)*; *R. v. Austen (Anthony)*; *R.v. Salter (Jeremy)*; *R. v. Preston (Zena)* [1993] 3 W.L.R. 891, H.L.
> s. 9, amended: 1989, c. 6 sch. 1; repealed in pt: *ibid.*, schs. 1, 2.

The Statute Citator for 1996 to 1999 has the following entry at p. 296:

> **56. Interception of Communications Act 1985.**
> see *Halford v. United Kingdom* [1997] I.R.L.R. 471 (ECHR), R. Bernhardt (President); see *R. v. Aujla (Ajlt Singh)* [1998] 2 Cr. App. R. 16 (CA (Crim Div)). Roch, L.J.
> applied: SI 1996/680 Art. 2, Sch. Part 1
> referred to: SI 1998 c.47 Sch. 2 para. 17
> s. 1, see *R. v.Owen (Darren Lea)* [1999] 1 W.L.R. 949 (CA (Crim Div)). Buxton, L.J.
> s. 1, amended: SI 1999/1750 Art. 6, Sch. 5, para. 6
> s. 2, applied: 1986 c.25, s.3, s.7, s.8, s.9, SI 1999/1748 Art. 3, Sch. 1, para. 6, SI 1999/1750, Art 2, Sch. 1
> s. 3, applied: SI 1999/1748 Art. 3, Sch. 1, para. 6
> s. 4, amended: SI 1999/1750 Art. 6, Sch. 5, para. 6
> s. 4, applied: SI 1999/1748 Art. 3, Sch. 1, para. 6, SI 1999/1750, Art 2, Sch. 1
> s. 5, amended: SI 1999/1750 Art. 6, Sch. 5, para. 6

6.53   The present collection of bound Statute Citators brings us up to the end of 1999. To find out about more recent statutory developments and about cases dealing with earlier statutes, consult the Current Awareness File of the *Current Law Statutes* which has a statute citator section for the year 2000. For very recent developments, see the citator sections of the *Current Law Monthly Digests*.

Current Law Statutes

6.54   This series has been mentioned earlier, but it is relevant in the present context because of its updating services. It is an annotated statute service, which began in 1947 and all the annotated statutes other than recent ones are kept in bound volumes. To trace the development of a statutory provision enacted since 1947, first check the original section and annotation in the relevant volume. Next, check the Statute Citators for the years since then to see if there have been any amendments. Finally, consult the annotations attached to any amending provisions in later versions of the *Current Law Statutes*. The Current Awareness Service, which is contained in loose-leaf volume, is updated annually and is particularly valuable. It contains in respect of the most recent full year – 2000 at present – (1) a list of statutes; (2) a subject index of those statutes; (3) a statute citator, thus updating the bound volumes of citators just described; (4) a statutory instrument citator; (5) a table of parliamentary debates (Commons and Lords) for public General Acts from 1950 to 1998; (6) commencement orders and (7) a numerical table of statutory instruments, of which there were over 3000 in the year 2000, published by the U.K. parliament

WORDS AND PHRASES DEFINED

6.55   Legal researchers often need to check if there is a statutory or judicial definition of a particular word or phrase. British lawyers are fortunate in having two major works answering this need: *Stroud's Judicial Dictionary* and *Words and Phrases Legally Defined*. Both are in several volumes with updating supplements. The third edition of *Words and Phrases*, for example, was published in four volumes by Butterworths in 1988, and there have been seven supplements in the meantime. It includes definitions from Canada, Australia and New Zealand as well as from the U.K. The sixth edition of *Stroud* was released in both paper and CD formats in October 2000. Judicial as well as statutory definitions are given in both works. Other sources include *Halsbury's Laws of England* (consult "words and phrases" in the subject index in volume 56 of the main work and in the various updates), the *Current Law Year Books* and *Current Law Monthly Digest*.

SCOTS LAW

The Scottish legal system

6.56   Scotland has always maintained its own distinct legal system, even after the creation of a legislative union with England in 1707. It has been strongly influenced by Roman law as well as English common law. Scholarly writings, known as institutional writings, have a higher status as a source of law than they would generally enjoy in a purely common-law system such as Ireland or England and Wales. At first sight, Scots law may seem difficult to understand because of its terminology. More often than not, however, the difficulty is just that, terminological rather than substantial. In Scots law, for example, the plaintiff in civil proceedings is known as the pursuer, a tort is known as a delict and an injunction as an interdict. The Lord Advocate is somewhat similar to the Attorney General in Ireland, although he also has overall responsibility for public prosecutions. Procurators fiscal are public prosecutors. The Faculty of Advocates is more or less equivalent to the Bar in Ireland. The best introduction to the Scottish legal system, and to its system of legal education, is Professor Hector MacQueen's *Studying Scots Law* 2nd edition (Edinburgh: Butterworths, 1999). There are also some useful reference works explaining the terminology used in Scots law, such as *Green's Glossary of Scottish Legal Terms* 3rd edition by A.G.M. Duncan (Edinburgh: W.Green/Sweet and Maxwell, 1992).

6.57   Irish lawyers have a tendency to ignore Scottish law, perhaps because of the terminological difficulties just mentioned. Scotland, however, is a jurisdiction worthy of closer study. Its population is much closer to Ireland's than that of England and Wales, and its legal procedures and structures are therefore of considerable interest for comparative purposes. Among the recent books on the Scottish legal system, apart from MacQueen's, are Walker, *The Scottish Legal System* 8th edition edition (Edinburgh: Green & Son, 2001), Marshall, *General Principles of Scots Law* 7th edition (Edinburgh: Green & Son, 1999), Young, *Crime and Criminal Justice in Scotland* (Edinburgh: The Stationery Office, 1997) and Duff and Hutton, *Criminal Justice in Scotland* (Ashgate/Dartmouth: Aldershot, 1999).

6.58   As noted at the beginning of this chapter, Scotland's constitutional status within the United Kingdom has changed significantly as a result of the Scotland Act 1998 which established at devolved parliament at Edinburgh. All the legislation, primary and secondary, made in Scotland since the Parliament began work in 1999 is available on the Internet at www.scotland-legislation.hmso.gov.uk/legislation/ .One can find the text of an Act simply by clicking on the title or, alternatively, use the search engine to find statutory material by topic. U.K. legislation made at Westminster before 1999, and applicable to Scotland, can be found in the sources mentioned at 6.06 *et seq.*

above, especially in the *Public General Acts and Measures*. Some pre-1707 legislation in still in force in Scotland. The best source is the collection, *Acts of the Parliament of Scotland 1424-1707* (HMSO, 1966). See also www.bailii.org for Scottish statutes and statutory instrumentes since 2000. Westlaw UK Scots Law contains full text fully consolidated legislation specific to Scotland, from Westminster and Holyrood and including the text of the Parliament House Book.

Citing an Act of the Scottish Parliament

6.59   An Act of the Scottish Parliament is cited in essentially the same way as an Irish or Westminster Act, except that there is an addendum indicating that it is an Act made in Scotland and assigning it a number, e.g.

Budget (Scotland) Act 2000 asp 2.

The addendum "asp 2" tells us that it is an Act of the Scottish Parliament and that it was the second Act made in 2000. Furthermore, before the word "Act" in the main body of the title, the word "Scotland" is placed in parentheses to indicate that it was made in and applies to Scotland.

Scottish case law

6.60   Before consulting Scottish law reports, it is necessary to know something about the Scottish courts system. The highest civil court is known as the Court of Session which sits in Edinburgh and consists of an Inner House and an Outer House, the latter being a trial court (more or less equivalent to our High Court) and the former being a court of civil appeal. The Inner House has two co-ordinate divisions, the first of which is presided over by the Lord President, and the second by the Lord Justice-Clerk. The High Court of Justiciary is a criminal court, similar to our Central Criminal Court, which has exclusive jurisdiction over certain serious crimes such as murder, rape and piracy. All trials are by solemn procedure, meaning that they are by judge and jury. There is now a Court of Criminal Appeal as well. The other major trial court is the Sheriff Court, somewhat akin to our Circuit Court. Scotland is divided into six Sheriffdoms, each with a Sheriff Principal. The Sheriff Court deals with all serious offences other than those reserved exclusively to the High Court of Justiciary, and also has a civil jurisdiction. The district courts, similar to ours, deal with minor civil and criminal cases. Finally, it should be recalled that the House of Lords, sitting in London, is entitled to hear appeals in civil cases from the Court of Session, but it does not hear criminal appeals from Scotland. There are usually two Scots Law Lords on the judicial committee of the House of Lords. For further information, see MacQueen, *Studying Scots Law* (6.56 above) and the information leaflet published by the Scottish Court Service which is available on the Internet at: www.scotscourts.gov.uk/forms/intro.htm

6.61   The present Scottish law reporting system is fairly straightforward. The main series of reports is known as the *Session Cases*, published in five parts a year, which are later cumulated in an annual volume. What must be remembered when using this series is that each volume is divided into three sections, each of which is paginated separately. The three sections are devoted to: (1) House of Lords cases from Scotland (SC(HL)); (2) High Court of Justiciary cases (JC) and (3) Court of Session cases (SC). The same arrangement is followed in each of the parts making up the annual volumes. Thus, Part v. for 2000 consists of HL 95-145, JC 413-554 and SC 407-525. Cases reported in the *Session Cases* are cited as follows:

> *Moffat v. Longmuir* 2001 SC 137 (a case reported in the 2001 volume of the *Session Cases* from the Court of Session section).

> *Advocate (HM) v. Burns* 2001 JC 1 (a case reported in the 2001 volume of the *Session Cases* from the High Court of Justiciary section)

> *Abnett v. Kennedy* 1997 SC (HL) 26 (a case reported in the 1997 volume of the *Session Cases* from the House of Lords section)

The other major law report series is the *Scots Law Times* which has been published since 1893, and which is organised like the former *Irish Law Times and Solicitors Journal* (ILTSJ) in the sense that it includes articles and news items as well as law reports. However, unlike the ILTSJ, there are two annual volumes, one of which is devoted to law reports. This law report volume, in turn, is divided into two main sections, each paginated separately. The first is devoted to House of Lords and Court of Session reports, and the second to Sheriff Court reports. There may also be short sections devoted to more specialized courts. House of Lords and Court of Session cases reported in the *Scots Law Times* are cited as follows:

> *Walker v. Normand* 1996 SLT 898.

Sheriff Court cases are cited as:

> *Belhaven Brewery Co Ltd v. Smith* 1996 SLT (Sh Ct) 127.

6.62   There are two other law report series, both of which are published by the Law Society of Scotland: the *Scottish Criminal Case Reports* (SCCR), begun in 1981 and the *Scottish Civil Law Reports* (SCLR), begun in 1987. The citation system is the same as for the others, e.g. .....1990 SCCR 123. Note that in Scotland, the year is not placed in sqaure brackets even in the case of reports cited primarily by year, as all them now are. From 1893 to 1908, the *Scots Law Times* reports were cited primarily by volume number with year in parentheses, again like the ILTSJ. A case reported in the SLT from this era is therefore cited as: *Wallace v. Kennedy* (1908) 16 SLT 486. When an article published in the *Scots Law Times* is being quoted, it is cited as follows:

Black, "The Scottish Parliament and the Scottish Judiciary" 1998 SLT
(News) 321.

Older Scottish law reports

6.63   The Scottish law reports published in the 19th century and earlier were
mainly nominate reports in the sense that they were known by the name of
editor, examples being Bell and Macqueen (abbreviated Macq). They are listed
in Hector MacQueen's *Studying Scottish Law* (6.56 above) at p. 138. Remember too that Raistrick's *Index to Legal Citations and Abbreviations* (6.35 above)
explains virtually all known abbreviations and provides some information about
the publications to which they refer.

Electronic sources of Scots law

6.64 The *Scots Law Times* reports from 1930 to date are available on Westlaw
UK (www.westlaw.co.uk) and are updated weekly. Reported Scottish cases since
1950 are available on LEXIS in the SCOT library. The same library has some
unreported cases of more recent vintage. A good deal of recent case law is also
available on the web site of the Scottish Court service. Court of Session opinions since 1998, criminal opinions of the High Court of Justiciary for recent
years and Sheriff Court decisions since September 1998 are available on a web
site which is usually admirably current. The relevant web pages are updated at
about 2.00 p.m. on any day on which new judgments are published. The home
page of the Courts Service is www.scotscourts.gov.uk/ . One can navigate from
there by way of hypertext. Judgments are under "opinions". The URL
www.scotscourts.gov.uk/html/links.htm provides access to other relevant courts
including the House of Lords, the Privy Council and the European Court of
Justice as well as to the Society for Computers and the Law, the Law Society of
Scotland and similar bodies. Also worth investigating is the SLORC website
(www.scottishlaw.org.uk/scotlaw/a1.html) which covers legislation and the
courts and provides links to dozens of other relevant sites.

Digests and current awareness services

6.65   The *Current Law Service* covers Scotland as well as England and Wales,
and Northern Ireland. There is a separate section for Scotland at the towards the
end of each issue of the *Current Law Monthly Digest* and again of the *Year
Book*. It provides the same kind of information and is used in the same way as
the section devoted to England and Wales (see 6.47 above). There is, however,
a separate series of *Scottish Current Law Case Citators* covering various periods from 1948 to 1995, with updates in *Current Law* for later years. Westlaw
UK Scots Law has the Scottish Law Journals index with abstracts.

WELSH LAW

6.66   The only distinctive Welsh law of any significance consists of the Statutory Instruments made by the Welsh Assembly since it came into operation in 1999. All of these are available on the Internet at: <u>www.wales-legislation.hmso.gov.uk</u>. See recent article by Kirby, "Welsh Legislation in Peril" in *Internet Newsletter for Lawyers* (July/August 2001).

CHAPTER 7

Secondary Sources of Irish and British Law

7.01 Secondary sources consist of books, periodicals, law reform documents and other legal literature apart from constitutions, legislation and case law. Our primary concern here is with scholarly literature, but reference will also be made to more general works that may be useful for legal research. The chapter is organised more or less in accordance with the steps that should be taken when researching a legal topic. As a rule, it is best to begin with a standard textbook providing a general statement of the present law. After that, one must seek out more detailed information from other books, reference works, periodicals, reports and similar sources. Accordingly, the secondary works to be described here are arranged in the following order: books, reference works, legal periodicals, government publications, law reform documents, parliamentary debates, theses, general publications.

BOOKS

7.02 A student should be able to identify the books relevant to a research topic in two ways: first, by ascertaining those books available in the library to which she has access and, secondly, by drawing up a bibliography of books otherwise available. Those on the second list, unless they are rare or particularly difficult to track down, can be borrowed by way of inter-library loan or consulted in another library. The same is true of periodical material described in 7.13 *et seq.* below

Searching in the library

7.03 Students should become familiar with the cataloguing systems in their own libraries. Nowadays, most libraries have their main catalogues on computer which allows the user to search by author, title, subject matter, and so forth. When searching by author, it is always helpful to have his or her full name. Typing in "Smith" will probably produce dozens, if not hundreds, of entries. "Smith, John" will narrow the search considerably; "Smith, John F", depending on the system, should narrow it even further. When using a computerised catalogue, two limitations should be borne in mind. First, this type of catalogue, no more than any other, cannot be guaranteed to identify all the books or other printed documents relevant to one's research topic. For example, a computer-generated list of books on tort law is unlikely to include Atiyah and Cane, *Accidents, Compensation and the Law* 6th edn (London: Butterworths, 1999) Yet this book will probably be found shelved in the general vicinity of other tort books. This is because the most common form of classification used in academic libraries is the Dewey Decimal system. This system was originally devised by Melvil Dewey (1851-1931) and published in 1876. It divides knowledge into 10 classes numbered 0 to 9. Class 3 is devoted to sociology which, for this purpose includes law. The numerical prefix "347. –" generally stands for law. At present, the 21st edition of the Dewey Decimal Classification is in force, with the 22nd scheduled to appear in 2002. It can be consulted on the Internet at www.oclc.org/fp/. The advantage of the Dewey system is that books relating to the same topic are grouped together. Therefore, in addition to consulting the library catalogue, it always pays to spend some time browsing among the book stacks. Often books relevant to a topic will have no a reference to it in their titles. Another consequence of the Dewey system is that there may be books germane to certain legal topics shelved elsewhere. Many criminology texts, for example, may be found in the sociology rather the law sections of the library. The same may be true of constitutional history, legal theory and other subjects with an interdisciplinary dimension.

7.04   The second limitation of computerised catalogues is that they may not cover all holdings. Older acquisitions, perhaps pre-1950, may still be catalogued in card form or in bound volumes or some combination of both. In the late 19th and early 20th centuries, many libraries produced their own printed catalogues in book form (see 7.07 below). Depending on the progress of computerisation in a given library, it may still be necessary to consult the older catalogues as well as the online version. Most academic libraries have information leaflets describing their cataloguing systems. If in doubt, seek assistance from the information desk.

On-line library catalogues

7.05   It is now possible to gain access to the computerised catalogues of many libraries through the World Wide Web. Access can generally be gained through the home pages of the relevant universities. Therefore, even if one does not have the exact Internet address (the URL) for say, the Trinity College Dublin library, one can just find Trinity College's home page using any of the usual search engines. It is then simply a matter of finding on-line library catalogue, which can easily be done by way of hypertext. This is a wonderful development, as most of the leading law libraries in the English-speaking world now have on-line catalogues. See the list of web sites in Appendix 8 of this book for a selection of the best on-line catalogues. Remember, of course, that they may not list all holdings; always check out how far back any on-line catalogue goes. Some on-line booksellers also have excellent web sites. Amazon (www.amazon.co.uk)

and Barnes and Noble (www.barnesandnoble.com) are probably the best. As-suming a book is in print, it is likely to be listed by one of them. But one cannot rely entirely on them; Irish books and books produced by smaller publishers may escape their attention. Leading bookshops such as Blackwells in Oxford, which has an extensive law collection, also have searchable on-line catalogues should also be checked out. Many Irish law books in print will be found on Fred Hanna's web site (www.hannas.ie). All the leading law publishers such as Sweet and Maxwell, Butterworths, Oxford University Press, Kluwer and others, have information about their recent publications on-line. However, except for titles that may just have been published, the Trinity College and U.C.D. catalogues are probably the most reliable guides to Irish law books.

Irish Legal Bibliographies

7.06   There is no comprehensive modern bibliography of Irish law books but there are some older ones. The best of these is Maxwell and Maxwell, *A Legal Bibliography of the British Commonwealth of Nations*, Volume 4. The second edition of this volume was published by Sweet and Maxwell in London in 1957, and includes more than 350 items which had come to light since the publication of the first edition some years earlier. There are very few subject-specific bibli-ographies apart from Hepple, Neeson and O'Higgins, *A Bibliography of Lit-erature on British and Irish Labour Law* (London: Mansell, 1975) with a later volume by Hepple, Hepple, O'Higgins and Stirling, *Labour Law in Great Brit-ain and Ireland to 1978* (London; Sweet and Maxwell, 1981).

7.07   There is an older, American-published, work, Marvin's *Legal Bibliog-raphy, or, A Thesaurus of American, English, Irish and Scotch Law Books* (Philadelphia: Johnson, 1847, reprinted in 1953). There is a short bibliography of Irish law books and government publications compiled by Joan Ryan in Twin-ing and Uglow (eds.), *Legal Publishing and Legal Information: Small Juris-dictions of the British Isles* (London: Sweet and Maxwell, 1981). The same book has a chapter by William Twining and Kevin Boyle on legal literature in Ireland, which is still a useful guide to some older sources. A list of Irish law books published since 1950 is provided in Appendix 4 of the present book, although it does not claim to be comprehensive. Raistrick's *Lawyers' Law Books* 3rd edition (London: Bowker Sauer, 1997) has a good, though by no means comprehensive, list of modern Irish law books. Not all of them are classified under "Irish law"; many of them are under the relevant subject headings. The *Index to Legal Periodicals and Books* (7.23 below) from 1994 onwards also lists some books published in Ireland. Certain printed catalogues are also useful in tracking down older Irish law books. These include *Catalogue of Books in the Library of the Honorable Society of Gray's* Inns (London, 1906), *Cata-logue of Books in the Library of the Incorporated Law Society of Ireland* (1895 and 1909) and the 9-volume catalogue of the Library of Trinity College

Dublin listing books wholly or partially published up to the end of 1872. Several other university library catalogues were produced in book form around the beginning of the 20th century and are to be found in many university libraries. There is now a major work by Tony Sweeney which will be of interest to anyone researching Irish legal history in the early modern period. It is entitled *Ireland and the Printed Word: A Select Descriptive Catalogue of Early Books, Pamphlets, Newsletters and Broadsides Relating to Ireland. Printed 1475 – 1700.* It was published in Dublin in 1997 by Eamonn de Burca for Edmund Burke Publishers. The first edition of this book was limited to 250 signed and numbered copies of which 235 were offered for sale. Copies should be available in the university libraries, and there is a copy in the library of the Honorable Society of King's Inns.

Bibliographies of English law books

7.08   The best source of information on recently published English law books is the *Current Law Year Book* (see 6.46 above). Towards the end of each annual volume (or, for recent years, the second annual volume), there is a list of books on English law published that year. The monthly editions of *Current Law* (6.46 above) list recently published articles under each subject heading, as well as some books under "Publications". But the Year Book is always the best guide. The problem is that it lists books by the names of authors and editors in alphabetical order, so one has to trawl through the entire list to locate relevant material. The *Index to Legal Periodicals and Books* (7.23 below) has listed books as well as periodicals since 1994. English books are included, although the *Index* is strongest on U.S. publications. Needless to say, Raistrick's *Lawyers' Law Books* (7.07 above), an English publication, is a very useful guide, as is *Law Books and Serials* in Print 2000 (7.10 below).

Recent books on European law

7.09   The best source of information on recently published European law books is the *European Current Law Year Book* which publishes annually a long list of recent books on European law in several languages, though mainly English. Shorter lists are to be found in each issue of the *European Current Law Monthly Digest*. See 8.18 below.

Other legal bibliographies

7.10   Legal bibliographies can be divided into two broad categories: general and subject-specific bibliographies. We shall begin with general works. For older and historical works, the five volumes of Maxwell and Maxwell, *A Legal Bibliography of the British Commonwealth of Nations*, the fourth of which, as noted, deals with Irish law, are a good starting point. The same is true of the various printed catalogues mentioned in para. 7.07. Beale's *Bibliography of Early English Law Books*, first published in 1926 by Harvard University Press, bound with a supplement by Anderson in 1943 and reprinted in 1966, has many interesting entries. One of the great works of modern bibliographical scholarship appeared within the past years. This is Morris Cohen's *Bibliography of Early American Law (BEAL)*, (Buffalo, NY: William S. Hein, 1998). This work, in the words of its introduction, "lists and describes the monographic and trial literature of American law published in [the USA] or abroad from its beginnings to the end of 1860". It also includes works on foreign, comparative and international law if published in the USA. There are six volumes, the last devoted to indexes.

Law Books 1876-1981 (New York and London, 1981) is a four-volume work listing about 130,000 books and 4,000 serials. The subject index occupies the first three volumes, while the fourth has an author and serials index. Various supplements have been issued since 1981.

Law Books and Serial in Print 2000: A Multimedia Sourcebook published annually by Bowker, is the best guide to law books in English that are still in print. There are three volumes. The first lists books with a subject index, the second has author, title, and publisher symbol indexes, and the third has a serials, audio cassette and video cassette index.

Bibliographic Guide to Law (Boston, Mass.) is a two-volume annual publication which lists the works catalogued in the US Library of Congress during the relevant year. It includes materials in all languages and forms.

General Bibliographies

7.11.   There is no comprehensive modern bibliography of books published in Ireland or about Irish issues. The *Irish Publishing Record* was an annual publication which began in 1967. The National Library of Ireland assumed responsibility for its publication from 1989 onwards, but the most recent issue appears to be that for 1994, published in 1996. In any event, online library and bookshop catalogues are now the most reliable source of information on recently published books. *Whitaker's Books in Print* is published annually in five volumes, with a single alphabetical index listing books by authors or editors and titles. The 2001 edition lists close on 1 million titles. Books are included if they are published in the U.K. and available to the general public through the book trade. Some English language titles published elsewhere are included. There is also a multi-volume US work, *Books in Print* which can be now has a web site as well: www.booksinprint.com .The *Cumulative Book List* has been published in monthly parts (later cumulating into annual volumes) since 1928 and which claims to give a "world list of books published in the English language". The issues for more recent years are available on CD. "Books in print" series list only those in print. For older books, the best print sources is *The British Museum Catalogue of Printed Books*. The main work comes up as far as 1955 and there are supplements for various periods since then. The American equivalent is the multi-volume *National Union Catalogue* published by the Library of Congress. There is a much shorter *English Catalogue of Books*, published by Sampson Low, and covering the period 1835 to 1916.

7.12   There are thousands of subject-specific catalogues published in various forms. *The Bibliographic Index: A Bibliography of Bibliographies* is published three times a year with an annual cumulation in December. It provides a subject list of bibliographies published separately, or as parts of books, pamphlets or periodicals. Selection is made from bibliographies with 50 more citations. It concentrates on titles in English and other Western European languages.

LEGAL PERIODICALS

7.13   Each university library will have available, in some format, a complete list of periodicals in stock and the years for which it has them. A library may not have a complete run of every periodical. Nowadays, many libraries have their periodical stocks listed on their computerised catalogues.

Irish Legal Periodicals (General)

7.14   During the 1990s, the number of Irish legal periodicals grew considerably. The *Irish Jurist*, which is the longest established, remains the most substantial. There have been several publications since the mid-19th century bearing the title *Irish Jurist*. In the 20th century, there was an *Irish Jurist* published from 1935 to 1965 which carried short articles and law reports (see 4.53 above). In 1966, it was transformed into a major academic journal under the editorship of the late Professor John Kelly. He was succeeded by Professor W.N. Osborough who, in turn, was succeeded by Professor Finbarr McAuley, the present editor. It is published annually and contains substantial articles and book reviews. The present series, begun in 1966, is referred to as the new series and is cited as …(1987) 22 *Irish Jurist* (n.s.) 123. In the early 1990s, the journal was appearing some years in arrears. Therefore, volumes 25 to 27 for the years 1990 to 1992 were published as a single issue as were volumes 28 to 30 for the years 1993 to 1995. Since then, it has been published in a single, though substantial, annual volume by Round Hall Sweet and Maxwell for the Law Faculty of University College Dublin.

7.15   The *Dublin University Law Journal* has been published since 1976. It assumed its present editorial format in 1978, and is now a very substantial journal. It is cited as … (1982) 4 D.U.L.J. (n.s.) 12, the new series having apparently begun in 1978. It is published by Round Hall Sweet and Maxwell for the Law School of Trinity College Dublin, and contains a good selection of scholarly articles, case-notes and book reviews. It is edited by Eoin O'Dell of the T.C.D. Law School. Two volumes of a *Dublin University Law Review* were published in 1969-70, also by the TCD law school.

7.16 The *Irish Law Times* has also gone through several changes in format and editorial policy. First, there was the *Irish Law Times and Solicitor's Journal* published from 1867 to 1981. This appeared weekly with news of general interest to the legal profession as well as articles which were often spread over several weeks. As noted earlier (4.52 above), the *Irish Law Times Reports* were published with this journal from 1871 until it ceased publication. Next came the *Irish Law Times* which was begun in 1981 and published by Round Hall Press. It was published monthly and contained articles, case notes and book reviews as well as digests of cases and legislation. It continues to be published by Round Hall Sweet and Maxwell, but during the past few years has now undergone some further changes. It is now published in 20 issues a year usually comprising one or two articles, a short digest of legislation and superior court decisions, a table of personal injury awards in the superior courts and, often, edited Circuit Court judgments.

7.17 *The Law Society Gazette* (formerly the *Gazette of the Incorporated Law Society of Ireland*) appears 10 times a year. It is produced essentially for members of the solicitor's profession, but is also in fact the only Irish law journal that goes on general sale in newsagents. At one time, it used to contain substantial academic articles. Nowadays, apart from a few short articles and comments, it is mainly devoted to providing information and news of interest to the legal profession. It performs that function remarkably well, and is attractively produced. Among its regular features is a digest of recent legislation and Superior Court decisions.

7.18 *The Bar Review* is published nine times a year by the Bar Council of Ireland. Each issues contains a good selection of articles as well as a legal update summarising recent legislation and judgments. Articles recently published in other law journals are also mentioned. There is an index for the first four volumes (1996 to 1999) arranged by subject and author, and compiled by Desmond Mulhere. Another general law journal, the *Hibernian Law Journal*, which it is planned to publish twice a year and which is based at the Law Society of Ireland, began in 2000.

Irish legal periodicals (subject specific)

7.19 Several new, subject-specific journals have been established in Ireland in recent years. They include:

Commercial Law Practitioner (begun in 1994) is published 11 times a year, containing articles as well as commentaries on commercial, company and banking law cases.

Irish Criminal Law Journal, published in two issues a year from 1991 to 1999. From 2000 onwards, it has appeared in four issues a year with articles, case comments and book reviews. Four issues of the *Criminal Law Journal* were published by the Association of Criminal Lawyers between 1981 and 1984.

Irish Business Law, begun in 1998, is published six times a year.

Irish Journal of European Law, begun in 1992, is published annually in one or two issues, and is now devoted mainly to articles, although some of earlier issues included law reports and case abstracts as well. It is a continuation of the *Journal of the Irish Society for European Law*.

The *Family Law Journal* is published a few times a year by the Family Lawyers Association. It usually consists of one or two articles and several judgments of which it is a very useful source.

The *Irish Journal of Family Law*, begun in 1998, is published six times a year. Each issue contains some articles as well as a section providing good summaries and analysis of recent cases.

The *Financial Services Law Journal 2001* is published 4 times a year.

The *Irish Intellectual Property Review*, begun in 1997, is published twice a year.

The *Medico-Legal Journal of Ireland*, begun in 1995, appears in two issues a year.

The *Conveyancing and Property Law Journal*, begun in 1996, and the *Irish Planning and Environmental Law Journal*, begun in 1994, appear four times a year.

All of the above journals with the exception of the *Law Society Gazette*, the *Bar Review*, the *Hibernian Law Journal*, *Irish Business Law* and the *Family Law Journal* are published by Round Hall Sweet and Maxwell.

Journal of the Irish Society of Labour Law, was published annually from 1992 to recent years containing articles, law reports and case summaries.

British Legal Periodicals

7.20 As in the case of Ireland, legal periodicals published in Britain can be divided into two broad categories: general and subject-specific. The leading general law journals include the *Law Quarterly Review*, the *Modern Law Review*, the *Cambridge Law Journal*, the *Oxford Journal of Legal Studies*, *Legal Studies* and *Current Legal Problems*. The *New Law Journal* appears weekly and includes summarised law reports as well as articles. It is one of the few British law journals available on LEXIS (in the UKJNL library). Nowadays, many university law schools are producing journals. Examples include the *King's College Law Journal* and the *Liverpool Law Review*. There are many specialist journals such as the *Criminal Law Review,* the *Conveyancer and Property Lawyer*, the *Journal of Business Law*, the *Company Lawyer*, *Family Law*, *the Industrial Law Journal* and many others. Some libraries provide a loose leaf folder containing the contents pages of all current journals, which helps readers keep up to date with what is being published. However, the best way is consult the indexes to legal periodicals listed at 7.23 *et seq.* below. Many journals now have web sites, some of which have online versions of some or all of their contents. There are now some good law journals published online. They include the *Web Journal of Current Legal Issues* (www.webjcli.ncl.ac.uk) which began in 1995 and is published five times a year and the *Mountbatten Journal of Legal Studies* (www.solent.ac.uk/law/mjls/default.html) which is published by the Southampton Institute. The *Journal of Information, Law and Technology* (http/elj.warwick.ac.uk/jilt) is also available online, but deals exclusively with law and information technology and the interaction between the two.

Student law reviews

7.21 A welcome development in recent years has been the appearance of student-edited law reviews. The first such publication in recent times was the *Irish Student Law Review*, produced by the Law Students' Debating Society of the King's Inns. More recently, similar journals have been produced by law students at NUI, Galway, Trinity College Dublin and the University of Limerick. Many of the articles appearing in those journals, which are of a high quality, began as student essays or dissertations.

Indexes of Legal Periodicals

7.22 Unfortunately, there is no current index to Irish legal periodicals. There is, however, an excellent work that has proved most valuable to researchers over the years. This is Professor Paul O'Higgins's *Bibliography of Periodical Literature Relating to Irish Law*, the main volume of which was published by the *Northern Ireland Legal Quarterly* in 1966. This lists articles and notes on all aspects of Irish law up until the mid-1960s. Two supplements have been published, one in 1973 and another in 1983 which update the main work and, indeed, include some pre-1966 material as well.

7.23   The two principal general indexes to legal periodicals are the *Index to Legal Periodicals and Books* (ILP) and the *Legal Journals Index* (LJI). The ILP has been published since 1908, and until the end of 1993 indexed periodicals only. Since then, it has included books as well. It appears 11 times a year, with quarterly and annual cumulations, The bound cumulative volumes run from September of one year to August of the next. There are four indexes in all. The first is a combined subject and author index, the second a case index, the third a legislation index and the fourth a book review index. At the beginning of each issue is a list of abbreviations for the journals indexed as well as a further list giving the publishers and the frequency of publication. The case list is valuable as it indicates articles and notes published (in the various journals indexed) on recent cases. However, the ILP has some drawbacks. It does not list articles under a certain length, and it concentrates largely on United States law. It is, therefore, of very limited use for research on Irish periodical literature, although it does index as few journals from Ireland as well as some from Australia, New Zealand and Canada.

7.24   The *Legal Journals Index* (LJI) was published monthly in paper form from 1986 to 2000. It now appears in electronic form only both as a CD-ROM and on the Internet. The LJI covers more than 400 journals published in the U.K. as well as 85 English language journals published elsewhere in Europe, including many Irish journals. The paper version had five separate indexes: (1) subject; (2) author; (3) cases; (4) legislation and (5) book reviews. The CD version is updated monthly, while the website is updated daily. Many academic libraries subscribe to both, and will have the CDs loaded on a central server. When using the CD version remember that there are, in fact, two disks one of which has material up until 1990 and that one can be accessed by clicking on the Archive button. One of the merits of the LJI is that it indicates briefly the subject matter of the articles, cases and other materials indexed. The following examples are taken from Vol. 4, No. 3 (March 1989):

Subject Index

JUSTIFICATION. Pleadings. Amendments, Defamation.
Look before you leap. (Whether allegedly defamatory words that local councillor had wasted ratepayers' money on 'a damn fool idea' a general allegation of squandering public money.) *Bookbinder v Tebbitt.* Times, December 23, 1988: *L.G.R.* 1989, 153 (4), 61-62

MERGERS. Law Firms
The Urge to Merge: Practical Pitfalls (Problems which may arise after

decision to merge has been taken) Micahel Simmons. *L.S.G.* 1989, 86(3) 29-33

CASE INDEX
Buxoo v R. [1988] 1 WLR 820
Principles applicable to Criminal Appeals. *J.Crim.L.* 1989, 53(1) 88-90.

7.25   As noted earlier, each issue of the *Current Law Monthly Digest* includes a list of recent articles under the various subject headings, although they are largely confined to English law.

ENCYCLOPAEDIAS, REFERENCE BOOKS AND DICTIONARIES

Halsbury's Laws of England

7.26   The major encyclopaedia of English law is *Halsbury's Laws of England*, now in its fourth edition, which sets out the entire law under broad subject headings. Some areas are treated in a few pages; others occupy a volume or more. The fourth edition of *Halsbury* has 52 main volumes, the last two of which are devoted to European Union law. Several volumes are reissued each year to take account of significant changes in the law. Then, there is the Cumulative Supplement, in two volumes, which summarises changes in the law since the main volumes were published. It is cumulative in the sense that it replaces all previous supplements. The Current Service, which is designed to be used with the Supplement, consists of a Monthly Review and a Noter-Up. The Monthly Review contains many cases not included in the Supplement, nor yet incorporated in the main volumes. In addition, there are Abridgement volumes which provide a detailed account of all Public General Acts as well as important statutory instruments and cases. Finally, there are several volumes of tables, lists of cases and subject index. When using *Halsbury*, consult the general subject index to identify the volume in which the subject being researched is covered. When using this volume, take note of the date on which it was published. Next, go to the Cumulative Supplement which is arranged under the same titles as the main work, then to the Current Service File. The Annual Abridgement is useful as a source of information on any particular statutes or cases on which further information is required. Remember that *The Digest* (6.43 above) also provides a good deal of information on cases, old and new.

The Laws of Scotland: Stair Memorial Encyclopaedia

7.27   This is a 25-volume encyclopaedia of Scots law which was completed in

1999 and is published by Butterworths. It is organised in much the same way as *Halsbury* covering 136 titles. Individual titles are reissued in booklet form from time to time and kept in separate binders. Each volume has its own tables and index, and there are also three consolidated volumes of tables and subject index for the entire work. These, too, are updated from time to time.

Doing Business in Ireland

7.28   *Doing Business in Ireland* is a two-volume loose-leaf work edited by Ussher and O'Connor and published by Matthew Bender as part of an extensive series on doing business in various countries. It is not, strictly speaking, an encyclopaedia, but consists of series of chapters written by specialists on key aspects of Irish law relating to business. Unfortunately, it is not always updated as quickly as it should be, so one must be careful when using it to check the release date of the particular part being consulted. (The date will be found at the bottom right-hand corner of the title page of each section). The topics it now covers are as follows:

1.   Introduction and Overview
2.   Investment Incentives
3.   Business Organisation
4.   Acquiring an Existing Irish Business
5.   Taxation
6.   Employment Law
7.   Social Security
8.   Land and Environmental Laws
9.   Contract
10. Product Liability
11. Agency and Franchising
12. Intellectual Property
13. Banks and Other Financial Institutions
14. Legal Aspects of Banking, Lending and Security
15. Competition Policy
16. Litigation and Arbitration
17. Public Control of Economic Activity: Miscellaneous Regulations
18. Termination of Business, Insolvency, Examinerships, Receiverships and Administrations.

Murdoch's Dictionary of Irish Law (A Sourcebook)

7.29   This dictionary, the third edition of which was published by Topaz Publications (Dublin) in 2000, cannot be praised too highly. It now runs to 896 pages and includes excellent entries on every aspect of Irish law. One of its many merits is that it provides up to date references to the relevant legislation and case law under each entry. It is very well cross-referenced, and explains virtually every Latin word and phrase that the lawyer is likely to encounter. The appendixes include a list of law report abbreviations and a list of books on Irish law as well as books published elsewhere of relevance to Irish law. A companion CD is also available which provides access to the texts of statutes and statutory instruments

The Oxford Companion to Law

7.30 This work, by David M. Walker, was published in 1980 and has not, unfortunately, been updated in the meantime. However, it remains very valuable as an authoritative source of information about many aspects of English, Scottish, American and Commonwealth law. It is a particularly good starting point for historical and biographical research and for further bibliographic references in relation to these matters. It also translates and explains many Latin words and phrases.

Other law dictionaries

7.31 Two major multi-volume dictionaries have been mentioned in the previous chapter, *Stroud's Judicial Dictionary and Words* and *Phrases Legally Defined*. These specialise in providing statutory and judicial definitions of words and phrases. Students, however, are more likely to need a general dictionary providing straightforward definitions of legal terms. The leading works in the latter category include the most recent editions of Osborn's *Concise Law Dictionary*, Mozley and Whiteley's *Law Dictionary*, and the *Concise Law Dictionary* published by Oxford University Press. Jowitt's *Dictionary of English Law* 2nd edition (1977) is a substantial two-volume work with some supplements, and is found in most law libraries. *Murdoch's Dictionary of Irish Law* is also, of course, a dictionary as well as a valuable reference work, as is the *Oxford Companion to Law.*

Biographical dictionaries

7.32 Legal study and research can often be enriched by having some knowledge of the lives of those who shaped the law. There are, of course, many full length biographies and memoirs such as V.T.H. Delany's biography of Chief Baron Palles (Dublin, 1960) and Sheldon M. Novick's *Honorable Justice: The Life of Oliver Wendell Holmes* (Boston, 1989). The best source of shorter biographical sketches is A.W.B. Simpson's *Biographical Dictionary of the Common Law* (London: Butterworths, 1984). Guy Holborn's *Sources of Biographical Information on Past Lawyers* (British and Irish Association of Law Librarians, 1999) is an excellent starting point for further research. The *Dictionary of National Biography* (DNB) published originally between 1885 and 1901, and now updated every five years, previously every 10 years, is a good source of information on notable British legal figures. Also worthy of note is F.E. Ball's *The Judges in Ireland 1221-1921*, first published in 1926, but reissued by Round Hall Press (Dublin) in two volumes in 1993.

Legal history

7.33   Many book-length studies of aspects of Irish legal history have been published during the past ten years or so, and these are listed in Appendix 4 of this book under "Legal History". The leading encyclopaedic work on legal history is Holdsworth's *History of English Law* published in 17 volumes, the last being a general index. The first volume was published in 1903 and the work had reached volume 12 by the time of the author's death in 1945. The remaining volumes were edited by Professors Goodhart and Hanbury. Some excellent legal history resources are now available on the Internet. The Orb web site for example has an enormous range of documents and sources relating to medieval law (http://orb.rhodes.edu/). Another excellent site is that of the Avalon Project at Yale Law School (www.yale.edu/lawweb/avalon/avalon.htm) which is devoted to documents in law, history and diplomacy. It is divided into four categories: pre-18th century, 18th century, 19th century and 20th century. It is a veritable treasure trove of historical documents, reproduced in many cases from the originals. Thus, in the pre-18th century section one can access Blackstone's *Commentaries on the Laws of England*, the Bull of Pope Adrian IV empowering Henry II to conquer Ireland, the Assize of Clarendon, 1166, the Code of Hammurabi, and a host of other documents. Under the 20th century, for example, one can find the inaugural address of every U.S. President for that century, among many other documents. Tucker's American edition of *Blackstone's Commentaries* is on the Web in full text at www.constitution.org/tb/tb-0000.htm . Since 1977, the *Cambrian Law Review* has published an annual bibliography of British and Irish legal history. See the internet site at www.aber.ac.uk.cambrianlaw/cambrian1.htm.

THESES

7.34   Many dissertations and theses submitted for higher degrees are never published, or not in monograph form at least. Yet they provide a rich source of research material, and almost always have extensive bibliographies. Most universities retain for their libraries a copy of every major dissertation for which a higher degree has been awarded. Certain copyright and ethical rules must be observed when consulting theses or making notes from them, especially if they are recent. The author of a thesis, after all, may be preparing it for publication as a book or series of articles. When in doubt, consult a member of library staff about the applicable rules. Theses from other universities can sometimes be obtained on inter-library loan or consulted on site. Fortunately, there are some very comprehensive indexes to theses completed in these islands, so it is easy to identify the postgraduate research that has already been completed on any particular topic. A literature search of this kind is, of course, essential for anyone beginning work on a research degree, as there is a general rule that any such work must be original. The *Index to Theses with Abstracts accepted for Higher Degrees by the Universities of Great Britain and Ireland* is published four times a year. Each part has a subject and author index. However, most of this is now available on the Internet at www.theses.com. This site covers theses accepted since 1970, covering all volumes from number 21 onwards. It is easily searched by author, subject, title, institution, year or any combination of these. Most university libraries have a subscription to this site, so it is readily available to students. Two older indexes are also useful. The *Retrospective Index to theses of Great Britain and Ireland 1716 –1950* is in five volumes, the first of which deals with social sciences and humanities, including law. *Legal Research in the United Kingdom 1905-1984* (London, 1985), published by the Institute of Advanced Legal Study, is a classified list of theses and dissertations successfully completed for postgraduate degrees awarded by UK universities and (former) polytechnics between 1905 and 1984.

LAW REFORM DOCUMENTS AND OFFICIAL REPORTS

7.35   Reports of law reform commissions and similar bodies can be very rich sources of information about particular branches of law. Although their primary purpose is to make suggestions for law reform, they often include a detailed survey of the existing law. Even today, reports and working papers of the Irish Law Reform Commission are often the best, and sometimes the only, accounts of certain areas of law. It is not uncommon to see lawyers going into court armed with one or more of these documents. Many academic authors are much indebted to them as well.

Irish Law Reform Commission

7.36   The Commission was established by statute in 1975, and it has produced a large number of reports and other documents in the meantime. Typically, the Commission publishes a working paper or consultation paper first, setting out the existing law and canvassing various options for reform. Then after members of the public have had an opportunity to make submissions, a final report is published. A full list of the Commission's publications to date is given in Appendix 5 of this book. In February 2001, the Commission launched its Second Programme outlining its proposed projects for the period 2000 to 2007. A complete up-to-date list of all the Commission's publications is included at the end of each of its reports, consultation papers and annual reports. The Commission now has a web site at www.gov.ie/lawreform/index.htm.

Other law reform documents

7.37   Occasionally, the Government or a Government Minister appoints a committee or working group to examine a certain area of law and make proposals for reform. In fact, the number of such groups has proliferated in recent years, and it is becoming difficult to keep track of their activities and publications. Often, the reports of these bodies are published by the Stationery Office (Oifig an tSoláthair in Irish). This, at least, means that they can be obtained either by post or by personal purchase in the Government Publications Sales Office. Furthermore, quarterly catalogues, later cumulated annually are published by the Stationery Office listing all recent publications. Official publications are also listed in *Iris Oifigiúil* which appears twice a week.

Official publications (Ireland)

7.38   Official publications include far more than law reform documents of the type just mentioned. They also include legislation and draft legislation, the debates of the Houses of the Oireachtas, as well as a whole range of annual reports and research findings by various public bodies. In the last mentioned category would be, for instance, the annual reports of the Adoption Board, the Report on Prisons and Places of Detention, reports of the Central Statistics Office and similar bodies. University libraries will generally have fairly comprehensive holdings of these documents in their government publications section. Most official publications carry codes similar to those for command papers in Britain (see 7.40 below). In Ireland, the codes are "P.", "Pr.", "Prl.", "PL" and "Pn.", depending on the date of publication. For example, the *Report of the Committee on Judicial Conduct and Ethics*, published in December 2000, carries the code "Pn 9449." There does not appear to be any standard way of citing official publications, but an acceptable way would be:

Report of the Second Commission on the Status of Women Pl. 9557 (Dublin, 1993)

There are some bibliographic guides to Irish official reports, although none of them is up to date. The leading work is Maltby and McKenna, *Irish Official Publications: A Guide to Republic of Ireland Papers with a Breviate of Reports* (Oxford: Pergamon Press, 1980). Ford's *Select List of Reports of Inquiries of the Irish Dáil and Seanad 1922-72* (Dublin; Irish University Press, 1974) provides a list of older parliamentary publications. More recent publications are listed in Finnegan and Wiles, *Irish Government Publications 1972-1992* (Dublin: Irish Academic Press, 1995) which includes a select list of serials as well as a list of publications by the National Economic and Social Council.

The Law Commission of England and Wales

7.39   This Commission was set up by statute in 1965, and has published some hundreds of reports and consultation papers since then. Some of its reports are published as command papers (see 7.40 below), some as House of Commons Papers and some as non-parliamentary papers. A complete list of all its publications is given in each of its annual reports, but there is now an easier way to consult this list, namely by checking out its web site (www.lawcom.gov.uk/library/library.htm) where under the general heading "Law Commission Library", one may view the entire list by clicking on that word. Better still, this web site has the actual texts of many recent reports and consultation papers which can be downloaded using an Adobe Acrobat Reader. Also on this site are the recent issues of *Law Under Review* which gives details of current law reform projects, and issues under consideration. This used to be published quarterly in paper form only and was seldom found in Irish libraries.

Official publications (U.K.)

7.40 Many thousands of official publications are produced in the U.K. every year, with an increasing additional number in the constituent jurisdictions of Scotland and Northern Ireland. As in Ireland, they are divided into parliamentary and non-parliamentary publications. The proceedings of the House of Commons and House of Lords will be considered later, but in the present context, the parliamentary publications of greatest interest are those of Select Committees which often deal with important questions of law and policy in their reports. See, example, the House of Lords Select Committee Report on Murder and Life Imprisonment (1989). Command papers are documents presented to Parliament on the initiative of some body, usually the Government, other than Parliament itself. They deal with a wide variety of legal and policy issues. They have been issued in six series, beginning with a new code when the number begins to approach 10,000. They are as follows (the numbers in square brackets and the years in parentheses);

1st series [1]-[4,222] (1833-1896)
2nd series [C.1]-[C. 9550] (1870-1890)
3rd series [Cd.1] – [Cd. 9293] (1910-1918)
4th series [Cmd. 1]-[Cmd. 9998] (1919-1956)
5th series [Cmnd. 1]-[Cmnd. 9927] (1956-1986)
6th series [Cm. 1] – [-] (1986 to date).

The Stationery Office publishes a monthly catalogue of publications with an annual cumulation. Another catalogue of particular interest to Ireland is the Home Office List of Publications, the Home Office being roughly equivalent to our Department of Justice. The Home Office has a very strong research department which produces an enormous number of reports and research findings, particularly, but not exclusively, in the area of criminal justice. As might be expected, much of this material for recent years is now available on the Internet. The Stationery Office web site is at www.official-documents.co.uk/menu/ bydept.htm, while the Home Office web site is at www.homeoffice.gov.uk . Both have good search engines.

PARLIAMENTARY PROCEEDINGS

Debates of Dáil and Seanad (Ireland)

7.41 The proceedings of the Dáil and Seanad for each sitting day are published separately, those of the Dáil having a green cover, those of the Seanad having a light orange cover. Later, bound volumes, covering the proceedings of each session, are published for both houses. There are usually several volumes for each session. Daily parts and volumes have been published in A4 format since late 1996. When working with a statute, it is sometimes helpful to read the Dáil and Seanad debates that preceded its adoption. The speech by the Minister or Minister of State while introducing the second stage of the Bill is generally helpful as it provides an official statement of what the Bill and its various sections are intended to achieve. Needless to say, the content of the Bill may change significantly between the second and final stages, something that should be borne in mind when reading second stage speeches. Many bills are now considered Dáil committees (as opposed to being sent to a committee of the full house). The proceedings of these committees are published separately, although libraries generally shelve them beside main volumes of the Dáil and Seanad debates. There is now an easy way of tracking down the relevant parliamentary debates on legislation enacted since 1984. *Irish Current Law Statutes Annotated* provides, as part of each annotation, references to all stages of the Bill in the Dáil and Seanad. Indeed, the annotations themselves often pick up the more important points raised in the course of the parliamentary debates. The entire text of the Dáil and Seanad debates from 1919 to the present are now available on the Internet at www.gov.ie/oireachtas/frame.htm.

7.42 Other useful information can also be gleaned from parliamentary proceedings, especially the Dáil debates which record written and oral answers from the Taoiseach and Ministers to questions put down by members of the House. This is often the only source of statistical information on a wide range of topics. Many questions, admittedly, are about purely local issues, but many others are about topics of national interest. Lawyers and law students, for example, are likely to be interested in the replies given by the Minister of Justice, Equality and Law Reform, the Minister for Foreign Affairs, and the Minister for Enterprise, Trade and Employment. It is most unfortunate therefore that the

debates are so badly indexed. There are six cumulative indexes of the Dáil
Debates covering the following periods:

Index	Volumes of Debates	Years
1	1-19	1922-27
2	20-68	1928-37
3	69-80	1938-40
4	81-109	1940-47
5	110-145	1948-54
6	146-160	1954-56

There are two cumulative indexes of Seanad Debates covering the following
periods:

Index	Volumes of Debates	Years
1	1-20	1922-36
2	21-34	1938-46.

7.43   For more recent years, one has to search through the legislation and subject indexes at the end of the bound volumes of which the most recent, at the
time of writing, appear to be volume 493 of the Dáil debates and volume 155 of
the Seanad debates, both dating from mid-1998. This can be very time-consum-
ing. Bound volumes are usually some time in arrears, so that for more recent
times, the only guide was the general table of contents on the front of each daily
part. However, since June 1997 the debates of the Dáil and Seanad have been
posted on the Internet at www.irlgov.ie/ (click on "Houses of the Oireachtas").
Some users have found that the references on this site are not always accurate,
so if using them for research purposes, it is better to check the electronic version
against the print version. As noted (7.41 above) all the earlier Oireachtas debates are now on the internet as well. The Parliamentary Archive 1919–1997 is
at www.gov.ie/oireachtas/frame.htm.

Citation of Dáil and Seanad Debates

7.44   Dáil and Seanad debates are cited primarily by volume and column numbers, never by page. There are two columns to each page. It is generally helpful
to include the date as well, so a typical citation might be

321 Dáil Debates 101 (28 May 1980)

Sometimes, "col." or "column" is inserted before the number, e.g. "col. 101" in
the above example.

Select Committees of the Dáil and Joint Oireachtas Committees

7.45   A Select Committee is one consisting of members of one House of the Oireachtas only. There are several Select Committees of the Dáil at present, including the Select Committee on Justice, Equality, Defence and Women's Rights (JEDWR), the Select Committee on Public Enterprise and Transport (PE), and the Select Committee on Tourism, Sport and Recreation (TSR). There are also several Joint Committees consisting of a Select Committee of each House working jointly. In law libraries, the reports of these Committees, when available, are usually shelved adjacent to the main volumes of the Dáil and Seanad Reports, although they are separate publications.

U.K. Parliamentary Debates

7.45   Since 1909, the debates of the House of Commons and the House of Lords have been published separately. Together they are known as the Official Reports of Parliamentary Debates or, more commonly, as Hansard (after the original printer of the debates in the early 19th century). Like the Irish Dáil and Seanad debates, they are numbered sequentially by column and not by page. They are cited in various ways, but one common way appears to be by House, session, volume number and column number, e.g.

HC Deb (1991-92) 123 col. 456

HL Deb (1991-92) 345 col. 798

Hansard is published daily, but the daily issues are later replaced by sessional volumes with an index for that session. Each bound volume has its own index. Official reports of Standing Committee debates are published separately. The U.K. Parliament web site is probably the most accessible source of Hansard since 1988 for the House of Commons and since June 1996 for the House of Lords. These sites allow the debates to be searched by date or by topic using the search engine. They can be entered through the Parliament home page at www.parliament.the-stationery-office.co.uk/ and are also available on CD.

OTHER SECONDARY MATERIAL

General Periodicals and Magazines

7.46   Periodicals and magazines as well as specialist periodicals in disciplines other than law will occasionally have material of legal interest. Irish journals such as *Studies*, *Administration* and the *Economic and Social Review*, are generally worth consulting from time to time, especially for material relating to public law. The same is true of many British, American and Commonwealth journals. Journals in philosophy, politics and women's studies are generally a ripe source of material on many aspects of law and legal thought. Academic libraries keep recent issues on display and some of the journals in question produce their own cumulative indexes from time to time. However, the *British Humanities Index* is a useful source of information. It is published four times a year with an annual cumulation. It began in 1962, succeeding the *Subject Index to Periodicals* which was published from 1915 to 1961. There is now a CD-ROM version of the Index covering over 300 British journals and newspapers from 1985 to date, and recently some abstracts have begun to be added to the records. The University of Edinburgh library has a useful web site giving instructions on how to use this CD-ROM. See www.lib.ed.ac.uk/lib/howto/bhi.shtml.

7.47   There is no general bibliography of Irish periodical literature. The best we have is the nine-volume *Sources of the History of Irish Civilisation – Articles in Periodicals* (Boston: Hall & Co., 1970) compiled by Richard Hayes, former Director of the National Library of Ireland. Volumes 1 to 5 deal with persons, volumes 6 to 8 with subjects and volume 9 with places. It has some material on law, but most, if not all, of this is included in O'Higgins' Bibliography (7.22 above). The *Administration Yearbook and Diary*, published by the Institute of Public Administration, gives a fairly comprehensive list of newspapers and journals currently published in Ireland.

7.48   For nineteenth-century periodical literature, the best guide is *Poole's Index to Periodical Literature* which, with supplements, comes up to 1907. Wall's *Cumulative Author Guide to Poole's Index to Periodical Literature 1802 to 1902* (Ann Arbor: Pierian Press, 1971) is useful for tracing the works of individual authors (somebody like, say, James Fitzjames Stephen who wrote a good deal on law in general periodicals). Cushing and Morris (eds.), *Nineteenth Century Reader's Guide to Periodical Literature*, a two-volume work published by Wilson in New York in 1944, is more broadly based and includes American writings. *The Waterloo Directory of Irish Newspapers and Periodicals 1800 – 1900* (Ontario: Waterloo, 1986) by J.S. North, gives a list of 19th century periodical publications but does not, of course, list their contents. Some years ago, the National Library of Ireland compiled an index of newspapers in stock. Copies of it are available for consultation in most university libraries. Early 19th century journals such as the *Edinburgh Review* founded in 1802, and *Westminster Review* founded in 1842, often carried material which is still of considerable interest, such as lengthy reviews of Bentham's various works. (See Twining, *Theories of Evidence: Bentham and Wigmore* (London: Weidenfeld and Nicolson, 1985) 100 *et seq.*)

PUBLICATIONS BY STATUTIRY AND VOLUNTARY BODIES

7.49   Many statutory, state-sponsored and voluntary bodies publish reports, working papers, pamphlets and the like which can of considerable interest to legal researchers, depending on their areas of interest. The organisations under consideration here would include, for example, the Economic and Social Research Institute, the National Economic and Social Council, the Institute of Taxation, Children's Rights Alliance and so forth. One of the more convenient sources of information about these bodies if the *Administration Yearbook and Diary*, published annually by the Institute of Public Administration. See under "Social, Cultural and Political Organisations".

CHAPTER 8

The European Union

8.01 In the aftermath of the Second World War, several international institutions were created in order to achieve closer co-operation between Western European countries. The Council of Europe, which is dedicated to the promotion of democracy and the protection of human rights, was one such institution and will be described in Chapter 10. Economic co-operation was secured by the treaties establishing the European Coal and Steel Community (ECSC) in 1952, the European Economic Community (EEC) in 1957, and the European Atomic Energy Community (Euratom) in 1958. From a legal perspective the most important of these is the EEC which was established by the Treaty of Rome. Article G of the Maastricht Treaty changed the name of the European Economic Community (EEC) to the European Community (EC). The Maastricht Treaty itself, or the Treaty on European Union (TEU) to give it its proper title, made significant changes to the pre-existing treaty system. First and foremost, it established the European Union which has three pillars. The first pillar consists of the European Communities (EC, ECSC and Euratom), the second consists of certain provisions dealing with common foreign and security policy, while the third deals with justice and home affairs. One distinguishing feature of the second and third pillars, however, is that they do not involve, as yet, the transfer of any additional powers from the member states to Community institutions. Instead, the institutions are confined to encouraging and supporting co-operative initiatives agreed by the member states themselves. Certain other changes brought about by the TEU will be noted in later sections of this Chapter. The next major development was the Treaty of Amsterdam which was agreed in 1997 at the end of an intergovernmental conference (IGC) which had lasted for 12 months. It finally entered into force on May 1, 1999 after a rather troubled ratification process. The original objectives of this treaty had been to prepare the way for enlargement by admitting several states, mainly from Central and Eastern Europe, and to make the European Union more "citizen friendly" by promoting institutional reform and improving policy-making procedures. The rather complex document that resulted can scarcely be said to fulfil either of those objectives. It did, arguably, facilitate the development of a multi-speed Europe by providing that member states that wished to establish closer co-operation between themselves could use the facilities of the institutions for that purpose. An Irish Government White Paper (Pn. 4931) on the Treaty of Amsterdam, published in 1998, gives a detailed account of the Treaty's provisions and implications.

8.02   The Treaty of Nice resulted from an IGC that lasted for most of the year 2000. It was signed on 14 February 2001 and will enter into force when all 15 member states have ratified it in accordance with their own constitutional procedures. This treaty proposes several concrete measures to cope with increased membership of the EU. At present, there are 12 countries from Eastern Europe, the Mediterranean and the Baltic negotiating accession to the EU, and Turkey has been recognised as a candidate for entry. The changes proposed by the Nice Treaty stem for an acknowledgement that a set of institutions that were originally established for a six-member community may not be able to cater effectively for a 30-member Union. For example, the European Parliament now has 626 members and the total number may not exceed 700. If all new member states were represented to the same degree as present members, the Parliament would become unworkable. The Treaty of Nice proposes to limit the number of members to 732 to be divided between member states and candidate countries. Germany will have 99 MEPS, Italy and the U.K. will have 72 each, Ireland will have 12, Malta (when admitted) will have five, and so forth. The Treaty also proposes to allow for qualified majority voting for Council decisions on 30 Articles of the EC Treaty that now require unanimity. The Commission, which is arguably the most powerful of the institutions, now has 20 members because the four larger countries are allowed two each. The Treaty of Nice proposes that with effect from 2005, there will be only one Commissioner for each member state. Once the Union has 27 member states, a ceiling will be placed on the number of Commissioners. The Council will decide, unanimously, on what the upper limit is to be. The end result will almost inevitably be that some member states will have no Commissioner from time to time, and that is likely to prove a controversial issue. These are just a few of the structural changes proposed by the Treaty. The Europa web site (8.26 below) has an excellent web page which contains the text of the Treaty as well as a clear explanatory booklet entitled *Who's Who in the European Union: What difference will the Treaty of Nice Make?*, also published in paper form by the European Communities (ISBN 92-894-0490-6). At a referendum held in Ireland in June 2001, the Nice Treaty was rejected by a majority of those voting. A Charter of Fundamental Rights of the European Union was proclaimed by the European Council at its Nice meeting in December 2000. The future of this Charter, in terms of how binding or otherwise it will be on member states, remains to be seen. The text is available on the Europa website (8.26 below).

European institutions

8.03   The EU has five principal institutions: the European Council, the European Parliament, the European Commission, the European Court of Justice and the Court of Auditors. There are two further advisory bodies: the Economic and Social Council, and the Committee of the Regions, each of which has 222 members. There are also two banks, the European Central Bank and the European

Investment Bank. Most general textbooks on European law describe the functions of these bodies in some detail. The European Commission recently published a short book by Klaus-Dieter Borchardt entitled *The ABC of Community Law* ISBN 92-828-7803-1 (Luxembourg, 2000) which gives a clear account of the various institutions and their functions. Further information can be found in Dinan's *Encyclopaedia of the European Union* (8.23 below). For those studying European law, the most significant institutions are the Court of Justice and the Commission, although the work of the Parliament is increasingly significant because of the enhanced co-decision procedure introduced by the Amsterdam Treaty in respect of legislative decisions under a wide range of articles of the EC Treaty.

SOURCES OF EUROPEAN UNION LAW

8.04 The primary sources of European law are the treaties (which are the primary legislation), secondary legislation and case law. Secondary legislation consists of Regulations, Directives, Decisions, Recommendations and Opinions. The case law is that of the Court of Justice and the Court of First Instance (8.13 *et seq*. below). Secondary sources of European law are, as might be expected, books, periodicals, digests, encyclopaedias and so forth. There are also, of course, many important judgments of the domestic courts in member states on aspects of European law. These will be found in the sources described in Chapters 4, 5 and 6 above in respect of Ireland, Northern Ireland, and Britain.

Treaties

8.05 The official texts of the treaties and amendments thereto are published in the *Official Journal* (8.08) which, as we shall see, has a rather complex indexing system. The most convenient source of the treaties is a collection of European legislation such as *Blackstone's EC Legislation* (London: Blackstone Press) which is edited by Nigel Foster, and a new edition of which is now published annually. For example, the 2000/2001 edition provides a consolidated version of the EC Treaty as established by the Treaty of Amsterdam. Another source available in many libraries is Sweet and Maxwell's *Encyclopaedia of European Law* in five volumes, and also available in CD form. The full text of the treaties is also available free of charge on the Europa web site: www.europa.eu.int/eur-lex/en/treaties/index.htm/ . However, anyone studying European law and who needs to refer constantly to treaty provisions would be well advised to invest in a collection such as *Blackstone* (above) which is reasonably priced.

Revised numbering of treaty articles

8.06   The numbering of the articles of the Treaty of the European Union and the EC Treaty was altered by the Treaty of Amsterdam in order to reflect the changes which had been made to them. Most textbooks published since 1998 or thereabouts have tables of equivalences setting out the old article numbers and the new ones by which they have been replaced. Thus, Articles 85 and 86 of the EC Treaty, dealing with competition law, are now Articles 81 and 82, while the former Article 177 is now Article 234. The articles of the TEU which has previously been lettered are now numbered Articles 1 to 53. It is still necessary to refer to the former numbering, especially in the case of the EC Treaty because, to mention just one reason, all ECJ cases and other European documents prior to the Treaty of Amsterdam will have used the old numbers. When referring to an article of the EC Treaty, one now writes, for example: "Article 220 (ex Article 164)". Among the many widely available books in which the new numbering system is given are those by Kennedy, Craig and de Burca, Borchardt, all of which are described at 8.23 below.

Secondary legislation

8.07   The more important forms of secondary legislation are regulations, directives and decisions. Their nature and effect is set out in Article 249 (ex Article 189) of the EC Treaty which states:

> "A regulation shall have general application. It shall be binding in its entirety and directly applicable in all Member States.
>
> A directive shall be binding, as to the result to be achieved, upon each Member State to which it is addressed, but shall leave to the national authorities the choice of form and methods.
>
> A decision shall be binding in its entirety upon those to whom it is addressed."

The European Commission has the right of initiative which means that it is the sole body entitled to propose new legislation although it may receive proposals in this regard from other institutions, including the Council and Parliament, as well as from Member States and non-governmental organisations. Legislative procedures are quite complex, but our main concern here is with their outcome in terms of finding the text of legislation once it is made. Again the principal source if the *Official Journal*, so it appropriate at this point to describe how this publication is organised.

The *Official Journal*

8.08   The *Official Journal of the European Communities* or the *Official Journal* as it is generally known, is published almost every day in several parts and in several languages. It is colour-coded by language, the colour for the English language version being purple. The two main parts, published separately, are known as Series L (for legislation) and Series C (for communications and information). There is a separate annexe containing the text of European Parliament debates. Each issue of Series L, containing legislative texts, is divided into two parts: Acts the publication of which is obligatory (such as regulations) and Acts the publication of which is not obligatory (such as directives). Series C contains a range of material but is likely to be of most interest to lawyers and law students for the text of legislation proposed by the Commission and reports of the European Parliament on proposed texts.

8.09   Each issue of Series L and Series C is numbered sequentially beginning with 1 for the first issue of January each year. An entry in either series is cited in the following form: OJ series (i.e. L or C), issue number, date of issue, page number, e.g.

Council Decision of 22 December 2000 establishing a European Police College (CEPOL), OJ L 336, 30.12.2000, p.1.

In this example, the Decision was published in the *Official Journal*, Series L, number 336 for 2000, in the issue published on 30 December 2000, at page 1. Likewise, one would refer to, say, OJ C 206 19.7.2000, p.3, this being the issue of Series C for July 19, 2000 at page 3. Most academic libraries subscribe to the *Official Journal*, but it is also available free of charge for the last 45 days on the Europa web site (8.26 below). Hopefully, this period will be extended in the future. The *Journal* is, after all, a public document.

8.10   An index to the *Official Journal* is published monthly with an annual cumulation. It is in two parts: the alphabetical index and the methodological tables. The alphabetical index is a type of subject index which directs the reader to the appropriate part of the *Official Journal* and indicates the legal form, i.e. whether it is the subject matter of case, a regulation or some other kind of instrument. Take "Abortion", the first entry in the cumulative alphabetical index for 1990. It is accompanied by the following information:

Document Number	C - 159/90
OJ Reference	C1/158/6
Legal Form	1/CJ

The relevant text, therefore, is to be found in issue 159 of Series C for 1990. It is important to understand the "legal form" entry as this tells us the nature of the document involved. The last part indicates the institution involved. In this case, it is the Court of Justice (CJ). If it were the Court of First Instance, the entry would read "1/T". The digit before the dash is also important in relation to court cases. 1 means that a case has been brought, 2 that a judgment was given, 3 that some order was made, and 4 that the case was removed from the register. The methodological index deals with several matters. It lists legislation contained in the *Official Journal* for that year. However, as in the case of the L Series, there are two separate lists for legislation depending on whether or not its publication is obligatory. This index is also a useful source of information on cases brought before the European Courts (see 8.13 below).

Directories of legislation in force

8.11   Such is the extent and complexity of European legislation that it is often difficult to be sure of the precise status of any legislative instrument, even one of fairly recent vintage. Fortunately, there is an indispensable guide available in most libraries, called *Directory of Community Legislation in Force*. It is published twice a year in two volumes. The first, a subject index is arranged under broad subject headings and will indicate the legislation in force, with any amendments (with cross-references to the *Official Journal*). The second contains chronological and alphabetical indexes. Much of this information is now available on the Eur-Lex web site: www.europa.eu.int/eur-lex/en/ .

Citing European legislation

8.12   A reference to a piece of European legislation must include several elements:

(a) the institutional origin (the Commission or Council)
(b) the form (e.g. Regulation, Directive or Decision)
(c) the number
(d) the year of enactment
(e) the treaty under which it was made (EC, ECSC or Euratom)
(f) the date.

The sequence of these elements varies. In the case of Regulations, the name of the Treaty comes first, followed by the number and year, e.g.

Commission Regulation (EEC) No 3158/92 of 30 October 1992 fixing the import levies on rice and imported rice.

Directives and Decisions are cited by reference to year, number and treaty, e.g.

Council Decision 91/384/EEC providing medium term financial assistance to Romania, OJ L208 30.7.1991.

Commission Decision 341/94/ECSC of 8 February 1994 implementing Directive No 3632/93/ECSC establishing Community Rules for State aid to the coal industry. OJ L049 19.02.1994 p. 1.

Commission Directive 2000/1/EC of 14 January 2000 adapting to technical progress Council Directive 89/173/EEC as regards certain components and characteristics of wheeled agricultural and forestry tractors.

As in the second last example, the citation is often accompanied by the OJ reference.

LAW REPORTS

8.13   The Court of Justice of the European Communities, or the European Court of Justice (ECJ) as it is more commonly known, sits in Luxembourg. It is composed of 15 judges, one from each member state, and eight advocates general, each of whom serves for a six-year renewable term. Article 223 (ex Article 167) of the EC Treaty provides that "Judges and Advocates General shall be chosen from persons whose independence is beyond doubt and who possess the qualifications required for appointment to the highest judicial offices in their respective countries or who are jurists of recognised competence". The Court has a number of different roles though all of them are designed to ensure that the law is observed in the interpretation of the EC Treaty, as the Treaty itself requires. First, the Court may hear cases brought against member states, usually by the Commission, for failure to fulfil a treaty obligation. Secondly, the Court is entitled to review the legality of acts of the Council and the Commission, essentially to ensure that these institutions do not act outside of their powers. Thirdly, there is the all-important power of the Court under Article 234 (ex Article 177) to give a preliminary ruling on the interpretation of a provision of the Treaties or of other Community legislation. Where such a question is raised before a national court, that court may request the ECJ to give a ruling on the matter. A great deal of European jurisprudence has been created by means of preliminary rulings which go a considerable way towards ensuring that EC law is applied in a reasonably consistent manner in all member states. The Irish courts have referred several cases to the ECJ for a preliminary ruling, e.g. *Campus Oil v. Minister for Energy,* Case 72/83 [1984] ECR 2727, and *Groener v. Minister for Education,* Case 379/87 [1989] ECR 3967.

8.14   In order to cope with the increased workload of the ECJ, the Single European Act (1987) provided for the creation of a Court of First Instance which came into existence in 1989. It is composed of a judge from each member state, and hears most cases brought by private individuals. There are no Advocates General attached to this Court, although one of the Judges may be called upon to play an Advocate General role if the complexity of a particular case so requires. This Court is not entitled to give preliminary rulings under Article 234 (ex Article 177), but it deals with most competition and anti-dumping cases of which there are many.

Case law of ECJ and Court of First Instance

8.15   Case reports of these two courts differ in layout from those of our own courts. Rudden and Phelan, *Basic Community Cases* 2nd edition (see 8.23 below) give some helpful advice on reading European cases. As a rule, a report of an ECJ judgment will consist of the opinion of the Advocate General, the judgment of the Court, and the decision or order of the Court in that order. Judgments and decisions of the European Court of Justice and the Court of First Instance are reported in the *European Court Reports* (E.C.R.). Until the establishment of the Court of First Instance in 1989, this series was devoted exclusively to the reports of the Court of Justice itself. Since then, it has included judgments from both courts. A case is cited by number, name, year, report series and initial page number. Thus, a pre-1989 case is cited as:

Case 272/86 *Commission v. Greece* [1988] E.C.R. 4875.

The number at the beginning is the case registration number. In this instance, *Commission v. Greece* was the 272nd case registered in 1986, and it was decided in 1988. With the advent of the Court of First Instance, a system had to be devised to distinguish between the proceedings of the two courts. Since 1989, therefore, a case number is prefixed with the letter C if it is an ECJ case, and with the letter T if it is a Court of First Instance case, e.g.

Case C-156/87 *Gestetner v. Council* [1990] E.C.R. I-781.
Case T-38/89 *Hochbaum v. Commission* [1990] E.C.R. II-43.

It will be noted that there is another new element in these citations, namely the presence of a Roman numeral, I or II, before the page numbers. The reason for this is that since the beginning of 1990, the E.C.R. have been divided into two parts. Part I has judgments of the Court of Justice, and Part II judgments of the Court of First Instance. These parts are paginated separately in both the individual parts and in the bound volumes. Cases are reported in the E.C.R. in strict chronological order. Furthermore, because the texts have to be translated into all eleven official languages, there is usually a delay of 18 months or so before a judgment appears in this series. They appear more quickly in the *Common Market Law Reports* (C.M.L.R.), which began in 1962 and are published weekly by Sweet and Maxwell. The format used in this series, which publishes only a selection of cases, is closer to that of a typical British or Irish law report, with headnotes and so forth. When citing a European case, therefore, it is preferable to include a reference to both the E.C.R. and C.M.L.R. reports, e.g.

Case C-316/91 *Parliament v. Council* [1994] E.C.R. I-625, [1994] 3
C.M.L.R. 149.

Obviously, this citation method is not suitable if one is including a European case in a general alphabetical index of cases drawn from a variety of jurisdictions. If the case just cited were included in such an index, it could be cited as: *Parliament v. Council* (Case C-316/91).

Commercially-published series

8.16   As already noted, the *Common Market Law Reports* (C.M.L.R.) usually publish cases more quickly than the E.C.R.. For several years now, there has been a companion series entitled the *C.M.L.R. Antitrust Reports* which appear in separate parts but which eventually constitute the fourth volume of the C.M.L.R. for each year. These reports are a useful source of information on EU competition law and policy. Each annual volume of the C.M.L.R. has several indexes, including a case list and subject index. In 1995, the *All England Law Reports* inaugurated a series entitled *All England Law Reports (European Cases)* which appears in ten parts a year and publishes a selection of cases in full text. Finally, there is a loose-leaf service which used to be called the *Common Market Reporter* but which is now known as the *European Union Law Reporter.* This service has the merit of providing the texts of cases shortly after they are delivered, although they do not have the official status of the E.C.R. Current cases are to be found in volume 4 of the *Reporter*. Since 1989, a bound volume entitled *European Community Cases* has been produced. A case reported in this series cited as *Merck & Co Inc. v. Primecrown Limited* [1997] 1 C.E.C. 261. Needless to say, if the case has been reported in the E.C.R., the C.M.L.R. or both, those citations should be included as well, with precedence given to the E.C.R. because of their official status.

Electronic sources of European law reports

8.17   The full texts of all E.C.J. cases since June 1997 are available free of charge on the Europa web site (8.26 below). Furthermore, so long as one has the case number, one can get the text of any E.C.J. decision from the beginning on a web site maintained by the University of Mannheim at www.uni-mannheim.de/users/ddz/edz/biblio/opace.html . The various subscription services provide much more extensive access to case law. Ellis Publications licenses information from the Office for Official Publications of the European Communities and in addition downloads publicly available data from websites of the EU institutions (www.ellispub.com). LEXIS (Chapter 2 above) has the full text of all E.C.J. judgments as well as the *Common Market Law Reports* and unreported judgments since 1980. They are available in the EURCOM library, CASES file of LEXIS and also in the ECCASE file of its INTLAW library.

CELEX, which is the official EC data base, is available on subscription only (which is unfortunate), but those with access to it will find there the full texts of all E.C.J. judgments and orders since the beginning as well as Advocate General opinions since 1965. There are also some CD services such as JUSTIS which provides the case law element of CELEX with weekly and quarterly updates, depending on the level of subscription. *Eurolaw* is much the same, although it includes lists of relevant journal articles as well.

Digests and summaries of European law

8.18   Volumes 51 and 52 of *Halsbury's Laws of England* are devoted to European Union law, and they frequently updated by means of supplements and updates as described at 7.26 above. The other major source is Sweet and Maxwell's *Encyclopaedia of European Union Law*, formerly the *Encyclopaedia of European Community Law*. This is a loose-leaf work divided into three main parts, A, B, and C. Part A consists of U.K. law in relation to the EU, part B is devoted to the European treaties, and part C, which now consists of 11 large volumes, is devoted to secondary legislation, with commentary and annotations. It is well indexed, with a detailed subject index in the last volume of part C. Naturally, it takes time to get accustomed to using a work of this length and complexity, but anyone working in the area of European law will find the effort well worth while. The *Encyclopaedia* is also available on a CD called *European Legal Information*. There is a shorter four-volume work called *EU Brief* by Gregg Miles, published by Locksley Press, Lisburn, Northern Ireland. It is now in its 17th edition and has a good updating service. The *European Current Law Monthly Digest* and the *European Current Law Year Book* are also excellent digesting services. Each is divided into three broad parts: a "focus" section at the beginning providing a comment on some recent development, a digest of EU law, and a digest of the European law in national jurisdictions. There are lists of Regulations, Directives and Draft Directives, classified by both numerical order and subject matter, and these are updated monthly. See also 8.21 below.

Finding European Cases by number, name and subject matter

8.19   One may encounter a reference to a European Court case by number only, by name only or, perhaps, by the volume and page number of the report series in which it was published. One may also find a case referred to simply by its common name, such as *Commercial Solvents* rather than by its official name. Many of the leading text books on European law have two case indexes, one listing cases by number in chronological order and the other listing them by name. Obviously, of course, they will list only those cases referred to in the text or footnotes. Fortunately, there is an outstanding reference work available in the form of *Butterworth's EC Case Citator and Service* which had its origins in

a personal database developed by Stuart Isaacs Q.C. but which is now published twice a year in June and December with a fortnightly case listing service.
The listing service consists of a few pink pages usually kept by libraries in a
folder located beside the main work. The main work lists cases under every
possible combination. First, and perhaps most valuably, Part A lists all cases by
number in chronological order by year and gives the full citation for each. Thus,
if one wanted to locate case number C375/92, one would simply go through the
first part of the *Citator* until one came to the /92 cases (i.e. cases registered with
in 1992) and then move on to number 375 where the full citation is given, *Commission of the European Communities v. Spain* [1994] 3 C.M.L.R. 500; [1994]
ECR I-923.

8.20   Part B of the *Citator* lists cases alphabetically by the name of the first
party cited in the official reports, and gives the full name and citation for each
case. Parts C, D, E. and F, list cases by treaty provision, regulation, directive
and decision respectively. This is a most useful way of identifying those cases
dealing with particular provisions of the EC Treaty and of the various forms of
secondary legislation. Part G lists cases by common name, which is a peculiar
feature of European cases. For example, most students will have heard of *Cassis
de Dijon,* a leading case on free trade under Article 28 (ex Article 30) of the EC
Treaty. The full name of this case is *Rewe-Zentrale v. Bundesmonopolverwaltung
fur Branntwein*. Many other cases are known by similar common titles, e.g. the
Chiquita Bananas Case, the *Centrafarm Case* or the *Buy Irish Campaign Case*.
A list of all of these is provided in Part G of the *Citator* with the official name
and full citation for each. Finally, Part H provides a list by key phrase/sector
which operates as a kind of subject index.

Current information on European case law

8.21   There are now many updating services on European case law in both
paper and electronic forms. As noted earlier, volume 21 of *The Digest* deals
with European case law, with updates in the equivalent sections of the Cumulative Supplement and the Quarterly Survey. However, this service is usually some
months behind time. The *Official Journal* (8.08 above), Series C provides a
summary of each case decided by the E.C.J. and the Court of First Instance.
One can then find the full text on the Europa web site (8.26 below). Another
very reliable source is *European Current Law* published monthly in its present
form since the beginning of 1992, and found in most law libraries. It began in
1973 and was known until the end of 1991 as the *European Law Digest.* It
cumulates in annual volumes known as the *European Current Law Year Books*.
Each issue provides an account of developments in European law, embracing
both case law and legislation, under broad subject headings. It includes material not only from the European institutions themselves but from individual states
as well (see 8.18 above). Volumes 51 and 52 of *Halsbury's Laws of England*

and the various updates (7.26 above) also deal with European law. The *Bulletin of the European Union*, published 10 times a year, provides summaries of recent cases and judgments as well as cross-references to the *Official Journal*. The *Bulletin* is also published in CD and on the Web, since 1996, at: www.europa.eu.int/abc/doc/off/bull/en/welcome.htm. Those with a subscription to Lawtel have access to a database containing summaries of all cases heard by the E.C.J. and the Court of First Instance since 1987. The *General Report of the Activities of the European Union* is a substantial document, published in the spring of each year, giving a fairly detailed account of all legal developments, among other things, for the previous year. This, too, has been available on the Web since 1997 at www.europa.eu.int/abc/doc/off/rg/en/welcome.htm .

Periodicals devoted to European law

8.22   At the outset, it should be noted that many general legal periodicals publish articles on European law. In recent years, for example, there have been many substantial articles on the topic in the *Irish Jurist*. Among the leading journals devoted exclusively to European law are the *Common Market Law Review* (cited as C.M.L. Rev. to avoid confusion with the *Common Market Law Reports*), the *European Law Review* and the *Yearbook of European Law*. Being an annual publication, the *Yearbook*, which began in 1981, tends to have quite substantial and authoritative articles. *European Competition Law Review* (ten issues a year) and *European Intellectual Property Review* (12 issues a year) are published by Sweet and Maxwell. There are other more specialist journals such as the *European Foreign Affairs Review*, published quarterly, and the *Journal of Common Market Studies* (also quarterly) which is devoted largely to issues connected with European integration.

Books on European Law

8.23   A list of recently published books will be found in each *European Current Law Year Book* (8.21 above). European law is certainly well served with textbooks, casebooks and collections of legislation. However, if one were to buy only one book, let it be Craig and de Burca, *EU Law: Text, Cases and Materials* 2nd edition (Oxford University Press, 1998) which provides an excellent commentary on all important aspects of European law as well as extracts from the relevant legislation and cases. The same authors have also edited a fine collection of articles in *The Evolution of EU Law* (Oxford University Press, 1999). There is a somewhat older, but still valuable, collection of articles in a two-volume work edited by Francis Snyder, *European Community Law* (1993). This is part of the International Library of Essays in Law and Legal Theory published by Dartmouth at Aldershot. Anyone embarking on the study of European law, and indeed many of those who are already familiar with it, will find Tom Kennedy's *Learning European Law* (London: Sweet and Maxwell,

1998) indispensable. The author, who is Principal Administrator in the Information Office at the Court of Justice in Luxembourg, shows remarkable insight into the issues and puzzles that confront most users of European law at one time or another. He covers the development of the European Union, the substance of the more important European laws, the courts, and the sources of law, and gives some sound advice to those thinking of a career in the European law or administration. Other leading textbooks and collections of materials include:

Weatherill and Beaumont, *EU Law* 3rd edition (London: Penguin Books, 1999)

Hartley, *The Foundations of European Community Law* 4th edition (Oxford: Clarendon Press, 1998)

Mathijsen, *A Guide to European Union Law* 7th edition (London: Sweet and Maxwell, 1999)

McMahon and Murphy, *European Community Law in Ireland* (Dublin: Butterworths, 1989)

Arnull, *Wyatt and Dashwood's European Union Law* 4th edition (London, Sweet and Maxwell, 2000)

Phelan, *Revolt or Revolution: the Constitutional Boundaries of European Law* (Dublin: Sweet and Maxwell, 1997).

Rudden and Phelan, *Basic Community Cases* 2nd edition (Oxford: Oxford University Press, 1997).

Forster, *Blackstone's EC Legislation 2000/2001* 11th edition (London: Blackstone Press, 2000), now published annually.

Brown and Kennedy, *The Court of Justice of the European Communities* 4th edition (London: Sweet and Maxwell, 1994).

There are many books dealing European competition law. Leading examples include:

Korah, *EC Competition Law and Practice* 7th edition (Oxford: Hart Publishing, 2000) Professor Korah is a leading expert on the topic and has published several more specialist works as well.

Whish's *Competition Law* is the standard work covering both U.K. and European competition law. The 4th edition is shortly due for publication by Butterworths.

Recently published books on European law

8.24   Each volume of the *European Current Law Year Book* (8.18 above) carries a long list of recently published books in several languages, though mostly English. Each issue of the *European Current Law Monthly Digest* also lists recent books. Check the index at the front of each issue (or volume in the case of the *Year Book*) for the precise location of these lists.

Encyclopaedias of European law

8.25   Sweet and Maxwell's *Encyclopaedia of European Union Laws* has already been described (8.18 above). There is a shorter reference work edited by Desmond Dinan, *Encyclopaedia of the European Union* (London, Macmillan, 1998). This is a single volume but it has substantial entries on most important aspects of European law. It is therefore particularly helpful to those who are beginning to study the subject or who are seeking general information on some aspect of it.

Electronic sources of European law

8.26 Many references have already been made to the Europa web site, which is a tremendous source of documentation on European law and policy. The URL is: www.europa.eu.int /. It contains the full texts of the treaties, the last 45 days of the *Official Journal* and the full texts of all judgments since 1997. To get direct access to the legal sources use www.europa.eu.int/eur-lex/en/ . There is a good deal of other information as well, in terms of policy documents, links to other sites and so forth. The best source of all is CELEX (an abbreviation of Communitatis Europae Lex) which is the official database of the European Community. It includes virtually every European document one would need to consult, as well as the Acts of accession of the various member states. Unfortunately, this is available by subscription only, and not every library may have access to it. There is another commercial version on CD called JUSTIS-CELEX, which some libraries also subscribe to. Westlaw UK (www.westlaw.co.uk) includes the full text of EU legislation from 1952, EU Treaties from 1951, EU Preparatory Acts from 1992, EU Parliamentary Questions from 1992 and the *Official Journal* from 1992, in addition to the case reports mentioned at paragraph 8-17, above. The EURCOM library of LEXIS also has a good deal of material, including all reported judgments and unreported judgments since 1980.

Irish Centre for European Law

8.27   The Irish Centre for European Law (ICEL), which is based in Trinity College Dublin, was established in 1988 to promote knowledge and discussion of European law in Ireland. It organises conferences on various aspects of European law and the proceedings of many of those conferences have been published. A list of available publications can be consulted on its web site: http://indigo.ie/~webworks.icel/ . The Centre can also be accessed through the Trinity College Law School site: www.tcd.ie/Law/lawhome.ie/ .

European Union offices in Ireland

8.28 Both the European Commission and the European Parliament maintain offices in each member state where general information, usually in the form of explanatory leaflets and pamphlets, can be obtained and where some enquiries can be answered. At the time of writing, the European Commission Representation in Ireland is at 18 Dawson Street, Dublin 2 (Telephone (01) 6625113) while the European Parliament Offices are at European Union House, 43 Molesworth Street, Dublin 2 (01 6057900).

CHAPTER 9

Public International Law

9.01 Public international law has traditionally been defined as the system of law governing relations between states. Throughout the 20th century, particularly with the development of international human rights law in the aftermath of the Second World War, individuals and bodies other than states acquired a much higher status, not to mention rights, under international law. Here, however, we shall concentrate on international law in the traditional sense. The sources of international human rights law are described in the next chapter. There is a separate body of law known as private international law or conflict of laws. It is not treated separately in this book because it is essentially a branch of domestic law dealing with the rules and principles to be applied in legal disputes with a foreign element. Public international law, at least as it applies to relations between states, is seldom encountered in domestic legal practice. But it is routinely applied by government officials and diplomats, and by international organisations. State departments of foreign affairs almost always have experts in international law on their staff. Students who are interested in international law should be aware of this career option. Disputes between states are generally resolved by international tribunals or, in serious cases, by the International Court of Justice (9.12 below). Lawyers representing states at this level are likely to be acknowledged experts in the relevant area and are usually either academics or senior foreign office lawyers.

SOURCES OF PUBLIC INTERNATIONAL LAW

9.02 The sources of international law are less clear-cut than those of domestic law. It is scarcely surprising therefore that most modern textbooks on international law devote a good deal of space to the discussion of sources. Article 38 of the Statute of the International Court of Justice (ICJ), which describes the law which the Court may apply, reads:

1. The Court, whose function is to decide in accordance with international law such disputes are submitted to it, shall apply:
   a. international conventions, whether general or particular, establishing rules expressly recognised by the contesting states;
   b. international custom, as evidence of a general practice accepted as law;

    c.   the general principles of law recognised by civilised nations;

    d.   subject to the provisions of Article 59, judicial decisions and the teachings of the most highly qualified publicists of the various nations, as subsidiary means for the determination of the rules of law.

2.   This provision shall not prejudice the power of the Court to decide a case *ex aequo et bono*, if the parties agree thereon.

Article 59 states: "The decision of the Court has no binding force except between the parties and in respect of that particular case". Before proceeding to examine the implications of Articles 38 and 59, it may be noted that the Statute of the ICJ forms part of the Charter of the United Nations and will be found in the sources mentioned at 10.02 below. Essentially, Article 38 (1) recognises five sources: treaties, customary law, general principles of law, judicial decisions and academic writings. Section 2 provides for a sixth source that may loosely be described as natural law or equity (although "equity" in this context does not have the technical meaning that it has acquired in common-law jurisdictions; rather it used in the broader sense of "justice"). However, the court may only decide a case on this last-mentioned ground with the agreement of the parties. Article 59 simply means that the doctrine of precedent or *stare decisis* as we know it in common-law jurisdictions does not apply to decisions of the ICJ. In reality, though, the Court usually relies heavily on its previous decisions when deciding particular cases.

TREATIES

9.03   Treaties are the first legal source mentioned in the Statute of the ICJ (*supra*), which is scarcely surprising in view of the wide variety of functions they serve in international law.[1] Most international treaties are bilateral, meaning that they are concluded between two states to govern some matter of mutual interest such as trade or extradition. Multilateral treaties, especially those concluded under the aegis of a major international organisations such as the United Nations, are more legally significant as they are likely to establish rules and principles of general application, at least in those states that are parties to them. From an academic perspective, therefore, multilateral treaties are the more important. But, international law practitioners, especially those working in government departments and the diplomatic service, must also be familiar with the sources of bilateral treaties, especially those entered into by their own states.

---

[1]   One of the classic pieces of writing on this topic is McNair, "The Functions and Differing Legal Character of Treaties" (1930) 11 *British Yearbook of International Law* 100.

Modern treaty series

9.04   International law has always striven to prevent secret treaties. Article 102 of the Charter of the UN provides that every treaty and international agreement entered into by any member state shall be registered with the Secretariat of the UN as soon as possible and published by it. Unregistered treaties may not be invoked before any organ of the UN including the International Court of Justice, although they remain binding between the states that are parties to them. Registration is also required by Article 80 of the Vienna Convention on the Law of Treaties, and was formerly required by Article 18 of the Covenant of the League of Nations. Treaties registered with the UN are published in the *United Nations Treaty Series* begun in 1946. This series now runs to over 2,000 volumes which appear some years in arrears. A treaty is not published in this series until it enters into force. As we shall see in Chapter 10 on International Human Rights Law, many years may elapse between the adoption of a treaty and its entry into force. The *United Nations Treaty Series* is referred to as the UNTS and a treaty published in it is cited as:

> *Abolition of Forced Labour Convention* 320 UNTS 291.

All of the UNTS volumes published since 1946 are available on the UN web site: http://untreaty.un.org/English/treaty.asp. However, this is a subscription site which costs about $500 a year for a university or a non-governmental organisation. It also describes the status of treaties deposited with the Secretary-General. The UN publishes a two-volume work entitled *Multilateral Treaties Deposited with the Secretary General: Status as of 31 December 1999* (to give the exact title of the most recent). Part I is devoted to multilateral treaties since the foundation of the UN, while Part II, towards the end of the second volume, is devoted to League of Nations treaties. This is a most valuable service as it provides lists of signatures, ratifications, reservations and declarations. The UN publication sales number of the most recent edition, published in 2000, is E.OO. V.2.

9.05   Some countries publish their own treaty series.[2] The *United Kingdom Treaty Series,* published by HMSO, provides the text of treaties entered into by the UK between 1892 and 1979. The *British Year Book of International Law*, which has been published annually since 1920 contains a list of treaties entered into during the year in question by the UK. The United States has several treaty series. *Treaties and other International Acts* (TIAS) has been published since 1945, while *United States Treaties and other International Agreements* (UST) has been published since 1950. A CD-ROM entitled *TIARA* has been produced by Oceana Publications since 1993 and contains the full texts of more than

---

[2]   For more detailed treatment, see Watt, *Concise Legal Research*, 3rd ed. (Annandale, NSW, 1997).

7,000 treaties entered into by the United States since 1783. The US Department of State publishes the *Treaties in Force*. This is a list (as opposed to the texts) of treaties to which the US is party, and has been published annually since 1929, with monthly updates. Part 1 deals with bilateral treaties, Part 2 with multilateral treaties. There are also various commercially-published lists and indexes including one produced by Oceana on CD-ROM.

Irish treaties

9.06   Ireland has its own treaty series, although it is seldom one sees any reference to it. Most treaties entered into by the Irish Government are published in pamphlet form by the Stationery Office, although libraries may keep the older treaties in bound volume form. Treaties and agreements entered into by the State are listed regularly in *Iris Oifigiúil*. An Irish treaty may be cited as:

Treaty of Extradition between Ireland and the United States of America (Irish Treaty Series, No 3 of 1987).

Some indexes to the Irish Treaty Series have been published, with both alphabetical and chronological lists. The most recent appears to be for the years 1977 to 1994. Some years ago, the Department of Foreign Affairs was planning to put the entire series on the Internet, but this has not yet been done. The Department has a small legal division the members of which are under constant pressure to deal with more immediate matters.

Shorter collections of treaties

9.07   There are several collections of international documents, including treaties, available in book form. Brownlie's *Basic Documents in International Law*, 4th edition (Oxford: Clarendon Press, 1995) includes the Charter of the United Nations, the Vienna Convention on the Law of the Sea, the Vienna Convention on Diplomatic Relations the Vienna Convention on the Law of Treaties, any other seminal sources of international law. This is a particularly useful and affordable collection. A more extensive collection of documents, including treaties, will be found in *The United Nations System and its Predecessors* (Oxford University Press, 1997), a two-volume work by Knipping, von Mangoldt and Rittberger. The first volume is devoted to documents connected with the foundation of the UN or produced by it. It is a particularly useful source of leading Security Council resolutions which are classified by the countries to which they applied. The founding documents of the various specialised agencies of the UN are also included. The second volume is devoted mainly to the League of Nations and includes the text of the Covenant of the League as well as the Statute of the Permanent Court of International Justice (9.12 below). This is an expensive publication but will be found in many academic libraries. Harris's *Cases* *and Materials on International Law* 5th edition (London, 1998), a superb work, includes extensive extracts from and commentary on all the major treaties to which students of international law, at least at undergraduate level, will need to refer.

Current status of treaties

9.08   When working with or referring to a treaty, it is always important to know its current status. One needs to know, for example, if the treaty is actually in force and, in the case of a multilateral treaty, which states have ratified it. One particularly useful source of such information is Bowman and Harris, *Multilateral Treaties: Index and Current Status* (London: Butterworths, 1984) with regular updates published by the University of Nottingham Treaty Centre.[3] However, much of this information, especially in relation to human rights treaties, is available on the Internet and described at 9.10 below.

Older treaties

9.09   Older treaties will be of interest to historians, but some may have contemporary legal significance as well. There are several collections and selections of historic treaties, one of the better compilations being *The Consolidated Treaty Series 1648-1967* by Clive Parry, published by Oceana in 1969. There are more than 230 volumes with several supplementary index volumes. Another useful work is Manley Hudson's *International Legislation 1919-1945* (Washington, 1931-). A much larger work, though perhaps of more contemporary significance, is the *League of Nations Treaty Series* published in 205 volumes and containing the texts of nearly 5,000 treaties registered with the League from 1920 to 1946. Those with a more antiquarian interest will doubtless find much to interest them in Peter Fischer's multi-volume *Collection of International Concessions and Related Instruments 595AD – 1974* (New York: Oceana Publications, 1974-1988)

Internet sources

9.10   There is now a great deal of international legal material on the Internet. It is advisable therefore to bookmark (see 2.11 above) certain sites which provide links to more specific sources. Professor Francis Auburn of the University of Western Australia maintains a particularly useful site: www.law.ecel.uwa.edu.au/intlaw. It has links to other sites dealing with the United Nations, the I.C.J., Treaties, Human Rights, Middle East Issues, International Trade Law and similar topics. Delia Venables' international law site is also excellent. It includes links to the I.C.J., the International Law Commission, the International Criminal Tribunal for Former Yugoslavia and many other bodies. The address is: www.venables.co.uk/legal/internat.htm . The Australian

Legal Information Institute also has an index of international law resources: www.austlii.edu.au. The address for the treaties library is: www.austlii.edu.au/ links/2366.html.

CASE LAW

9.11   Article 38 of the Statute of the ICJ (9.02 above) refers to "judicial deci- sions", as opposed to decisions of international courts, as a source of interna- tional law. Decisions of national courts as well as international courts and tribunals may therefore be cited to support a point of international law. Certain leading decisions of national courts such as that of the District Court of Jerusa- lem in *Attorney-General for the Government of Israel v Eichmann* (1961) 36 I.L.R. 5 are often cited as authority for points of international law. *Eichmann* was primarily concerned with state criminal jurisdiction. The same point arose in *Joyce v D.P.P.* [1946] A.C. 347 in which the House of Lords held that it had jurisdiction to try William Joyce (Lord Haw Haw) for treason although he was a US citizen born of Irish parents. In terms of sources, decisions of national courts will obviously be found in the relevant law report series. However, the leading English texts listed at 9.18 below will probably refer to most interna- tional law decisions of any significance by courts in English-speaking coun- tries. We shall concentrate here on the case law of the ICJ and its predecessor, as well as on the decisions of certain international tribunals.

9.12   The International Court of Justice (ICJ), also known as the World Court, was established in 1946 in accordance with a Statute contained in the Charter of the United Nations. Compared with national courts or, indeed, with other international courts such as the European Court of Human Rights, it deals with relatively few cases, but its judgments are usually lengthy and of considerable legal significance. Its proceedings are published in two series, the first of which contains its judgments and opinions. This is officially entitled *International Court of Justice: Reports of Judgments, Advisory Opinions and Orders*, and began in 1947. The second series, also begun in 1947, is entitled *International Court of Justice: Pleadings, Oral Arguments and Documents*. The latter se- ries is obviously of great value to researchers as it contains the arguments of the parties who are usually represented by top international lawyers. The Court also publishes an annual *Yearbook* containing information about its organisa- tion, jurisdiction, activities and administration, as well as an account of cases before the Court and a list of the Court's publications, including its judgments. Judgments of the ICJ will also be found in other sources. *International Legal Materials* (9.15 below) reproduces many ICJ judgments and orders shortly af- ter their delivery. Reports of ICJ decisions are also included in *International Law Reports* (9.16 below). Nowadays, the most convenient source of recent ICJ judgments is the Internet where the Court has an excellent web site: www.icj-cij.org/icjwww/igeneralinformation.htm. The full texts of judgments delivered since 1996 can be found through this site. It continues to develop; for example, there is now a list of all decisions and advisory opinions brought before the Court since 1946. This can be found at www.icj-cij.org/icjwww/idecisions.htm. The cases are listed by year. For some there is a full case overview, for others there are summaries of judgments and opinions. The first of these web sites contains a good deal of general information about the Court, including biographies of the judges. Links to the I.C.J. web site are also contained in the various sites mentioned at 9.10 above.

9.13   The ICJ had a predecessor in the form of the Permanent Court of International Justice (PCIJ) which lasted from 1922 to 1946. It delivered 32 judgments and 27 advisory opinions. These, together with other documents associated with the Court, are available in official publications which were published in six series, A, B, A/B, D, E. and F. The first three contain the judgments and advisory opinions; D and E contain documents relating to the organisation of the Court and annual reports, while Series F contains general indexes. However, the most accessible source of the PCIJ judgments, and one that is found in many libraries, is Manley Hudson's *World Court Reports: A Collection of the Judgments, Orders and Opinions of the Permanent International Court of Justice* which was published in four volumes between 1934 and 1943 by the Carnegie Endowment of International Justice.

Summaries and analyses of I.C.J. cases

9.14   Summaries and analyses of I.C.J. cases will be found in many legal periodicals but two journals which will be found in most libraries deserve particular mention. The *International and Comparative Law Quarterly* is an excellent source; occasionally an issue devotes an entire section to expert commentary on recent I.C.J. cases. This is a good source of information on the substance and importance of recent cases which are not yet treated in any of the leading textbooks. Useful commentaries will also be found in the *American Journal of International Law* (9.21 below).

OTHER INTERNATIONAL LAW MATERIALS

9.15   Certain journals and yearbooks devoted to international law include a current awareness service. The *British Year Book of International Law*, begun in 1920 and now published by the Clarendon Press, Oxford, provides information on decisions of the British courts involving questions of public or private international law during the year under review. Decisions of the European Court of Justice and the European Court of Human Rights are also covered. *The Hague*

Yearbook of International Law which began in 1988 (succeeding the *Yearbook of the Association of Attenders and Alumni of The Hague Academy of International Law)* covers decisions of the I.C.J., the Permanent Court of Arbitration, the Iran-US Claims Tribunal and other bodies. Both yearbooks include substantial academic articles and, in the case of the *British Year Book,* book reviews as well. Each issue of the *American Journal of International Law* has a "Current Developments" section which covers, among other things, recent developments in international organisations and at the various UN committees.

International legal materials

9.16 *International Legal Materials* (I.L.M.) is published six times a year by the American Society of International Law. It reproduces significant international law documents including treaties, judicial decisions, legislation, reports and resolutions of international organizations and similar material. The November issue of each year includes an annual table of contents and an annual index. It is a remarkably useful service. Many of the documents reproduced in recent issues are available on the Internet, but students and practitioners of international law will still find the hard copy convenient to have to hand. In fact, I.L.M. has become a valuable source of Internet addresses. Whenever it takes a document from the Internet, it helpful provides the address of the relevant site. The following is just a small selection of documents that have been reproduced in I.L.M. during the past two years or so: the text of the Good Friday Agreement re Northern Ireland (37 I.L.M. 751 (1998)), the Optional Protocol to the Convention on the Elimination of All Forms of Discrimination against Women (38 I.L.M. 763 (1998)), the judgments of the High Court of Australia in the *Chen* case on refugee law (39 I.L.M. 769) (2000), the report of the WTO Appellate Body on Import Prohibition of Certain Shrimp and Shrimp Products into the United States (38 I.L.M. 118 (1999)), the OSCE Charter on European Security (39 I.L.M. 255) (2000). Decisions of arbitral tribunals and international criminal tribunals are also routinely reported. As will be noted from the foregoing, the approved citation system is by volume and page number with the year in parentheses at the end. There are also some cumulative indexes, or decennial indexes as they are known, to I.L.M. Three have been published to date covering the periods 1962 to 1969, 1970 to 1979 and 1980 to 1989. Presumably there will shortly be one for the period 1990 to 1999.

International law reports

9.17 *International Law Reports* (I.L.R.) was established in 1919 and known at first as the *Annual Digest of Public International Law Cases*, later as the *Annual Digest and Reports of Public International Law Cases.* From Volume 17 onwards, it has been known by its present title and is edited by Lauterpacht and Greenwood and published by Cambridge University Press. The aim of the series, in the words of the present editors is "to provide within a single series of volumes comprehensive access in English to judicial materials bearing on public international law". Unlike *International Legal Materials*, therefore, it does not provide the texts of treaties or legislation. However, it gives a broad interpretation to "cases". Decisions and reports of international courts, arbitral tribunals and national courts are included. A particularly useful feature of this series is its coverage of decisions and judgments of many national courts in the English-speaking world and elsewhere on international law issues. Nowadays, there is a good deal of human rights material as well.

ACADEMIC WRITINGS

9.18   The fifth source of international law listed in the Statute of the ICJ consists of "the teachings of the most highly qualified publicists of the various nations". In fact, the ICJ seldom, if ever, quotes from writers in its decisions although members of the Court frequently do so in their separate opinions, whether concurring or dissenting. Scholarly writings tend to be more widely quoted by states engaged in diplomatic disputes with the result, as Malanczuk says, that "writers quote states and states quote writers, at least when it suits their interests".[4] Indeed, as he also notes, it is becoming increasingly difficult in a modern multicultural world to identify the most authoritative writings.[5] The Statute of the ICJ may refer to publicists of all nations but until recently the most highly esteemed writings were almost invariably those of European or Anglo-American authors. Be that as it may, certain scholars are widely acknowledged as "highly qualified publicists", at least by traditional standards. They include O'Connell,[6] Schwarzenberger,[7] Oppenheim, and Brierly.[8] International law as we know it was largely formed by European scholars such as Grotius (1583-1645), Pufendorf (1632-94) and Vattel (1714-67) and their works are still occasionally cited. Modern scholars from the English-speaking world whose works are widely respected include Bowett, Brownlie, Henkin, Higgins, Jennings, McDougal and Reisman. A selection of their works is given at 9.19 below. The ninth edition of the first volume of *Oppenheim's International Law: Peace* was published in two sub-volumes in 1996 under the editorship of Sir Robert Jennings, former President of the I.C.J. and Sir Arthur Watts, former Legal Advisor to the Foreign and Commonwealth Office. It is published by

---

[3]   The web address for this Centre is: www.nottingham.ac.uk/law/TREATY.HTM .

[4]   *Akehurst's Modern Introduction to International Law* 7th revised ed. by Malanczuk (London, 1997) 52.

[5]   *Ibid.*

[6]   O'Connell, *International Law* 2nd ed., 2 vols. (London, 1970).

[7]   Schwarzenberger, *A Manual of International Law* 6th ed. (Milton: Professional Books, 1976) and *International Law* 3rd ed. (London: Stevens, 1957).

[8]   *The Law of Nations* 6th ed. by Waldock (Oxford, 1963).

what is now the Pearson Education Group. The paperback edition costs about £90 sterling while the hardback costs over £600 sterling. The cost of *War*, as the second volume may well be entitled, remains to be seen.

SECONDARY LITERATURE ON INTERNATIONAL LAW

Textbooks and casebooks

9.19   During the past decade there has been a remarkable growth in the number of scholarly publications on international law. Developments in international relations, particularly in matters such as humanitarian intervention, international peace-keeping and the establishment of war crimes tribunals have doubtless fuelled academic interest, not to mention research and publishing opportunities, in this field of knowledge. Nevertheless, certain leading textbooks remain the most reliable guides to the basic principles of international law. *Akehurst's Modern Introduction to International Law,* 7th revised edition by Peter Malanczuk (London, 1997) is exactly what the title says and has long been a favourite introductory text. Rebecca Wallace's *International Law* 3rd edn (London: Sweet and Maxwell, 1997) is another good introduction. More detailed works include Ian Brownlie's *Principles of International Law* 5th edn (Oxford, 1998) and Malcolm Shaw's *International Law* 4th edn (Cambridge UP, 1997). Rosalyn Higgins' *International Law and How We Use It* (Oxford, 1998), based on a series of lectures delivered at the Hague Academy of International Law, is a particularly thought-provoking introduction which more advanced students will also find useful. (Professor Higgins is now a member of the ICJ). Leading American works include Henkin's *How Nations Behave*, 2nd edn (New York, 1979) and Henkin, Pugh, Schachter and Smit, *International Law: Cases and Materials* 3rd edn (West Publishing, 1993). As mentioned earlier, Harris's *Cases and Materials on International Law* 5th edn (London, 1998) is a splendid piece of work and indispensable to anybody engaged in the study or practice of international law. There are, of course, many more detailed works on various aspects of international law. Examples include Brownlie's *International Law and the Use of Force* (Oxford: Clarendon Press, 1963) which has been reissued in the meantime, Gray's *Judicial Remedies in International Law* (Oxford: Clarendon Press, 1990), McCorquodale's *Self-Determination in International Law* (Dartmouth: Ashgate Publishing, 2000) and Bowett's *The International Court of Justice: Process, Practice and Procedure* (London: British Institute of International and Comparative Law, 1997).

9.20   International lawyers are generally luckier than their domestic law counterparts in having *Festschriften* and other celebratory or memorial volumes of essays dedicated to them. These collections generally include scholarly and original contributions from leading academic experts and practitioners. Fortunately, there is a convenient source of information about the contents of these various volumes. The review section of the *American Journal of International Law* often has a "Collected Essays" heading under which the contents of recent collections of essays and yearbooks are listed.

Journals

9.21   Articles on international law will be found in a wide variety of periodicals in the areas of law, politics and international relations. The leading English-language journals devoted to international law include the *American Journal of International Law*, begun in 1907 and published quarterly, the *British Year Book of International Law,* published annually since, the *European Journal of International Law*, published since 1990 by Oxford University Press, the so-called *Hague Receuil,* properly known as *Receuil des cours de l'Academie de droit international,* and *The Hague Yearbook of International Law.* The *International and Comparative law Quarterly* also publishes a good deal of material on international law. Many US law schools produce journals devoted exclusively to international law. They include the *Yale Journal of International Law*, the *Harvard International Law Review,* the *Denver Journal of International Law and Politics* and the *Cornell International Law Journal.* Another useful publication, nowadays sold in shops, is *Foreign Affairs*, which appears six times a year. It is aimed at the general reader, but students of international law should also find it interesting, if only for its book reviews. Most academic libraries also subscribe to it. However, this is no more than a small selection of periodicals dealing with international law.[9] The entire series of the *American Journal of International Law* from 1907 up until to 1994 is now available online on JSTOR. More recent volumes continue to be added. The URL is: www.jstor.ac.uk/.

9.22   One of the more respected and frequently-cited periodicals is the *Recueil des Cours – Academie de Droit International*, commonly known as *The Hague Recueil.* The Hague Academy of International Law was established in 1923 with support from the Carnegie Endowment. It hosts an annual summer school which is divided into two sessions, one devoted to Private International Law and the other to Public International Law. Lectures and seminars are given by specialists from various countries. All courses given at the Academy are generally published in the language in which they are delivered. So far, 276 volumes of the *Recueil* have been published, the most recent for 1999. There are also several consolidated indexes. The first, a substantial work in itself, is the *General Index to the Recueil des Cours of the Hague Academy of International*

---

[9]   The bibliographies, especially the first, listed in /// will give full lists of journals, but another useful and accessible source is the Table of Abbreviations in Harris's *Cases and Materials on International Law*, 5th ed., p. lxxv.

Law, Volumes 1 – 101, published in 1968 by A.W. Sijthoff, Leyden. The most recent, published in 1999 by Martinus Nijhoff, The Hague, is for volumes 241 to 250. The Proceedings of the International Law Association (I.L.A.) are another useful source of current ideas and information about many aspects of international law. The Association was founded in 1873 and holds a major conference every second year. The most recent volume contains the proceedings of the 68th Conference held in Taipei, Taiwan in May 1998.

REFERENCE WORKS

9.23   Parry and Grant's *Encyclopaedic Dictionary of International Law* (London, 1986) explains many terms and provides brief accounts of some ideas and institutions associated with international law. The *Encyclopaedia of Public International Law,* published under the auspices of the Max Planck Institute for Comparative Public Law and International and under the direction of Rudolf Bernhardt, will appear in several volumes. The first, A-D, was published in 1992 and two more have been published in the meantime. This looks set to become the standard work in the area.

BIBLIOGRAPHIES OF INTERNATIONAL LAW

9.24   The most comprehensive current bibliography is *Public International Law: A Current Bibliography of Books and Articles*, published twice a year since 1975 by the Max Planck Institute at Heidelberg. The *Bibliography of the International Court of Justice* is published annually by the Court itself listing such works and documents relating to the Court as have come its attention during the year. *A Collection of Bibliographic and Research Resources: International* Law (New York; Oceana) in several volumes, covers most areas of international law. A number of other bibliographies in book form have been published, though must of them are rather dated by now. Still useful, however, is Elizabeth Beyerly's *Public International Law: A Guide to Information Sources* (London, 1991) which is available in many libraries.

INTERNATIONAL LAW DIGESTS

9.25   Several multi-volume digests of international law have been published by the U.S. State Department (something which should be borne in mind when using them, as they are naturally U.S. biased in terms of coverage). The first was edited by Hackworth, *Digest of International Law* (1940-1944), covering the period 1906 to 1939. The second was edited by Whiteman, *Digest of International Law* (1963-1973), covering the period 1940-1960. Since 1973, the

U.S. Department of State produces an annual publication entitled *Digest of United States Practice in International Law.*

OTHER INTERNATIONAL INSTITUTIONS

International Criminal Court (ICC)

9.25 The Rome Statute of the International Criminal Court was adopted by a UN Diplomatic Conference of Plenipotentiaries on the Establishment of an International Criminal Court, on 17 July 1998. The ICC maintains a very comprehensive web site. The background to the establishment of the Court is set out at www.un.org/law/icc/general/overview.htm. The text of the statute is to be found at www.un.org/law/icc/statute/romefra.htm while the current status of the statute in terms of signature, ratification and so forth can be checked at www.un.org/law/icc/statute/status.htm . The ICC has already been subject to a great deal of scholarly discussion and analysis. *The Statute of the International Criminal Court. A Documentary History* (New York: Transnational Publishers Inc, 1998) compiled by M. Cherif Bassiouni, includes the text of the Statute and a detailed account of the drafting process. Ireland's ratification of the Rome Statute was made possible by a constitutional referendum held in June 2001.

International Labour Organisation (ILO)

9.26 The International Labour Organisation (ILO) was founded in 1919, having been created by the Treaty of Versailles, and it became a specialised agency of the United Nations in 1946. It is essentially concerned with developing labour standards through the medium of conventions and recommendations. These instruments generally set minimum standards for a range of labour-related issues such as freedom of association, equal opportunities and so forth. It also provides technical assistance towards vocational training, labour administration and many other issues. The ILO has a website outlining its history, policies and activities: www.un.or.id/ilo/english/general.htm. This, in turn, allows access to the ILO-NORMES website which has the texts of several conventions and recommendations. The ILO has published a three-volume work, *International Labour Conventions and Recommendations* 1977-1995 (ILO Office, Geneva, 1996).

World Trade Organization (WTO)

9.27 In the late 1940s, it had been intended to create an institution, similar to the World Bank and the International Monetary Fund, to deal with international economic cooperation. This was to be known as the International Trade Organisation (ITO), but it was to prove an elusive goal. Between 1948 and 1994, world trade was regulated by the General Agreement on Tariffs and Trade (GATT). GATT was never intended to be anything other than provisional, but it lasted for almost 50 years. Eventually the World Trade Organisation was established in 1995 following negotiations during the eighth (Uruguay) round of GATT. The WTO's mission is to ensure that trade between states flows "as smoothly, predictably and freely as possible". As an organisation, the WTO has been far more controversial than anticipated. In late 1999, its Seattle meeting was thrown into disarray by public protests, with the result that it is now difficult to predict its future effectiveness. Be that as it may, the WTO has an excellent web site which sets out its history and objectives and makes most of its documents available on line. The address is: www.wto.org. To gain direct access to its main web page which sets out its history and provides links to more further sources, use: www.wto.org/english/thewto_e/tif_e/fact4_e.htm.

CHAPTER 10

International Human Rights Law

10.01   The concept of human rights and the liberal philosophy it reflects may be traced back to the Eighteenth Century and possibly earlier, but it was only in the late 1940s, with the foundation of the United Nations, that a coherent body of international human rights law began to emerge. This body of law has grown exponentially during the past 50 years and may be divided into two broad categories, the global and the regional. For all practical purposes, global human rights law consists of the rules, principles and standards developed by the United Nations and its agencies. Alongside this is an important and ever-growing body of regional human rights law developed under the aegis of the Council of Europe, the Organisation of American States and the Organisation of African Unity. The focus of this Chapter is on *international* human rights law, but there are two points worth mentioning at the outset. First, human rights belong primarily to individual human beings. Consequently, they should be of as much concern to states and to non-governmental organisations operating within states as they are to the international community. Most countries, including Ireland, have several organisations devoted to protecting civil liberties and promoting the welfare of disadvantaged or marginalised groups. Material published by these organisations, many of which interact, formally or otherwise, with international human rights bodies, can be particularly useful for identifying domestic human rights issues and suggesting policy initiatives. Secondly, it should be noted that there is a rich theoretical literature on the concept of rights themselves and the political philosophy underpinning them. During the past twenty years or so, American scholars in particular have produced many challenging works criticising rights-based public philosophies (which generally hold that the state should be neutral as to the personal goals to be pursued by individuals) and advocating a return to more communitarian or civic-spirited policies.[1] Communitarian philosophy is, of course, itself open to criticism on a number of grounds, but it still provides a welcome antidote to conventional human rights scholarship much of which tends to assume too readily the validity of the liberal position, and is often devoid of any significant critical or empirical dimension.

---

[1]   Leading works include Kautz, *Liberalism and Community* (London: Cornell U.P., 1995) and Sandel, *Democracy's Discontent: America in Search of a Public Philosophy* (Cambridge, Ma: Belknap Press of Harvard U.P. 1998).

THE UNITED NATIONS

10.02   The United Nations (UN) is a global international organisation. Membership, according to Article 4 of its Charter, is open to all "peace-loving States which accept the obligations contained in the present Charter and, in the judgment of the Organisation, are able and willing to carry out these obligations".[2] At present, it has 189 members which means that almost every country in the world belongs to it.[3] The UN was established on 25 October 1945 by the original 51 member states. It is a vast and complex organisation, although it consists essentially of six main organs: the General Assembly, the Security Council, the Economic and Social Council, the Trusteeship Council, the Secretariat and the International Court of Justice.[4] The first five are based at the UN headquarters in New York while the International Court of Justice (which was dealt with in the previous Chapter) is based at The Hague. From a human rights perspective, the more important organs are the Economic and Social Council, to which many subsidiary bodies report, and the Secretariat although both of these report ultimately to the General Assembly.

United Nations human rights instruments

10.03   The *fons et origo* of modern human rights law is the Universal Declaration of Human Rights adopted by the General Assembly of the United Nations on 10 December, 1948. Although it is merely a declaration as opposed to a binding treaty, much of it may now be said to have become part of customary international law. If this is so, then many of the Declaration's provisions are binding on every state irrespective of whether it has ratified or acceded to any of the international human rights treaties. Complementing the Universal Declaration are three human rights treaties which were adopted by the General Assembly in 1966 and entered into force in 1976. They are the International Covenant on Economic, Social and Cultural Rights, the International Covenant on Civil and Political Rights and the Optional Protocol to the International Covenant on Civil and Political Rights. There is now a second Optional Protocol, aimed at abolishing the death penalty, adopted in 1990. These treaties, together with the Universal Declaration, are collectively known as the International Bill of Rights.

---

[2]   For a detailed article-by-article commentary on the Charter, see Simma (ed.), *The Charter of the United Nations: A Commentary* (Oxford, 1994).

[3]   A list of all member states with dates of accession until 1998 will be found in Harris, *Cases and Materials on International Law*, 5th edn. (London, 1998) 1080-1081.

[4]   A useful chart describing the structure of the UN will be found on the web site of the UN High Commissioner for Human Rights: www.unhchr.ch/hrostr.htm. The Trusteeship Council no longer has any real function now that all of the former trust territories have achieved either self-government or independence.

10.04   Many of the fundamental rights protected by the Bill of Rights are defined in fairly general terms. Other human rights treaties have, however, been
adopted to provide enhanced or more explicit protection for particular rights or
certain groups of people. The more important supplementary treaties are: the
International Convention on the Elimination of All Forms of Racial Discrimination (1966), the Convention on the Elimination of All Forms of Discrimination Against Women (1979), the Convention Against Torture and Other Cruel,
Inhuman or Degrading Treatment or Punishment (1984), and the UN Convention on the Rights of the Child (1989). There are also several declarations and
resolutions on human rights issues which, while not legally binding, are important indicators of acceptable human rights norms. They include the Declaration
on the Elimination of All Forms of Intolerance and of Discrimination Based on
Religion or Belief (1981) and the Declaration on the Rights of Persons Belong-
ing to National or Ethnic, Religious or Linguistic Minorities (1992). The documentation associated with all the main treaties are described in later paragraphs.

Charter-based and treaty-based institutions

10.05   Students of human rights are often confused by the maze of conventions, declarations, resolutions, enforcement mechanisms and institutions established by the UN or its specialised agencies to deal with human rights problems
and issues. In order to bring some conceptual clarity to this bewildering array of
documents and institutions, it is best to begin by noting that some institutions
are treaty-based while others are charter-based. As will be apparent from later
sections of this Chapter, the UN, since its foundation, has adopted several major human rights conventions which are available for ratification by all member
states. Each of these conventions contains its own enforcement mechanism, a
central element of which is a committee or similar body established to monitor
the observance and enforcement of the convention. For example, the International Covenant on Civil and Political Rights (10.13 below) establishes the
Human Rights Committee, and the UN Convention on the Rights of the Child
(10.19 below) establishes the Committee on the Rights of the Child. These are
all treaty-based bodies. They owe their existence solely to the treaties under
which they were established, and their functions are confined to those specified
in the conventions which established them.

10.06   Alongside these there are Charter-based institutions and procedures
which have their constitutional basis in the Charter of the UN.[5] Chapter X of
the Charter established the Economic and Social Council which now consists of

---

[5]   Burgenthal, *International Human Rights in a Nutshell* 2nd edn. (St. Paul, Minnesota,
1995), an unduly modestly entitled book. For a more detailed account of charter-based
and treaty-based bodies, see Alston (ed.), *The United Nations and Human Rights: A
Critical Appraisal* (Oxford, 1992).

54 UN member states. It was given particular responsibility for human rights (Art. 62) and required to set up commissions for the promotion of human rights (Art. 68). In fulfilment of this requirement, the Council established the Human Rights Commission (now consisting of 53 member states) in 1946. A Sub-Commission on the Prevention of Discrimination and the Protection of Minorities and a Commission on the Status of Women were established in 1947.[6] More recently, the High Commissioner for Human Rights (the post currently held by Mary Robinson) was established in 1994, pursuant to Resolution 48/141 of the UN General Assembly (7 January 1994). Charter-based bodies usually have more general and inclusive remits than those of treaty-based bodies. They are typically charged with investigating, studying, reporting on and attempting to find solutions to a wide variety of human rights problems and issues throughout the world. The main sources of the vast documentation produced by these bodies will be outlined at 10.13 – 10.20 below

The structure and terminology of human rights treaties

10.07 There is no official template determining the structure or content of international human rights treaties, but most of the major treaties follow a similar pattern. A treaty generally begins by setting out the rights that it aims to protect. In the case of a general convention such as the International Covenant on Civil and Political Rights or the European Convention on Human Rights, the first part will set out an extensive list of rights. If the convention is concerned with a more specific right such as protection from racial discrimination or freedom from torture, the first part will simply set out this right, though perhaps in some detail. In the International Convention on the Elimination of All Forms of Racial Discrimination (1966), for example, Article 1 defines racial discrimination while Articles 2 to 7 specify the measures that states must adopt to prevent and combat it. The second major component of a human rights treaty is the enforcement mechanism. As noted earlier, a UN-sponsored treaty will generally provide for a committee, to be appointed from among the state parties, to which reports must periodically be submitted and which may be empowered to take other steps to ensure compliance with the treaty. In the case of the European Convention on Human Rights, the Court of Human Rights and the Council of Ministers are the established enforcement mechanisms. The third major component of a human rights treaty will usually be the set of provisions dealing with signature, ratification and entry into force. When reading a treaty, it is important to note which states may become parties to it; for example, the European Convention on Human Rights is open to member states of the Council of

---

[6] The Sub-Commission has earned a good deal of international respect, largely because its members, unlike those of the Commission, serve in a personal capacity. Its 26 members are elected by the Commission from a list designated by the member states of the UN.

Europe only. This part of a treaty will also indicate the number of ratifications required before it can enter into force, the circumstances in which a state may withdraw from it and, possibly, the procedures to be followed in respect of proposals to amend it.

10.08   Certain terminology associated with treaties should also be noted. In international law, the terms "treaty", "convention", "covenant" and "protocol" are more or less synonymous. However, human rights treaties are almost always known as conventions or covenants. The term "protocol" is usually reserved for an ancillary treaty added to an existing one. State parties to the existing treaty may decide to ratify, although they are not obliged to do so. Thus, we have the First and Second Optional Protocols to the International Covenant on Civil and Political Rights and the various protocols to the European Convention on Human Rights. Adhesion to a human rights treaty generally involves a two-stage process, signature and ratification or accession. A state which signs a human rights treaty is not thereby bound by it, although its signature may be taken to indicate agreement with its contents and, according to some writers, implies a commitment to ratify sometime in the future. The terms "ratification" and "accession" are often used interchangeably although, strictly speaking, a state *accedes* to a treaty when it did not take part in the negotiations leading to its adoption but later becomes a party at the invitation of the negotiating states. Ireland, therefore, *ratified* the European Convention on Human Rights (because it was party to its adoption in the early 1950s) whereas it *acceded* in 1989 to the two UN Covenants of 1966. A state is solemnly obliged under international law to observe in good faith the terms of any treaty it ratifies or accedes to.

Finding the texts of UN human rights instruments

10.09   Electronic sources of international human rights law continue to expand. The United Nations has produced an excellent CD-ROM entitled *Human Rights* (4th edn, 1999) which contains 5,000 full-text documents, 95 international instruments and a bibliography. It retails at about £75 sterling. Meanwhile, all the major international organisations, including the UN and the UN High Commissioner for Human Rights, having been placing large amounts of valuable material on the World Wide Web. The High Commissioner's web site is particularly impressive and we shall be returning to it presently in the context of reporting procedures. The URL (address) for the UN is www.un.org while that for the High Commissioner is www.unhchr.ch. There is little point in providing here a detailed description of all the web pages maintained by these organisations. Once they are entered through the addresses just given, it is easy to navigate one's way through them. However, for quick access to the main UN treaties, a particularly useful address is that of the research guide: www.un.org/Depts/dhl/resguide/spechr.htm. Through the use of hypertext (2.11 above), this site grants access to the texts of the main treaties and the proceedings of the various treaty-based bodies. There are other excellent web sites maintained by universities and human rights organisations. The Human Rights Internet, a Canadian organisation, has web site with 95 international human rights treaties in full text. The address is: www.hri.ca/uninfor/treaties/index.htm. The University of Minnesota Human Rights library has more than 6, 500 documents on its web site (www1.umn.edu/humanrts/) with an enormous number of links to centres for human rights teaching and research, and to NGOs. Another outstanding source of human rights material is the University of Queensland (Australia) database. This will be found at: www.library.uq.edu.au/law/subjects/weblawhr.html and includes UN, European, American and African human rights instruments as well as material dealing with the UN High Commissioner for Refugees, the International Labour Organisation, UNESCO and similar bodies. The Australian Legal Research Institute also has a good collection of human rights material at www.austlii.edu.au/links/48.htm. The Minnesota and Queensland sites are particularly worth bookmarking.

Printed collections of human rights documents

10.10   The most comprehensive and up-to-date collection of documents is the second edition of *Blackstone's International Human Rights Documents* by P.R. Ghandi (London: Blackstone Press, 2000). The documents in this collection are grouped under two main headings, international and regional. Those under the former heading are mainly United Nations instruments, while those under the latter are drawn from European, American, African and Arab organisations. All treaties and declarations of any significance are included, as well as UN resolutions for handling human rights complaints (including the 1503 procedure for dealing with gross violations of human rights),[7] instruments emerging from UN World Conference such as the Proclamation of Teheran, and the U.K. Human Rights Act 1998. The documents are arranged in chronological order under each of the main headings, beginning with the human rights provisions of the Covenant of the League of Nations (1919) under the international heading, and the European Convention on Human Rights (1950) under the first regional heading. The Rome Statute of the International Criminal Court is also included. While this book has a short subject index, it provides no commentary whatever and no information on the status of the individual instruments in terms of entry into force or number of ratifications.

10.11   Ian Brownlie's *Basic Documents on Human Rights,* 3rd edn (Oxford, 1992) is preferable in many ways to Ghandi's collection. The layout and printing style make it easier to use, and it contains a judicious selection of human rights treaties and other instruments. It includes all the UN-sponsored conven-

---

[7] On this topic, see A.P. Schmid, *Research on Gross Human Rights Violations* (Leiden: COMT, 1989).

tions and declarations, the more important documents of the International Labour Organisation, European, Latin American and African instruments and a few relevant documents touching on international trade. Its greatest asset however is the short commentaries preceding most of the instruments giving useful background and explanatory information as well as some bibliographical references. There is another very comprehensive collection of documents entitled *The Raoul Wallenberg Compilation of Human Rights Documents* edited by Goran Melander and Gudmundur Alfredson (London: Martinus Nijhoff Publishers, 1997). With a price tag of £160.00 it is unlikely to be a best-seller among students (or academics) but is stocked by many libraries. Another useful collection is van der Wolf's *Human Rights: Selected Documents* published in 1994 by the Global Law Association in the Netherlands.

HUMAN RIGHTS INTSRUMENTS OF GLOBAL APPLICATION

10.12   The first set of instruments to be considered under this heading is the International Bill of Rights which, as noted earlier, consists of the Universal Declaration of Human Rights (1948), the International Covenant on Economic, Social and Cultural Rights (1966), the International Covenant on Civil and Political Rights (1966) and the two Protocols to the latter Covenant. Then there are the more specific UN treaties mentioned at 10.04 above. The sources of the texts of these instruments have been described at 10.09 and 10.10. Here we shall deal with the documentation associated with the more important of the UN treaties. Much of this documentation is now available on the Internet, particularly on the web site of the UN High Commissioner for Human Rights (10.09 above), but it is still useful to be familiar with the coding system used to identify the paper version of the documents. The main codes are as follows:

Committee on Economic and Social Rights	E/C.12/-.
Human Rights Committee	CCPR/C/-
Committee on Rights of the Child	CRC/C/-
Committee on Elimination of Racial Discrimination	CERD/C/-
Committee on Elimination of Discrimination against Women	CEDAW/C/-
Committee against Torture	CAT/C/-
Commission on Human Rights	E/CN.4/-

For further details, see www.un.org/Depts/dhl/resguide/spechr.htm.

The International Covenant on Civil and Political Rights and the Optional Protocols

10.13 Article 28 of this Covenant provides for a Human Rights Committee of which there are 18 members. This Committee is charged with the implementation of the Covenant and the Optional Protocols, the first of which allows individuals to make complaints (or, in the language of the Covenant, communications) alleging a violation of a right under the Covenant by a state provided the state in question has ratified the Protocol. Irrespective of whether or not it has ratified the Protocol, every state party to the Covenant must submit periodic reports to the Human Rights Committee setting out the measures they have adopted to give effect to the rights protected by the Covenant and related matters. The Committee has decided that its own general reports and formal decisions as well as reports and additional information received from state parties should be documents of general circulation, meaning that they should be available to the public, unless it is decided otherwise in a particular case. The response of the Committee to individual communications received under the Optional Protocol are also published as a rule. The session papers of the Committee provide all of this information, but their sheer bulk often makes it difficult to extract pertinent information from them. There is, however, a more convenient source. The official records of the Human Rights Committee are published periodically in bound volumes. The records of the first 30 sessions were published in the *Yearbooks of the Human Rights Committee* for the years 1977 to 1987. At its 32nd session in 1988, the Committee decided to change the title from *Yearbook* to *Official Records*. Therefore, to take one of the more recently available (there is a long delay in publication), the *Official Records of the Human Rights Committee 1992/93* in two volumes includes the documents of the 46th to the 48th sessions of the Committee, held between October 1992 and July 1993. Included in these volumes is Ireland's first report (at page 225 *et seq.*) as well as the Committee's comments on this report (at page 453 *et seq.)* There are also some bound volumes of decisions taken under the First Optional Protocol. Important decisions of the Committee under the First Optional Protocol are also occasionally published in the *Human Rights Law Journal* (10.73 below) and in the *International Law Reports* (see 9.16, previous chapter). The Second Optional Protocol, adopted in 1990, deals with the abolition of the death penalty.

10.14 Working documents produced by the Human Rights Committee are coded CCPR/C/-. A number of book-length studies of the Committee have been published, including McGoldrick's *The Human Rights Committee: Its Role in the Development of the International Covenant on Civil and Political Rights* with updated introduction (Oxford: Clarendon Press, 1996). Some governments publish their own periodic reports to the Human Rights Committee and similar monitoring bodies. Ireland has, in fact, published its two reports to date.

The International Covenant on Economic, Social and Cultural Rights

10.15   Under Articles 16 to 25 of this Covenant, States Parties are required to submit periodic reports setting out the measures adopted and the progress made towards giving effect to the Covenant. Reports are submitted to the Economic and Social Council (ECOSOC) which is made up of government representatives unlike, for example, the Human Rights Committee which consists of independent experts acting in a personal capacity. For many years after the Covenant entered into force (in 1976), state reports received little scrutiny because of the time constraints under which ECOSOC was operating. In 1985, however, ECOSOC established a committee of 18 experts acting in an independent capacity to examine state reports, and comment on them. This body, known as the UN Committee on Economic, Social and Cultural Rights, held its first meeting in 1987. The session papers of this Committee and of ECOSOC are documents of general circulation. They are coded E/C/12/-. A report on each session of the Committee on Economic, Social and Cultural Rights is published by the United Nations. At the time of writing, the reports for the 16th and 17th sessions, ending in November 1997, appear to be the most recent. Reports submitted by Ireland under the Covenant are published by the Government. There are several textbooks and commentaries on the Covenant, including Craven, *The International Covenant on Economic, Social and Cultural Rights* (Oxford: Clarendon Press, 1998), Arambulo, *Strengthening the Supervision of the International Covenant on Economic, Social and Cultural Rights* (Oxford: Hart Publishing, 1999) and Eide, *Economic, Social and Cultural Rights* (Dondrecht: Martinus Nijhoff, 1994).

The International Convention on the Elimination of All Forms of Racial Discrimination

10.16   This Convention, adopted by the UN General Assembly in 1965 and in force since 1969, is one of the more widely ratified of all human rights treaties. By early 2001, it had been ratified by 157 states including Ireland, which ratified in December 2000. The implementation of this Convention is supervised by the Committee on the Elimination of Racial Discrimination (CERD) which is composed of 18 independent experts elected by states parties. The reporting procedure is the main implementation mechanism. A state party must submit a report within one year of the Convention entering into force for it, and thereafter every two years or on request. A state party may lodge a complaint against another (Article 11). A party may also declare that it recognises the competence of CERD to consider communications from individuals subject to its jurisdiction alleging a violation of the Convention (Article 14). One of the interesting features of this Convention is that it provides (Article 22) for disputes between parties to be referred to the International Court of Justice if they cannot be settled under procedures established by the Convention itself. The code for UN documents produced in accordance with the Convention is *CERD*. Thus the code for a state report would be *CERD/C/192/Add.2* (this being the text of Italy's sixth periodic report).

The Convention Against Torture and Other Cruel, Inhuman and Degrading Treatment or Punishment.

10.17 This Convention was adopted by the UN General Assembly in 1984 and entered into force in 1987. It provides for the creation of a Committee against Torture, consisting of 10 experts elected by the States Parties, to supervise its implementation. Each party must submit a report within one year of ratification setting out the steps taken to give effect to its obligations under the Convention. Thereafter, a report must be submitted every four years. A State Party may declare that it recognises the competence of the Committee to receive communications from one State Party to the effect that another is not fulfilling its obligations under the Convention (Article 21). Likewise, a State Party may recognise the competence of the Committee to receive communications from individuals subject to its jurisdiction (Article 22). Working documents of the Committee are coded CAT/C/-. At the time of writing, Ireland had not ratified this Convention although it had paved the way for doing so with the enactment of the Criminal Justice (United Nations Convention against Torture) Act, 2000. More than 120 states have now ratified. A volume entitled *Conclusions and Recommendations of the UN Committee Against Torture*, edited by Holmstrom, and covering the 11th to 22nd sessions (1993 to 1999) was published in 2000 by Martinus Nijhoff Publishers in co-operation with the Raoul Wallenberg Institute of Human Rights and Humanitarian Law. Other leading textbooks include Boulesbaa's *The UN Convention against Torture and the Prospects of Enforcement* (Dondrecht: Martinus Nijhoff Publishers, 1999), and Rodley, *The Treatment of Prisoners under International Law* 2nd edn (Oxford, Oxford University Press, 1999).

The Convention on the Elimination of All Forms of Discrimination against Women

10.18 This Convention (CEDAW), which was adopted by the General Assembly in 1979 and entered into force in 1981, has been ratified by 167 states, including Ireland. It imposes a wide range on obligations on states parties in relation to the elimination of discrimination and the adoption of positive measures to promote equality. It provides for the establishment of a Committee on the Elimination of Discrimination against Women, consisting of twenty-three experts who are selected by the states' parties who sit in an independent capacity. A state which has ratified the Convention is obliged to submit a report to this Committee within one year of the entry into force of the Convention for itself, and thereafter every four years. Reports submitted by Ireland have been published by the Stationery Office. The Convention itself makes no provision for inter-state complaints or for individual petitions. However, in 1999, the General Assembly adopted an Optional Protocol to the Convention, which entered into force on 22 December 2000, having received the necessary number of ratifications (10, in accordance with the terms of Article 16). Article 2 of the Protocol allows the Committee on the Elimination of Discrimination against Women to receive communications by or on behalf of individuals or groups claiming to be victims of a violation of any of the rights set forth in the Convention by a state party to the Protocol. The Committee, assuming it finds the communication to be admissible, shall examine the matter and communicate its views to the parties concerned. Within six months, the state party shall submit a written response to the Committee including information on any action taken in light of the Committee's findings. Further information may then be requested by the Committee. Article 8 of the Protocol allows the Committee to investigate grave or systematic violations by a state party of the rights set forth in the Convention. However, a state party when ratifying the Protocol may indicate that it does not recognise the competence of the Committee in relation to the provisions of Article 8. Working documents of the Committee are coded CEDAW/C/-. Summary records of meetings bear the code CEDAW/C/SR.123.

The UN Convention on the Rights of the Child

10.19   This Convention was adopted by the General Assembly of the United Nations in September 1989 and has since become the most widely ratified of human rights conventions, with 192 states parties, including Ireland. It provides a comprehensive catalogue of the rights to which children are entitled – civil, political, economic, social and cultural. It establishes a Committee on the Rights of the Child composed of 10 independent experts elected by the states parties. Under Article 44, each state party must submit a report to this Committee within two years of the entry into force of the Convention for the state party concerned, and thereafter every five years. Two optional protocols have recently been adopted, one on the involvement of children in armed conflict, and the other on the sale of children, prostitution and child pornography. The texts are available on the High Commissioner's website (10.09 above) and in *International Legal Materials*[8] (9.16 above). Shortly after Ireland ratified the Convention, a voluntary body called Children's Rights Alliance was formed to monitor the application of the Convention within the country, This organisation has produced some interesting material including a report called *Small Voices: Vital Rights* (Dublin, 1997) which it submitted to the UN Committee on the Rights of the Child when the Government presented its first report. The latter report was published as well, and was available from the Government Publications Sales Office.

---

[8]   [2000] 39 I.L.M. 1285

10.20 There are now several textbooks on the Convention including Detrick's *A Commentary on the United Nations Convention on the Rights of the Child* (Dondrecht: Martinus Nijhoff Publishers, 1999), and van Bueren's *The International Law on the Rights of the Child* (Dondrecht: Martinus Nijhoff Publishers, 1993). The *Concluding Observations of the UN Committee on the Rights of the Child* (Martinus Nijhoff Publishers in association with the Raoul Wallenberg Institute of Human Rights and Humanitarian Law) has been published in a single volume edited by Holmstrom, and covering the third to 17th sessions (1993-1998). Geraldine van Bueren has also edited a very comprehensive collection of documents entitled *International Documents on Children* 2nd edn (Dondrecht: Martinus Nijhoff Publishers, 1998). Some of the documents included are not easily obtainable elsewhere.

INTERNATIONAL HUMANITARIAN LAW

10.21 Humanitarian law may be defined as that body of rules and principles that limit the use of violence in times of armed conflict. It origins may be traced back to the battle of Solferino between the Italian and Austrian armies in June 1859 in which one of the wounded was a young man called Henri Dunant. He went on to found the International Committee of the Red Cross and to organise a diplomatic conference in Geneva in 1864 at which the first Geneva Convention was adopted. This was revised and augmented on a number of occasions, but after the Second World War, it became clear that a fresh start was needed. Hence the four Geneva Conventions of 1949.

Humanitarian law treaties

10.22 Nowadays, international humanitarian law is based on four Conventions adopted at an international diplomatic conference in Geneva in 1949 and two Protocols adopted in 1977. The four Conventions are very ratified by every member state of the UN, and are as follows:

Convention (I) for the Amelioration of the Condition of the Wounded and the Sick in Armed Forces in the Field (189 ratifications).

Convention (II) for the Amelioration of the Condition of the Wounded, Sick and Shipwrecked Members of Armed Forces at Sea (1989 ratifications).

Convention (III) relative to the Treatment of Prisoners of War (189 ratifications)

Convention (IV) relative to the Protection of Civilian Persons in Time of War (189 ratifications).

The two Protocols are:

Protocol (I) relating to the Protection of Victims of International Armed Conflicts (157 ratifications).

Protocol (II) relating to the Protection of Victims of Non-International Armed Conflicts (150 ratifications).

Sources of Conventions and Protocols

10.23   The most convenient source of the texts of the Conventions and Protocols is the web site of the International Committee of the Red Cross: www.cicr.org/eng/ihl. This is an excellent web site with the texts of 91 treaties together with commentary, analysis and information about national implementation measures. The leading paper source is Roberts and Guelff, *Documents on the Laws of War* 3rd edn. (Oxford: Clarendon Press, 2000). Other useful sources include, Schindler and Toman, *The Laws of Armed Conflicts: A Collection of Documents* 3rd edn revised (Dondrecht: Martinus Nijhoff, 1988), and the International Committee of the Red Cross, *International Red Cross Handbook,* published periodically in Geneva. One of the leading texts on the subject is McCoubrey, *International Humanitarian Law: Modern Developments in the Limitation of Warfare* (Aldershot: Ashgate, 1998).

THE COUNCIL OF EUROPE

10.24   The Council of Europe was established by a statute signed in London on May 5, 1949 with the aim of achieving "a greater unity between its Members for the purposes of safeguarding and realising the ideals and principles which are their common heritage".[9] Since its foundation, the Council has concentrated largely on the promotion and protection of human rights and the advancement of democracy.[10] It has formulated and adopted several major human rights instruments including the European Convention on Human Rights (1950), the European Social Charter (1961), the European Convention for the Prevention of Torture and Inhuman or Degrading Treatment or Punishment (1987) and the European Convention on the Exercise of Children's Rights (1996). During the past ten years, with the collapse of communism and the growth of democracy in Eastern Europe, the membership of the Council of Europe has grown significantly. In late 1999, there were 41 member states. The Council is also, of course, a political body consisting of a Committee of Ministers (consisting of

---

[9]   The text of the Statute is to be found on the Internet at www.coe.fr/eng/legaltxt/le.htm.
[10]   See Quinn, "Ireland begins a Six Month Presidency of the Council of Europe" (December 1999), *Gazette of Law Society of Ireland.*

the Foreign Affairs Ministers of all member states), the Parliamentary Assembly (consisting of 286 representatives and the same number of substitutes from the parliaments of the member states), and the Congress of Local and Regional Authorities in Europe, also with 286 representatives and the same number of substitutes, and composed of two chambers, one representing local authorities and the other representing regions. Further information can be found on the Council's web site: www.coe.fr/eng/present/about.htm.

Texts of Council of Europe Treaties

10.25 As noted earlier, the Council of Europe web site has a great deal of useful information. The primary address of this site is www.coe.fr/eng/legaltxt/treaties.htm. This is the home page for Council of Europe treaties the texts of which can be accessed by way of hypertext (2.11 above). A good collection of texts will be found in *Blackstone's International Human Rights Documents* (10.10 above) and while those of main treaties will be found in a Council of Europe Publication entitled Europe entitled *Human Rights Today; European Legal Texts* (Strasbourg, 1999) which costs 120FF or 18 Euros.

General information on European human rights law

10.26 The main sources of information on selected human rights instruments of the Council of Europe will be described in the paragraphs that follow. The Human Rights Information Centre of the Council has produced an indispensable general guide called *Documentation Sources in Human Rights*. At the time of writing, the most recent edition, H(98) 1, dates from May 1998. It consists of a full and detailed bibliography of virtually everything produced by the Council in relation to human rights, including texts of decisions and judgments of the former Commission and the Court. An enormous number of documents, including the texts of resolutions, explanatory memoranda, information leaflets and conference proceedings, have been produced by the Council since its foundation, but especially in recent years. They deal with a wide range of issues including equality, racism, prisons, policing, health and medical issues, and are all listed in *Documentation Sources in Human Rights*. Some of the earlier documents are now out of print, but should be available in libraries. Much of this information will also be found on the Information Centre's web site: www.dhdirhr.coe.int but a hard copy of the guide is still very useful to have to hand when researching any human rights issue.

10.27 In terms of current information, the *Human Rights Information Bulletin* is published three times a year by the Council of Europe, both in paper and on the Internet (www.humanrights.coe.int/). One can get the paper version by writing to Directorate General II – Human Rights, Council of Europe, F-67075 Strasbourg Cedex. The recent Special Issue No 50, published to mark the 50th anniversary of the Convention, has many interesting articles, including an account of some of the legal changes made in some member states as a result of European Court decisions.

The European Convention on Human Rights

10.28   The official title of this treaty is the Convention for the Protection of Human Rights and Fundamental Freedoms, but it is better known as the European Convention on Human Rights. It was adopted by the Council of Europe in 1950 and entered into force on 3 September 1953 by which date it had been ratified by 10 states as required by Article 66.[11] The text of the Convention must now be read in conjunction with the various protocols adopted in the meantime,[12] and especially the Eleventh Protocol which made significant changes to the text and layout of the Convention. A protocol may guarantee additional rights, reform convention procedures or both. The First Protocol, for example, in force since 18 May 1954, guarantees rights to private property, education and free elections with secret ballot. The Fourth Protocol prohibits imprisonment for debt and guarantees certain rights connected with freedom of movement. The Sixth abolishes the death penalty while the Seventh provides various due process rights including the right of everyone convicted of a criminal offence to have his or her conviction reviewed by a higher tribunal. These four Protocols exist separately from the Convention and not all States Parties have ratified all of them. The Third, Fifth, Eighth and Eleventh Protocols effected changes to the text of the Convention itself. The Convention, which now consists of 59 Articles, was significantly amended by the Eleventh Protocol which entered into force on 1 November 1998. The impact of this Protocol will be considered in later paragraphs, especially those dealing with the Court of Human Rights. The Second, Ninth and Tenth Protocols no longer exist. On 26 June 2000, the Committee of Ministers of the Council of Europe adopted Protocol No 12 to the European Convention on Human Rights, and this will enter into force when 10 ratification have been received.[13] This is potentially a very important Protocol because it contains a general prohibition on discrimination based on a wide range of grounds. Strangely enough, there is no such prohibition in the main Convention itself. It is available on the web at http://194.250.50.202/Prot12/.

Text of the European Convention on Human Rights

10.29   The present text of the Convention will be found in Clements, Mole and Simmons, *European Human Rights* (10.51 below), *Blackstone's Guide to the*

---

[11] Now Article 59 of the amended text of the Convention (see para. 10.32).
[12] On the background to the Convention and its Protocols, see Beddard, *Human Rights and Europe* 3rd edn. (Cambridge, 1993), Chap. 2.
[13] See Bharania, "Who's Afraid of Protocol 12?" (2001) 151 *New Law Journal* 65.

Human Rights Act 1998 (10.52 below) and *Blackstone's International Human Rights Documents* (10.25 above). The Council of Europe's *Human Rights Today* (10.25 above) also has the full text of the Convention and Protocols, an explanatory memorandum to the all-important Eleventh Protocol, the Rules of the Court, and a chart of signatures and ratifications as they stood on 1 January 1999. It is available on the Internet at http://conventions.coe.int. If all else fails, it can be had by writing to the Council of Europe Publishing, F-67075 Strasbourg Cedex, France.

Status of the Convention on Human Rights and other European treaties

10.30 Charts setting out the state of signatures and ratifications of the Convention, its Protocols and the other main European human rights treaties are available on the Internet at www.coe.fr/eng/legaltxt/treaties.htm. A hard copy version entitled *Charts of Signatures and Ratifications of Selected Human Rights Instruments* is available from the Council of Europe. This information will also be found in Council of Europe, *Human Rights Today* (10.25 above) in respect of the Convention on Human Rights, the Convention against Torture (10.56 below), the Framework Convention for the Protection of National Minorities and the relevant Protocols to these treaties. Another useful web site is that of the Treaty Office of the Council of Europe, maintained by the Directorate General for Legal Affairs at http://conventions.coe.int. This site includes a section entitled "Recent Changes" which is updated following each signature, ratification, accession or other development in respect of any Council of Europe Treaty. By consulting this site in early July 2000, for example, we discover that Georgia signed the European Social Charter on 30 June, while France signed the European Convention on Nationality on 4 July. Given the speed of change in adhesion to treaties because of the growth in membership of the Council of Europe and the increasing number of treaties, one can no longer rely entirely on paper sources. It is necessary to check out the web site just mentioned in order to update any information otherwise available.

General information on the Convention

10.31 The Council of Europe has produced various information leaflets and booklets about the European Convention and these had be had by writing to the Council itself, although they should be available in most university and professional law libraries. The Council has also published a *Short Guide to the European Convention on Human Rights* 2nd edn (Strasbourg, 1998) which costs FF60 or about 9 Euros. More detailed information will be found in the various textbooks listed at 10.49 below, but note that any book published before 1998 may be outdated in so far as the enforcement mechanisms of the Convention are concerned.

Enforcement of the Convention

10.32   The European Convention on Human Rights is often said, with some justification, to have a more effective enforcement mechanism than any other international human rights instrument. This mechanism has changed substantially since the revised Convention (to be described below) entered into force on 1 November 1998. However, one must also be familiar with the enforcement machinery as it existed between 1953 and 1998, as the decisions and judgments issued during that period remain good law. We shall therefore deal with the old system first.

The old system

10.33   Under the old Article 24 of the Convention, one state party could lodge a complaint against another with the European Commission of Human Rights. The Commission consisted of a number of members equal to that of the state parties to the Convention, each state appointing one member. It was the body to which all complaints had to be submitted. Article 24 was seldom invoked, although there were some celebrated inter-state cases such as that taken by Ireland against the United Kingdom alleging that certain interrogation practices by the Northern Ireland security forces violated the Convention. {NOTE} The vast majority of cases were taken by virtue of old Article 25 which authorised the Commission to receive petitions from individuals or groups claiming to be victims of a violation of the Convention, provided the State against which the complaint was made had made a declaration recognising the competence of the Commission to receive petitions under Article 25. Once a petition was received under Article 25, the Commission had first to decide on its admissibility. The vast majority of admissions were declared inadmissible for one reason or another. Some, for example, failed to disclose a violation of any article of the Convention, others were out of time, and others failed to show that domestic remedies had been exhausted. Those declared admissible were then examined, and if the Commission failed to secure a friendly settlement between the parties, it issued an opinion as to whether there was a violation of the Convention. Within three months of the issue of the Commission's report, the complaint could be referred to the European Court of Human Rights by the Commission itself or by any of the relevant parties. Otherwise, it was up to the Committee of the Ministers of the Council of Europe to decide if there had been a violation of the Convention.

10.34   The European Court of Human Rights consisted of a number of judges equal to the number of member states of the Council of Europe (which could be greater than the number of state parties to the Convention). The Court's decision was final and binding, although it was up to the Committee of Ministers to supervise the execution of the Court's judgment. From the mid-1980s onwards, there was a vast increase in the number of petitions being lodged with the Commission and in the number of cases referred to the Court. In 1990 alone, for example, more cases were referred to the Court than in the first 24 years of its existence. Needless to say, from 1990 onwards, the situation got worse as many more states from Eastern Europe joined the Council of Europe and ratified the Convention. There were long delays, usually of several years, in hearing cases, which often defeated the entire purpose of the Convention. By the mid-1990s, it was abundantly clear that structural changes were needed, and these were effected by Protocol 11 which entered into force on 1 November 1998.

10.35　The best guide to changes brought about by Protocol 11 is the *Explanatory Report to Protocol No. 11 to the European Convention on Human Rights*, republished in *Human Rights Today: European Legal Texts* (10.25 above). The text of the Convention, particularly in regard to enforcement mechanisms, has undergone considerable change as a result of the Protocol. The rights remain the same, except that each Article now bears a heading, e.g. Article 5 is headed "Right to liberty and security". Perhaps the most significant change was the abolition of the Commission and the creation of a new single Court. The number of judges on the Court is equal to the number of states' parties to the Convention. They serve for a six-year period and may be re-elected. The Court will sit in committees (consisting of three judges), Chambers (consisting of seven judges) and Grand Chambers (consisting of 17 judges). The sole power of a committee will be to declare a case inadmissible or to strike it off the list. If a committee does not decide to exercise one of these powers, the application is referred to a Chamber.

10.36　Decisions on the admissibility and merits of an application will ordinarily be taken by a Chamber (Article 29). However, if a case raises a serious question affecting the interpretation of the Convention or where the resolution of the question might lead to a result inconsistent with the a previous judgment of the Court, the Chamber may relinquish its jurisdiction and refer the matter to a Grand Chamber (Article 30). The Grand Chamber has two other functions, one in relation to appeals and the other in relation to advisory opinions. Within a period of three months from the judgment of a Chamber, any party to the case may, in exceptional cases, request that the case be referred to a Grand Chamber (Article 43). A panel of five judges of the latter shall decide if the case raises a sufficiently serious issue to merit consideration. If it decides in the affirmative, the Grand Chamber shall decide the case. The Grand Chamber may also give advisory opinions in accordance with Article 47, at the request of the Committee of Ministers.

10.37　The Court may still receive and deal with inter-state applications (Article 33) and applications from "any person, non-governmental organisation or group of individuals claiming to be a victim of a violation by one of the High Contracting Parties of one of the rights set forth in the Convention or the protocols thereto" (Article 34). Since Protocol 11 came into force, states no longer have the option of accepting or rejecting the right of individual petition. This is now an integral part of the Convention. The same admissibility criteria apply save that the decision on admissibility is made by a committee or a Chamber as outlined in the previous paragraph. The Committee of Ministers is still responsible for supervising the execution of judgments. A Declaration adopted by the Ministerial Conference on Human Rights at Rome (December 3-4, 2000) called upon the Council of Ministers to pursue ways of supervising the enforcement of judgments more effectively.

10.38   From this short account, it will be clear that when investigating the jurisprudence of the Convention for the period 1953 to 1998, one must have regard to decisions and reports of the former Commission on Human Rights as well as to judgments of the Court. The judgments are, of course, the more authoritative sources, but the Commission's reports often dealt with important legal points and are widely quoted.

Primary sources of European Convention law

10.39   Following the establishment of the European Commission on Human Rights, various systems were introduced for reporting its decisions. The preliminary volume of what was to become the *Yearbook of the European Convention on Human Rights* was entitled *European Commission on Human Rights: Documents and Decisions 1955/1956/1957*. It was published by Martinus Nijhoff at The Hague in 1959. The following year, the first volume of *The Yearbook* was published which covered Commission decisions for 1958-1959. The European Court of Human Rights was set up in 1959, so from then on, the *Yearbook* covered its judgments and decisions. In 1960, the Council of Europe established a series devoted exclusively to the work of the Commission. At first, it was called *Collection of Decisions* which appeared in 46 volumes between 1960 and 1974. It was succeeded by *Decisions and Reports of the European Commission on Human Rights* published by the Council of Europe from 1975 onwards. The stated purpose of this series was to provide "complete texts of, or extracts from, the most significant decisions on the admissibility of applications as well as the Commission's Reports where they have been made public". Volumes 94A and 94B appeared in January 1999, and they seem to be the last. Three volumes of *Summaries and Indexes* of the *Decisions and Reports* have so far been published: for volumes 1 to 20 in 1981, for volumes 21 to 40 in 1987 and for volumes 41 to 60 in 1993.

European Court judgments and decisions

10.40   The case law of the European Court of Human Rights is more extensively reported. With the establishment of the Court in 1959, an official series of its judgments was launched, and published by Carl Heymanns Verlag. There were, in fact, two series. Series A carried the judgments and decisions of the Court, as well as the opinions of the Commission. At first, the practice was to publish a separate volume for each case. Series B contained the submissions of the parties, a record of the public hearing and the report of the Commission. Again, there was usually one volume for each case, though generally published several years in arrears. A case published in Series A is cited as:

Tyrer v U.K., Series A, No. 26.

However, if one were referring to a case such as this in a work that was not dealing predominantly with human rights, it would be wise to add a reference to the Court to alert the reader to the fact that this is a European case, e.g. *Tyrer v U.K.*, Eur. Ct. H.R., Series A, No 26. Indeed, it is generally helpful to include a parallel citation to the *European Human Rights Reports* (below) as these are widely available, e.g. *Tyrer v U.K.*, Series A, No. 26, (1978) 2 E.H.R.R. 1.

10.41 This series ended in 1995 with volume 329. Thereafter, the series became known as *European Court of Human Rights: Reports of Judgments and Decisions* which are cited primarily by year, with a number of volumes each year. Therefore, the judgment of the Grand Chamber in *Murray v United Kingdom*, delivered on 8 February 1996 was published in this new series at "1996–I" at page 30, and could be cited as:

Murray v U.K. ECHR, 1996-I, p. 30.

A new citation system for this series was officially adopted following the entry into force of Protocol 11 and the consequent changes made to the organisation of the Court. This new system has the following pattern: case name (in italics), application number, paragraph number of judgments, abbreviation of European Court of Human Rights, year and volume number. Furthermore, unless the judgment is one on the merits, the name of the case will be followed by an abbreviation in brackets indicating the nature of the decision or judgment involved, e.g. "(dec)" for a decision on admissibility, "[GC]" to indicate a decision or judgment of a Grand Chamber, or "just satisfaction" to indicate a case dealing with this matter. If ever there was a citation system designed by a committee, this is it! The following are examples given in the reports themselves as to how a case should now be cited:

Court judgment on merits

Campbell v Ireland, no. 45678/98, § 24, ECHR 1999-II

Grand Chamber judgment on merits

Campbell v Ireland [GC], no. 45678/98, § 24, ECHR 1999-II

Chamber decision on admissibility

Campbell v Ireland (dec), no. 45678/98, ECHR 1999-II

Grand Chamber decision on admissibility

Campbell v Ireland (dec) [GC}, no. 45678/98, ECHR 1999-II

This is the official line. One cannot help suspecting however that most people will, quite sensibly, omit the registration number, and place the paragraph number after the year and volume number. It is difficult to see what is lost by citing such a case as:

Campbell v Ireland, ECHR 1999-II, § 24.

10.42   The *European Human Rights Reports*, published by Sweet and Maxwell, first appeared in 1979-80. This series provides the English text of Court judgments together with headnotes and summaries. The first two volumes reproduced all the major judgments from 1960 onwards, beginning with *Lawless v Ireland*. All the big cases, including *Golder, Handyside, Ireland v United Kingdom,* the *Belgian Linguistic Case, Klass,* and *Airey* are to be found in these volumes. The series quickly came up to date and now provides a fast and efficient system of reporting the Court's judgments. It is cited primarily by volume number, e.g. *Hussain v U.K.* (1996) 22 E.H.R.R. 1.

10.43   Of course, the fastest and, often, the most convenient way of gaining access to the Court's recent judgments is through the Internet. The Council of Europe itself maintains an excellent web site with all the judgments of the Court. The address is: www.echr.coe.int/hudoc. This gives a complete list of judgments in reverse chronological order, so that *Lawless v Ireland* is, in fact, the last. At the time of writing, it is numbered 1428. By simply clicking on the title of the case, the full judgment will come up on the screen. Another useful site maintained by the Council of Europe lists the effects which decisions of the Court have had on the laws of states found to be in violation of the Convention. Each relevant case is listed with a short account of measures adopted by the state in question. The address for this site is: www.echr.coe.int/eng/Edocs/Effectsof Judgments.html.

Digests of case law of European Commission and Court of Human Rights

10.44   There are several digests of European human rights case law. Peter Kempees' *A Systematic Guide to the Case Law of the European Court of Human Rights* has been published in four volumes. The first two, published in 1996, cover the period 1960 to 1994. Volume 3 published in 1998 deals with the period 1995 to 1996, while Volume 4, published in 2000, covers the years 1997 and 1998. All are published by Martinus Nijhoff Publishers. This work is well produced and easy to use. It deals with the Convention and Protocols article by article, and provides of summary of all the significant decisions of the Court under each. It does cover the former Commission's decisions and reports, some of which are still valuable but remains nonetheless a reliable guide to the jurisprudence of the European Convention. Also useful is the recently-published Volume 41A of the *Yearbook of the European Convention on Human Rights* by Gilles Dutertre and Jacob van der Velde which consists of "key extracts from a selection of judgments of the European Court of Human Rights and Decisions and Reports of the European Commission on Human Rights". It is not as detailed as Kempees' work, but makes a good starting point for research on Convention case law.

10.45   Vincent Berger's *Case Law of the European Court of Human Rights* deals with the case law of the European Court on a case by case basis. It provides a concise summary of the facts and judgment in each case and, valuably, includes a bibliography of published articles and comments on the individual cases, with a comprehensive bibliography at the end of each volume. Three volumes have been published covering the years 1960 to 1987, 1988 to 1990 and 1991 to 1993. All three were published by Round Hall Press in Dublin.

10.46   The *Human Rights Digest: The European Convention System* is published six times a year by Kluwer Law International in co-operation with the British Institute of Human Rights. It covers all human developments at Council of Europe level, but from a lawyer's perspective it is most useful for its coverage of the case law of the European Convention on Human Rights.

10.47   Finally, the Council of Europe itself publishes a good deal of information, usually available free of charge, on recent developments. One particularly valuable service is the *Information Note on the Case Law of the Court* published monthly which provides an article-by-article summary of the case law for the month in question. It provides abstracts of judgments and decisions, indications of friendly settlements and so forth.

Electronic digest (Beagle)

10.48   One of the best law sites on the Internet is "Beagle", originated by Judge Sean Overend, which classifies the jurisprudence of the European Convention by article and topic. The URL is www.beagle.org.uk. It is particularly useful for locating cases on, say, Articles 5 and 6 which have generated an enormous jurisprudence. Thus, if one were looking for cases on bail under Article 5, one can simply search by that word and find the relevant case titles. By use of hypertext (2.11 above) one can locate the texts of the cases themselves.

This site allows for searches by article of the Convention, by case or by key word. It also covers the U.K. Human Rights Act 1998 and has other useful links.

Books on European Convention on Human Rights

10.49   There are many books, in several languages, on the European Convention. Obviously, no one of them can claim to be entirely up to date, because of the constant stream of judgments emanating from the Court. On the other hand, relatively few judgments make any significant contribution to the jurisprudence of the Convention, so any major textbook published within the past few years will generally provide a fairly reliable guide to the meaning of the Convention. However, anyone interested in the practical operation of the Court and the procedures for lodging an application should consult one of the books mentioned under the next heading below. Harris, O'Boyle and Warbrick, *Law of the European Convention on Human Rights* (London: Butterworths, 1995) is a magisterial piece of work, widely esteemed by human rights scholars and practitioners. It provides a detailed analysis of the entire convention with reference to the case law of the Court and the former Commission. Both the procedural and substantive aspects of the Convention are therefore well covered. The second edition of this text is due for publication shortly as is a companion volume of cases and materials by Harris and O'Boyle, also due for publication by Butterworths. Van Dijk and van Hoof, *Theory and Practice of the European Convention on Human Rights,* the most recent edition of which was published by Kluwer Law International in 1998, is also excellent. Janis, Kay and Bradley, *European Human Rights Law: Text and* Materials 2nd edn (Oxford: Oxford U.P., 2000) is a shorter work but still a good introduction. A text on the European Convention by Stephen Livingstone of Queen's University Belfast is due for publication by the Oxford University Press in 2000. Andrew Drzemczewski's *The European Human Rights Convention in Domestic Law* (Oxford U.P., 1985 and reissued in 1997) describes the status of the Convention in each of the countries that has ratified it. Blackburn and Polakiewicz (eds.), *Fundamental Rights in Europe. The European Convention on Human Rights and its Member States 1950-2000,* which is due for publication by Oxford University Press in 2001 will provide a more modern account of the domestic impact of the Convention. The chapter on Ireland is contributed by Donncha O'Connell, Director of the Irish Council for Civil Liberties.

Information for applicants and legal practitioners

10.50   Compared with the procedures to be followed when instituting legal proceedings in the Irish courts, the complaints system under the European Convention on Human Rights is quite informal. A simple letter setting out the complaint will often be sufficient to set the machinery in motion. However, applicants and their legal representatives are well advised to undertake a certain amount of research and investigation in advance. The first and most obvious point to check is that the complaint alleges a violation by a State Party of the one of the articles protected by the Convention or the Protocols. (Remember that not all States have ratified all of the Protocols). The right must have been violated by a public authority, and all domestic remedies must have been exhausted by the complainant. Certain time limits and procedural rules must also be observed. A complaint should be submitted to: The Registrar, European Court of Human Rights, Council of Europe, F-67075 Strasbourg Cedex. Information and guidance on the submission of complaints will be found on the Court's web site: http://194.250.50.200/Notices%20for%20Applicants/Notice%20eng.html or from www.echr.coe.int/eng/.general.html and clicking on "information" for persons wishing to apply to the European Court of Human Rights.

10.51 There is also an excellent book on the topic by Luke Clements, Nuala Mole and Alan Simmons, *European Human Rights: Taking a Case under the Convention*, the second edition of which was published in 1999 by Sweet and Maxwell in London. It is written specifically for those planning to make a complaint to the European Court of Human Rights, and provides a detailed account of the complaints procedure, admissibility criteria and remedies. It also includes a good description, with reference to the principal case law, of the rights protected by each of the articles and protocols. The amended text of the Convention and the Rules of Court as they stood in November 1998 are also included. Practitioners will find the precedents and draft bills of costs contained in the appendices particularly useful. There is a more general work edited by Hurst Hannum, *Guide to International Human Rights Practice* 3rd edn (Ardsley, New York: Transnational Publishers Inc., 1999) which has chapters dealing with practice before all the major human rights bodies. It provides good general descriptions, but practitioners before the European Court will certainly find Clements, Mole and Simmons (above) to be the best guide.

Incorporation of the European Convention in United Kingdom and Ireland

10.52 The European Convention on Human Rights was incorporated into U.K. law by the Human Rights Act 1998. As a result of this Act, the courts are bound to interpret legislation in such a way as to uphold the rights protected by the Convention. They may strike down subordinate legislation that is incompatible with the Convention but, because of the supremacy of parliament, may not strike down a statute. What the courts may do is to declare that a statutory provision is incompatible with the Convention which in turn will place an obligation on the political branches government to take remedial action. Equally significantly, public authorities are obliged to act in conformity with the Convention and failure to do so may lead to an action for damages by a person who has suffered as a result of that failure. As might have been expected, the incorporation of the Convention proved a major boost to the publishing industry, and it is difficult to keep track of the various "practitioner guides", to both the Convention and the Act that continue to appear. They include Baker, *Human Rights Act 1998: A Practitioner's Guide* (London: Sweet and Maxwell, 1998); Hunt and Singh, *A Practitioner's Guide to the Impact of the Human Rights Act* (Oxford: Hart Publishing) due for publication in Autumn 2001; Wadham and Mountfield, *Blackstone's Guide to the Human Rights Act 1998* (London: Blackstone Press, 1999), a particularly useful work; Clayton and George, *The Law of Human Rights* 2 vols. (Oxford: Oxford U.P., 2000). This is an expensive work, but a worthwhile investment for a practitioner. It includes not only a detailed account of the 1998 Act but also of the Convention. It analyses the Convention case law in detail and makes comparative references to rights law in New Zealand, Ireland and elsewhere. The second volume is a compendium of relevant human rights instruments, statutes and extracts from state constitutions, including Ireland's.

10.53 Many cases coming before the European Convention on Human Rights arise from criminal proceedings. The "Case and Comment" section of the *Criminal Law Review* (published monthly by Sweet and Maxwell in London) now includes European human rights cases dealing with criminal law and procedure. The comments are by Professor Andrew Ashworth, the leading expert on the topic. Due for publication shortly is a book by Professor Ashworth and Ben Emmerson, Q.C., entitled *Criminal Law and the European Convention on Human Rights* (London: Sweet and Maxwell). The Irish Government has undertaken to incorporate the European Convention into Irish law. It appears that the Convention will be subordinate to the Constitution, but that the State will be permitted to make *ex gratia* payments to applicants who succeed in proving before one of the superior courts that they have been victims of a violation of the Convention by a public authority.[14]

THE EUROPEAN SOCIAL CHARTER

10.54 The European Convention on Human Rights is devoted mainly to civil and political rights, though the Protocols protect certain rights connected with property and education. The European Social Charter, on the other hand, is devoted to the protection of social and economic rights. It was adopted in 1961, and three further protocols were added in 1988, 1991 and 1995. Finally, in 1996, a revised European Social Charter was adopted which incorporates these protocols. The revised charter entered into force on 1 July 1999 and, as of the

---

[14] *Irish Times*, February 12, 2001, p. 12.

beginning of 2001, had been ratified by nine states, including Ireland. The original Charter had been ratified by 20 other states. The enforcement mechanism of the Charter is less effective than that of the European Convention on Human Rights. For example, Part I of the Revised Charter, like that of the original Charter, contains a long list of workers' rights which states parties "accept as the aim of their policy, to be pursued by all appropriate means". Part II consists of 30 articles covering a wide range of social and economic rights. Under Part III, each party must undertake to accept Part I as a declaration of the aims to be pursued, and to consider itself bound by at least six of Articles 1, 5. 6, 7, 12, 13, 16, 19 and 20 of Part II. It must consider itself bound by other articles as well such that it is bound by not less than 16 articles or 63 numbered paragraphs. Parties must submit periodic reports under the Charter, and these reports are examined by the European Committee on Social Rights (ECSR). Collective complaints may be submitted by international and national NGOs.

10.55 The web site of the European Social Charter is at www.socialcharter.coe.int. It includes official documents, state reports on the application of the Charter, the Conclusions of the ECSR, and decisions on collective complaints. The Council of Europe publishes a newsletter on the Charter entitled *Social Rights = Human Rights* which is sometimes accompanied by a Fact Sheet. It is available on the Web at the same address. In 2000, the Council of Europe published a good introductory text, *Short Guide to the European Charter*. The leading textbook, though now dated, is D.J. Harris, *The European Social Charter* (Charlottesville: University of Virginia Press, 1984). Lenia Samuel's *Fundamental Social Rights: Case Law of the European Social Charter* (Strasbourg: Council of Europe, 1997) is more up-to-date. The Council of Europe has also published some useful guides on specific aspects of the Charter, including *Conditions of Employment in the European Social Charter* (2000) and *Equality between Women and Men in the European Social Charter* (2001).

EUROPEAN CONVENTION AGAINST TORTURE

10.56 The European Convention for the Prevention of Torture and Inhuman or Degrading Treatment or Punishment was adopted by the Committee of Ministers of the Council of Europe in 1987. It has been ratified by all (41) member states of the Council of Europe. Unlike other human rights instruments, it neither defines any legal rights nor establishes a complaints or reporting system. Instead, it establishes the European Committee for the Prevention of Torture and Inhuman or Degrading Treatment and Punishment consisting of a number of independent experts equal in number to that of the Parties. This Committee is charged with the task of making periodic and other visits to member states to examine the treatment of persons deprived of their liberty by a public authority. As such, detainees in prisons, police stations and patients involuntarily committed to hospitals come within the Committee's remit. The purpose of the exercise is to ensure, in so far as possible, that such persons are not subject to torture or inhuman or degrading treatment. Those subject to such treatment may, of course, seek redress from their own state or, ultimately, make a complaint to the European Court of Human Rights alleging a violation of Article 3 of the European Convention on Human Rights.

10.57   Under the terms of the Convention, reports forwarded by the Committee to the States visited are confidential. The Committee may, however, make a public statement if a state fails to improve specified conditions of detention or refuses to co-operate. However, a state may request publication of the Committee's report together with the state's own comments, and this in fact has become the norm. About 70 such reports have been published to date. The Committee's annual report to the Committee of Ministers is a public document. Persons working or carrying out research in this field can readily obtain the published reports. However, the Committee maintains an excellent website which includes most of its documentation to date www.cpt.coe.int/en/about.htm. It also has a CD with most of this information and that too is easily available from the Committee. Two short Protocols have recently been added to the Convention. The first opens the Convention for ratification by non-member states of the Council of Europe. The second introduces certain technical changes, such as allowing half of the Committee's membership to be renewed every two years. Most member states, including Ireland, have ratified both of them.

10.58   The paper sources of the text of the Convention and its Protocols include *Blackstone's International Human Rights Documents* and *Human Rights Today: European Legal Texts* (both at 10.25 above), the latter including the explanatory report to the Convention. Writings on the topic include Evans and Morgan, *Preventing Torture: A Study of the European Convention for the Prevention of Torture and Inhuman or Degrading Treatment or Punishment* (Oxford: Clarendon Press, 1998). The background to the Convention and its drafting are described by Cassese in "A New Approach to Human Rights: The European Convention for the Prevention of Torture" (1989) 83 A.J.I.L. 128-153. The text of the Convention (though not, of course, of the recent Protocols), the explanatory report, the proceedings of a seminar on a topic held at Strasbourg, and an extensive bibliography will be found in (1989) 10 *Human Rights Law Journal*. A short account of the Convention is given by O'Malley, "A Ray of Hope for Prisoners: The New European Convention against Torture" (1990) 9 *I.L.T.* 216.

FRAMEWORK CONVENTION FOR THE PROTECTION OF NATIONAL MINORITIES

10.59   This is one of the lesser known European human rights treaties. It was adopted in 1995 and, so far, has been ratified by 33 states, including Ireland which ratified in 1999. As the name suggests, it is devoted to protecting the rights of national minorities, and there is a strong emphasis on the protection of language rights. The enforcement procedure is set out in Article 25 which requires each party, within one year of the entry into force of the Convention in respect of itself, to submit to the Secretary General of the Council of Europe a report setting out the measures adopted to give effect to the Convention. Thereafter, reports must be submitted on a periodical basis and whenever the Committee of Ministers so requests. There is an Advisory Committee consisting of persons with recognised expertise in the field of protecting national minorities to assist the Committee of Ministers in supervising the implementation of the Convention. The text of the Convention and other information is available on the Web at http://conventions.coe.int/treaty/en/Treaties/Html/157.htm or through the Council of Europe Treaty web site at 10.30 above. The paper sources of the Convention are the same as those for the European Convention against Torture (see 10.58 above). There is also a European Charter for Regional or Minority Languages (ETS No. 148) which entered into force on 1 March 1998 and which has been ratified by 13 states though not, as yet, by Ireland.

HUMAN RIGHTS IN THE AMERICAS

10.60   The human rights system of the Organisation of American States (OAS) derives from three main sources, the Charter of the Organisation which was adopted at Bogota in 1948,[15] the American Declaration of the Rights and Duties of Man, also adopted in 1948, and the American Convention on Human Rights which was adopted at San Jose in 1969, together wits Protocols. The two principal human rights organs are the Inter-American Commission on Human Rights and the Inter-American Court of Human Rights. The Commission, based in Washington, D.C., began in 1960, and is a part-time body composed of seven members, who act in an independent capacity. They are nominated by OAS member states and appointed by the OAS General Assembly. It has several functions, the most important of which are the preparation of reports on the state of human rights in the various member states (country reports) and dealing with individual petitions (somewhat akin to the function exercised by the former European Commission on Human Rights (10.33 above). Because the Commis-

---

[15] The Charter was amended by the Protocol of Washington (1997) which allows the OAS to suspend a member state whose democratically elected government has been overthrown by force.

sion is part-time and meets for only eight weeks a year, much of its work is actually carried out by the permanent Secretariat. The OAS itself has 35 member states and four official languages: English, Spanish, French and Portuguese. Apart from the protection of human rights, the OAS also has important programmes dealing with free trade, combating drugs, promoting sustainable development and strengthening democracy. Information about these programmes can be found on its web site, the address of which is given at 10.64 below.

10.61   With the entry into force of the American Convention on Human Rights, the Inter-American Court of Human Rights was established in 1979. It is located at San Jose, Costa Rica, and is composed of seven judges who sit in a part-time capacity, and who are empowered to give advisory opinions as well as deciding contentious cases. Cases may be referred to the Court by the Commission or by a state party to the Convention. Until recently, relatively few cases were being referred to the Court, particularly by the Commission, but this is now changing. The Court has had some impact, though not as much as might have been anticipated. But given that it is still just over 20 years in existence, a fairly short time in legal history, it may well develop in the years ahead. Under the American Convention on Human Rights, the right of individual petition is obligatory – it must be accepted by member states. However, the right of inter-state petition is optional, the exact opposite of what used to be the case under the European Convention on Human Rights.

10.62   Both the Commission and the Court submit annual reports to the General Assembly of the OAS. The Commission's report includes the decisions it has taken during the year in response to individual petitions. These reports, in green-covered A4 format, are available in many libraries. The Court's judgments and decisions are published in three series. Series A contains advisory opinions and judgments, Series B contains written submissions, summaries of oral arguments and other documents, while Series C contains decisions and judgments in contentious cases. Few libraries in these islands will have all of this documentation, but it should be recalled that important decisions and judgments of the Commission and the Court, and other OAS documents are likely to be reproduced in publications such as *International Legal Materials* (9.16 above), *International Law Reports* (9.17) and, occasionally, in the *Human Rights Law Journal* (10.72)

10.63   Publications of the OAS are usually available in English and Spanish. The work of the Inter-American Commission on Human Rights since its foundation is charted in a number of works published by the OAS in Washington, D.C.. First, there was a three-volume work, *The Organisation of American States and Human Rights* covering the decade 1960-1970. This was followed by *The Inter-American Commission on Human Rights: Ten Years of Activities 1971-1981*, published in 1982. The *Inter-American Yearbook on Human Rights* began in the late 1960s, and is now published in two annual volumes covering in detail the work of both the Commission and the Court of Human Rights. There are some retrospective volumes covering the periods 1960-1967, 1968 and 1969-70. For the electronic sources, see immediately below.

Electronic sources of Inter-American human rights law

10.64 The OAS has a web site providing general information about its history and activities, with links to more specific sites. The address is www.oas.org/en/ . The web site of the Inter-American Commission on Human Rights has a wide range of documents and reports at www.cidh.oas.org/spanish.htm. If this produces Spanish text, just click on English in the list of languages at the top of the document. Meanwhile, the University of Minnesota Human Rights Library has excellent pages devoted to the Inter-American Court of Human Rights at www.umn.edu/humanrts/iachr/iachr.html. If any of these addresses proves difficult to access, just use a search engine to find the University of Minnesota web site, and proceed from there.

Books on human rights in the Americas

10.65 The best introductory account is the chapter on the American system of human rights in Thomas Buergenthal's *Human Rights in a Nutshell* 2nd edn (St Paul, Minn: West, 1998). *The Inter-American System of Human Rights* (Oxford: Clarendon Press, 1998) edited by David Harris and Stephen Livingstone is an outstanding piece of work. It contains a good selection of essays on the American system, embracing both legal and political perspectives. Reproduced in the appendices are all the primary documents including the Charter of the OAS, the American Declaration on the Rights and Duties of Man, and the American Convention on Human Rights with its protocols. Other useful works include Scott Davidson's *The Inter-American Human Rights System* (Aldershot: Dartmouth Publishing, 1997) and Thomas Burgenthal and Dinah Shelton, *Protecting Human Rights in the Americas*, 4th edn (Kehl, Germany: N.P. Engel, 1995). During the past twenty years or so, several Latin American countries have been making the transition from dictatorship of one kind or another to democracy. A great deal has been written about this process. One particularly interesting book is *Transition to Democracy in Latin America: The Role of Judiciary* (Boulder: Westview Press, 1993) edited by Irwin P. Stotzky. It includes some very interesting essays, many of them by leading US judges and academics, on the role of the judiciary in democratic systems.

HUMAN RIGHTS IN AFRICA

10.66 The African Charter on Human and People's Rights was adopted in

Nairobi, Kenya in June 1981 by the Organisation of African Unity and entered into force on 21 October 1986. From a cultural perspective, the Charter is of particular interest because, in addition to the usual civil and political rights found in other international instruments, it sets out individual duties and collective rights. Article 27, for example, states that "every individual shall have duties towards his family and society, the State and other legally recognised communities and the international community". It establishes a commission, the African Commission on Human and Peoples' Rights which is responsible for enforcing the Charter through the investigation of communications submitted to it, principally by states, and the preparation of reports on its findings. For several years after the establishment of the Charter, many commentators and activists were dissatisfied with its effectiveness, although this seems to have improved in recent years. In 1998, there was adopted a Protocol on the Establishment of an African Court on Human and Peoples' Rights which is open for signature and ratification or accession by any state party to the Charter. Cases may be submitted to the Court by state parties, the African Commission on Human and Peoples' Rights and African intergovernmental organisations.[16] However, when ratifying the Protocol or at any time thereafter, a state shall make a declaration accepting the competence of the Court to receive cases from NGOs with observer status before the Commission and from individuals. The Court may not however entertain such a case involving a state party until the state in question has made the necessary declaration.[17]

10.67 Another fairly recent addition to African human rights law is the African Charter on the Rights and Welfare of the Child (1990). This Charter sets out a wide range of children's rights similar in many ways to those contained in the UN Convention on the Rights of the Child (10.19 above), but with some provisions clearly inspired by regional considerations. Article 26, for example, specifically guarantees protection against *Apartheid* and discrimination. The Charter is open for signature and ratification by member states of the Organisation of African Unity, and entered into force in November 1999. Its enforcement is entrusted to the African Committee of Experts on the Rights and Welfare of the Child (Art. 32). Each state party must submit periodic reports to the Committee setting out the steps being taken to give effect to the Charter[18] (again similar to the reporting requirements under the UN Convention on the Rights of the Child). The Committee may also receive communications from any person, group, NGO, member state or the United Nations in respect of any matter covered by the Charter. The Committee has broad powers of investigation although compared with, say, the European Court of Human Rights, its enforcement powers are very limited.

---

[16] Art. 5.1.
[17] Arts 5.3 and 34.6.
[18] Art. 43.

Texts of African human rights documents

10.68   The text of African Charter on Human and Peoples' Rights will be found in the collections of human rights documents by Brownlie and Ghandi described at 10.10 and 10.11 above. It is also reproduced in (1982) 21 *International Legal Materials* 58 and in Appendix 2 of Ankumah's *The African Commission on Human and Peoples' Rights: Practice and Procedure* (London: Martinus Nijhoff Publishers, 1996). Ghandi's book also includes the texts of the Protocol on the Establishment of an African Court and the African Charter on the Rights and Welfare of the Child. The best web site on human rights in Africa is www.umn.edu/humanrts/africa/index.htm.

Secondary material on African human rights law

10.69   Evelyn Ankumah's book, mentioned in the previous paragraph, contains a good, critical account of the African Charter and Commission as they operated up until the year of publication, 1996. It also has a valuable bibliography. Other good accounts are provided by U.Oji Umozurike, *The African Charter on Human and People's Rights* (The Hague: martinus Nijhoff, 1997) and W. Benedek, "The African Charter and Commission on Human and Peoples' Rights: how to make it more effective" (1993) *The Netherlands Quarterly of Human Rights* 30. Books on all aspects of African law, including human rights law, are distributed by African Books Collective (ABC) which has several member publishers. Its web site address is www.africanbookscollective.com.

SECONDARY SOURCES OF HUMAN RIGHTS LAW

10.70   The following are lists of selected books, periodicals and bibliographies dealing with international human rights law in general. More specific bibliographies have been given earlier in relation, for example, to the European Convention on Human Rights, (10.49), the UN Human Rights Committee (10.14) and humanitarian law (10.23)

Introductory texts

10.71 Thomas Buergenthal, *International Human Rights in a Nutshell* 2nd edn (St. Paul, Minnesota: West, 1998).

J. Donnelly, *International Human Rights Law* 2nd edn (Boulder, Colorado: Westview Press, 1998).

A.H. Robertson and J.G. Merrills, *Human Rights in the World: An Introduction to the Study of the International Protection of Human Rights* 4th edn (Manchester: Manchester U.P., 1996).

P. Sieghart, *The Lawful Rights of Mankind* (Oxford: Oxford UP, 1985). Paperback edition, 1986.

Rebecca Wallace, *International Human Rights: Text and Materials* (London: Sweet and Maxwell, 1997).

More detailed texts

10.72 Henry J. Steiner and Philip Alston, *International Human Rights in Context: Law, Politics, Morals. Text and Materials* (Oxford: Clarendon Press, 1996).

Philip Alston (ed.), *The United Nations and Human Rights: A Critical Appraisal* (Oxford: Clarendon Press, 1992). This includes good essays on the various human rights organs of the United Nations.

Philip Alston (ed.), with M. Bustelo and James Heenan, *The EU and Human Rights* (Oxford: Oxford UP, 1999).

Philip Alston (ed.), *Promoting Human Rights Through Bills of Rights* (Oxford: Clarendon Press, 1999).

Philip Alston (ed.), *The Future of UN Human Rights Treaty Monitoring* (Cambridge: Cambridge University Press, 2000).

Hurst Hannum (ed.), *Guide to International Human Rights Practice* 3rd edn (Ardsley, NY: Transnational, 1999).

Theodor Meron (ed.), *Human Rights in International Law: Legal and Policy Issues* 2 vols. (Oxford: Clarendon Press, 1984).

Frank Newman and David Weissbrodt, *International Human Rights: Law, Policy and Process* (Cincinnati, Ohio: Anderson, 1996).

Carlos S. Nino, *The Ethics of Human Rights* (Oxford: Clarendon Press, 1991)

Michael O'Flaherty, *Human Rights and the U.N.: Practice before the Treaty Bodies* (London: Sweet and Maxwell, 1996).

Periodicals

10.73 Articles, case notes and commentaries on human rights issues are nowadays to be found in a wide range of journals, especially those wholly or partly devoted to public law. They are likely to become more prevalent once the European Convention on Human Rights is incorporated into the domestic law of all the jurisdictions in these islands. There are many journals devoted entirely to human rights of which the following are merely a few. The *Human Rights Quarterly*, currently published by Johns Hopkins University Press, is one of the leading journals in the field. It has been known by its present title since Volume 3 (1981). Before that, it was known as *Universal Human Rights*. The *European Human Rights Law Review* has been published six times a year by Sweet and Maxwell (London) since 1996. The *Human Rights Law Journal* is published by Engel in Kehl in association with the International Institute of Human Rights in Strasbourg. It includes scholarly articles as well as a wide variety of other information – texts of leading documents, case reports and material from the European Parliament. There are several national and university-based journals devoted to human rights e.g. *Israel Yearbook on Human Rights*, the *Netherlands Quarterly of Human Rights,* the *Canadian Human Rights Yearbook,* the *Columbia Human Rights Law Review*, the *Harvard Human Rights Law Journal* and the *New York Law School Journal of Human Rights*. An *Irish Human Rights Yearbook 1995* was published by Round Hall Sweet and Maxwell for the Irish Human Rights Centre at NUI, Galway. It is anticipated that this will shortly become an annual publication. It has already been noted that the *Criminal Law Review* (10.53 above) carries regular commentaries on judgments of the European Court of Human Rights in respect of criminal cases.

Encyclopaedia

10.74 Edward Lawson's *Encyclopaedia of Human Rights* 2nd edn (New York and London: Taylor & Francis Inc., 1996) is a major 1900-page compilation of human rights material arranged by subject. It includes the texts of many human rights instruments and has extensive bibliographies arranged by both subject and country, although Ireland is not particularly well treated. It also provides extensive information on both intergovernmental and non-governmental organisations.

Bibliographies

10.75 Several of the leading works already mentioned, including Lawson's *Encyclopaedia*, most of the books edited by Alston (10.71above) and Newman and Weissbrodt's *International Human Rights* (*ibid.*) contain extensive bibliographies. Entries on human rights will be found in the various indexes and bibliographies mentioned in Chapter 7 above. The most recent one-volume bibliography appears to be Carrtington's *Human Rights: A Bibliography* (New York: Nova Science Publishers, Inc., 2000). There are some older ones which may still be useful occasionally, such as Friedman and Sherman (eds.), *Human Rights: An International and Comparative Law Bibliography* (Westport, Connecticut: Greenwood Press, 1985).

Principal human rights treaties ratified by Ireland.

10.76 International Covenant on Economic, Social and Cultural Rights (8 Dec. 1989)

International Covenant on Civil and Political Rights (8 Dec. 1989)

First Protocol to Covenant on Civil and Political Rights (8 Dec. 1989)

Second Protocol to Covenant on Civil and Political Rights (18 June 1993)

Convention on the Elimination of All Forms of Racial Discrimination (29 Dec. 2000)

Convention on the Elimination of All Forms of Discrimination Against Women (23 Dec. 1985)

Optional Protocol to the Convention on the Elimination of All Forms of Discrimination Against Women (8 Sept. 2000).

Convention on the Rights of the Child (22 Sept. 1992).

Genocide Convention (June 22, 1976)

Slavery Convention (June 18, 1950)

Convention relating to the Status of Refugees (October 1, 1954)

Convention on the Political Rights of Women

Convention on the Nationality of Married Women (November 25, 1957)

The Four Geneva Conventions on Humanitarian Law

The two Protocols to the Geneva Conventions on Humanitarian Law

The European Convention on Human Rights (February 25,1953)

Protocols 1, 4, & 6 to the European Convention on Human Rights

The European Social Charter (Revised) (July 5, 1999)

The European Convention for the Prevention of Torture (March 14, 1988)

The (European) Framework Convention for the Protection of National Minorities (June 7, 1999).

CHAPTER 11

United States Law

STRUCTURE OF GOVERNMENT

11.01   The United States of America is a federal jurisdiction, which means that there are several legal systems operating side by side. The federal or national government based in Washington DC has responsibility for certain matters such as national government taxes, immigration and naturalisation, printing money, control of postal systems, control of the armed forces and the declaration of war. It exercises these and many other powers over the entire country. Additionally, each of the states has its own government and legal system with control over certain other matters. The federal government has complete control over the District of Columbia (DC), and its actual power over the states is more extensive that a strict reading of the federal Constitution might suggest. A concise account of the US legal system is provided by Walker in *The Oxford Companion to Law* (Oxford, 1980) under the heading "U.S.A. law". A more detailed and modern account is provided by Jay M. Feinman, *Law 101: Everything You Need to Know about the American Legal System* (New York: Oxford UP, 2000). Further information on the sources of US law is provided by the books listed at 11.29 below.

FEDERAL SYSTEM

11.02   The powers of the federal government are set out in the Constitution of the United States which was drawn up at Philadelphia in 1787 and entered into force in 1789. The federal government is divided into three branches: the legislature, the executive and the judiciary. The United States is often said to provide the best example of the separation of powers. The legislature is known as Congress and consists of the House of Representatives and the Senate. The Senate has two representatives from each of the fifty states while the number of members elected from each state to the House of Representatives depends on population. Congress is responsible for the making of federal law, and the Executive is responsible for its implementation. The Executive is headed by the President of the United States, together with the Vice-President and the various Secretaries of State who make up the cabinet. The President has, of course, assumed and acquired many other powers over the years and is much more than a mere executor of congressional law. The federal judiciary consists of the nine members of the US Supreme Court (also based in Washington DC), the federal Court of Appeal, the federal District Court and judges of other specialised federal courts.

THE STATES

11.03 Each state has its own legal system largely similar in structure to the federal system. Each has its own constitution, legislature, executive and judiciary. The boundary between the powers of the states and those of the federal government is seldom a matter free of controversy. The 10th Amendment of the US Constitution reads:

> The powers not delegated to the United States by the Constitution, nor reserved by it to the States, are reserved to the States respectively, or to the People.

In theory, therefore, the states have power over every matter that is not expressly consigned by the Constitution to the Federal Government. In reality, the power of the Federal Government is very extensive, especially in areas of public law and finance. Still, there are many areas of law over which the states have control. Each has its own law of contract, property, tort, business transactions and so forth. Each has its own criminal code, although there is also a federal criminal code dealing with crimes involving federal interests.

SOURCES OF US LAW

11.04 The primary sources of both federal and state law are constitutions, legislation and case law. There are also many specialised agencies, but we shall concentrate here on the three primary sources because they are likely to be of most interest to lawyers on this side of the Atlantic.

Constitutions

11.05 The text of the Constitution of the United States, which consists of seven articles and 27 amendments, is included in several leading textbooks and casebooks on US Constitutional law, and in *Constitutions of the Countries of the World* (New York: Oceana, 1971-1974). It is also widely available on the Internet. Two valuable sites are: http://caselaw.findlaw.com/data/constitution/articles.html which provides annotations to the text of each article, and www.law.emory.edu/FEDERAL/usconst.html which also includes the text, with commentary, of draft amendments which have been submitted to the states, but have not been ratified. Before the advent of the World Wide Web, the texts of state constitutions were sometimes difficult to locate, although they are available in *Constitutions of the U.S.: National and State* (New York: Oceana, 1974-75). Now, there are electronic versions of them available on the Internet at www.findlaw.com . Click on "State Cases and Codes".

Statutes

11.06   Again, it is necessary to distinguish between federal and state law. In most jurisdictions, however, including the federal system, statutes become available in three forms. Shortly, after being enacted, a statute is issued as a "slip law", meaning as a single document. Later, all the statutes enacted during a congressional or legislative session are issued in volumes, known as session laws, in which statutes are arranged chronologically according to the date on which they were enacted. The session laws of the US Congress are known as the *Statutes at Large*. Finally, statutes are issued in code form. Codes, which are the most widely available of the three forms, arrange statutes according to subject matter. Often different sections of a statute will appear under different sections of a code. The *United States Code* is the official version of the federal code. There are also two unofficial codes published commercially, which are particularly useful because of their annotations. They are the *United States Code Annotated (USCA)* published by West, and the *United States Code Service (USCS)* published by Lawyers Co-op. The *United States Code* is divided into 50 sections, known as Titles. Thus, Title 2 deals with Congress, Title 3 with the President, Title 18 with crimes and criminal procedure, Title 21 with food and drugs, Title 50 with War and National Defence. The commercially-produced, annotated codes, the *USCA* and *USCS*, follow the same pattern.

11.07   Like the Irish and U.K. parliaments, the United States Congress enacts both public and private laws, the latter dealing with particular individuals or localities. Private laws are not, however, included in the codes. Public law statutes are cited by reference to congressional session during which they were passed and the chronological number of the statute during that session. Thus, the Comprehensive Crime Control Act of 1984 is cited as *Pub. Law No. 98-73* (the 73rd statute enacted during the 98th congress). Lengthy statutes are often divided into broad parts or, indeed, more specific statutes, known as Titles, in the same way as the codes. So, Title II of the Comprehensive Crime Control Act is the Sentencing Reform Act 1984. Or, to take a better-known example, Title VIII of the Civil Rights Act 1968 deals with the removal of discrimination in housing policy. As noted earlier, the laws for a congressional session are later published in volumes known as the *Statutes at Large*. A statute in one of these volumes is referred to by volume and initial page number. The Freedom of Information Act 1967 is referred to as 80 *Stat.* 383, i.e. beginning at page 383 of the Volume 80 of the *Statutes at Large*. Once published, the *Statutes at Large* become the authoritative texts of the statutes they contain, superseding the slip laws. But to complicate matters further, certain titles of the *United States Code* have been re-enacted as law by congress, so these Titles provide the authoritative texts of the statutory provisions in question.

Federal Statutes on the Internet

11.08   Few libraries in Ireland or, indeed, in Britain have extensive collections of U.S. statutory law. Fortunately, however, a great deal of it is now available on the Internet. The U.S. Code is available electronically from a number of sources, one of the more helpful being the Legal Information Institute at Cornell University. For users in these islands, this site can be accessed via Warwick University at http://liiwarwick.warwick.ac.uk/uscode/. In it, each of the 50 sections of the code is listed by number and name and each is searchable. Furthermore, if one already has a reference, such as "42 U.S.C. 2000aa" for sections of the Privacy Protection Act 1980, one simply types "42" and "2000aa" in the boxes provided, and that section of the Code will come up on screen. The code is also among the documents available at www.netlizard.com/yourlaw/55fed.htm. The U.S. Government Printing Office has a web site entitled *U.S. Code: Helpful Hints,* which describes how to use the code and understand its abbreviations and citations. The address is www.access.gpo.gov/su_docs/aces/desc007.html. The U.S. Congress web site, known as Thomas (in honour of Thomas Jefferson) has a document describing how U.S. laws are made: http://thomas.loc.gov/home/lawsmade.bysec/publication.html. New editions of the Code are published every six years, and cumulative supplements are published at the conclusion of each regular session of Congress. The texts of more recent laws are also available on the Internet. The Congress web site has all the recent legislation at http://thomas.loc.gov/ . This site also provides access to the Congressional Record (essentially the same as parliamentary debates in these islands) and to Committee reports for recent years. Finally, it should be noted that U.S. statutes are often known by popular names such as the Sherman Act or the Mann Act. The web site of the Legal Information Institute at Cornell (see above) has a table of popular names which enables one to get direct access to the relevant legislation.

FEDERAL CASE LAW

11.09   Federal case law consists primarily of the judgments and decisions of the United States Supreme Court, the United States Courts of Appeals and the United States District Courts. Our main concern here is with the reported case law. One point to note about the United States Supreme Court is, that no matter how important the case, the lawyers presenting each side are confined to 30 minutes for their oral presentations, although extensions are occasionally granted by the Court. Cases are taped as they are presented; that practice began many years ago. Some of the tapes have been published. For example, in 1993, the Free Press in New York produced a collection of cassettes with the transcripts of 23 live recordings of oral arguments and judicial questioning in leading cases such as *Gideon v Wainwright* 372 U.S. 335 (1963), *Miranda v Arizona* 384 U.S. 436 (1966), *Roe v Wade* 41 U.S. 113 (1973) and *United States v Nixon* 418 U.S. 683 (1974). The six cassettes are accompanied by a book setting out the text as well as background information. The entire collection is entitled *May It Please the Court* and is edited by Peter Irons and Stephanie Guitton. Because there is so little time for oral argument, the written submissions made to the Court in advance of the hearing are crucially important. There are published series of these briefs, although few libraries in these islands would have them. There is, however, on series entitled *Landmark Briefs and Arguments of the Supreme Court of the United States.* Some are now being published on the Internet as well at www.oyez.com which also provides access to tape recordings. Summaries of legal arguments are given in the *Supreme Court Reports: Lawyer's Edition* (see 11.10 below).

United States Supreme Court

11.10 The judgments of the Supreme Court are published in several formats, the three most important print series being the *United States Supreme Court Reports,* the *Supreme Court Reporter* and the *Supreme Court Reports, Lawyer's Edition.* The first of these, commonly known as the *U.S. Reports,* is the official series, as it is commissioned by Congress. Most American courts require citation to this series when reference is being made to a Supreme Court case. The others are equally accurate, but they are published commercially, *Supreme Court Reporter* by West and the *Lawyer's Edition* by Lexis Law Publishing. The *U.S. Reports* started in 1790 and became official in 1817. Until 1874, they were known by the name of the official reporter (rather like the Irish and English nominate reports described at 6.16 above). Thus, *Marbury v Madison* (the leading case on judicial review of legislation, decided in 1803) was reported at 1 Cranch 137. Nowadays, however, the citation includes the volume number of the US Reports as well, so this case would be cited as *Marbury v Madison* 5 U.S. (1 Cranch) 137 (1803). From volume 91 onwards, they have been cited simply as: *Powell v Texas* 392 U.S. 514 (1968), and all the earlier volumes were retrospectively renumbered, as illustrated by the reference just given for *Marbury v Madison.* Just for the record, the names of the reporters for the first 90 volumes (1789 to 1874) were as follows, with the standard abbreviations in parentheses:

Name	Volumes of U.S. Reports
Dallas (Dall)	1 – 4
Cranch	5 – 13
Wheaton (Wheat)	14 – 25
Peters (Pet)	26 – 41
Howard (How)	42 – 65

Black	66 – 67
Wallace (Wall)	68 – 90.

11.11   The *Supreme Court Reporter*, published by West, begins with volume 106 of the *U.S. Reports*. It is abbreviated as "S. Ct." and cited by reference to volume and initial page number, e.g. *Roe v Wade* 93 S. Ct. 705 (1973). The *Lawyer's Edition* contains all Supreme Court decisions since 1791 with summaries of the arguments of counsel and other annotations. It is cited as "L.Ed.", e.g. *Roe v Wade* 35 L. Ed. 2d 147 (1973). It is customary to cite a U.S. Supreme Court case by reference to all three series, beginning with the official reports, e.g.

Roe v Wade 410 U.S. 113, 93 S. Ct 705, 35 L.Ed.2d 147 (1973).

There is usually a considerable time lag before judgments appear in these three series, especially the *U.S. Reports*. The *U.S. Law Week*, a loose-leaf publication, generally provides the full text of Supreme Court decisions within a week or two of their release. Nowadays, however, the quickest way of getting them is on the Internet, and the relevant web sites will be described presently.

Meaning of "2d"

11.12   One often sees "2d" as part of an American or Canadian case citation. It simply stands for "second series". Sometimes, when a report series reaches a certain volume number, say 300, it begins afresh with a new series, "2d", starting again with volume 1. The *U.S. Reports* have never done this, but when the *Lawyer's Edition* reached volume 100, it started a second series. So, *Morisette v New York* is cited as 96 L.Ed 288 (1952), while *Patterson v New York* is cited as 53 L. Ed 2d 281 (1977).

Supreme Court Cases on the Internet

11.13   The Internet has some outstanding sites devoted to the U.S. Supreme Court. The best of these is *Findlaw: Supreme Court Opinions* (www.findlaw.com/casecode/supreme.html) which is a searchable database of all decisions since 1893. It is an excellent site and can be searched by volume and initial page number of the *U.S. Reports*. One need only insert these numbers in the boxes provided to bring the full text of the case up on the screen. Thus, to read or print out *Roe v Wade*, simply type 410 in the first box, and 113 in the second. One can also search by year, and by title. When searching by title, it is often sufficient to indicate the name of either party. The Legal Information Institute at Cornell University (LII) also has an excellent site (www.law.cornell.edu/federal/opinions.html) with nearly all opinions issued since May 1990. There is another web site devoted to very recent opinions:

www.supremecourtus.gov/opinions/opinions.html. This currently lists all opinions for the 1999 term by name and date. By simply clicking on the name, the full text comes up on screen. When dealing with the US Supreme Court, remember that the term begins in October of one year and ends 12 months later. The 1999 term began on October 4, 1999 and ended on October 1, 2000. Therefore, many opinions of the 1999 term were in fact issued in the year 2000. The sites just mentioned can also be accessed through various search engines and portals. The best way is through Yahoo, www.yahoo.com (see 2.09 above). Scroll down through the Yahoo menu, and under the general heading "Government", click on "Law". Then, under "Categories", click on "US Judiciary and Supreme Court". Once this site is entered, one can, by way of hypertext, enter any of the Supreme Court sites mentioned above.

11.14   As noted, *Findlaw* lists U.S. Supreme Court opinions since 1893. To get earlier opinions, one must consult the printed volumes of the *U.S. Reports* or the *Lawyer's Edition*. However, there is a valuable web site entitled *Selected Historical Decisions of the Supreme Court* which gives the text of many leading pre-1893 cases such as *Marbury v. Madison* (1803). The URL is http://supct.law.cornell.edu/supct/cases/name.htm. There is another site entitled *Specific Cases* found through the Yahoo site which, at last count, had 74 entries. This includes cases which, for one reason or another, are particularly important or happen to be in the news. For example, when the film *Amistad*, was being shown in cinemas, someone helpfully provided the text of the actual case (40 U.S. 518 (1841) on the Internet and it will be found under the *Specific Cases* heading. Both of the web sites mentioned can easily be accessed through *Yahoo* by following the steps outlined in the previous paragraph. Another interesting collection of historic Supreme Court decisions is provided by the 'Lectric Law Library', one of the Internet's more entertaining law sites, at: www.lectlaw.com/tcas.htm.

Other federal case law

11.15   Immediately below the Supreme Court in the federal system is the U.S. Court of Appeals which is divided into 12 circuits, including the District of Columbia Circuit. There is, in addition, a Federal Circuit that deals with patent and customs cases. Apart from the District of Columbia, the entire country is divided into 11 circuits. The First, for example, consists of Maine, Massachusetts, New Hampshire, Rhode Island and Puerto Rico. The Second consists of Connecticut, New York, and Vermont; and so on throughout the fifty states. The Court of Appeals wields considerable authority in all aspects of federal law. Remember that only a small percentage of appeals to the Supreme Court are actually granted a hearing. Below the Court of Appeals is the U.S. District Court, a federal court of first instance. There is no official reporting series for either the Court of Appeals or the District Court. Instead, decisions and judgments are reported in series published by West. Between 1894 and 1897, West published *Federal Cases* which contained about 20,000 federal Appeals and District Court decisions from 1789 to 1880. In 1880, it began to publish the *Federal Reporter* which included decisions of both of these courts. In 1932, it established a further series, the *Federal Supplement*, devoted to District Court cases. The present situation is that the *Federal Reporter* carries Court of Appeals cases as well as decisions of a few other courts, while the *Federal Supplement* carries selected decisions of the U.S. District Court. Needless to say, only a small proportion of District Court cases are formally reported.

Citation of federal reports

11.16   A case reported in the *Federal Reporter* is cited as:

> *Kramer v United States* 408 F.2d 837 (8th Cir. 1969).

Note, again, that this is in the second series (2d) of the *Federal Reporter.* A case reported in the *Federal Supplement* is cited as:

> *Mitchell v Untreiner* 421 F Supp. 886 (Fla. 1976)

The information in parentheses tells us that it was decided in Florida in 1976.

Federal cases on the Internet

11.17   Some cases from all of the Circuits are now available free of charge on the Internet. The best source is the Legal Information Institute at Cornell University (www.law.cornell.edu/federal/opinions.html) which lists all the circuits giving the years for which opinions are available in each case, as well as indicating alternate sites. Findlaw at www.findlaw.com/casecode/courts/index.html is also useful. There are some web sites devoted to particular circuits. For example, Emory University (www.law.emory.edu/10circuit/) has hosted a site for 10th Circuit opinions from 1995 to October 1997. From October 1997 onwards, the service is provided by Washburn University School of Law. However, the Cornell site remains the best and most comprehensive, as it covers all the circuits. Some subscription services are also available, in the United States at least, which go back further. Versuslaw, for example, has some federal appeal cases going back to 1950 (www.versuslaw.com) but one must pay to get access to it.

STATE CASE LAW

11.18   As in the federal system, judicial decisions of the states are published in both official and unofficial reports, the official reports being the authoritative version. The leading commercially-produced series is West's *National Reporter System* which will be explained presently as it is often to be found, in part at least, in Irish and British law libraries. In most states, the official reporters include appellate decisions only. Some of the larger states have separate series devoted to decisions of the intermediate courts. A typical citation for a state report would be:

State v Almeda 189 Conn. 303

This case is reported at page 303 of volume 189 of the *Connecticut State Reports*.

West's National Reporter System

11.19 This series publishes most of the decisions of the appellate courts of the 50 states, an enormous body of case law. To make it more manageable, the Reporter system divides the country into seven regions as follows:

Atlantic Reporter (abbreviation A) covers Maine, Vermont, New Hampshire, Connecticut, Pennsylvania, Delaware, Maryland, Rhode Island, New Jersey.

Northeastern Reporter (abbreviation N.E) covers New York, Illinois, Indiana, Massachusetts and Ohio.

North Western Reporter (abbreviation N.W.) covers Michigan, Wisconsin, Minnesota, Iowa, North Dakota, South Dakota, Nebraska.

Pacific Reporter (abbreviation P) covers Montana, Washington State, Oregon, Idaho, Wyoming, Kansas, Oklahoma, Utah, Nevada, Colorado, California, New Mexico, Arizona, Alaska, Hawaii.

South Western Reporter (abbreviation S.W.) covers Texas, Arkansas, Kentucky, Tennessee, Missouri.

Southern Reporter (abbreviation S) covers Florida, Alabama, Mississippi, Louisiana.

South Eastern Reporter (abbreviation SE) covers Georgia, South Carolina, North Carolina, Virginia and West Virginia.

West also publishes two special reporters for New York and California. The *New York Supplement* (abbreviated as N.Y.S) covers all New York Supreme and intermediate appellate cases. Incidentally, the highest court in New York is the Court of Appeals, not the Supreme Court. The *California Reporter* (abbreviated as Cal. Rptr.) covers a similar range of cases from California. A case reported in one of the Reporters is cited as:

People v Bryant 100 N.E.2d 598 (1951)

However, the citation to the official state reports is usually included as well, e.g.

People v Bryant 409 Ill. 467, 100 N.E.2d 598 (1951)

This case was decided in 1951, reported in volume 409 of the Illinois State Reports, beginning at page 467, and also in the 100th volume of the *North Eastern Reporter*, 2nd series, beginning at page 598. Other examples would be:

Elmore v State 269 Ind. 532, 382 N.E.2d 893 (1978)
Bell v Commonwealth 220 Va. 87, 255 S.E.2d 498 (1979)

The first of these cases was decided in Indiana, the second in Virginia. The National Reporter system sometimes carries judgments not found in official state reports. Thus, the citation

State v Williams 395 A.2d 1158 (Me. 1978)

means that the case is to be found in volume 395 of the *Atlantic Reporter*, 2nd series, and was decided in Maine in 1978.

Electronic sources of state cases

11. 20   For researchers on this side of the Atlantic, LEXIS and Westlaw are the most convenient sources of American state case law. Some of it is now becoming available on the Internet as well, although few of the relevant web sites have material extending back more than a few years. Once more, the best source is the Legal Information Institute at Cornell University (www.law.cornell.edu/opinions/html#state) which lists all the states and by clicking on the relevant name, one can discover and access whatever is available by way of case law.

DIGESTS OF U.S. CASE LAW

11.21   If one had access to a major law library, the best way of finding U.S. case law on any topic would be to consult the *American Digest* system. In reality, outside of America, the best of way of drawing up a case list is by gaining access to LEXIS which has extensive online libraries and search facilities for both the federal system and the states. There are many digests of state law, regional law and federal law, e.g. the *Supreme Court Digest* and the *Federal Practice Digest*. However, the most comprehensive is the series of *Decen-*

nial Digests published by West. These run to hundreds of volumes and provide an index of all the case law of the United States with headnotes. The following are the main units of this Digest system, each unit running to between 25 and 50 volumes.

Years	*Digest Unit*
1658-1896	Century Digest
1897-1906	First Decennial
1907-1916	Second Decennial
1916-1926	Third Decennial
1926-1936	Fourth Decennial
1936-1946	Fifth Decennial
1946-1956	Sixth Decennial
1956-1966	Seventh Decennial
1966-1976	Eighth Decennial
1976-1981	Ninth Decennial (Part 1)
1981-1986	Ninth Decennial (Part 2)
1986-1991	Tenth Decennial (Part 1)
1991-1995	Tenth Decennial (Part 2)
1995-2000	Eleventh Decennial (Part 1)*

* Projected.

ENCYCLOPAEDIAS

11.22   The two major encyclopaedias of United States law are *American Jurisprudence 2d* and *Corpus Juris Secundum.* Many Irish and British libraries stock one or other of them. They are quite similar, the main difference being that they are published by different companies. *American Jurisprudence* (often abbreviated as *Am. Jur.*) is published by Bancroft-Whitney/Lawyers Coop, while *Corpus Juris Secundum* (often abbreviated as *C.J.S.*) is published by West. It should be noted that both of these encyclopaedias use pocket parts, which are not a common feature of Anglo-Irish legal publishing. Inside the front or back cover of each volume, there are paperback inserts that are frequently updated. Therefore, when using any volume with a pocket part, one should first consult the text of the main volume on the topic being researched, and then turn to the equivalent section of the pocket part to discover any recent developments. Both encyclopaedias have several index volumes with subject and case indexes. There are topical indexes within each volume. So, for example, under "Negligence", there is an index of more specific headings. In terms of content, the encyclopaedias give a concise account of the law on each topic covered, together with extensive reference to cases and statutes. It is this reference material which constitutes the main value of the encyclopaedias for the researcher.

11.23   In 1983, West published a short, 12-volume encyclopaedia entitled *Guide* *to American Law – Everyone's Legal Encyclopaedia.* As the title suggests, it is primarily concerned with giving an introduction to American law, but some international and comparative law is also covered. There are many short articles by leading American legal scholars and good accounts of many leading cases. The second volume, for example, has an essay by Louis Pollak on *Brown v Board of Education* 347 U.S. 483 (1954), the leading case on racial desegregation in schools.

11.24   The *American Law Reports (A.L.R.)* are, in fact, a set of law reports somewhat akin to West's National Reporter System, but they serve a different purpose. There are two series, *American Law Reports (A.L.R)* and *American Law Reports, Federal (A.L.R. Fed.)*, the latter having been first published in 1969. Unlike, the National Reporter system, which aims to report most state cases, the *A.L.R.* concentrates on certain cases which it regards as particularly important, and subjects them to detailed annotations. In a sense, therefore, it resembles an encyclopaedia as much as a law report series, except that, unlike, an encyclopaedia, it does not claim to provide a comprehensive coverage of the law, as its content depends on the actual cases decided.

CASE CITATORS

11.25   Although case and statute citators are essential tools of U.S. legal research, they will be described very briefly here as they are unlikely to be available to many Irish lawyers. The process of using citators is known as "Shepardizing", because the leading series of citators are known as *Shepard's Citations*. At first sight, a citator may seem incomprehensible, consisting as it does of closely-printed columns of letters and numbers. In fact, they are remarkably easy to use. What a citator will not give, as a rule, is the name of a case. It is necessary to have the citation in terms of the volume and page number before consulting a citator. So, to take a fictitious case, suppose one wished to trace the history of *Brown v Kelly* 987 U.S. 345. From this citation, we know that it was reported in volume 987 of the *U.S. Reports*, beginning at page 345. One would therefore begin by finding the set of *Shepard's Citations* for the Supreme Court. Then find the volume and page where volume 987 of the *U.S. Reports* is treated. The look for a heading in bold type saying **345**. What one will find is something like this:

345

993US 342
f876 F2d123
j995US325
d996US786
c897F2d123

o997US346

It will be noted that each entry in this column is, in fact, a case citation. They are all cases in which *Brown v Kelly* was considered in some way. What matter most are the small letters preceding each citation: **f** means followed; **e** means explained; **j** means mentioned in a dissent; **c** means criticised; **o** means overruled; **d** means distinguished. Obviously, one must look out especially for **o** because it means that the cited case (*Brown v Kelly* in this instance) has been overruled by a citing case (997 US 346, which is a later decision of the U.S. Supreme Court). There are many different series of *Shepard*, dealing with federal law, state cases, state statutes and so forth. In fact, nowadays, there is an easy way of shepardizing U.S. Supreme Court opinion on the Internet. When one brings up the text of a Supreme Court case on Findlaw, one will notice near the top left-hand corner two notices, one saying Cases citing this case: Supreme Court, the other, Cases citing this case: Circuit Courts. Using this service, one can easily trace the subsequent history of the case in question. There is also a useful web site of Supreme Court decisions overruled by subsequent decisions (www.access.gpo.gov/congress/senate/constitution/scourt.html). This is also available on the *Yahoo* Supreme Court page (see 11.13 above).

SECONDARY SOURCES

Books

11.26 The number of law-related books published annually in the United States is enormous. Many of the legal and general bibliographies mentioned in Chapter 7 cover books published in the United States as well as in other English-speaking countries. For law students and practitioners in Ireland, the most valuable and accessible U.S. law books are casebooks, treatises and hornbooks. In a U.S. law school, the casebook is the main text used for teaching purposes. There are casebooks on virtually every area of law from agricultural law to water law. A casebook will typically include key extracts from all the important cases relevant to the subject, extracts from academic commentaries and copious references to additional cases and materials. Casebooks do not, as a rule, aim to give a comprehensive account of the law in the sense of describing every relevant legal rule and provision. Their primary purpose is to provide a well-chosen selection of case extracts to illustrate fundamental principles and to provoke discussion and analysis. For Irish readers, casebooks are valuable compilations of important judgments, especially those of state courts, which can otherwise be difficult to obtain. A treatise is comprehensive account of a particular area of law, while a hornbook is a shorter treatise written as a student text. As in so many other areas, the Internet is now a great source of information on American law books. All the leading publishers such as West and Foundation Press have their catalogues online. Barnes and Noble, the leading book-seller, has probably the biggest online catalogue followed closely by Amazon. Also, as mentioned earlier (7.05), one can browse through the online catalogues of leading U.S. law schools, and they are likely to have everything of any value that has recently been published.

Legal periodicals

11.27   There are hundreds of legal periodicals published in the United States. They include university law reviews, bar association journals, and subject-specific journals. Virtually every law school produces at least one law review, the bigger ones produce several. Most of them appear in at least four issues a year, some of them have up to nine, which are later cumulated in one or more annual volumes. Law reviews are edited entirely by students; this is one of the peculiarities of the American system. Membership of a law review editorial board or, better still, being an editor-in-chief or case note editor, is a considerable academic achievement and therefore much sought after. It is generally awarded on the basis of a draft case note or other piece of writing completed in the first or second year of the law degree programme. The basic U.S. law degree is the J.D. (*Juris Doctor)* equivalent to the B.C.L. or the LL.B. here. There are various sites on the Internet listing U.S. law reviews and journals. In fact, the most convenient source of information for this purpose is the list given at the beginning of each issue of the *Index to Legal Periodicals and Books* (7.23 above) which is stocked by most law libraries. There is a similar work entitled *Current Law Index* which seems to be more U.S.-oriented, and is not found in many Irish or British libraries. As noted earlier (2.15 *et seq.* above), LEXIS has very good search facilities for periodical material as well. For a list on law journals on the Internet (though not all of them have their contents online), see www.yahoo.com/Government/Law/Journals.

Dictionaries and reference books

11.28   The leading U.S. law dictionary is *Black's Law Dictionary*, published by West and now in its seventh edition (1999). It is, among other things, an excellent source of information on the meaning of Latin words and phrases. Another useful work is *West's Legal Desk Reference* (1990) which has a wealth of information, including definitions of about 10,000 legal terms and phrases, selected statutes and court decisions, and much else besides. Wests's *Legal Thesaurus /Dictionary* has over 125,000 entries, while the Mellinkoff's *Dictionary of American Legal Usage*, also published by West in 1992, is helpful to those writing for American publications. Another dictionary sometimes cited is *The Leff Law Dictionary: A Fragment*. This work was cut short by the untimely death of its author, Professor Arthur Leff of Yale Law School. At the time of his death, the dictionary extended from "A" to "Chiltern Hundreds", and the text was published in the *Yale Law Journal*, Volume 94, No. 8 (July 1985). It provides some very detailed definitions, some of which are mischievously comprehensive. For example, the final paragraph of the first entry, "A", reads:

> In legal hypotheticals, "a", usually capitalised, is ordinarily one of the important parties, with a composite personality more aggressive than that of any other letter, e.g. "A hits B", "A offers to B" and so on. Cf. b, c, ...z.

Further reading on sources of American law

11.29 There are many books on this topic, but the following are particularly useful:

> Morris Cohen and Kent C. Olsen, *Legal Research in a Nutshell* 7th edn (St. Paul, Minn: West Group, 2000).
>
> Stephen Elias and Susan Levinkind, *Legal Research: How to Find and Understand the Law* 6th edn (Berkeley, California, Nolo Press, 1998).
>
> Robert C. Berring and Elizabeth A. Edinger, *Finding the Law* 11th edn (St Paul, Minn: West Group,1999).
>
> Yvonne J. Chandler, *Guide to Finding Legal and Regulatory Information on the Internet* (New York: Neal-Schuman, 1998).
>
> Robert Watt, *Concise Legal Research* 3rd edn (Annandale, NSW: Federation Press, 1997). This has a chapter on U.S. law.

New editions of all of the above books are likely to be published from time to time.

CHAPTER 12

Commonwealth Law

12.01   There is a growing interest among Irish lawyers in the law of certain Commonwealth countries, especially Australia, Canada and New Zealand. Ireland has much in common with these countries including a language (English), a legal system (the common law) and, in some cases, a written constitution. Indeed, it is interesting to note that the Privy Council which has the same membership as the House of Lords (6.20 above) is sometimes called upon to adjudicate on the constitutionality of certain legislative provisions in those Commonwealth countries which allow for an appeal to the Privy Council, an exercise which has traditionally been alien to the British constitutional tradition itself. This chapter will concentrate on Australia, Canada and New Zealand, the three countries that are of most interest for comparative purposes. Furthermore, we shall concentrate largely on sources of case law, again because they are the more likely sources to be consulted in order to find a variety of judicial perspectives on fundamental common-law principles. Law reform commission documents from these countries are always worthy of study as well.

12.02   Before dealing individually with our three chosen jurisdictions, mention should be made of a particularly valuable law report series which began in 1985, the *Law Reports of the Commonwealth* (LRC). The editorial policy is to collect together in five annual volumes law reports that "will travel" in the sense of having a wide comparative interest. Reports are included from many different commonwealth countries including some smaller ones the official reports of which are unlikely to be found in many foreign libraries. There are usually alphabetical and subject indexes in each volume. Another useful publication, also found in many libraries, is the *Commonwealth Law Bulletin,* begun in 1974, which appears in four substantial parts a year. It summarises legislation, judicial decisions and law reform documents from many Commonwealth countries. It is cited as .... (1992) 18 C.L.B. 123. The *Annual Survey of Commonwealth Law* was published from 1965 to 1977 and contained essays on legal developments in Commonwealth countries.

AUSTRALIA

12.03   Australia is a federation which means that users of Australian legal materials must be careful to distinguish between laws and judicial decisions made within the federal system on the one hand, and on the other, in the states, of which there are six, and the territories, of which there are two. It must be said at the outset that Australia has been in the vanguard of the electronic revolution in so far as the provision of legal materials is concerned. The Australian Legal Research Institute (ww.austlii.edu.au) has blazed a trail in terms of providing vast amounts of well-organised primary and second sources free of charge on the Internet. Indeed, the main British and Irish system, *Bailii*, appears to have been inspired by the Australian initiative. Australia has also been to the fore in devising neutral citation systems described at 3.30 above, and to which we shall return presently.

12.04   Australian courts may be divided into two broad categories: Commonwealth courts, and state and territory courts. The High Court of Australia is the country's most senior court. It has original as well as appellate jurisdiction, but foreign lawyers are most likely to be interested in its appellate judgments. It may hear appeals from other federal courts, from courts exercising federal jurisdiction (as state courts are allowed to do in certain circumstances) and from state supreme courts. The Federal Court of Australia, the next in the hierarchy, was created in 1976 and began work in early 1977. It, too, has original and appellate jurisdiction. There are also some specialised Commonwealth courts such as the Family Court of Australia and the Industrial Relations Court of Australia. Each state and inhabited territory has its own court structure typically consisting of a Supreme Court, an intermediate appellate court and various trial courts.

Legislation

12.05   Few libraries in these islands have comprehensive collections of Australian legislation in paper form. However, a good deal of modern legislation, both Commonwealth and state, is now available on the AustLII database (12.03 above). It includes, for example, all commonwealth acts consolidated in 1973 and all later Commonwealth acts since 1973. The same database has an extensive collection of consolidated legislation from the states and territories.

Case law

12.06   The leading law report series, and the one found in most libraries, is the *Commonwealth Law Reports* (CLR) which began in 1903. It contains judgments of the High Court and is well indexed with several cumulative indexes, the first of which covers the first 150 volumes from 1903 to 1982 and the later ones covering shorter periods. Cases reported in this series are cited primarily by volume number, e.g.

Ramsay v Watson (1961) 108 C.L.R. 642

Another useful series, also found in many Irish and British libraries, is the *Australian Law Journal*. This is a journal with articles and news items, but it also includes some law reports in each issue, rather like the *Irish Law Times and Solicitors Journal* of old. However, the law reports are paginated and indexed separately, and in some libraries are bound separately from the remainder of the journal. Otherwise, the law reports are usually bound together at the back of the individual volumes. It is also cited primarily by volume number, e.g.

Van Leeuwen v R (1981) 55 A.L.J.R. 726.

Butterworths publish a more general series entitled *Australian Law Reports* (ALR) which include High Court reports and other federal decisions. This series, begun in 1973, is a continuation of the *Australian Argus Law Reports* (1960-1973) and the *Argus Law Reports* (1895-1959). The present series also includes reports of the Supreme Courts of the Australian Capital Territories and the Northern Territory.

12.07   There are also some specialist series of law reports, including *Administrative Law Decisions,* begun in 1976 and cited as (1983) 7 ALD 83 in the case of a law report, and (1983) 7 ALN 4 in the case of a note, *Australian Criminal Law Reports,* begun in 1979 and cited as (1981) 5 A. Crim R 34, and *Australian Company Law Reports*, begun in 1974 and cited as (1987) 12 ACLR 336. There are various consolidated indexes to these series. Each of the states has a law report series, e.g. the *New South Wales Law Reports* (NSWLR), the *Victorian Reports* (VR), *South Australian State Reports* (SASR), *Queensland Reports* (Qd R), *Western Australian Reports* (WAR), and *Tasmanian Reports* (Tas. R).

Electronic Reports and neutral citation

12.08   In order to facilitate the publication and later citation of electronic law reports, the High Court of Australia has facilitated a method of citing reports in a neutral way when the decision has now been reported in a printed series. First, it has adopted the practice of laying out judgments in numbered paragraphs. Secondly, it has allowed for the citation of cases by year, court and judgment number, e.g.,

Crimmins v Stevedoring Industry Finance Committee [1999] HCA 59

This means that the judgment was delivered in 1999 by the High Court of Australia (HCA), and that it is the 59th case in which judgment was delivered that year. If referring to a specific paragraph of the judgment, say paragraph 21, one writes " ...... [1999] HCA 59 at [21]".

As already noted, the web site of the Australian Legal Research Institute contains a wealth of material of which the following is but a sample:

High Court of Australia decisions from 1947
Federal Court decisions from 1977
Australian Competition Tribunal decisions from 1997
Refugee Tribunal decisions from 1993
Supreme Court of New South Wales decisions since 1995
Supreme Court of the Northern Territory decisions since 1986
Supreme Court of Victoria decisions since 1998
Supreme Court of Tasmania decisions since 1987.

The web site address is: www.austlii.edu.au.This is one address that should certainly be bookmarked. The High Court database is especially valuable, not least because it extends back to 1947. LEXIS has an extensive range of Australian legal materials. AUSMAX, the first file in the library, is a good starting point as it covers a wide range of Australian case law.

Law Reform Commission documents

12.09   Many law reform commission documents and related material are also available on the internet. The best site is maintained by the Council of Australian and New Zealand Law Reform Agencies which was established in 1996. By means of this site, one can gain access to the web site of virtually any law reform body in Australia and New Zealand. The address is http://home.vicnet.net.au/~lawref/council.htm.

Digests

12.10   The *Australian Digest* is a collection of case digests and related research tools. It describes itself as "a library in miniature of the Australian Law Reports and Periodicals since 1825". The third edition, begun in 1988, is the most recent. It is published by the Law Book Company in loose-leaf volumes, with updated material added as necessary. The same company publishes the *Australian Legal Monthly Digest*. Butterworths publish *Australian Current Law* which began in 1963. It appears monthly with cumulative annual volumes in loose-leaf format. It is in five parts, the most substantial being the current law digest, the others being mainly indexes and tables.

CANADA

12.11   Canada is a federation of ten provinces. There are also two territories for which the Federal Government has direct responsibility. Canadian public law has been of particular interest to Irish lawyers since the 1982 when a Charter of Rights and Freedoms was adopted as part of the Constitution Act of that year. There are several books on the Canadian legal system, one of the more recent being Fitzgerald and Wright, *Looking at Law – Canada's Legal System* 5th edn (Butterworths, 2000). A great deal of background information is also available free of charge on the Internet. The Supreme Court maintains a particularly useful site at www.scc-csc.gc.ca/aboutcourt/system/ which includes a detailed account of the judicial system. That system is a rather complex one as it involves both federal and provincial courts

12.12 The federal courts are the Supreme Court of Canada, established in 1875, the Federal Court of Canada, established in 1971 and the Tax Court of Canada, established in 1983. The Federal Court has both a trial division and an appeal division. Each province has its own set of trial courts and superior courts with extensive jurisdiction. As in Ireland, all members of the Canadian judiciary are drawn from the legal profession and they enjoy security of tenure. The Supreme Court of Canada consists of a Chief Justice (currently the Honourable Beverley McLachlin) and eight puisne judges.

Statutes

12.13 With statutes as with case law, a distinction must be drawn between federal and provincial law. Federal legislation is published in both annual volumes and in revised volumes. The same system is followed in most of the provinces. A good deal of modern legislation, provincial and federal, is now becoming available on the Internet. For example, the *Consolidated Statutes of Canada* are now available at: www.canada.justice.gc.ca .When seeking revised statutes of the various provinces, try the web site www.qp.gov/. For example, the revised statutes and consolidated regulations of British Colombia will be found at www.qp.gov.bc.ca/statreg/ while those of Alberta will be found at www.qp.gov.ab.ca/ . They are constantly updated. If unsuccessful in accessing any of these sites, one can always use a good search engine such as Google (www.google.com), typing in the name of the Province (Alberta, British Colombia, Manitoba, New Brunswick, Newfoundland, Nova Scotia, Ontario, Prince Edward Island, Quebec, or Saskatchewan) and "legislation" or "statutes". The two territories are the Northwest Territories and Yukon.

Case law

12.14 Many libraries in these islands stock one or more series of Canadian law reports. The *Canada Supreme Court Reports* have been published in one form or another since 1876 and are the official series with the texts of judgments in both England and French. They are abbreviated as "S.C.R." and are available on the Internet from 1985 onwards at: www.lexum.umontreal.ca/csc-scc/en/. Alternatively, one can just use a search engine to find the Supreme Court of Canada and proceed from there. The *Canada Federal Court Reports* have been published since 1971, and cited as .... [1991] 2 CF 117. There is a commercially produced series, the *National Reporter*, established in 1974, which appears quickly and includes judgments of both the Supreme Court and Federal Court.

Dominion Law Reports

12.15 The various series of the *Dominion Law Reports* are found in many libraries. This series includes leading decisions of both federal and provincial courts. It has been in existence since 1912 and is divided into an Old Series, New Series, Second Series, Third Series, and Fourth Series. It appears in several parts and bound volumes a year and has an excellent indexing service. When using it, however, it is important to bear in mind that it contains only a selection of cases and cannot be relied upon to report all the decisions of any one court, even the Supreme Court. The *Dominion Law Reports* since 1912 are available on LEXIS (Canada library).

Provincial Reports

12.16 Each of the provinces and territories now has its own law report series although, rather surprisingly, many of them have only begun since the early 1970s. Only very big law libraries are likely to stock these reports. A complete list, with dates, is given in Watt's *Concise Legal Research* 3rd edn (Sydney: The Federation Press, 1995) at p. 134. The *Ontario Reports*, for example, a Butterworths publication, have been published in their present form since 1974 and are now in their third series. They are published in parts 50 weeks a year. There are also two major series of selected reports. The *Western Weekly Reports,* begun in 1912, includes reports from Alberta, British Colombia, Manitoba, Saskatchewan and the territories. The *Atlantic Provinces Reports*, begun in 1975, includes reports from New Brunswick, Newfoundland, Prince Edward Island, and Nova Scotia.

Canadian Rights Reporter

12.17 This is a reporting service published by Butterworths which is devoted to decisions and reports of the Canadian courts under the Charter of Rights and Freedoms. It contains a selection of edited cases and digests of others. There are ten parts a year, and a cumulative index is published annually.

LEXIS

12.18 LEXIS has a reasonably good collection of Canadian case law, including Supreme Court reports since 1876 and, as noted, the *Dominion Law Reports* since 1912. When searching, it is always useful to use the CANCAS file which is a group file of reported and unreported Canadian cases.

Specialist reports

12.19   There are several series of specialist reports, e.g. *Reports of Family Law, Canadian Criminal Cases* and *Criminal Reports,* the last-mentioned of which includes articles as well as reports.

Abridgements and digests

12.20   The *Canadian Abridgement* is available in over 50 bound volumes with several supplements. It is divided into about 120 subject titles, and digests almost all reported federal and provincial decisions with the exception of civil law cases from Quebec, and is updated quarterly. There are two encyclopaedic digests. The *Canadian Encyclopaedic Digest (Ontario)* 3rd edn, published in 34 loose-leaf volumes, is a compilation of the federal laws of Canada and the provincial laws of Ontario organised by subject matter. The *Canadian Encyclopaedic Digest (Western)* 3rd edn covers the laws of Alberta, British Columbia, Manitoba, Saskatchewan and the territories.

Indexes and citators

12.21   *Canadian Case Citations 1876-1990*, published in ten volumes by Carswell, provides a service similar to the *Current Law Case Citator* in England and Wales. *Canadian Current Law* is published in three parts:

> *Case Law Digest* (12 times a year) containing case digests, words and phrases, and a general index.
>
> *Legislation* (eight times a year)
>
> *Canadian Legal Literature* (eight times a year).
>
> *Canadian Case and Statute Citations* is published separately in 12 issues a year.

Law Reform Commissions

12.22   Canada has several very active law reform commissions, and their work has occasionally influenced recommendations of the Irish Law Reform Commission. Most of these commissions now have web sites. The Law Reform Commission of Canada has a particularly good site which contains many of its more recent reports and discussion papers. It can be found at www.lcc.gc.ca/en/.

Law Journals

12.23   The better-known Canadian law journals are *Canadian Bar Review, McGill Law Journal, Manitoba Law Journal, Osgoode Hall Law Journal, Ottawa Law Review, Queen's Law Journal, Alberta Law Review, Canadian Business Law Journal, Canadian Journal of Family Law*. The contents of these and many others are listed in *Canadian Legal Literature* (12.21 above) and *Index to Canadian Legal Literature*. Many are also included in the *Index to Legal Periodicals and Books* (7.23 above).

NEW ZEALAND

12.24   New Zealand is a constitutional monarchy with Queen Elizabeth II, represented by the Governor-General, as head of state. It has a single chamber parliament, the House of Representatives, with 120 members. New Zealand does not have a written constitution in the form of a single document. Instead, its constitution, rather like that of the United Kingdom, consists of a combination of key statutes, judicial decisions and constitutional conventions. The statutes include the Constitution Act 1986, the New Zealand Bill of Rights 1990, the Human Rights Act 1993 and the Treaty of Waitangi (1840) which deals with the relationship between the government of New Zealand and the Maori people. There is also a Waitangi Tribunal for that purpose.

12.25   The principal courts are the District Court, High Court and Court of Appeal. There are also some specialist courts such as the Maori Land Court, the Environment Court and the Land Court. New Zealand is one of those Commonwealth countries which still allows appeals to the Privy Council (which sits in London) in relation to certain matters. Judgments of the New Zealand Court of Appeal always make interesting reading for lawyers in other common-law jurisdictions, particularly in core areas such as tort, contract and criminal law. Useful books on the legal system include: McDowell and Webb, *The New Zealand Legal System: Structures, Process and Legal Theory* 2nd edn (Wellington: Butterworths, 1998) and Greville, Davidson and Scragg, *Legal Research and Writing in New Zealand* (Wellington: Butterworths, 2000). Margaret Greville, a co-author of the latter text and a law librarian, has an excellent document on the Internet entitled "An Overview of New Zealand Law", dating from March 2000. It includes a list of leading textbooks on New Zealand law as well as a detailed account of primary sources. It is at : www.llrx.com/features/nz.htm . The Ministry of Justice web site (at 12.30 below) also has some helpful material. Further information about the courts can be found at www.courts.govt.nz/courts/.

Legislation

12.26   Statutes are published in pamphlet form at first and then in annual bound volumes. Some electronic versions are available and can be accessed through the "Knowledge Basket" at www.knowledge-basket.co.nz/. However, the two better ones, published by Brooker's and Status, are available on subscription only.

Case law

12.27   This is the source lawyers in other jurisdictions are most likely to use. There are several series, all of which are clearly described in a web site created by the University of Waikato Law Library at: www.waikato.ac.nz/lawlib/deci-sions/lrptinfo.html (entitled "Directory of Decisions - Law Report Series"). The series most commonly found in Irish and British libraries, *New Zealand Law Reports* (NZLR), has been published since 1883 and is available on LEXIS since 1958. Some libraries may have the *District Court Reports* (DCR) published under their present title since 1980,and available on LEXIS since 1997. However, the series began in 1939 and was known until 1979 as *Magistrates Courts Decisions* (MCD). There are four main law publishers in New Zealand: Butterworths, Brooker's, CCH and Legislation Direct. Between them, they publish a large number of specialist law reports, many of which have begun during the past twenty years or less. They include *Criminal Reports of New Zealand* (CRNZ), published by Brooker's since 1993, *Employment Reports of New Zealand* (ERNZ), published by Brooker's since 1991, *Family Reports of New Zealand* (FRNZ), published by Brooker's since 1983, *Human Rights Reports of New Zealand* (HRNZ), published by Brooker's since 1995, and *New Zealand Company Law Cases* (NZCLC), published by CCH New Zealand since 1981. Some report series incorporate both Australian and New Zealand decisions, such as the *Australian and New Zealand Equal Opportunity Cases* (EOC) published by CCH Australia since 1984.

Digests and Encyclopaedia

12.28   There is a relatively new encyclopaedia, begun in 1993 and not yet fully completed, entitled *The Laws of New Zealand*. It is a loose-leaf publication, also available on CD-ROM. Until this began, the main reference work was the *Abridgement of New Zealand Law* in 16 main volumes with annual supplements. However, it digests only those cases reported in the *New Zealand Law Reports*. The main current awareness service is *Butterworth's Current Law,* which appears twice a month. This is also available on LEXIS in the New Zealand library under NZCL. However, the indexing system of the *New Zealand Law Reports* is very efficient and generally up-to-date, and makes an excellent reference system.

Law journals

12.29   A full list of law journals will be found at http://library.canterbury.ac.nz/law/ . The *New Zealand Law Journal*, begun in 1928 is largely practice-oriented. Leading academic journals include the *Otago Law Review*, and the *New Zealand Universities Law Review*. There are two retrospective indexes of legal writings published by the Legal Research Foundation: Northey (ed.), *Index to New Zealand Writing 1954-1981*, and Palmer (ed.), *Index to New Zealand Writing 1982-1985*. The *Index to Legal Periodicals and Books* (7.23 above) should be consulted for more recent writings.

Electronic sources

12.30   When searching for electronic sources anywhere in the Southern Hemisphere, it is always best to begin with AustLII. As yet, few primary sources of New Zealand law are available free of charge on the Web. However, there is a database for the Court of Appeal which contains all decisions released by that Court since 1998. To find them, it is best to enter www.austlii.edu.au and then follow "links", "World", "Countries", "New Zealand". The Ministry for Justice has an excellent web site at www.justice.govt.nz. Click on "Publications" which contains a the full texts of many documents and reports on a variety of areas, but especially criminal law. As noted earlier, LEXIS has a reasonably good New Zealand library with Court of Appeal judgments since 1958 and some material from other courts as well as *Butterworths Current Law*. Other useful web sites include those of the New Zealand Human Rights Commission (www.hrc.co.nz) and the Legal Information Institute of New Zealand (www.liinz.org.nz).

CHAPTER 13

Researching a Legal Topic

13.01 The approach to be adopted towards researching a legal topic depends on the nature of the problem to be solved. Sometimes, a lawyer or student will simply need to track down a case, a statute or other legal document for which they have the name but not the citation. At other times, they may need to know if a particular case has been followed or overruled, or if a statute has been amended or judicially interpreted, or if there are any recent academic writings on a particular topic. More commonly, however, they will simply want to find out what the law is, whether in relation to a case with which they are dealing, or a topic they have been assigned to research. In that event, they must first identify the primary legal materials, i.e. statutes, statutory instruments and case law. They may then find it helpful to consult books, articles, reference works and other secondary materials. Nowadays, the ease with which a topic can be researched depends considerably on the range of electronic resources at the researcher's disposal. Throughout this chapter, each section will begin by describing the various paper sources which are still the most reliable. The various electronic services are also indicated.

The scope of research

13.02 One of the first questions to be addressed when researching a legal topic is how widely the research should extend. In other words, should the research be confined to Irish law or should it also embrace English or European Union law or, perhaps, the laws of other countries? The answer obviously depends on the purpose and the nature of the research itself. When researching a common-law area such as contract or tort, it is almost invariably necessary to examine English as well as Irish law, because of the close connection between the two. The same is true of many aspects of administrative law and criminal law. Other areas, such as family law and labour law are more statute-bound, so one is more likely to concentrate on the Irish law itself. Even so, many Irish statutes are modelled in part at least on British precedents, so some English case law may still be relevant. What can seldom be ignored nowadays is the law of the European Union which is likely to be relevant to any topic touching on economic relationships between parties or between the individual and the State. Likewise, the law of the European Convention on Human Rights is likely to be relevant when dealing with any rights-based issue, and its relevance will obviously increase once the Convention is incorporated into Irish law. Finally, of course, one should never underestimate the value of comparative research into the laws of other jurisdictions, especially common-law jurisdictions. Electronic sources are now rendering the laws of the United States, Canada, Australia and New Zealand more accessible than ever before

LOCATING LEGAL MATERIALS

Finding a case by citation or by name

13.03   Finding a case for which one has the citation or name should be simple enough. If one has the citation of case without the name, one can identify the report series by checking one of the many lists of law report abbreviations available in most libraries. Sources include the first volume of *Halsbury's Laws of England*, Raistrick's *Index of Legal Citations and Abbreviations*, *Current Law Monthly Digest* and *Irish Current Law Monthly Digest*. Abbreviations for many current law report series are given in Appendix 2 of this book. Difficulties are most likely to be encountered with older reports, especially the nominate reports (6.16 above) with their unfamiliar citations. The best source for these (and indeed, for all citations) is Raistrick's *Index*. A shorter list of older Irish report series, with abbreviations, is given at the end of *Murdoch's Dictionary of Irish Law* while some of the English law dictionaries, such as Curzon's *A Dictionary of Law* 2nd edn (London: Pitman, 1983), have short lists of English nominate reports. So, if one finds a citation such as "(1856) 23 Beav. 195", one should know straight away that it is a nominate report. One can check Raistrick's *Index* or, if that it not to hand, the index of abbreviations in *The Digest* or *Halsbury*. It so happens that this particular abbreviation is given in Curzon's *Dictionary* as well. It stands for *Beavan's Reports*, published between 1838 and 1866. The next matter to be checked is whether these reports are included in the *English Reports* (6.17 above). One can do this by checking the chart accompanying these reports, if it is available. Obviously, if one had the name of the case in question, which happens to be *Kell v Charmer*, one would begin by checking the index of cases in volumes 177 and 178 of the *English Reports* , because if *Beavan* has been reprinted in this series (as it has been in Volume 53 at p. 76), one can find the case straight away in the relevant volume.

13.04   Finding the citation of a case for which one has the name alone, but not the citation or perhaps even the jurisdiction, may be more problematic. The name itself may provide some clue to the jurisdiction, although this is not an infallible guide. For example, *McLoughlin v O'Brian*[1] and *O'Brien v Gillespie*[2] may sound like Irish cases, when in fact the first is a decision of the House of

---

[1]   [1983] A.C. 410.
[2]   (1997) 41 N.S.W.L.R. 549.

Lords and the second a case from New South Wales. Unless one knows the jurisdiction in which a case was decided, the best starting point is the most recent case index of *The Digest* (6.43 above). Here one will find the name of virtually every English case as well as many from other common-law jurisdictions. Failing this, one could check through the various Case Citators in the *Current Law Service* (6.48 above). If there is reason to believe the case may be Irish, check through the case indexes (*including* tables of cases judicially considered) in the various *Irish Digests*, the two bound volume indexes to *Irish Law Reports Monthly* which cover the period 1976 to 1995, the case lists in *Irish Current Law* (both year books and monthly digests) from 1995 onwards, and the Red, Green and Blue indexes (4.73 *et seq.* above). When consulting these reference works, remember to consult not only the table of cases actually digested or reported, but also the table of cases judicially considered, as the latter table is usually far more extensive. It generally gives a citation for each case listed, which is what we are looking for. Often, of course, the fastest way to find a case citation is to consult the table of cases in a standard, up-to-date, textbook, assuming one has some idea of the area of law involved. Generally, one can be confident that standard texts such as those by Casey, or Kelly, Hogan and Whyte on the Constitution (4.10 above), McMahon and Binchy on torts, McAuley and McCutcheon, or Charleton, Bolger and McDermott on criminal law, Clark on contract or Shatter on family law[3] will list every case relevant to those areas. If one has access to electronic sources such as LEXIS or the JUSTIS version of the *Irish Reports*, one can simply type in the name as a search term, and if the case is any way modern, the data base in question should either have the text or some reference to it.

Find statutes by name and year

13.05   Finding statutes, whether by year or by name, is seldom a problem. Obviously, if one has the year of a British or Irish statute passed in the past two hundred years or so, one simply consults the relevant volume of the U.K. or Irish statutes (6.06 and 4.18 above). Even at a time when British statutes were cited by regnal year, the calendar year was usually given on the spine or title page of the annual volumes. If one has the regnal year only, one must work it out from a list of regnal years such as those given in Walker's *Oxford Companion to Law* or Raistrick's *Lawyers' Law Books* (7.07 above). So, if the reference is to 23 & 24 Vic. c. 12. One must calculate that the statute was passed in the 23rd and 24th years of the reign of Queen Victoria who ascended to the throne in 1837. The Act is the 12th passed in the parliamentary session in question.

13.06   If one has the name of an Irish statute, but not the year, say "the Suc-

---

[3]   See book list in Appendix 4 of this book for the full titles and publication details of the books mentioned.

cession Act", the best way of checking out the date (or dates, as there may be several statutes of the same name) is use the search facility on the *Irish Statute Book* on the Attorney General's web site or on the equivalent (CD). The name of the statute will generally indicate the area of law involved, so again, one could safely rely on a standard textbook. Any one of Professor Wylie's standard texts on land law, conveyancing law or landlord and tenant law, for example, will give the year for the Succession Act (for the record, it's 1965). In case the statute has been passed very recently, check through the *Irish Current Law Year Book* for recent years and *Irish Current Law Monthly Digest* for recent months. Remember, too, that there are tables of statutes from 1984 onwards in the Prelims and Tables volume of *Irish Current Law Statutes Annotated.*

13.07   If the statute was made at Westminster, it will probably be listed in the table of statutes volume in *Halsbury's Statutes* (6.07 above), if it is to hand. Otherwise, one could check in the tables of *Halsbury's Laws of England* which is much more widely available, or in the Statute Citators of the *Current Law Service* together with the *Current Law Statutes Annotated* and *Current Law Monthly Digest* for more recent years and months. Many libraries have the (English) *Index to the Statutes,* which is no longer published, but the last edition of which listed English statutes from 1235 to1990. If that volume is available, it is a good place to start, and one can move on to the more current reference works just mentioned for the years 1990 to the present. Those with access to LEXIS can simply use STAT file of the ENGGEN library (see 2.19 above).

Finding the law on a topic

13.08   When researching the law on any topic, it is best to start with a good general textbook if one is available. Thankfully, there are now textbooks on most areas of Irish law, and they provide reliable starting points for research. A textbook should, at the very least, direct the reader to the relevant legislation and case law. The footnotes or bibliography will generally indicate more detailed writings in the form of books, articles and reports on the topics covered. From that point on, the direction to be taken depends on the jurisdiction and the nature of the topic.

Irish law

13.09   The absence of an encyclopaedia of Irish law, equivalent to *Halsbury*, can make the investigation of a legal topic more difficult in Ireland than in England or other common-law jurisdictions. However, *Murdoch's Dictionary of Irish Law* (7.29 above) compensates remarkably well for the absence of an encyclopaedia. Not only does it explain legal terms and indicate the law on hundreds of topics, it also mentions the relevant legislation and case law, which means that it is an excellent starting point. At the outset, however, it should be acknowledged that legal research often involves a fair amount of detective work. The standard reference works described below are indispensable but, more often than not, the researcher must find leads and follow them. Law reports, for example, usually include lists of other cases cited or considered as well as references to statutes, statutory instruments and rules of court. By following these through, one can often built up a reasonable picture of legal issues involved, if not the current law actually governing them. To find that law, the following are the standard sources.

13.10   Statutory provisions are now most easily found by using the various search facilities attached to the *Irish Statute Book* on the Attorney General's web site, or the equivalent CD (2.27 and 4.30 above). Subject indexes to the Statutes are available for the period up until 1989 (4.31 above), and there is a broad subject index for the period 1985 to 2000 in the Prelims and Tables volume of *Irish Current Law Statutes Annotated*. Case digests (below) can also be helpful in tracking down relevant statutes in the sense that a judgment may mention the statutes most relevant to the subject matter of the case. Digests are by no means the most reliable guide to statutory material, but it can help to consult them in any event. For recent developments, check the *Irish Current Law Year Books* and *Monthly Digests* which give the titles of recent statutes and statutory instruments under the relevant subject headings, as well as a brief indication of subject matter. Most extensive and detailed accounts of recent legislation will be found in the *Annual Review of Irish Law* (4.83 above) which began in 1987, and will usually describe legal developments up to a year or 15 months before the date of one's research.

13.11   To find Irish case law on a topic, the various *Irish Digests* are the best point of departure for the period up until 1999, though bearing in mind all the time that they usually cover reported cases only. One should therefore supplement the *Digests* with the Red, Green and Blue Indexes (4.73 *et seq.* above) for the period 1966 - 1989. The *Irish Law Log* should be consulted for the years 1988-1991 inclusive, and *Irish Current Law Year Book and Digests* from the beginning of 1995 onwards. However, the best guide of all, for the years 1987 onwards is the *Annual Review of Irish Law* (4.83 above). *Irish Current Law* can then be used to bring the law up to date. Remember, too, to consult journals such as the *Commercial Law Practitioner,* the *Irish Criminal Law Journal* and the *Irish Family Law Journal* (7.19 above), all of which have extensive notes on recent cases in their respective subject areas. The various subject indexes to *Irish Current Law Monthly Digest* (4.79 above) should also be consulted, but bear in mind that they cover only those cases reported in that series.

13.12   LEXIS has all reported Irish cases since 1950 and unreported cases since 1985. One can use the search facility to find case law since those dates on any topic. The JUSTIS version of the *Irish Reports* (3.28 above) can be used for the same purpose, bearing in mind that only cases reported in that series are covered. Another useful source nowadays is the statute citator in the Prelims and Tables volume of *Irish Current Law Statutes Annotated*, as noted earlier (4.33 above), this citator covers the statutes for the years 1993 to 1999, and includes, among other things, the cases in which each section of any of the statutes in force was mentioned. Do not, however, rely on this citator unless looking for *recent* cases on a particular statutory provision. It serves this particular purpose excellently, but because of the narrow time frame involved, it must be supplemented by consulting the older sources such as the *Irish Digests* or, from 1987 onwards, the *Annual Review of Irish Law* (4.83 above).

English case law

13.13   The two great sources of English case law are *The Digest* and *Current Law*. One can begin by checking the subject index to *The Digest* to identify the relevant volumes and parts. One should then check the various update volumes as well. The *Current Law Monthly Digest* and *Year Books* should also be consulted, as they generally contain a wider selection of English cases. Furthermore, the monthly parts will be more up to date than *The Digest* as a rule. *Halsbury's Laws of England* (7.26) is a useful starting point for getting a general knowledge of most subject areas, though it is always important to check the currency of the volume being consulted. Is it a recent reissue or was it published several years ago? In the latter event, one must consult the various updates. There is scarcely any area of English law on which there is not at least one modern textbook, and this will usually be the best starting point. To identify any developments that have occurred since the publication of the book, turn to *Current Law* (both the *Year Books* and *Monthly Digest*) as well as to the Case and Statute Citators (6.46 *et seq.* above). Obviously, LEXIS, if one has access to it, is best for identifying English case law, especially since the mid-20th century, while a great deal of modern case law from the late 1990s onwards is available free of charge on the Internet (6.33 above). If one has access to the electronic *Current Legal Information* service, one can research *Current Law* since 1986, and then use the paper version for the years before that. If all else fails, the general subject indexes to the *Law Reports* and to the *All England Law Reports* (6.40 and 6.41 above) are good sources of information on case law, although not as comprehensive as *The Digest*, and they do not go back as far.

English statutes

13.14   Once more, a good modern textbook is the best starting point for identifying relevant statutes. *Halsbury's Law of England* and its updates should serve the same purpose. If all else fails, one can consult the Index to the Statutes (6.11) or, somewhat more laboriously, the subject indexes to the various volumes of the *Current Law Year Books*. LEXIS also has the statutes in force, which are easily searchable. The Internet sources of modern U.K. statutes are described at 6.09 above. One indispensable source, however, is the *Current Law Statute Citator* (6.51 above) which allows one easily to trace the history of most English statutes. The *Current Law Legislation Citator* from 1989 onwards is available as part of the *Current Legal Information Service.*

Secondary sources

13.15   Nowadays, the best way of identifying books relevant to a particular topic is to use consult the various online university catalogues on the Internet (2.14 above). One can supplement these by consulting the web sites of leading publishers such as Amazon, Oxford University Press, Butterworths, Sweet and Maxwell, and so forth. Paper sources are still worth consulting as they often have more reliable classification systems, even if their content goes out of date rather quickly. Most libraries have Raistrick's *Lawyers' Law Books* 3rd edn (7.07 above) which is well classified. Other legal bibliographies are listed at 7.10 above. Each volume of the *Current Law Year Book* has a list of recently published books.

13.16   For periodical literature, the best sources are the *Legal Journals Index,* available on CD, and *Index to Legal Periodicals*, both described at 7.24 above, although the *Legal Journals Index* is better for English and Irish material, and carries abstracts as well. Remember, too, that the *Current Law Monthly Digest* has lists of recent articles published in the various subject areas covered.

Law reform documents

13.17   Reports and consultation papers of law reform commissions and similar bodies are always worth consulting, both for the present content of the law and for a critical analysis of it. Sources of Irish and British law reform documents are provided at 7.35 *et seq.* above, the equivalent sources of Australian, Canadian and New Zealand reports have been given in Chapter 13. Many of these reports are now available on the Internet at http://home.vicnet.net.au/~lawref/council.htm. Another very useful web page is maintained by the University of Cambridge Faculty of Law which gives access to many law reform commissions throughout the world. The address is www.law.cam.ac.uk/urllists/reform.htm.

CHAPTER 14

Legal Writing

14.01   John Sparrow, who began his professional life as a chancery lawyer and later became Warden of All Souls College, Oxford as well as a prolific writer and broadcaster, once said that "good English" should be understood as "the efficiency with which the words give expression to the meaning".[1] That is sound advice for any aspiring writer but especially for lawyers who must, as part of their work, write about a wide variety of topics in a clear and understandable fashion. Good writing should not be confused with a flowery or ornate prose style or with long, involved sentences. The first duty of a writer is to communicate effectively, to convey to the reader as clearly and exactly as possible the idea or the message forming the substance of the communication. The challenge, therefore, as Sparrow said, is to find the most appropriate words to give effect to the meaning. Naturally, the writing style adopted will depend on the nature of the document. But it is always a mistake to assume that clear and simple writing, or speech for that matter, must be devoid of effect. One of the more memorable commencement addresses at Yale Law School was delivered in 1979 by Professor Leon Lipson. It was a short address, about 750 words, and contained passages such as this:

> "When you start to close that deal, to write that brief, to press that claim, to draw that deed or that bond, to break that will or that bank, pause first and weigh the worth of the end to which you bend your strength. You will, it may be, toss that bright hard coin that James wrote of, a coin of which the front face is some man's right and ease and the back face is his peer's pain and wrong; and you will help one face to come up. What aim will you have in view? To do Right? – to help Might? – to earn a Fee? No more than that? When you look back on what you have done, will it have brought you pride, shame or guilt? Or just plain wealth?"[2]

The remarkable thing about this passage, like the entire address, is that it consists entirely of one-syllable words (fortunately he was speaking at Yale rather than Harvard!). Yet, it can hardly be said to lack effect.

---

[1]   Sparrow, *Words on the Air. Essays on Language, Manners, Morals, and Laws* (Chicago: University of Chicago Press, 1981) 36.
[2]   Reprinted in *Yale Law Report*, Fall 1996, p. 3.

14.02   Clarity is the first hallmark of good writing, whether in law or any other discipline. Since the middle of the 20th century, many philosophers and literary critics have come to regard obscurity and impenetrability as badges of academic excellence, or so it would appear. As Bryan Magee argues in a powerful essay in defence of clarity in philosophical writing, there seems to be an assumption that to write clearly amounts to an admission that the subject matter is not difficult, and therefore not very impressive.[3] However, as he says, difficulty and lack of clarity must be distinguished. It is not always possible to express difficult concepts in simple language, but that does not relieve the writer from attempting to do so in *clear* language. This is a point that legal theorists would do well to bear in mind. Some leading members of the Critical Legal Studies Movement that flourished in the United States, especially in the 1980s, seemed incapable of expressing their theories and opinions in anything other than the most obscure terms, a practice that certainly diminished their influence. That was a great pity because many of them had challenging and worthwhile things to say.

14.03   It is also a mistake to confuse good legal writing with legalese, meaning the kind of technical language found in formal legal documents. When drafting a deed for the sale of house, for example, certain technical language must be used and certain precedents followed. But when writing about such a transaction, whether in a letter to a client or in an academic article, the best way of conveying a clear message is to use clear language. Consequently, expressions like "to wit", "as aforesaid", "as heretofore provided" should be avoided at all costs. They can always be replaced with simple words like "this" or "that", depending on the context. Matthew Arnold once said that the only secret of style is to have something to say and to say it clearly as you can. That is good advice for all writers, lawyers included.

14.04   Traditionally, legal writers relied heavily, and often unnecessarily, on Latin words and phrases. Few of today's legal writers will have studied Latin, so they would be well advised to observe two golden rules. First, never use a Latin word or phrase without knowing what it means. *Corpus delicti*, for example, does not mean the corpse of the deceased; it means the circumstances constituting the offence. Secondly, never use Latin when the meaning can be conveyed just as effectively in English. There is little point in using *inter alia* when "among other things" will do. Likewise, *in extenso* simply means "in full" or "at length", so it is difficult to see any advantage in using the Latin phrase. There are, to be sure, some well-recognised Latin phrases, such as *mutatis mutandis*, that have no convenient English equivalents, so one should not hesitate to use them. There are also certain legal principles encapsulated in

---

[3]   "Sense and nonsense", (February 2000) *Prospect*.

Latin phrases, such as *res ipsa loquitur* or *res peruit domino*. These can, and should, be used when appropriate.

14.05 So far, we have been discussing "good English"; let us now turn to "correct English" which is concerned with observing conventional rules of spelling, grammar and syntax. Up until the late1960s, schoolchildren were taught English in a rule-based manner. Every word had a correct spelling, and sentences were analysed in terms of subject, predicate and object. On no account could an infinitive be split or a sentence end with a preposition. Everyone knew what a subordinate clause was. Very few people under the age of 40 now know what it is, and very few of them know much about infinitives and prepositions either. The abandonment of this formal approach to English teaching was not a bad thing as it allowed more scope for self-expression. But a working knowledge of grammar and syntax is still essential for effective writing. Syntax, for example, is about the ordering of words within a sentence. It goes without saying that in English unlike, say, Latin, word order determines meaning. Take the following two sentences: *The man hit the car. The car hit the man.* They contain the exact same words, but the meaning of the first is different from the second on account of the way the words are ordered.

Spelling

14.06 Most English words have correct spellings in the sense that if one were to look up any one of them in several different modern dictionaries, the spelling in each case would be the same. That is true, for example, of every word in this sentence and in the previous one. But it is not necessarily true of words like "colour" "programme" or "analyze". A dictionary of American English would spell "colour" as "color" and "programme" as "program" while a British English dictionary would spell "analyze" as "analyse". Ireland and Britain follow the same spelling conventions, and in both countries the various Oxford English dictionaries are widely accepted as a sure guide to correct spelling. Occasionally, a word may have two different spellings, both of which are acceptable. This is true, for example, of "recognize" and "recognise" both of which are given in The Concise Oxford Dictionary (9th edition) although it seems to prefer the first, "z", spelling. On the other hand, words such as "compromise", "chastise" or "advertise" are always spelt with "s" rather than "z". Some words end with "-able", others with "-ible", e.g. "durable", "immutable" and "impeccable", but "accessible", "defensible" and "permissible". Words which look or sound the same or very similar may have very different meanings. To "forbear" means to tolerate, while "forebear" means an ancestor. "Biannual" means half-yearly while "biennial" means two-yearly. "Credible" means believable, but "creditable" means worthy of praise or respect. Compound words often cause problems. Should one write "letterhead", "letter-head" or "letter head"? The first is correct. At present, it seems more correct to refer to a "web site" than a "website" though this may change. One might own an "oil-colour", an "oil-field" or an "oil well". "Common-law" is usually hyphenated when it is used as an adjective, as in a "common-law rule" but not when used as a noun - "the common law". The best reference book for matters such as these is the *Oxford Dictionary for Writers and Editors* (4.18 below), but most problems can be solved by consulting any of the standard English dictionaries (4.17 below). One spelling distinction particularly important for lawyers is that between "judgment" (with one "e") in the sense of a judgment delivered by a court, and "judgement" meaning the exercise of a critical faculty, as in a matter of judgement.

14.07   The possessive of a singular noun is formed by adding "'s", e.g. "John's coat" or "the book's cover". Many writers insist, probably rightly, on following this rule even when a proper noun ends with "s". e.g. "James's coat". It seems to be accepted, however, that there is an exception to the rule in the case of biblical or classical characters, e.g., Jesus' teaching" or "Socrates' death". The possessive of plural nouns is formed by adding an apostrophe to the nominative plural, e.g. "the judges' opinions" or "the books' covers". Remember that there is no apostrophe in "hers", "ours", "theirs", "yours" "its". One therefore writes "yours sincerely" not "your's sincerely". Note, in particular, the distinction between "its" and "it's". The first, "its" is a possessive. One would write that "the court reversed its earlier decision". "It's", on the other hand, is a contraction of "it is". One would therefore write; "it's true that its purpose is unclear". Also, when dealing with institutions or place-names, always check the position of any apostrophes. In Ireland, for example, aspiring barristers are educated at "The Honorable Society of King's Inns", not at "The Honourable Society of the Kings' Inns". One refers to "Queens' College Cambridge" which was named after two queens, but "The Queen's College, Oxford" which was named after one.

Grammar and syntax

14.08   The following are among the mistakes most commonly encountered in essays and other writing assignments. As noted earlier, opinions differ over their seriousness, but it is as well to be aware of them at least.

14.09   *Split infinitives* The infinitive form of a verb is its basic form, e.g. "to read", "to write". A split infinitive occurs when an adverb is inserted between those two words, e.g. "to slowly read" or "to quickly write". The traditional view was that split infinitives should be avoided, so one should say, for example, "to read slowly" or "to write quickly". This, however, is only a general rule. As a visiting American colleague of mine used to say, "I do not like to unnecessarily split infinitives"!

14.10 *Terminal prepositions* The traditional rule was that, whenever possible, a clause or sentence should not end with a preposition. In stylistic terms, this often makes sense. A sentence, especially a long one, can read awkwardly if it ends with a short preposition such as "of" or "in". Final prepositions can sometimes be avoided by the use of a relative pronoun, so instead of writing "there was no one I could turn to", one could write "there was no one to whom I could turn". Much depends on the style being adopted. The more formal the document, the more final prepositions could be avoided. Often they cannot be, as exemplified by a phrase such as "the bed had not been slept in", and there is little point in engaging in elaborate circumlocution in order to do so. Not surprisingly, therefore, *The Oxford Companion to the English Language* (0xford, 1984) says (p. 166) that the "alleged rule that forbids the placing of the preposition at the end of a phrase or sentence should be disregarded".

14.11   *Participial clauses* A common error in writing (and one that can affect meaning) is to begin a sentence with a participial clause in which there is one implied subject, and then continue with a main clause that has a different subject. Take the following sentence: "Turning around, she saw her husband fall off his bicycle". Here, "turning around" is known as a participial clause, as it tells us something about the subject of the sentence "she", but does not, in itself, tell us who the subject is. The difficulty arises with sentences like this: "Having got drunk before the lecture, the professor threw Peter out of the classroom". Now, this may or may not be correct. If it was the professor who got drunk, the sentence is unobjectionable, more than can be said for the professor's behaviour. But if it was Peter who got drunk, then the sentence conveys the wrong meaning. It should read something like: "Having got drunk before the lecture, Peter was thrown out of the classroom by the professor". Another example would be: "Having read the relevant cases, the judge appears to have applied the wrong law". Here the subject of the sentence is "the judge" which implies that it is she who has been reading the cases. What the writer probably intended to convey was that as a result of his own reading of the cases, he believes that the judge was wrong. Therefore, the sentence should be rewritten along these lines: "Having read the relevant cases, I believe that the judge applied the wrong law".

14.12   *Location of adverbs* An adverb qualifies a verb. It often, though not always, ends in *-ly*. Thus, "recent" is an adjective while "recently" is an adverb. Many common adverbs, such as "fast", "high", and "well" do not, of course, end in -ly. Our concern here is with the proper location of adverbs in clauses or sentences. This, to a degree, is a matter of individual style, but there are a few general rules that make sense, because the location of an adverb may affect the meaning of a sentence. To borrow an example from a leading English grammar,[4] there is a clear difference between "they secretly decided to leave the town" and "they decided to leave the town secretly". As a rule, an adverb of

---

[4]   A.J. Thomson and A.V. Martinet, *A Practical English Grammar* (London: Guild Publishing, 1991) p. 52.

manner, describing how something is done, comes after the verb that it qualifies, e.g. "he played brilliantly". If there is an object, it comes after that, e.g.
"he played the piano brilliantly".

14.13 *"Only"* In a recent article in *The New York Times Magazine*, William
G. Connolly, a senior editor of that newspaper, described the word "only" as
perhaps the most misplaced word in the English language. To illustrate the point,
he asks the reader to take the following seven-word sentence, "Thelma told
Standish that she loved him", and then consider how it would change meaning
by placing "only" before any one of those seven words. Thus "Only Thelma
told Standish that she loved him" has a different meaning from "Thelma only
told Standish that she loved him" (she may not have meant it) or "Thelma told
Standish that she loved only him". Needless to say, when drafting or interpreting legal documents, particular care must be taken to ensure that "only" qualifies the right word. A clause in a contract providing that "the vendor only shall
be liable for any losses incurred in transit" could differ in meaning from "the
vendor shall be liable only for any losses incurred in transit".

14.14 *"Shall" and "will"* The use of these words is no longer governed by
strict rules. But, for the record, the rule used to be that when used with the first
person, singular or plural, shall expressed the simple future, as in "I shall see
you tomorrow". *I will* or *we will*, on the other hand, was used to express an
intention, a determination or a promise, e.g. "I will buy you a present for your
birthday" or "I will never be persuaded to drink". When the second or third
person is involved, the rule is the direct opposite. *Will* used to describe the
simple future, e.g. "they will arrive here tomorrow" whereas *shall* is used to
express an intention, a promise or, sometimes, a direction, e.g. "you shall be
here by noon at the latest". Strunk and White in *The Elements of Style* (14.18
below) give the example of a swimmer in distress shouting "I will drown; no
one shall save me" which implied an intention to commit suicide, when he probably meant "I shall drown; nobody will save me".

14.15 *Use of singular and plural* A singular noun takes a singular verb and
a plural noun takes a plural verb. That's logical enough, but there are certain
aspects of the rule that call for comment. Sometimes, a compound subject will
take a singular verb. This occurs when two items make up the same thing. To
borrow examples from *The Little Oxford Guide to English Usage* (Oxford,
1994), one would say that "the bread and butter was scattered on the floor" or
that "the Stars and Stripes was flying at half-mast". Likewise, the singular verb
is used when referring to the same person in different capacities, e.g. "her pride
and joy is home at last" or "his son and heir is safe". A more common error is to
use the plural instead of the singular when the subject of the sentence is singular. This usually happens when a plural noun occurs somewhere between the
subject and the verb. Nobody would write "the volume are missing", but one

occasionally sees statements like "the volume of statutes are missing". This is incorrect; the subject of the sentence is "volume", not "statutes", and therefore the verb should be in the singular.

14.16 *Collective nouns can cause problems* These are singular words that denote a group of individuals such as "committee", "jury" "company", "parliament", "congregation", "public". The various Oxford guides to English usage claim that the singular verb and pronouns should generally be used with collective nouns. So, they would recommend writing "the cabinet has made its decision" rather than "the cabinet have made their decision". They are more insistent (and logically so) that singular should be used when a collective noun is qualified by "this", "that" or "every". So, one would write "this family is large " or "that jury was unanimous". They accept, however, that the plural should be used when a collective noun is used to refer to the separate individuals who make up the collectivity, so it would be proper to write that "the jury are now taking their places in the jury box". Sometimes, however, the use of the singular simply does not sound right in which case the plural should be used. "Police", for example, will always be treated as plural. Some words are the same in the singular and plural. "Counsel" is a good example. One might say that "counsel has made her submission" or "counsel have made their submissions", depending on how many were involved.

REFERENCE BOOKS

Dictionaries and thesauri

14.17 All writers, legal writers included, need access to a good dictionary and other reference books. A standard dictionary such as the *Concise Oxford English Dictionary* or the *Collins English Dictionary* is an excellent investment. A dictionary of this kind will provide much more than spellings and definitions. The *Collins*, for example, has 170,000 entries including 15,000 encyclopaedia entries. A thesaurus, which is also useful to have available, performs a different function; it provides alternative words. Thus, if one looks up "justice" in a thesaurus, one will find several similar words which may be equally appropriate, or more so, depending on the context. The best-known thesaurus is Roget's which is organised thematically. This is now available on the Internet (www.bartleby.com) and hard copies will be found in most libraries. However, there are more modern thesauri which are easier to use, the best being *The Oxford Paperback Thesaurus*, published in 1994, in which the entries are in straightforward alphabetical form.

Books on writing and style

14.18   There are three outstanding reference books which every writer will find valuable. The first is Strunk and White, *The Elements of Style*' 3rd edn. This is a short book, running to just over 90 pages, and it contains some excellent uncomplicated advice on writing style. It is also available on the Internet. The second is the *Oxford Dictionary for Writers and Editors* which is an excellent source of information on correct spellings, and is particularly useful when dealing with compound words (see 14.06 above). It states clearly if compound words are to be hyphenated or written as one word or two. It also explains abbreviations from several languages and gives brief, but helpful information, on famous places and persons. The third book is *The Little Oxford Guide to English Usage*, published in 1994. It does not replace either of the other two, but is a good guide to basic spelling, grammar and syntax. Other useful reference books include *Hart's Rules for Compositors and Editors*. Although written primarily for editors of publishing houses, it has good advice on punctuation, quotations, abbreviations and the use of capital and lower-case initials. *The Oxford Guide to the English Language*, first published in 1984, is a more substantial volume, but excellent value in paperback at about £7 sterling. It combines a guide to English usage and a dictionary in one volume.

Handbooks on legal writing

14.19   Garner's *A Dictionary of Modern English Usage* is an excellent book. It is arranged in alphabetical order, giving the etymology and legal meanings of words, and the correct use of words and phrases. If one were to buy only one book after Strunk and White, this should be it, as it is a legal encyclopaedia and a writing manual in one volume. Another book by Garner, *The Elements of Legal Style* (Oxford, 1991) adopts an approach similar to that of Strunk and White, but is written specially for lawyers and law students. Finally, reference should be made to *Chambers' Legal Spelling Checker*, a short book costing a few pounds, which contains a list of words commonly used by lawyers. It does not provide any definitions, just correct spellings.

PRESENTATION OF ESSAYS

14.20   Essays should obviously be presented in the manner stipulated in any instructions furnished by the department or instructor for whom they are being written. A common requirement, however, is that they should be typed on A4 paper with adequate margins on both sides and at the top and bottom of the page. As a rule, the text of the essay should be double-spaced; footnotes or endnotes should be single-spaced.

Footnotes and endnotes

14.21   Footnotes are placed at the bottom of the page, endnotes at the end of the essay, the book or individual chapters as the case may be. Either approach may be adopted in essays. Nowadays, word processing packages make it easy to insert footnotes, so they have become more common than endnotes. In the remainder of this chapter, the term footnotes will be used to cover endnotes as well. In an essay, footnotes should be numbered consecutively, beginning with number 1. The sequence should begin anew at the beginning of each chapter in the case of a book or dissertation. Again, word processing packages now perform this task automatically, assuming each chapter is a separate document.

14.22   What should be contained in footnotes? There are few hard and fast rules, except that footnotes should be as economical as possible. Some authors (and publishers), for example, prefer to incorporate case citations in the main text so as to keep footnotes to a minimum. They would write, for example, "*Berkeley v. Edwards* [1988] I.R. 217", while others would write simply "*Berkeley v. Edwards*" and then have a footnote containing the citation. The latter approach is now the more widely used, and certainly makes sense when parallel citations are being included. The more difficult question is how extensively footnotes should be used to provide supplementary information. American law reviews are famous, indeed notorious, for the extent of their footnoted material. In fact, the word count of the footnotes can be higher than that of the main text. Extensive footnotes are often treated as a sign of scholarship. Certainly, in a larger treatise aiming to provide a comprehensive treatment of some aspect of law, footnotes allow the author to give references for all or most of the relevant primary and secondary material which users, especially practitioners, may find useful. Generally, however, the best advice is probably that recorded by Hector McQueen in his book, *Studying Scots Law*, namely that "discursive material which cannot be firmly bonded into the text should be ruthlessly discarded, at least from the current piece of work".

14.23   References in the text to books and other secondary sources, and probably to cases (see preceding paragraph), should be accompanied by relevant publication details, and case citations where relevant, in the footnotes. Suppose one refers to an author in the main text, e.g.

> Wylie has argued that this is an unduly restrictive interpretation of the statute.

The footnote will cite in the prescribed way (14.28 *et seq.* below) the book or article in which Wylie made this argument. Sometimes, it will be appropriate to mention the title of a book or article in the text, in which case the relevant footnote will contain the publication details. Thus, one might write that

MacQueen's *Studying Scots Law* provides an excellent introduction to the Scottish legal system.

A footnote would then indicate the edition, place and date of publication and, perhaps, the publisher of that book.

Abbreviations

14.24   Time and space can be saved by the sensible use of abbreviations. The key consideration should be to ensure that the meanings of any abbreviations used are readily understood by the reader. If, for example, a document, an organisation or an institution is being referred to by initials or by an acronym, then unless every reader can be presumed to understand the abbreviation, the meaning should be indicated somewhere in the text. In an essay or article, the first time the document or institution in question is mentioned, its full name should be given followed by the abbreviation that will henceforth be used. One might refer at first to the Police and Criminal Evidence Act 1984 (PACE), to take a well-known English example. Thereafter it will be sufficient to refer to PACE. Some abbreviations will be so well known to likely readers that there is no need to explain them. Everyone reading a legal book, article or essay will probably know that the UN stands for the United Nations. Not everyone might know that OSCE stands for the Organisation for Security and Co-operation in Europe, so it might be as well to indicate this the first time a reference is made to it. In longer pieces of writing, especially in monograph form, certain works may be referred to repeated throughout. In such circumstances, a list of abbreviations can be included in the introductory pages providing a key to the abbreviations used. Such a list would read something like this:

McAuley and McCutcheon	F. McAuley and P. McCutcheon, *Criminal Liability: A Grammar* (Dublin: Round Hall Sweet and Maxwell, 2000).
Smith and Hogan (1992),	J. Smith and B. Hogan, *Criminal Law*, 7th edn (London: Butterworths, 1992).
Smith and Hogan (1996),	J. Smith and B. Hogan, *Criminal Law*, 8th edn (London: Butterworths, 1996).
Willams, *Textbook*	G. Williams, *Textbook of Criminal Law*, 2nd edn (London: Sweet and Maxwell, 1983)

Throughout the text then, one need only refer to McAuley and McCutcheon, Smith and Hogan, or Williams, followed by the relevant page number. However, this arrangement is really only suited to longer works. In shorter works, such as articles and letters, it is better to use standard abbreviations of which the following are the more common.

op. cit.   "in the work cited" (referring, as a rule, to a book or article already cited in full).

loc. cit.   "in the place already cited" (referring to a passage, as opposed to a book or article, cited in a previous note. Since it refers to a particular passage, it should not be followed by a page number).

ib. or *ibid.* "in the same place" (in the same book, article or, perhaps, case that has been cited in the immediately preceding note).

passim   "here and there" (throughout the text mentioned). Sometimes, *et passim*, after a particular page number, meaning "and here and there", as exemplified in the final sample footnote in 4.26 below.

14.25   The following examples illustrate the use of the above abbreviations in a little more detail. If, in an essay on constitutional law, one were making frequent references to Casey's *Constitutional Law in Ireland*, one would provide the full title and publication details in a footnote on the first occasion it was cited. In subsequent footnotes, it would be sufficient to write: "Casey, *op. cit.* p. 120". This is acceptable to long as one is referring to a single work by the same author. Suppose, however, that in the same essay, one were also referring to Casey's *The Irish Law Officers*. Obviously, the full title and publication details would be given the first time it was cited, but it would be confusing for the reader to find later references saying simply "Casey, *op. cit.* p. 120". It would be unclear as to which of the two books were being referred to. To avoid such confusion, one can adopt the following strategy. The first time the book on constitutional law is mentioned, one would write:

> Casey, *Constitutional Law in Ireland* 3rd edn (Dublin, 2000), hereinafter referred to as Casey, Constitutional Law.

Likewise, the first reference to the book on Law Officers would read:

> Casey, *The Irish Law Officers. Roles and Responsibilities of the Attorney General and the Director of Public Prosecutions* (Dublin, 1996), hereinafter referred to as Casey, *Law Officers*.

In later footnotes, one need only refer to "Casey, *Constitutional Law*, p. 120" or "Casey, *Law Officers*, p. 120", as the case may be. This system is useful, but only really suitable when they are to be many references to different works by the same author.

14.26   A series of footnotes in such an essay might therefore read as follows:

21. Casey, *Constitutional Law in Ireland* 3rd edn (Dublin, 2000), here-
    inafter referred to as Casey, *Constitutional Law*.

22. Forde, *Constitutional Law of Ireland* (Dublin, 1987) p. 12.

23. Casey, *The Irish Law Officers. Roles and Responsibilities of the At-
    torney General and the Director of Public Prosecutions* (Dublin,
    1996), hereinafter referred to as Casey, *Law Officers*.

24. Casey, *Constitutional Law*, p. 124.

25. *Ibid*. p. 126.

26. Forde, *op. cit*. p. 350.

27. *Ibid*.

28. Casey, *Law Officers*, p. 234.

29. Morgan, *The Separation of Powers in the Irish Constitution* (Dub-
    lin, 1997) p. 125 *et passim*.

Note that *ibid*. is used only to refer to a work cited in the footnote immediately
preceding the one in which it is used. One must be careful when the preceding
footnote contains more than one reference. For example, in footnote 25 above,
it is quite clear that the reference is to Casey's *Constitutional Law,* as that is the
only work cited in footnote 24. But if footnote 24 also referred to, say, Kelly,
Hogan and Whyte, *The Irish Constitution*, footnote 25, as it is now written,
would make no sense. Instead, it would have to read something like "Casey,
ibid. p. 126". When referring to a work cited in a footnote other than the immediately preceding one, use *op. cit*. as illustrated by the reference to Forde in
footnote 26 above.

14.27   These abbreviations are used when referring to books, articles and other
secondary sources. A different approach must be adopted when referring to
cases. One never uses op. cit., for example, to refer to a case already cited.
Some authors and publishers follow the practice of giving the full citation of a
case every time it is cited. It is, however, logically permissible to use *ibid*. to
refer to a single case cited in the immediately preceding footnote. Therefore, a
series of case citations might read:

32. [1984] I.R. 123.

33. [1997] 2 I.L.R.M. 345.

34. *Ibid*.

35. [1984] I.R. 123.

36. [1997] 2 I.L.R.M. 345.

Parallel citations were explained in Chapter 3 above. Whether or not one includes all citations for a case, as opposed to just one, depends on the practice followed by the publisher or journal editor, or on the instructions to be followed when writing essays, as the case may be.

14.28   Citing books. In a footnote, a book is generally cited by reference to its author(s), full title, place and date of publication, and page number where relevant. The title is placed in italics (or underlined in a typescript), while the place and date of publication are placed in italics. A typical citation would therefore be:

> Redmond, *Dismissal Law in Ireland* (Dublin, 1999).

Some publishers prefer to have the first name or initials of the author included, while others include the publisher as well as the place of publication. So the above work might also be cited as:

> M. Redmond, *Dismissal Law in Ireland* (Dublin: Butterworths, 1999).

When the second or later edition of a book is being cited, the edition number is also included as part of the reference. Thus, one would write:

> Wylie, *Irish Conveyancing Law*, 2nd edn (Dublin, 1996).

Again, certain variations are permissible; "2nd ed." is more often used than "2nd edn". Nowadays, the edition number is placed inside the parentheses along with the place and date of publication, but is it better left outside.
A book may consist of a collection of essays written by several authors. Such a book is cited in the same way as any other, except that the author is replaced by the editor(s), e.g.

> O'Dell (ed.), *Leading Cases of the Twentieth Century* (Dublin, 2000).

Citing articles and essays

14.29   A journal article is cited by reference to the name(s) of the author(s), title of the article, year and volume of journal, journal title and initial page number. The title of the article is placed in inverted commas, the journal title is italicised if given in full, and the year is placed in parentheses.

> Craig, "Negligent Misstatements, Negligent Acts and Economic Loss" (1976) 92 L.Q.R. 213.

This, at least, is the conventional way of citing articles. Again, some publishers may require the first name or initial of the author, or that the name of the journal be given in full. However, most of the leading journals, such as the *Law Quarterly Review* in the example just given, have well known abbreviations which can always be used in the absence of instructions to the contrary. But when referring to a little-known law journal, or a non-legal periodical, it may be helpful to give the full title. Abbreviated journal titles, such as L.Q.R. or Crim. L.R., are not, as a rule, italicised. Italics are used only when the title is given in full.

14.30   An essay from an edited collection is cited by reference to the author(s) of essay, title of essay, editor(s) and title of book, place and date of publication, and initial page number. The name of the essay, as in the case of an article, is placed in parentheses and the title of the collection is placed in italics.

> Keogh, "Church, State and Society" in Farrell (ed.), *De Valera's Constitution and Ours* (Dublin, 1988) 103.

Quotations

14.31   A short quotation, generally meaning one of five lines or less, may be incorporated in the text using single or double quotation marks. Longer quotations are indented with, though sometimes without, quotation marks. Quotation marks are inverted commas, and may be single or double, namely '' or "". The more predominant practice is to employ double inverted commas for the main quotation and single marks for any quotation within a quotation, although the reverse system is sometimes used as well. The following two examples[5] illustrate the use of shorter and longer quotations.

1.   In *Mehigan v. Duignan* [1997] 1 I.R. 340, Shanley J. said (at p. 357) that where the matters listed in s. 204 of the Companies Act, 1990 had been satisfied, "the court may, if it thinks it proper to do so, declare that such officer or officers be personally liable without limitation of liability for all or such part as may be specified by the court of the debts and other liabilities of the company". In that case, he declared the respondent to be personally liable to the company.

2.   In *P & F Sharpe Ltd. v. Dublin City and County Manager* [1989] I.R. 701, the same point was considered by the Supreme Court. The submission was rejected. Chief Justice Finlay said at p. 721:-

> "The powers of An Bord Pleanála on the making of an appeal to it would be entirely confined to the consideration of the matters before

---

[5]   The second passage is taken from *McGoldrick v. An Bord Pleanála* [1997] 1 I.R. 497 at 509.

it on the basis of the proper planning and development of the area and it would have no jurisdiction to consider the question of the validity, from a legal point of view, of the purported decision by the county manager. It would not, therefore, be just for the developers who are respondents in this appeal [applicants] to be deprived of their right to have that decision quashed for want of validity."

Similar reasoning led to a refusal to grant relief by way of certiorari in *The State (Abenglen Properties) v. Corporation of Dublin* [1984] I.R. 381.

14.32   A few other points about quotations should be noted. Sometimes, one will not wish to quote an entire passage because some of it may be irrelevant to the purpose for which it is being used. Take, for example, the following passage:

"It is only in exceptional circumstances such as illness on the part of the applicant - though I am not necessarily accepting that the applicant in the present case was as ill as he claims to have been - that an extension of the time limit will be granted."

One could quote this sentence, while omitting the parenthetical part, by writing:

The judge said that "it is only in exceptional circumstances such as illness on the part of the applicant ... that an extension of the time limit will be granted."

The three dots used to indicate that part of the quotation has been omitted are known as ellipsis points. Three points are used to indicate the omission of part of a sentence. Four points are used to indicate that the sentence ends with the quoted passage or that the ellipsis extends into a new sentence.

14.33   Sometimes, it is necessary to insert a word into a quotation to clarify its meaning. This is known as interpolation. Suppose the original passage read:

In circumstances such as these, Mr. Jones is entitled to succeed once he proves negligence on the part of Mrs Doyle.

If quoting this passage in isolation, it will be helpful to indicate who Mr Jones and Mrs Doyle are. The appropriate words can be interpolated in square brackets after, or instead of, the names, e.g.

The judge said that "(i)n circumstances such as these, [the plaintiff] is entitled to succeed once he proves negligence on the part of the [defendant]".

As this example also illustrates, parentheses are used indicate that a lower-case letter is being used instead of the capital letter appearing in the original quotation, e.g. "(i)n" instead of "In".

14.34 Finally, a quotation may contain a mistake or a misspelling. The general practice is to reproduce the passage exactly as it is, but to insert "sic" in parentheses after the mistake to show that it occurred in the original, e.g.

> The judge said that "there is (*sic*) many exceptions to the rule against hearsay."

Sometimes, however, "sic" is used rather too pedantically. If one is quoting from a law report, for example, and there is a clear misspelling, such as "injucntion" instead of "injunction", just use the correct spelling when quoting it, as the error in the original is merely typographical.

BIBLIOGRAPHIES

14.35 A bibliography is a list of secondary sources mentioned in a book or essay, or consulted in the course of its preparation. Primary sources of law are never included in bibliographies attached to legal works. If necessary, there can be separate tables of statutes, cases, statutory instruments, constitutional provisions and so forth. As a rule, all secondary sources are included in the same bibliography, listed by author in alphabetical order. Some authors and publishers prefer to have separate bibliographies, one for books, one for articles, and perhaps another for official reports. It's really a matter of choice, although if all the works to be listed are relatively small in number, it is probably better to include them in a single bibliography. There are few hard and fast rules for the compilation of bibliographies provided certain basic information is included, and provided it is in alphabetical order by author. Remember that the main purpose of a bibliography is to help the reader track down the items listed. It follows therefore that for periodical material, the same information should be given as when citing an article in a footnote (14.22 above) and that for books the usual publication details, including the edition if there has been more than one, should be given (14.28 above). When citing two or more works by the same author in successive entries, one should arrange them in order of date of publication, beginning with the earliest. Sometimes, instead of repeating the same author's name, a dash is used for second and subsequent items, but the modern tendency seems to be to repeat the author's name for each entry. It is also helpful when listing books in a bibliography to include the publisher as well as the place of publication, as this may help a reader trying to locate or buy the book in question. For the same reason, the first name or initials of an author should always be included. When there are several authors or editors, they should be given exactly as they appear in the original work, except of course that first names may be replaced by initials. Finally, when listing a report, working paper or the like, the committee, body or organisation that produced it is treated as the author. Sometimes, however, government departments or voluntary organisations publish research papers produced by named individuals. In such a case, those individuals should be listed as authors, whereas the department or organisation will generally be the publisher. Obviously, when inserting the publisher's name, one goes by whatever information is given in the work itself, usually on the reverse of the title page. The following sample bibliography illustrates most of the principles just mentioned.

American Friends Service Committee,	*Struggle for Justice* (New York: Hill and Wang, 1972).
Alston, P., Parker, S. and Seymour, J (eds),	*Children, Rights and the Law* (Oxford: Oxford University Press, 1992).
Ashworth, A.,	"Prosecution and Procedure in Criminal Justice" [1979] Crim L.R. 480
Ashworth, A.,	*Sentencing and Criminal Justice* 2nd edn (London: Butterworths, 1995)
Ashworth, A.,	*Principles of Criminal Law* 2nd edn (Oxford: Oxford U.P., 1995)
Ashworth, A. and Gostin, L.,	"Mentally Disordered Offenders and the Sentencing Process" [1984] Crim L.R. 195.
Department of Justice,	*The Management of Offenders: A Five-Year Plan* Pn 0789 (Dublin, 1994)
Home Office,	*Criminal Justice: Plans for Legislation* (London: HMSO, 1986)
Law Reform Commission	*Report on the Law Relating to Dishonesty* LRC 43-1992 (Dublin, 1992)
McConville, M. and Baldwin, J.,	*Courts, Prosecution and Conviction* (Oxford: Oxford U.P., 1991)
McEwan, J.,	*Evidence and the Adversarial Process: The Modern Law* 2nd edn (Oxford: Hart Publishing, 1998).
Murray, B.,	"Director Disqualification and the Criminal Law" (1992) 2 I.C.L.J. 165
Tribunal of Inquiry (Dunnes Payments)	*Report* Pn 4199 (Dublin: Stationery Office, 1997)

14.36 As noted earlier (at 14.28), some publishers prefer to include the date of publication immediately after the author's name. As a result, the footnotes may then refer to secondary materials solely by reference to the author and the date. The reader will be able to identify the full citation by checking out the relevant entry in the bibliography. When two or more pieces of writing were published by the same author in one year, say 1995, they are listed as1995a, 1995b and 1995c. Thus, some of the entries in the sample bibliography given above would read as follows:

American Friends Service Committee (1972),	*Struggle for Justice* (New York: Hill and Wang).
Ashworth, A. (1979)	"Prosecution and Procedure in Criminal Justice" Crim L.R. 480
Ashworth, A. (1995a)	*Sentencing and Criminal Justice* (London: Butterworths)
Ashworth, A. (1995b)	*Principles of Criminal Law* 2nd edn (Oxford, Oxford University Press)
Murray, B. (1992)	"Director Disqualification and the Criminal Law" 2 I.C.L.J. 165.

One advantage of this approach is that it allows one to be more economical with footnotes. Thus, instead of giving the full reference in every case, one could refer simply, for example, to 'Ashworth (1995a)', referring the reader to the appropriate entry in the bibliography.

APPENDIX 1

Specimen Sources of Law

1. STATUTE

Number 25 of 1982[1]

EXCHANGE CONTROL (CONTINUANCE) ACT, 1982[2]

[3]AN ACT TO CONTINUE IN OPERATION THE EXCHANGE CONTROL ACT, 1954. [27*th December*, 1982][4]

BE IT ENACTED BY THE OIREACHTAS AS FOLLOWS:[5]

[6]Continuance of Exchange Control Act,1954

1.—The following subsection is hereby substituted for section 2(2) of the Exchange Control Act, 1954, as amended by section 2 of the Exchange Control (Continuance and Amendment) Act, 1978:

"(2) This Act shall continue in operation until the 31st day of December,1986, and shall then expire".

Short title and collective citation

[7]**2.**—This Act may be cited as the Exchange Control (Continuance) Act, 1982.

[8](2) The Exchange Control Acts,1954 to 1978, and this Act may be cited together as the Exchange Control Acts, 1954 to 1982.

---

[1] Number and year
[2] Title
[3] Long title
[4] Date signed into law

[5] Enacting formula
[6] Marginal note
[7] Statement of short title
[8] Collective citation

2. STATUTORY INSTRUMENT

S.I No. 33 of 1990[9]

HOUSING ACT, 1988 (COMMENCEMENT) ORDER, 1990.[10]

The Minister for the Environment, in exercise of the powers conferred on him by section 31(9) of the Housing Act, 1988 (No. 28 of 1988), hereby orders as follows:[11]

1. This order may be cited as the Housing Act, 1988 (Commencement) Order, 1990.[12]

2. Sections 3, 25 and 26 of the Housing Act, 1988, shall come into operation on the 16th day of February, 1990.[13]

GIVEN under the Official Seal of the Minster for the Environment this 16th day of February, 1990[14]

PADRAIG FLYNN,
Minister for the Environment[15]

EXPLANATORY NOTE.[6]

(This note is not part of the instrument and does not purport to be a legal interpretation.)

This Order brings sections 3, 25 and 26 of the Housing Act, 1988, into operation with effect from 16th February, 1990.

Notice of the making of this Statutory Instrument was published Iris Oifigiúil *of 23rd February, 1990.*

---

[9] Number
[10] Title
[11] Minister responsible and enabling Act
[12] Mode of citation
[13] Substance of instrument
[14] Date of signature
[15] Name of Minister
[16] Explanatory note

3. LAW REPORT

Michael Ryan, Applicant, v. **The Director of Public Prosecutions,**[4] Respondent
[1988 J.R. No. 56][5]

High Court[6]   21st October, 1988[7]

Judicial review – Jurisdiction – Evidence – Ruling of inadmissibility – Statement of accused – Inadmissible statement accidentally given to jury – Retrial – Whether High Court entitled prior to retrial to restrain prosecution from adducing same statement – Whether such attempt an abuse of process of court[8]

[9]At a trial upon indictment in the Circuit Criminal Court on charges of rape and other offences a statement of the accused was ruled inadmissible by the trial judge, but given in error to the jury when it retired to consider its verdict. The accused applied in the High Court for orders by way of judicial review restraining the respondent from seeking to have the same statement admitted as evidence in the retrial.

Held by Barron J., in refusing the orders sought, that the admissibility of evidence in any trial is a matter solely within the jurisdiction of the presiding trial judge and the High Couour has no jurisdiction, whether by judicial review or otherwise, to make advance rulings upon matters which may or may not arise in a trial before another tribunal.
    The State (O'Callaghan) v. O hUadhaigh [1977] I.R. 42 and *Kelly v. Ireland* [1978] l.L.R.M. 318 considered.[10]

Cases mentioned in this report–[11]
The State (O'Callaghan) v. O hUadhaigh [19771 I.R. 42.
Kelly v. lreland [1978] I.L.R.M. 318.

---

[1]   Title of law report series
[2]   Year (of *Irish Reparts)*
[3]   Page number
[4]   Name of case
[5]   Registration number of case
[6]   Court in which case was heard
[7]   Date on which judgment was delivered
[8]   Catch-words
[9]   Headnote (summary of facts and judgment)
[10]   Cases considered
[11]   Cases mentioned in this report

Judicial Review.
[12]The facts are as stated in the judgment of Barron J., *post.* On the 14th March, 1988, the High Court (Hamilton P.) gave the applicant leave to apply for judicial review on the grounds set out in the judgment of Barron J. Full grounds of opposition, grounded upon the afffidavit of Detective Garda Thomas Lillis exhibiting the transcript of the original three day trial, were filed and pursuant to originating notice of motion dated the 28th March, 1988, the matter came on for hearing on the 25th July, 1988, before the High Coun (Barron J.).

Paul Carney S.C. (with *him Anthony Sammon)* for the applicant
James O'Relily for the respondentt[13]

Cur. adv. vult.[14]

Barron J.[15]   21st October, 1988
[16]The applicant was put on trial in the Circuit Criminal Court on charges of rape and other offences. His trial commenced on the 18th November, 1987, and continued for three days. In the course of the trial, the trial judge was required to rule *inter alia* on the admissibility of certain verbal statements and a written statement made by the accused. He ruled each of these statements to be inadmissible. . . .

The present application is to restrain the Director of Public Prosecutions on the retrial from seeking to have these statements admitted in evidence. . . .

The relief sought is refused.

Solicitors for the applicant: *Michael J. Staines & Co.*
Solicitor for the respondent: *Chief State Solicitor*[17]

Eanna Mulloy, B.L.[18]

---

[12] Description of the form of action
[13] Names of counsel appearing for the parties
[14] Indicates that this is a reserved judgment (see 'Glossary of Latin and French Law Terms' in Appendix 3 below).
[15] Name of judge
[16] Text of judgment
[17] Names of solicitors for the parties
[18] Name of reporter

APPENDIX 2

Abbreviations

The following is a list of abbreviations commonly encountered in legal literature. The full titles of periodicals are given in italics. Most of the other abbreviations are for law report series or legal institutions of various kinds. In certain cases, paragraph numbers have been inserted after the title, referring the reader to the paragraph in this book in which the item in question is described in more detail. Abbreviations for United States law reviews and journals have not been included here, as most of them are self-explanatory, e.g. Yale L.J. clearly stands for the *Yale Law Journal*. In any event, a comprehensive list of abbreviations for U.S, and other legal periodicals is provided at the beginning of each issue of the *Index to Legal Periodicals and Books* (7.23 above). Another good list of abbreviations will be found at the beginning of the first volume of *Halsbury's Laws of England* (7.26), while the most comprehensive of all is Raistrick's *Index to Legal Citations and Abbreviations* (14.03 above).

A.B.A.	American Bar Association
A.C.	Appeal Cases (6.20)
A.C.T.R.	Australian Capital Territory Reports
A.D.R.L.J.	Arbitration and Dispute Resolution Journal
Admin L.R.	Administrative Law Reports
A.J.I.L.	*American Journal of International Law*
A.L.J.	*Australian Law Journal*
A.L.J.R.	Australian Law Journal Reports
All E.R.	All England Law Reports
All E.R.(EC)	All England Law Reports (European Cases)
A.L.R.	American Law Reports (11.24)
	Australian Law Reports (12.06)
Am. J. Comp. L.	*American Journal of Comparative Law*
App. Cas.	Appeal Cases (1875-1990)
A.Y.I.L.	*Australian Yearbook of International Law*
B.A.C.R.	Brooker's Accident Compensation Reports (NZ)
B.C.C.	*British Company Law and Practice*
B.C.R.	Butterworths Company Law Reports (NZ)
B.C.L.C.	Butterworths Company Law Cases
B.H.R.C.	Butterworths Human Rights Cases
Bl. Comm.	Blackstone's *Commentaries on the Laws of England* (1765)
B.L.R.	Building Law Reports
	Business Law Review
B.P.I.R.	Bankruptcy and Personal Insolvency Reports
Bract.	Bracton, *De Legibus et Consuetudinibus Angliae* (13th century)

B.T.C.	British Tax Cases
B.T.R.	*British Tax Review*
B.Y.B.I.L.	*British Year Book of International Law*
Brit. J. Criminol.	*British Journal of Criminology*
B.U.I.L.J.	*Boston University International Law Journal*
Bull. J.S.B.	*Bulletin of the Judicial Studies Board*
Bus. L.R.	*Business Law Review*
B.Y.I.L.	*British Yearbook of International Law*
c.	Chapter (of an Act of U.K. Parliament)
C., Cd., Cmd, Cmnd, Cm.	Command Paper (U.K.)
CA	Court of Appeal (England and Wales)
Can. C.L.	*Canadian Current Law*
C.C.A.	Court of Criminal Appeal (Ireland)
C.C.C.	Canadian Criminal Cases
CCH T.C.	CCH Tax Cases
C.D.	Collection of Decisions of European Commission on Human Rights (1959-1974).
CDE	*Cahiers de Droit Europeen*
C.E.C.	European Community Cases (8.16)
C.F.I.	Court of First Instance (8.13)
Ch.	Law Reports, Chancery Division (6.20)
C.I.L.	*Contemporary Issues in Law*
C.J.Q.	*Civil Justice Quarterly*
C.L.	*Current Law Monthly Digest*
C.L.B.	*Commonwealth Law Bulletin*
C.L.C.	Commercial Law Cases
C.L. & P.	*Computer Law and Practice*
C.L. Pract.	*Commercial Law Practitioner* (Ireland)
C.L.J.	*Cambridge Law Journal* (also Camb. L.J.)
C.L.P.	*Current Legal Problems*
	Commercial Law Practitioner (alternative abbreviation)
C.L.R.	Commonwealth Law Reports (Australia)
CLRC	Criminal Law Revision Committee (England and Wales).
C.L.Y.	*Current Law Yearbook* (6.47)
C.M.L. Rev.	*Common Market Law Review*
C.M.L.R..	Common Market Law Reports (8.16)
Co. Inst.	Coke, *Institutes of the Laws of England* (1628-1644)
C.O.D.	Crown Office Digest
C.P.L.J.	*Conveyancing and Property Law Journal*
C.R.N.Z.	Criminal Reports of New Zealand
C.R.	Criminal Reports (Canada)
C.T.L.R.	*Computer and Telecommunications Law Review*
Ch.	Law Reports, Chancery Division (6.20.)
C.M.A.C.	Court Martial Appeal Court (England and Wales)
Co.Law	*Company Lawyer*

Comp. & Law	*Computers & Law*
Con. L.R.	Construction Law Reports
Conv.	*Conveyancer and Property Lawyer*
Cox C.C.	Cox's Criminal Cases (6.31)
Cr. App.R.	Criminal Appeal Reports (England and Wales)
Cr. App.R. (S)	Criminal Appeal (Sentencing) Reports (England and Wales)
Crim L.J.	*Criminal Law Journal* (Australia)
Crim L.Q.	*Criminal Law Quarterly* (Canada)
Crim.L.R.	*Criminal Law Review* (England)
Crim. Law	*Criminal Lawyer*
CSCE	Conference on Security and Co-operation in Europe
CSO	Community Service Order
D.C.R.	District Court Reports (New Zealand)
D.L.R.	Dominion Law Reports (Canada)
	Discrimination Law Reports (U.K.)
D.R.	Decisions and Reports of the European Commission on Human Rights (1975-1998)
D.U.L.J.	*Dublin University Law Journal*
EAT	Employment Appeals Tribunal (Ireland)
	Employment Appeal Tribunal (England and Wales)
E. & P.	*International Journal of Evidence and Proof.*
E.B.L.R.	*European Business Law Review*
EC	European Community
ECB	European Central Bank
E.C.H.R.	European Convention on Human Rights
ECJ	European Court of Justice
E.C.R.	European Court Reports (8.15)
E.C.R. – S.C.	European Court Reports – Staff Cases.
E.C.L.R.	*European Competition Law Review.*
EEA	European Economic Area
EEC	European Economic Community (now EC)
EEIG	European Economic Interest Grouping
E.F.A.Rev.	*European Foreign Affairs Review*
EFTA	European Free Trade Association
E.G.	*Estates Gazette*
E.G.L.R.	Estates Gazette Law Reports
E.H.R.L.R.	*European Human Rights Law Review*
E.H.R.R.	European Human Rights Reports
EIR	European Investment Bank
E.I.P.R.	*European Intellectual Property Review*
E.I.R.R.	*European Industrial Relations Review*
E.J.H.L.	*European Journal of Health Law*
E.J.I.L.	*European Journal of International Law* (9.21)
E.L.J.	*European Law Journal*
E.L.R.	Education Law Reports
	Employment Law Reports (Ireland)

	European Law Review (also E.L. Rev.)
E.L.R.N.Z.	Environmental Law Reports of New Zealand
E.M.L.R.	Entertainment and Media Law Reports
EMU	European Monetary Union
E.O.C.	Australian and New Zealand Equal Opportunity Cases.
E.O.R.	*Equal Opportunities Review*
E.O.R. Dig.	Equal Opportunities Review and Discrimination Case Digest.
E.L.P.	*European Public Law*
E.P.O.R.	European Patent Law Reports
E.R.	English Reports (6.17.), also Eng. Rep.
E.T.M.R.	European Trade Marks Reports
Ed.C.R.	Education Cases Reports
Eng. Rep.	English Reports (6.17), also E.R.
Ent. L.R.	*Entertainment Law Review*
Env.L.R.	Environmental Law Reports
ECSC	European Coal and Steel Community
E.R.N.Z.	Employment Reports of New Zealand
EU	European Union
Euratom	European Atomic Energy Agency
Eur. J. Crime Cr.L. Cr.J.	*European Journal of Crime, Criminal Law and Criminal Justice.*

F. (or Fed.R.)	Federal Reporter (U.S.) (11.15)
Fam.	Law Reports, Family Division (6.20)
F.C.R.	Family Court Reporter
	Federal Court Reports (Australia)
Fed. Supp.	Federal Supplement (U.S.) (11.15).
F.L.R.	Family Law Reports
	Federal Law Reports (Australia)
Frewen	Judgments of Irish Court of Criminal Appeal (1924 to 1989) (4.57).
F.S.R.	Fleet Street Reports
Fem L.S.	*Feminist Legal Studies*

GATT	General Agreement on Tariffs and Trade
G.I.L.S.I.	*Gazette of the Incorporated Law Society of Ireland* (now *Law Society Gazette*)
Glanv.	Glanville, *De Legibus et Consuetudinibus Regni Angliae* (c. 1189).
GmbH	(German) Gesellschaft mit beschrankter Haftung. (Limited company).

Hale CL	Hale's *Common Law* (c. 1713)
Hale PC	Hale's *Pleas of the Crown* (c.1736)
Hawk. PC	Hawkin's *Pleas of the Crown* (c.1716)
H.L.R.	Housing Law Reports
HL	House of Lords

	House of Lords Appeals (1866-1875)
HL Cas.	House of Lords Cases (1847-1866)
H.L.R.	Housing Law Reports
HMSO	Her Majesty's Stationery Office (for UK official publications)
Hold.L.R.	*Holdsworth Law Review*
Holdsworth HEL	Holdsworth's *History of English Law* (7.33)
H.R.L.J.	*Human Rights Law Journal*
I.B.L.	*Irish Business Law*
I.B.R.	*Irish Banking Review*
I.C.C.L.R.	*International Company and Commercial Law Review*
I.C.J.	International Court of Justice (9.11)
	International Commission of Jurists
I.C.J. Rep.	International Court of Justice Reports (9.11)
I.C.L.J.	*Irish Criminal Law Journal*
I.C.L.R.	Irish Common Law Reports, 1849-1866
	Incorporated Council of Law Reporting (England and Wales)
I.C.L.Q.	*International and Comparative Law Quarterly*
I.C.L.S.A.	*Irish Current Law Statutes Annotated.*
I.C.R.	Industrial Cases Reports
IH	Inner House of Scottish Court of Session (6.60)
IEA	International Energy Agency
I.I.L.R.	*Irish Insurance Law Review*
I.I.P.R.	*Irish Intellectual Property Review*
I.J.E.L.	*Irish Journal of European Law*
I.J.L. & I.T.	*International Journal of Law and Information Technology*
I.J.R.L.	*International Journal of Refugee Law*
ILC	International Law Commission
I.L.J.	*Industrial Law Journal.*
I.L.M.	*International Legal Materials* (9.16)
I.L.O.	International Labour Organisation (9.26)
I.L.P.	*International Legal Practitioner*
I.L.R.	Irish Law Reports 1838-1850
	International Law Reports (9.17)
I.L.R.M.	Irish Law Reports Monthly.
I.L.T.	*Irish Law Times*
I.L.T.R.	Irish Law Times Reports (7.16)
I.L.T.S.J.	*Irish Law Times and Solicitor's Journal*
I.M.L.	*International Media Law.*
I.P.	*International Peacekeeping*
I.P.E.L.J.	*Irish Planning and Environmental Law Journal*
I.P.Q.	*Intellectual Property Quarterly*
Iran-U.S.C.T.R.	Iran-U.S. Claims Tribunal Report
I.R.	Irish Reports
I.R.C.L.	Irish Reports, Common Law, 1867-1877
Ir. Ch.R.	Irish Chancery Reports, 1850-1866
I.R. Eq.	Irish Reports, Equity, 1866-1877
Ir. Eq. R.	Irish Equity Reports, 1838-1851

Ir. Jur.	*Irish Jurist*
Ir. Jur. Rep.	Irish Jurist Reports, 1935-1965 (4.53)
I.R.L.R.	Industrial Relations Law Reports
I.R. Term Rep.	Irish Term Reports, 1793-1795
I.S.L.R.	*Irish Student Law Review*
ITLOS	International Tribunal for the Law of the Sea.
I.T.L.Q.	*International Trade Law Quarterly*

J.A.C.L.	*Journal of Armed Conflict Law*
J.B.L.	*Journal of Business Law*
JC	Justiciary Cases (Scotland) (6.61)
J. Com. Mar. St.	*Journal of Common Market Studies*
J. Crim. L.	*Journal of Criminal Law* (Canada)
J.I.B.L.	*Journal of International Banking Law*
J.I.E.L.	*Journal of International Economic Law*
J.I.L.T.	*Journal of Information, Law and Technology* (7.20)
J.I.S.E.L.	*Journal of the Irish Society for European Law* (7.19)
J.I.S.L.L.	*Journal of the Irish Society for Labour Law* (7.19)
J.L.S.S.	*Journal of the Law Society of Scotland*
J. Law & Soc.	*Journal of Law and Society*
J. Leg. Hist.	*Journal of Legal History*
J.M.L. & P.	*Journal of Media Law and Practice*
J.P.	*Justice of the Peace*
J.P.N.	Justice of the Peace Reports and Local Government Notes of Cases
J.P. Rep.	Justice of the Peace and Local Government Law Reports
J.S.B.J.	*Judicial Studies Board Journal*
J.S.P.T.L.	*Journal of the Society of Public Teachers of Law*
J.S.S.L.	*Journal of Social Security Law*
J. Soc. Wel. & Fam. L.	*Journal of Social Welfare and Family Law*
Jur. Rev.	*Juridical Review* (Scotland)

K.B.	Law Reports, King's Bench. (6.20)
K.C.L.J.	*King's College Law Journal*
K.I.R.	Knight's Industrial Reports.

L.Ed.	Lawyer's Edition (U.S. Supreme Court Reports) (11.10)
L.G. Rev.	*Local Government Review*
L.J.	*Law Journal* 1866-1965.
L.J. Ir	Law Journal, Irish Supplement, 1931-1934.
L.N.T.S.	League of Nations Treaty Series
L.Q.R.	*Law Quarterly Review*
L.R. App. Cas.	Law Reports Appeal Cases
LRC	Law Reform Commission (Ireland)
	Labour Relations Commission (Ireland)
	Law Reports of the Commonwealth (12.02)
L.S.	*Legal Studies*
L.S.G.	*Law Society Gazette* (England and Wales)

Law Lib.	*The Law Librarian*
Lit.	*Litigation*
M.J.L.S.	*Mountbatten Journal of Legal Studies* (7.20)
M.L.B.	*Manx law Bulletin*
M.J.L.I.	*Medico-Legal Journal of Ireland*
M.L.R.	*Modern Law Review*
Med. Sci. Law	*Medicine, Science and the Law*
M.U.L.R.	*Melbourne University Law Review*
NATO	North Atlantic Treaty Organisation
N.I.	Northern Ireland Law Reports
N.I.J.B.	Northern Ireland Judgments Bulletin (5.08)
N.I.L.Q.	*Northern Ireland Legal Quarterly*
N.I.L.R.	*Netherlands International Law Review*
N.L.J.	*New Law Journal*
Nott. L.J.	*Nottingham Law Journal.*
N.R.	National Reporter (Canada)
N.S.W.L.R.	New South Wales Law Reports
N.Z.L.R.	New Zealand Law Reports
	New Zealand Law Review
N.Z.C.L.D.	*New Zealand Case Law Digest*
OECD	Organisation for Economic Co-operation and Development
O.J.L.S.	*Oxford Journal of Legal Studies*
OJ	*Official Journal* (of the European Communities).
OSCE	Organisation for Security and Co-operation in Europe
P.	Probate, Divorce and Admiralty Law Reports (England and Wales) (6.19)
P.C.	Privy Council
	Peace Commissioner (Ireland)
P.C.I.J.	Permanent Court of International Justice (9.13)
P. & C.R.	Property, Planning and Compensation Reports
P. & P.	*Practice and Procedure*
P.L.	*Public Law*
Proc. A.S.I.L.	*Proceedings of the American Society of International Law*
Proc. R.I.A.	*Proceedings of the Royal Irish Academy*
Qd. R.	Queensland Reports (Australia)
Rev. I.C.J.	*Review of the International Commission of Jurists*
S.A.	
S.A.L.R.	South African Law Reports
S.A.S.R.	South Australia State Reports
S.A.L.J.	*South African Law Journal*
SC	Session Cases (Scotland) (6.61)

	Senior Counsel (Ireland)
	Supreme Court (Ireland)
SC (HL)	Session Cases (House of Lords) (6.61.)
SCCR	Scottish Criminal Cases Reports (6.62)
SCLR	Scottish Civil Law Reports (6.62)
SCOLAG	*Bulletin of the Scottish Legal Action Group*
S. Ct.	Supreme Court Reporter (U.S.) (11.10)
SEA	Single European Act
S.I.	Statutory Instrument
S.L.T.	Scots Law Times (
Sol. J.	*Solicitors' Journal*
S.R. & O.	Statutory Rules and Orders (4.37)
S.T.C.	Simon's Tax Cases
St. Tr.	State Trials 1163-1820
T.C.	Tax Cases
Tax Cas.	Tax Cases
TEU	Treaty of the European Union (8.01)
T.L.R.	The Times Law Reports (1884-1950)
UD	Unfair Dismissal (4.58)
U.K.T.S.	United Kingdom Treaty Series
UCLOS	United Nations Convention on the Law of the Sea
U.N.T.S.	United Nations Treaty Series
U.S.	United States Supreme Court Reports
U.S.C.C.A.N.	*U.S. Code Congressional and Administrative News*
U.S.T.	*U.S. Treaties and Other International Agreements*
V.A.T.T.R.	Value Added Tax Tribunal Reports,
V.R.	Victorian Reports (Australia) (12.07)
W.A.L.R.	Western Australian Law Reports (1898-1959)
WIPO	World Intellectual Property Organisation
W.L.R.	Weekly Law Reports (6.23)
W.N.	Law Reports. Weekly Notes (1866-1952)
WTO	World Trade Organisation (9.27)
Y.B.I.L.C.	*Yearbook of the International Law Commission*

Glossary of Latin and French Law Terms

The following is a list of Latin and Law French words and phrases commonly found in legal writing. These and many other terms are explained in the various dictionaries and reference books mentioned in 7.31 above, such as the *Oxford Companion to Law* and *Murdoch's Dictionary of Irish law.* Curzon's *Law Dictionary* is particularly good for this purpose as well.

a fortiori	with a yet stronger reason; more compellingly.
a aver et tener	(Law French) to have and to hold.
a mensa et thoro	"from table and bed", a form of divorce or separation which did not dissolve a marriage.
a vinculo matrimonii	from the bond of marriage (a divorce dissolving a marriage).
ab initio	from the beginning
actor sequitur	*actor sequitur forum rei,* the plaintiff follows the defendant to the jurisdiction to which the defendant is subject.
actus reus	the outward act, as opposed to the mental element, of a crime.
ad hoc	for this purpose
ad idem	to the same effect, or of the same mind (as in consensus *ad idem*)
ad rem	to the point, relevant.
ad valorem	according to value (used in context of levying tax or excise duty)
aliunde	otherwise or from another source. A person might know *aliunde* why a decision was being taken, and could not therefore complain if not expressly informed of the reason by the decision-maker.
amicus curiae	a friend of the court (a person who is not a direct party to an action but who is permitted to make submissions).
animus furandi	the intention to steal
animus possidendi	the intention to possess
animus testandi	the intention to make a will
ante	before
arguendo	for the sake of argument, as in "assuming *aguendo* that this is so ......"
audi alteram partem	hear the other side. One of the two traditional principles of natural justice; see *nemo iudex* below.
autre vie	(Law French) other life (as in estate *pur autre vie,* a life estate measured by the life of somebody other than the

	holder)
autrefois	on an other occasion (as in *autrefois acquit/convict*, acquitted or convicted on a previous occasion).
avizandum	In Scottish law, the time taken by a court to consider the judgment to be delivered in a case.
bona fide	in good faith
bona vacantia	goods without an owner. Usually become property of the State.
caveat emptor	let the buyer beware
certum est quod	*certum est quod certum reddi potest*. A thing is certain if it can be made certain.
cestui que trust	(Law French) the beneficiary of a trust
ceteris paribus	other things being equal
colore officii	by colour of office.
commorientes	dying at the same time.
consensus	agreement
contra bonos mores	against good morals.
contra legem	against the law
contra proferentem	against the person proferring (the principle that an ambiguous provision, such as a contractual term, is construed against the person relying on it)
coram	in the presence of.
corpus delicti	the substance of the crime (*not* the body of the deceased).
corpus iuris	a body of law (usually refers to a legal encyclopedia such as the *Corpus Juris Hibernici*, a compendium of early Irish law)
corpus juris	alternative spelling for *corpus iuris*
cujus est solum....	*cuius est solum, ejus est usque ad coelum et ad inferos* (he who owns the land owns everything above it and everything beneath it).
cur. adv. vult	the court took time to deliberate before delivering judgment (indicates a reserved as opposed to an *ex tempore* judgment)
curia regis	the King's Court.
custos morum	guardian of morals
damnum absque injuria	loss without injury, also *damnum sine injuria*
de bonis non.....	*de bonis non administrandis* (describes a situation where a previous administrator has failed to complete the administration of an estate)
de facto	in fact, or in reality
de jure	in law, or as a matter of legal right.
de minimis...	*de minimis non curat lex*, the law does not concern itself with trifles.
de novo	starting again, anew or afresh.
delegatus non potest...	*delegatus non potest delegare*. A delegate cannot delegate.
dictum	a saying or statement
dicta	plural of *dictum* (as in *obiter dicta*, q.v.)
doli capax/incapax	capable/incapable of wrongdoing (used in relation to crimi-

nal liability of children).

dominus litis	the master of the suit (i.e. of the legal action)
donatio mortis causa	gift made in anticipation of death
duces tecum	bring with you. (A *subpoena duces tecum* orders a person to bring certain documents or materials for production in court).
dubitante	doubting (in a law report, an indication that a judge expressed doubts about the soundness of a particular legal rule).
dum casta	while she remains chaste.
dum bene se gesserint	see *quamdiu se bene gesserint* (below).
ejusdem generis	of the same kind.
ex aequo et bono	according to equity and good conscience
en banc	in full court.
ex abundante cautela	out of abundant caution.
ex debito justiciae	as of right (contrast with *ex gratia*).
ex facie	on the face of it.
ex gratia	given as a favour (without conceding any legal entitlement on the part of the recipient)
ex hypothesi	following from the hypothesis stated.
ex officio	by virtue of an office held (e.g. the Taoiseach is *ex officio* a member of the Council of State).
ex parte	on the part of or on behalf of. Generally used to indicate an application made by one party without notice to the other, e.g. an *ex parte* application for leave to apply for judicial review or for an interim injunction.
ex post facto	after the event, or retrospectively.
expression unius…	*expressio unius (est) exclusio alterius*. Express mention of one means the exclusion of the other; a principle of statutory interpretation.
ex turpi causa…	*ex turpi causa non oritur actio*. A person cannot seek a remedy when the transaction was illegal.
factum probans	an evidentiary fact from the existence of which a court may infer the existence of the principal fact to be proved (*factum probandum*).
factum probandum	the principal fact to be proved. Plural: *facta probanda*.
felo de se	(Anglo Latin) meaning with (1) suicide and (2) a person who committed suicide.
ferae naturae	of a wild nature. One refers to "animals *ferae naturae*" to indicate wild as opposed to domesticated animals which said to be *mansuetae naturae*.
fiat	let it be done. (Often used to indicate official permission, e.g. the *fiat* of the Attorney General is required).
fiat justitia	let justice be done
fieri facias (fi fa)	cause to be done (an order or writ for the execution of a judgment, usually directed to a sheriff to seize goods belonging to the defendant). Usually abbreviated to *fi fa*.
filius nullius	nobody's son (a term formerly used to describe a child

	born outside of marriage).
flagrante delicto	caught in the act of committing an offence.
force majeure	(French) circumstances beyond one's control; an unforeseeable event, usually one preventing a person from performing an obligation or fulfilling a contract.
functus officio	having fulfilled the task. (A judge who has brought a case to its conclusion is said to be *functus officio*, having no further role in the matter).
generalia specialibus...	*generalia specialibus non derogant.* A general statutory provision does not repeal an earlier specific provision.
habeas corpus	have the body of... (an order directing a person who is detaining another to bring the detainee before a court for a decision on the legality of the detention).
habendum	to be had (the part of a conveyance of land denoting the amount of interest conveyed, e.g. fee simple or life estate).
ignorantia legis	*Ignorantia legis neminem/haud/non excusat*; ignorance of the law is no excuse.
In b./In bonis	In the goods of. (Used in titles of probate cases, e.g. *In bonis Murphy*).
in camera	in private. (A court hearing *in* camera is one from which everybody other than the parties is excluded. *Camera* in Latin means a chamber or a room).
in consimili casu	in a like case. *In consimili casu, consimile debet esse remedium*, in like cases the remedy ought to be the same.
in extenso	at full length.
in forma pauperis	procedure (now abolished) whereby an impoverished litigant could seek free legal representation and exemption from court fees.
in loco parentis	in place of a parent.
in medias res	in the middle of things.
in pari delicto	equally culpable. The maxim *in pari delicto potior est causa defendentis* means that when both parties are at fault, the defendant has the stronger case.
in pari materia	in an analogous case.
in personam	a right or claim against a specific person only (as opposed to a claim on property), leading to personal liability on the part of the defendant, usually to pay monetary compensation.
in re	in the matter of
in rem	a right or claim *in rem*, as opposed to *in personam*, is a right against persons generally, and imposes a duty on everyone to respect the claimant's right, usually over certain property.
in situ	in its place, or in its original place.
in toto	in full.
infra	below.
inter alia	among other things
inter alios	among other persons.

inter partes	between (the) parties.
inter se	among themselves.
inter vivos	among living persons. An *inter vivos* gift is one effected while the parties are alive.
intra vires	within one's powers, as opposed to *ultra vires* (q.v.)
ipse dixit	he himself/she herself said. An unsupported assertion.
ipsissimis verbis	in the exact same words
ius/iuris	law/of law. The words *ius* and *jus* are the same, sometimes spelled with "i", sometimes with "j".
jus accrescendi	the right of survivorship in a joint tenancy.
jus gentium	the law of nations. Used nowadays to refer to the law governing relations between states - public international law.
jus quaesitum tertio	right acquired by a third party to a contract.
jus tertii	the right of a third party.
lex fori	the law of the forum, the place where the case is heard. Used in context of a conflict of laws.
lex loci	the law of the place. *Lex loci celebrationis* means the law of the place in which a marriage was celebrated.
lex loci delicti	the law of the place where the wrong occurred.
lex loci solutionis	the place at which the contract is to be performed or the payment made.
lis	a legal action or lawsuit.
lis pendens	a pending action.
locus poenitentiae	a place for repentance. An opportunity to change one's mind, to reconsider a planned course of action or, more commonly, to withdraw from a contract before it becomes fully binding.
locus regit actum	the place governs the act. A principle of private international law.
locus sigilli (L.S.)	in place of the seal. Often found at the end of statutory instruments of various kinds indicating where seal was placed on original.
locus standi	standing. Refers to a requirement that a person must have a sufficient interest in legal proceedings in order to initiate them.
mala fide	with bad faith
mare clausum	a closed sea. A sea under the jurisdiction of one particular country.
mens rea	the mental element of a crime.
motu proprio	of his/her own accord.
mutatis mutandis	the necessary changes having been made.
ne exeat regno	let him/her not leave the kingdom. An order prohibiting a person from leaving the jurisdiction.
nec vi, nec clam, nec precario	without violence, without secrecy, without permission. The conditions under which one party may acquire adverse possession of another's land.
nemo dat....	*nemo dat quod non habet.* Nobody can give what he/she has not got. A principle of law relating to sale of goods.

nemo debet bis vexari   nobody should be twice trouble (for the same offence). The rule against double jeopardy.

nemo iudex...   *nemo iudex in causa sua* or *nemo debet esse iudex in propria sua causa.* Nobody should be a judge in his/her own case. A principle of natural justice; see *audi alteram partem* above.

nemo tenetur seipsum accusare   nobody should have to incriminate him/herself. The privilege against self-incrimination.

nisi   unless. In English matrimonial law, a decree *nisi* of divorce is a temporary decree which may be followed by a decree absolute dissolving the marriage.

nisi prius   unless before. In modern times referred to a commission conferred on assize judges to try cases. It therefore came to mean a case tried by a jury with one judge as opposed to a case tried by a full court with several judges.

nolle prosequi   unwilling to prosecute. A decision of the D.P.P. or other prosecuting authority not to proceed with a prosecution.

non est factum   it is not his deed.

non obstante   notwithstanding.

noscitur a sociis   it is known by its associates. A principle of statutory interpretation whereby the meaning of a doubtful word may be ascertained by reference to the meanings of words closely associated with it.

novus actus interveniens   a new act intervening.

nudum pactum   an unenforceable agreement.

nulla bona   no goods. The words endorsed by a sheriff on an order of *fieri facias* (q.v.) indicating that there were no goods to be seized.

nullum crimen   *nullum crimen sine lege/nulla poena sine lege.* There shall be no crime unless created by law/no penalty unless specified by law. The principle of legality.

obiter dictum   a statement made in passing. A judicial statement not forming part of the *ratio decidendi* (q.v.) of judgment.

omnia praesumuntur...   *Omnia praesumuntur rite et solemniter esse acta.* Everything is presumed to have been done properly and solemnly. The presumption of legality.

onus probandi   the onus of proof.

pacta sunt servanda   agreements must be honoured. A principle of international treaty law.

pari passu   with equal speed or in equal measure. Usually refers to right of creditors to receive a share of assets without preference.

passim   here and there (throughout a text).

pendente lite   while a lawsuit is pending.

per   *per* is often used in legal texts to mean "by", to indicate that a statement was made or a judgment delivered by a particular person e.g. "*per* Walsh J."

per annum	a year, as in "he was paid £12,000 per annum".
per capita	each. Literally "by heads".
per curiam	by the court
per diem	a day, as in *per annum* (q.v.). A *per diem* allowance is a payment made on a daily basis.
per incuriam	through carelessness or oversight. Usually refers to a decision reached by a court through the application of the wrong legal rule or principle.
per minas	by threats or menaces
per quod servitium amisit	as a result of which he lost the services [of a servant or a wife (in former times)]. A person could sue for loss resulting from injury to a servant. If the plaintiff was suing for the loss of his wife's "society" (her company), the action was entitled *per quod consortium amisit*.
per se	in itself, or of itself.
per stirpes	by the stocks. A term of succession law. See Succession Act, 1965, s. 3(3).
post	after, as in *post mortem*, after death.
post hoc, ergo...	*post hoc, ergo propter hoc*, meaning "after this, therefore because of this". A logical fallacy of thinking that because one thing follows another, it must have resulted from that other.
praecipe	a document containing the particulars of an instrument which the plaintiff wishes to have prepared or issued, such as a writ for the execution of a judgment.
pro forma	as a matter of form.
pro rata	proportionately.
pro se	on one's own behalf.
pro tanto	to that extent.
probandum	the fact or matter to be proved.
quamdiu se bene gesserint	as long as they are of good behaviour. Describes the tenure of judicial office.
quia timet	because he/she fears. A *quia timet* injunction is one sought because of apprehended harm.
quo warranto	with what authority. An action (nowadays by way of judicial review) challenging the validity of the respondent's tenure of a particular office.
quoad	with regard to. *Quoad hunc* (with regard to this male), *quoad hanc* (with regard to this female), *quoad hoc* (with regard to this thing).
quod vide (q.v.)	which see. Usually referring reader to a word or phrase explained earlier in the text.
quantum meruit	the amount earned or the amount something was worth.
R.	In U.K. and some Commonwealth case titles, *R* stands for *Rex* (King) or *Regina* (Queen), depending on the incumbent of the throne.
ratio decidendi	the reason for a judicial decision. The principle of law applicable to the facts of a case. Contrast with *obiter dictum* (q.v.)

ratio legis	the rationale or reason behind a law.
ratione materiae	by reason of the subject matter. A complaint made to the European Court (or formerly to the Commission) of Human Rights may be dismissed *ratione materiae* (subject matter not covered by Convention on Human Rights), *ratione temporis* (by reason of time), *ratione loci* (by reason of place) or *ratione personae* (by reason of person).
rebus (sic) stantibus	in these circumstances. An implied condition of a treaty that it will no longer be binding when the conditions under which it came into existence have changed substantially.
recte	correctly.
res	thing or matter.
res furtivae	stolen goods.
res gestae	things done. In the law of evidence, it refers to the circumstances surrounding the fact in issue.
res integra	a question on which there is no existing legal rule or precedent and which therefore must be decided in accordance with first principles. Same as *res nova*.
res judicata	a case judicially decided. The phrase *res judicata* refers to principle whereby a case can be reopened once it has finally been decided.
res ipsa loquitur	the thing or matter speaks for itself. A principle of tort law.
res nova	see *res integra*.
res peruit domino	the loss falls on the owner (principle of sale of goods law).
respondeat superior	let the master answer, or be responsible. The principle of vicarious liability.
restitutio in integrum	restoration to the original position.
scienter	knowingly.
sed quaere	but enquire further.
semble	it seems.
sic	thus. Often used to indicate a factual or grammatical error in a passage being quoted, e.g. he said that "the plaintiffs was (*sic*) in error".
sine die	without a day, indefinitely, e.g. adjourned *sine die*.
spes successionis	the hope of succeeding to property.
statim	immediately.
status quo	the situation as it is now.
status quo ante	the situation as it was before.
sua sponte	of his or her own accord. A court is said to act *sua sponte* when it decides a matter not raised by the parties to the proceedings.
sub judice	under judicial consideration. Prejudicial statements made about a matter of which a court has seisin may constitute contempt of court.
sub nom.	under the name of. Sometimes a case may be reported under different names, e.g. *D.P.P. v Morgan* [1975] 2 All E.R.

	347 is reported *sub nom. D.P.P. v McDonald* [1976] A.C. 182.
sui generis	one of a kind.
sui juris	of full age and capacity.
supra	above. Used to refer reader to earlier passage in a book or article.
terminus a quo	the boundary from which.
terminus ad quem	the boundary to which.
terra nullius	no-man's land. Territory not owned or claimed by any state.
uberrima fides	the utmost good faith. *Uberrima fides* is the nominative case. The genitive case is used in expressions like "a conract *uberrimae fidei*", a contract of the utmost good faith.
ubi ius, ibi remedium	where there is a right, there is a remedy.
ultra vires	beyond one's powers. Contrast with *intra vires* (q.v.)
ut res magis....	*Ut res magis valeat quam pereat.* It is better that a legal instrument or thing should survive rather than perish.
venditioni exponas	Put up for sale (imperative). An order directing a sheriff to sell seized goods at the best price available. See *fieri facias* above.
venire de novo	a writ directing a new trial.

Irish Law Books Published since 1950

Abortion Law

All Party Oireachtas Committee on Constitution	*Fifth Progress Report: Abortion* pn 9183 (Dublin: Stationery Office, 2000) 124 & 592 & 8 pp.
Doctrine and Life	*Abortion. Law and Conscience* Special issue of *Doctrine and Life* Vol. 42:5, pp. 229-348 (Dublin: Dominican Publications, 1992)
Flannery, A. (ed.),	*Abortion and the Law* (Dublin: Dominican Publications, 1983)
Glendon, M.A.	*Abortion and Divorce in Western Law* (Cambridge, MA.: Harvard UP, 1987) 197 pp.
Hadley, J.,	*Abortion: Between Freedom and Necessity* (Philadelphia, Temple UP, 1996) xiv + 250 pp. Contains chapter partly devoted to Ireland.
Kingston, J. and Whelan, A. with Bacik, I.,	*Abortion and the Law* (Dublin: Round Hall Sweet and Maxwell, 1997) xxxiii + 347 pp.
Lee, E.,	*Abortion Law and Politics Today* (Basingstoke: Macmillan, 1998) xviii + 233 pp. (Chapter on Ireland by T O'Brien).
McDonagh, S. (ed.),	*The Attorney General v X and Others: Judgments of the High Court and Supreme Court. Legal Submissions made to the Supreme Court* (Dublin: ICLR, 1992) 103 pp.
Smyth, A. (ed.),	*The Abortion Papers: Ireland* (Dublin: Attic Press, 1992) 207 pp.

Administrative Law

Barrington, T.J.,	*The Irish Administrative System* (Dublin: I.P.A., 1980) x + 242 pp. Bibliog.
Bradley, C.,	*Judicial Review* (Dublin: Round Hall Ltd, 2000) lxxiv + 787 pp.
Delany, H.,	*Judicial Review of Administrative Action: A Comparative Analysis* (Dublin: Round Hall Sweet and Maxwell, 2000) xl + 281 pp.

Grogan, V.,   *Administrative Tribunals in the Public Sector* (Dublin, I.P.A., 1961) 76 pp.

Hadfield, B. (ed.),   *Judicial Review: A Thematic Approach* (Dublin: Gill and Macmillan, 1995) xxxv + 408 pp. Contains chapter (by Dr G. Hogan) on Republic of Ireland.

Hogan, G. and   *Administrative Law in Ireland,* 3rd ed. (Dublin: Round Hall
   Morgan, D.G.,   Sweet and Maxwell, 1998) xc + 992 pp. [1st ed. 1986]

Keane, R.,   *The Law of Local Government in the Republic of Ireland* (Dublin: ILSI, 1982) xliv + 423 pp

Stout, R.M.,   *Administrative Law in Ireland* (Dublin, I.P.A., 1985) xxix + 514 pp.

Adoption Law

O'Halloran, K.,   *Adoption Law in the Two Jurisdictions of Ireland: A Comparative Perspective* (Aldershot: Avebury, 1994) xxiii + 234 pp.

O'Halloran, K.,   *Adoption Law and Practice* (Dublin: Butterworths Ireland Ltd, 1992) xxvii + 384 pp.

Agricultural Law

Sheedy,   *A Farmer's Affairs in Order: Wills, Titles of Land, Estate Duty* (Dublin: Irish Farmer's Journal, 1967).

Sheedy   *The Law of the Land: A Practical Guide to the Laws that Control Farm Ownership and Land Transfers* (Dublin: Agribooks, 1981).

Walsh, E.S. (ed.),   *Agriculture and the Law* (Dublin: Round Hall Sweet and Maxwell, 1996) x + 273p

Annual Reviews

Byrne, R. and Binchy, W.,   *Annual Review of Irish Law* (an annual publication by Round Hall Sweet and Maxwell beginning with the year 1987).

Arbitration Law

Carrigan, M.W.,   *Handbook on Arbitration in Ireland* (Dublin; Law Society of Ireland, 1998) viii + 44 pp.

Forde, M.,   *Arbitration Law and Procedure* (Dublin: Round Hall Press, 1994) xxvi + 159 pp.

Auctioneering Law

Mahon, A.P.,   *Auctioneering and Estate Agency Law in Ireland* (Dublin: The Irish Law Log, 1990) 195 pp.

Banking Law

Breslin, J.,   *Banking Law in the Republic of Ireland* (Dublin: Gill and Macmillan, 1998) xcvi + 913 pp.

Donnelly, M.,   *The Law of Banks and Credit Institutions* (Dublin: Round Hall Sweet and Maxwell, 2000) lxxxvi + 586 pp.

Johnston, W.,   *Banking and Security Law in Ireland* (Dublin: Butterworths, 1998) lxxix + 702 pp.

O'Connor, E.R.,   *The Law and Practice in Ireland relating to Cheques and Analogous Instruments: The Paying and Collecting Banker* (Dublin: The Institute of Bankers in Ireland, 1993) xii + 286 pp.

Bankruptcy Law, see Commercial Law

Bibliographies and related works

Eager, A.R.,   *A Guide to Irish Bibliographical Material* 2nd ed. (London: Library Association, 1980) xvi + 502 pp. [1st ed. 1964]

Finnegan, R.B. and   *Irish Government Publications. A Select List 1972-1992*
    Wiles, J.L.,   (Dublin: Irish Academic Press, 1995) 58 pp.

Ford, P. and Ford, G.,   *Select List of Reports of Enquiries of the Irish Dáil and Senate 1922-1972* (Shannon, IUP, 1974) 64 pp.

Hepple, B.A., Neeson,   *A Bibliography of the Literature on British and Irish La-*
    J.M., and O'Higgins, P.,   *bour Law* (London: Mansell, 1975) xxv + 331 pp.

Hepple, B.A.,   *Labour Law in Great Britain and Ireland until 1978* (Lon-
    O'Higgins, P. *et al.*   don: Sweet and Maxwell, 1981) xxii + 131 pp.

Jones, D.L. and Pond, C.,   *Parliamentary Holdings in Libraries in Britain and Ireland* (Westminster: House of Commons Library, 1993) viii + 202 pp.

Maltby, A. and   *Irish Official Publications: A Guide to Republic of Ire-*
    McKenna, B.,   *land Papers with a breviate of reports 1922-1972* (Oxford: Pergamon, 1980) xi + 377 pp.

Marvin, J.G.,   *Legal Bibliography, or, A Thesaurus of American, English, Irish and Scotch Law Books* (Buffalo, New York, 1953) vii + 800 pp. First published in 1847.

Maxwell, L.F. & Maxwell, W.H.,	*A Legal Bibliography of the British Commonwealth of Nations* Volume 4, *Irish Law to 1956* 2nd ed. (London, Sweet and Maxwell, 1957) [1st ed. 1936]
O'Higgins, P.,	*A Bibliography of Periodical Literature Relating to Irish Law* (Belfast: NILQ, 1966) xvi + 401 pp.
O'Higgins, P.,	*A Bibliography of Periodical Literature Relating to Irish Law: First Supplement* (Belfast: NILQ, 1973) x + 149 pp.
O'Higgins, P.,	*A Bibliography of Periodical Literature Relating to Irish Law: Second Supplement* (Belfast: SLS Legal Publications, 1983) xx + 140 pp.
O'Higgins, P.,	*Bibliography of Irish Trials and other Legal Proceedings* (Abingdon: Professional Books, 1986) xxvii + 504 pp.
O'Higgins, P & Partington, M.,	*Social Security Law in Britain and Ireland: A Bibliography* (London: Mansell, 1986) xxvii + 417 pp.
O'Malley, T.,	*The Round Hall Guide to the Sources of Law: An Introduction to Legal Research and Writing* (Dublin: Round Hall Press, 1993) 10 + 217 pp. 1st ed. of present book.
Raistrick, D.,	*Lawyers' Law Books: A Practical Index to Legal Literature* 3rd ed. (London: Butterworths, 1994) xxxv + 604 pp. Contains many Irish entries.
Twining, W.L. and Uglow, J. (eds.),	*Law Publishing and Legal Information: Small Jurisdictions of the British Isles* (London: Sweet and Maxwell, 1981). 188 pp. Contains chapter on Ireland as well as a short select bibliography of Irish law books.
Winterton, J, and Moys, E.M. (eds.),	*Information Sources in Law* 2nd ed. (London: Bowker Sauer, c. 1997) xxii + 673 pp. Contains chapter by John Furlong on Ireland.

Biographies and Memoirs

Ball, F.E.,	*The Judges in Ireland 1221- 1921* (Dublin: Round Hall Press, 1993) xxii + 365 + 408 pp. (First published by John Murray (London), 1926).
Comyn, J.,	*Their Friends at Court* (Chicester: Barry Rose, 1973) viii + 143 pp.
Comyn, J.,	*Summing It Up: Memoirs of an Irishman at the English Bar* (Dublin: Round Hall Press, 1991) 232 pp.
Comyn, J.,	*Watching Brief: Further Memoirs of an Irishman at Law in England* (Dublin: Round Hall Press, 1993) 170 pp.
Comyn, J.,	*Leave to Appeal: Further Legal Memoirs* (Dublin: Round Hall Press, 1994) 168 pp.

Comyn, J.,   *"If Your Lordship Pleases": Legal Recollections* (Dublin: Round Hall Sweet and Maxwell, 1996) viii + 196 pp.

Delany, V.T.H.,   *Christopher Palles, Lord Chief Baron of Her Majesty's Court of Exchequer in Ireland 1874-1916. His Life and Times* (Dublin: Figgis, 1960).xii + 200 pp.

Golding, G.,   *George Gavan Duffy 1882-1951: A Legal Biography* (Dublin: Irish Academic Press, 1982) 224 pp.

Hale, L.,   *John Philpot Curran: His Life and Times* (London: Jonathan Cape, 1958) 287 pp.

Healy, M.,   *The Old Munster Circuit* (Dublin and Cork: Mercier Press, 1979) 272 pp. First published by Michael Joseph Ltd in 1939.

Hostettler, J.,   *Sir Edward Carson: A Dream Too Far* (Chicester: Barry Rose, 1997) xvii + 334 pp.

Lee, G.A.,   *A Memoir of the South Western Circuit* (Dublin: Moytura Press, 1990) 55 pp.

Lindsay, P.,   *Memories* (Dublin: Blackwater Press, 1992) vii + 200 pp.

McArdle, J.,   *Irish Legal Anecdotes* (Dublin: Gill and Macmillan, 1995) x + 230 pp.

MacKenzie, P.,   *Lawful Occasions: The Old Eastern Circuit* (Cork and Dublin: Mercier Press, 1991) 151 pp.

Mackey, R.,   *Windward of the Law* 2nd ed. with new material (Dublin: Round Hall Press, 1991). 203 pp. First edition published by Allen in 1965).

Matthews, A.C., (ed.),   *Immediate Man: Cuimhni ar Chearbhaill O Dalaigh* (Dublin: Dolmen Press, 1983) 79 pp.

Montgomey Hyde, H.,   *Carson: The Life of Sir Edward Carson, Lord Carson of Duncairn* (London: William Heinemann Ltd, 1953) 515 pp. Bibliog.

O'Higgins, T.F.,   *A Double Life* (Dublin: Town House and Country House, 1996) 308 pp.

Sheehy, E.,   *May it Please the Court* (Dublin, 1951).

Sullivan, A.M.,   *The Last Sergeant: Memoirs of Sergeant A.M. Sullivan QC* (Dublin: MacDonald & Co., 1952) viii + 320 pp.

Building Law

Keane, D.,   *Building and the Law* (Dublin: Institute of Architects of Ireland, 1993) 244 pp.

Lyden, J.M.E. & McGrath, M.,	*Irish Building and Engineering Case Law* (Dublin: Society of Chartered Surveyors, 1989) xii + 595 pp.
Meghen, P.,	*A Guide to Building Contracts in Ireland* (Limerick: Meghen Hayes and Co, 1985) 176 pp.
O Cofaigh, E.,	*The Building Regulations Explained* (Dublin: Royal Institute of Architects of Ireland, 1993) 224 pp.

Building Societies

Murdoch, H.,	*Building Society Law in Ireland: A Guide* (Dublin: Topaz Publications, 1989) xxxiv + 214p

Business Law, *see* **Commercial Law**

Capital Markets, *see* **Commercial Law** and **Financial Services**

Charities. See **Equity and Trusts.**

Children and the Law. See also **Family Law** and **Juvenile Justice**.

CARE,	*Children Deprived: The Care Memorandum on Deprived Children and Children's Services in Ireland* (Dublin; CARE, 1972) 112 pp.
CARE,	*Planning for Our Children: The Report of the Care Conference* (Dublin: CARE, 1977) 101 pp.
Children's Rights Alliance,	*Small Voices: Vital Rights. Submission to the United Nations Committee on the Rights of the Child* (Dublin: Children's Rights Alliance, 1997) ix + 62 pp.
Children's Rights Alliance	*Children's Rights: Our Responsibilities. Concluding Observations of the UN Committee on the Rights of the Child on Ireland's First Report* (Dublin: Children's Rights Alliance, 1998) 9 pp.
Cooney, T. and Torode, R (eds.),	*Report of the ICCL Working Party on Child Sexual Abuse* (Dublin: ICCL, 1988) 116 pp.
Council for Social Welfare,	*The Rights of the Child: Irish Perspectives on the UN Convention* (Dublin: Council for Social Welfare, 1991) xii + 124 pp. Bibliographies.
Cousins, M.,	*Seen and Heard: Promoting and Protecting Children's Rights in Ireland* (Dublin: Children's Rights Alliance, 1996) viii + 75 pp. Bibliog.
Department of Foreign Affairs,	*United Nations Convention on the Rights of the Child: First National Report of Ireland* (Dublin: Dept of Foreign Affairs, 1996) 121 + 4 pp.

Ferguson, F., Gilligan, R.   *Surviving Childhood Adversity: Issues for Policy and*
  & Torode, R.,   *Practice* (Dublin: Social Studies Press, TCD, 1993) xii +
                                  372 pp. Bibliographies.

Gilligan, R.,   *Irish Child Care Services: Policy, Practice and Provi-*
                                  sion (Dublin: I.P.A., 1991) xvi + 263 pp.

Kilkelly, U.,   *The Child and the European Convention on Human Rights*
                                  (Aldershot, Ashgate, 1999) xiv + 353 pp.

Martin, F.,   *The Politics of Children's Rights* (Cork, Cork U.P., 2000)
                                  xii + 97 pp.

Mollan, C.,   *Children First; A Sourcebook for Parents and Other Pro-*
                                  fessionals (Dublin: Arlen House, 1979) 198 pp.

Robins, J.,   *The Lost Children: A Study of Charity Children in Ire-*
                                  land 1700-1900 (Dublin: I.P.A., 1980) viii + 366 pp.
                                  Bibliog.

Task Force,   *Task Force on Child Care Services: Final Report* Prl 9345
                                  (Dublin: Stationery Office, 1980) 446 pp. Bibliog.

Tuairim,   *Some of Our Children: A Report on the Residential Care*
                                  of the Deprived Child in Ireland (London Branch of
                                  Tuairim, 1966) 54 pp.

Civil Liberties. See also Constitutional Law, Criminal Law, Discrimination and Equality Law, and Human Rights.

IACL,   *Your Rights as an Irish Citizen* (Dublin: Irish Association
                                  of Civil Liberty, 1972)

ICCL,   *The Emergency Powers Act 1976: A Critique* (Dublin:
                                  ICCL, 1977).

ICCL,   *Equality Now for Lesbians and Gay Men* (Dublin: ICCL,
                                  1990) vi + 71 pp.

ICCL,   *Know Your Rights* (Dublin: ICCL, 1992)

Commercial Law, *see also* Banking Law and Personal Property.

                                  Principles and General and Mercantile Law (Irish) (Dub-
                                  lin: Professional Examination Aids Ltd, 1976)
                                  Bankruptcy Law: Committee Report Prl 2714 (Dublin;
                                  Stationery Office, 1972).

Ashe, M. and Murphy, Y.,   *Insider Dealing* (Dublin: Round Hall Press, 1992) 231pp.

Byrne, R.,   *Cases and Comment on Irish Commercial Law and Le-*
                                  gal Technique 2nd ed. (Dublin: Round Hall Press, 1988)
                                  218pp. [1st ed. 1985]

Courtney, T.B.,   *Mareva Injunctions and Related Interlocutory Orders*
                          (Dublin: Butterworths, 1999) lx + 569pp.

Doolan, B.,   *A Casebook on Irish Business Law* (Dublin; Gill and
                          Macmillan, 1989) xvi + 208 pp.

Forde, M.,   *Commercial Law* 2nd ed. (Dublin: Butterworths, 1997) lxxv
                          + 691pp. [1st ed. 1990]

Forde, M.,   *Bankruptcy Law in Ireland* (Dublin and Cork: Mercier
                          Press, 1990) xxix + 214 pp.

Forde, M.,   *Re-Organising Failing Businesses – The Legal Frame-
                          work* (Dublin and Cork: Mercier Press, 1991) 218 pp.

Forde, M.,   *Commercial Legislation* (Dublin: Round Hall Sweet and
                          Maxwell, 1998) viii + 658pp.

Foy, A.,   *The Capital Markets: Irish and International Laws and
                          Regulations* (Dublin: Round Hall Sweet and Maxwell,
                          1998) lxviii + 709pp.

Grogan, V., King, T and   *Sale of Goods and Supply of Services: A Guide to the
Donelan, E.J.,   Legislation* (Dublin: ILSI, 1983) xxii + 133 pp.

Keenan, A.,   *Essentials of Irish Business Law* 2nd ed. (Dublin: Gill and
                          Macmillan, 1997) xii + 322 pp.

Linehan, D.,   *Irish Business and Commercial Law* (Cork: Irish Legal
                          Publications, 1981) 248 pp.

McHugh, K. *et al.,*   *Regulation of Investment Capital Markets. Irish and Eu-
                          ropean Regulatory Arrangements and Law* (Dublin:
                          Blackhall Publishing, 1999) x + 496 pp.

McNeece, S. (ed),   *Commercial Law* (London: Blackstone Press/Law Soci-
                          ety of Ireland, 2001) xxv + 284 pp.

Murphy, E.,   *Irish Legal Framework for Business Students* 2nd ed. (Dub-
                          lin: Gill and Macmillan, 2000) xxx + 520 pp.

O'Malley, L.,   *Business Law* (London: Sweet and Maxwell, 1982) xxxii
                          + 222 pp.

O'Reilly, P.F.,   *Commercial and Consumer Law* (Dublin: Butterworths,
                          2000) xix + 1070 pp.

Quinn, S. E.,   *Statutes Revised on Commercial Law 1695 –1913* (Bray,
                          Co Wicklow: Irish Law Publishing, 1992) xliii + 371 pp.

Sanfey, M. and Holohan, B., *Bankruptcy Law and Practice in Ireland* (Dublin: Round
                          Hall Press, 1991) lv + 292 pp.

Sheeran, N.,   *Essentials of Irish Business Law* (Dublin: Gill and
                          Macmillan, 1992) 293pp.

Ussher, P., O'Connor, B.J.   *Doing Business in Ireland* (New York: Matthew Bender,
& McCarthy, C.,   loose-leaf).

Waldron, K.,   *Guidelines on the Law of Agency and the Sale of Goods*
                                (Dublin, 1969). Published by author.

Waldron, K.,   *Guidelines on the Sale of Goods* (Dublin, 1971). Pub-
                                lished by author.

Wegan, G and   *Insider Trading in Western Europe: Current Status* (Lon-
Assman, H-D.(eds.),   don: Graham and Trotman, 1994) xiv + 211 pp. Contains
                                chapter by J.N. Dudley and K. Casey on Ireland.

Whalley, M. and   *International Business Acquisitions: Major Issues and*
Heymann, T.,   *Due Diligence* (London; Kluwer Law International, 1996)
                                xv + 376 pp. Contains chapter on Ireland.

Company Law

Bastow Charleton,   *Combined Companies Acts* (Dublin: Bastow Charleton,
                                loose-leaf).

BPP (NI)   *Irish Company Law and Partnership Law* 3rd ed.
                                (Newtownabbey: BPP(NI), 1992) xxix + 517 pp.

Brazil, L., Egan, P. and   *Jordan's Irish Company Secretarial Precedents* 2nd ed.
Horan, P.,   (Bristol: Jordans, 1999) xxi + 440 pp.

Brennan F,   *A Company Purchasing its Own Shares* (Dublin:
                                Brilton Publications/Oak Tree Press, 1991) 290 pp.

Cahill, D.,   *Corporate Finance Law* (Dublin: Round Hall Press, 2000)
                                li + 589 pp.

Callanan, G.,   *An Introduction to Irish Company Law* (Dublin: Gill and
                                Macmillan, 1999) (Dublin: Gill and Macmillan, 1999) xxv
                                + 293 pp.

Courtney, T.B. with   *The Law of Private Companies* (Dublin: Butterworths,
Hutchinson, G.B.,   1994) lxxxix + 916 pp.

Courtney, T.B.   *Company Law Review 1994* (Dublin: Brehon Publishing,
                                1995) xiii + 73 pp.

Courtney, T.B.,   *Company Law Review 1995* (Dublin: Round Hall Sweet
                                and Maxwell, 1996) xv + 95 pp.

Craig Gardiner   *Accounting, Disclosure and Publication Requirements of*
                                the Companies (Amendment) Act, 1986 (Dublin: Craig
                                Gardiner Price Waterhouse, 1986)

C.I.S.   *The Companies Act, 1963* (Series of Lectures arranged by
                                the College of Commerce Rathmines and C.I.S.) (Lon-
                                don: C.I.S., 1965)

Crowley, T.P.,   *A Guide to the Companies Act,1963* (Dublin: Irish Soci-
                        ety of Certified Accountants, 1965) 126 pp.

Daly, B.,   *Irish Company Law Reports (1963-1993)* (Dublin: Round
                        Hall Sweet and Maxwell, 1996) xi + 726 pp.

Deloitte Touche   *Responsibilities of Directors in Ireland: Your Questions
                        Answered.* Prepared by M Fulton (Dublin: Deloitte Tou-
                        che, 1991) 56 pp.

Doolan, B.,   *A Casebook on Irish Company Law* (Dublin: Gill and
                        Macmillan, 1987) xxii + 249 pp.

Doyle, C.,   *The Company Secretary: A Guide to the Law* (Dublin:
                        Round Hall Press, 1994) xxvi + 317 pp.

Egan, P.,   *The Companies Acts of Ireland and U.K.* 2nd ed. (Bristol:
                        Jordan Publishing Ltd, 1995) xiv + 284 pp.

Egan, P.,   *Irish Corporate Procedures. The Organisation and Regu-
                        lation of Business Enterprises in Ireland* 2nd ed. (Bristol:
                        Jordan Publishing Lrd, 1996) xiv + 203 pp.

Ellis, H.,   *Irish Company Law for Business* (Bristol: Jordans, 1998)
                        lxxiii + 483 pp.

Ernst & Young,   *Guide to the Companies Act 1990, including guide to
                        Companies (Amendment Act, 1990)* (Dublin: Ernst &
                        Young, 1991) 61 pp.

Flynn, J. & O'Carroll, S.P., *Irish Company Law and Partnership Law* (Brittas, Co.
                        Wicklow, 1979) iii + 72 pp.

Forde, M.,   *Reorganising Failing Businesses: The Legal Framework*
                        (Cork: The Mercier Press, 1991) xxi+ 218 pp.

Forde, M.,   *The Law of Company Insolvency* (Dublin: Round Hall
                        Press, 1993) lviii + 518 pp.

Forde, M.,   *Cases and Materials on Irish Company Law* 2nd ed. (Dub-
                        lin: Round Hall Sweet and Maxwell, 1998) xl + 645 pp.

Forde, M.,   *Company Law* 3rd ed. (Dublin: Round Hall Sweet and
                        Maxwell, 1999) ciii + 774 pp.

Keane, R.,   *Company Law in the Republic of Ireland* 3rd ed. (Dublin:
                        Butterworths, 2000) lxii + 590 pp.

Kelleher,   *Companies (Amendment) Act 1986: A Guide to Account-
                        ing, Reporting and Filing Requirements* (Dublin: Insti-
                        tute of Chartered Accountants, 1987)

MacCann, L.,   *A Casebook on Company Law* (Dublin: Butterworths (Ire-
                        land) Ltd, 1991) xxxvii + 664 pp.

MacCann, L.,	*Butterworths Ireland Companies Acts 1963-1990* (Dublin: Butterworths (Ireland) Ltd, 1993) xxxii + 1256 pp.
McConville, C.,	*Company Law* Round Hall Nutshells (Dublin: Round Hall Sweet & Maxwell, 2001) xvi + 148 pp.
McCormack, G.,	*The New Companies Legislation* (Dublin: Round Hall Press, 1991) xxiv + 252 pp.
McGahon, D.,	*Irish Company Law Index* (Dublin: Gill and Macmillan, 1991) 256 pp.
Murphy, E.,	*Make that Grade. Irish Company Law Revision* (Dublin: Gill and Macmillan, 1999) xiv + 114 pp.
O'Donnell, J.L.,	*Examinerships: The Companies Amendment Act 1990* (Dublin: Oak Tree Press, 1994) xxii + 292 pp.
O'Kane, B.,	*How to Form a Limited Company* (Dublin: Oak Tree Press, 1993) 118 pp.
Peat, Marwick, Mitchell	*Basic Information, Classification of Companies, Share Capital and Distributions: Implementation of Directives 1&2 in the Republic of Ireland* (Dublin and Brussels: Peat, Marwick, Mitchell & Co, 1984)
Phelan, M.,	*Guide to the Irish Companies Acts 1990* (Dublin: Gill and Macmillan, 1991) 395 pp.
Power, B.J.,	*Accounting Law and Practice for Limited Companies* (Dublin: Gill and Macmillan, 1987)
Power, B.J.,	*Company and Partnership Law for Builders* (Dublin: An Foras Forbartha, 1987)
Power, B.J.,	*Irish Company Law 1973-1983: A Guide and Handbook* (Dublin: Gill and Macmillan, 1984) xxiii + 184 pp.
R.I.C.I.S.,	*Index to the Companies Act, 1963* (Dublin: Hely Thom for Republic of Ireland Council of Incorporated Secretaries, 1968)
Ussher, P.,	*Company Law in Ireland* (London: Sweet and Maxwell, 1986) xlvii + 577 pp.
William Fry Solicitors	*Companies Act 1990 – A Commentary by William Fry Solicitors* (Dublin: Oak Tree Press, 1993) xxiv + 187 pp.

Competition Law

| Allan, W. and Hogan, G., | *Competition Law of United Kingdom and Republic of Ireland* (New York: Matthew Bender and Co, (1989) loose-leaf). |

Brown J.,   *Competition Law and Regulation in Ireland: The New Business Requirements* (Dublin: Competition Press, 1991) 133 pp.

Cregan, B.J.,   *Competition Law in Ireland: Digest and Commentary* (Dublin: Gill and Macmillan, loose-leaf).

Fair Trade Commission,   *Study of Competition Law* (Dublin: Stationery Office, 1990).

Findlater, J.(ed.),   *The New Competition Legislation* (Dublin: ICEL, 1991) 143 pp.

McNutt, P. and   *Competition Policy and the 1991 Irish Competition Act*
   Doherty, M.,   (Galway: SSRC (NUI, Galway), 1992) 70 pp.

Maher, I.,   *Competition Law: Alignment and Reform* (Dublin, Round Hall Sweet and Maxwell, 1999) lxvii + 514 pp.

Maitland-Walker, J.,   *Competition Laws of Europe* (London: Butterworths, 1995) xxxiv + 425 pp. Contains chapter by J. Meade on Ireland.

Massey, P. and O'Hare, P.,   *Competition Law and Policy in Ireland* (Dublin: Oak Tree Press, 1996) xxx + 427 pp.

O'Connor, T.(ed.),   *Competition Law Source Book* 2 vols. (Dublin: Round Hall Sweet and Maxwell, 1996) x + xiv + 1432 pp.

Power, V,   *European Union Competition Law and Ireland: the first 21 years* (Dublin: Irish Society for European Law, 1994) 25 pp.

Schuster, A. (ed.),   *Key Aspects of Irish Competition Law and Practice* (Dublin: ICEL, nd) vi + 141pp.

Stationery Office,   *EC policy of Competition: A Guide for Irish Business* 4th ed., Pl 8783 (Dublin, 1991).

Stationery Office,   *Competition Authority: A Guide to Irish Legislation* Pl 9199 (Dublin, 1992)

Compulsory Purchase

McDermott, S. and   *Compulsory Purchase and Compensation in Ireland: Law*
   Woulfe, R.,   *and Practice* (Dublin: Butterworths (Ireland) Ltd, 1992) xxxv + 397 pp.

Confiscation of Assets *See* Criminal Justice

Conflicts of Law

Binchy, W.,	*Irish Conflicts of Law* (Dublin: Butterworths (Ireland) Ltd., 1988) lxxiv + 691pp. Bibliog.
North, P. M.(ed.),	*The Private International Law of Matrimonial Causes in the British Isles and the Republic of Ireland.* Vol. 1 of Problems in Private International Law Series (Amsterdam: North Holland, 1977) xxiii + 465 pp.

Constitutional Law

All-Party Oireachtas Committee,	*First Progress Report* Pn 3795 (Dublin: Stationery Office, 1997) ix + 226 pp.
All-Party Oireachtas Committee,	*Second Progress Report: Seanad Éireann* Pn 3835 (Dublin: Stationery Office, 1997) vii + 120 pp. Bibliog.
All-Party Oireachtas Committee,	*Third Progress Report: The President* Pn 6250 (Dublin: Stationery Office, 1998) v + 360 pp.
All-Party Oireachtas Committee,	*Fourth Progress Report: The Courts and the Judiciary* Pn 7831 (Dublin: Stationery Office, 1999) vii + 118 pp.
All-Party Oireachtas	*Fifth Progress Report: Abortion* (Dublin: Stationery Office, 2000) 124 + 592 + 8 pp.
Beth, L.P.,	*The Development of Judicial Review in Ireland 1937-1966* (Dublin: I.P.A., 1967) 75 pp. Bibliog.
Beytagh, F.X.,	*Constitutionalism in Contemporary Ireland* (Dublin: Round Hall Sweet and Maxwell, 1997) xxvii + 213p
Boyle, K. & Hadden, T.,	*The Anglo-Irish Agreement: Commentary, Text and Official Review* (London: Sweet and Maxwell/Edwin Higel Ltd, 1989) 100 pp.
Casey, J. P.	*The Office of the Attorney General in Ireland* (Dublin: I.P.A., 1980) 247 pp. Bibliog.
Casey, J.	*Constitutional Law in Ireland* 3rd ed. (Dublin: Round Hall Sweet and Maxwell, 2000) lxx + 733 pp.
Casey, J.,	*The Irish Law Officers. Roles and Responsibilities of the Attorney General and the Director of Public Prosecutions* (Dublin: Round Hall Sweet and Maxwell, 1996) xxxv + 374 pp.
Chubb, B.,	*The Constitution and Constitutional Change in Ireland* 3rd ed. with new material (Dublin: IPA, 1978) 122 pp. Bibliog.
Chubb, B.,	*The Politics of the Irish Constitution* (Dublin: I.P.A., 1991) 153 p Bibliog.

Clarke, D. (ed.),   *Morality and the Law* (Dublin & Cork: Mercier Press, 1982) 125 pp. Bibliog.

Clifford,   *The Constitutional History of Eire/Ireland* (Belfast: Athol Books, 1987)

Constitution Review Group, *Report of the Constitution Review Group* (Dublin: Stationery Office, 1996) xiv + 701. Bibliog.

Curtin, D. and   *Constitutional Adjudication in European Community and*

  O'Keeffe, D. (eds.),   *National Law: Essays for the Hon Mr Justice T.F. O'Higgins* (Dublin: Butterworths (Ireland), 1992)

Dept of Environment,   *Presidential Elections 1937-1990* (Dublin: Oifig an tSolathair, c. 1991).

Dept of Environment,   *Referenda in Ireland 1937-1987* (Dublin: Oifig an tSolathair, c. 1991)

Dept. of Environment,   *Referendums in Ireland 1937- 1999* Pn 8976 (Dublin: Department of the Environment and Local Government, 2000) 59 pp.

Doctrine and Life   *Abortion.* Special Issue of *Doctrine and Life* (Dublin, 1992)

Donaldson, A.G.,   *Some Comparative Aspects of Irish Law* (Durham, NC, Duke UP and London: Cambridge UP, 1967) xii + 293 pp.

Doolan, B.,   *Constitutional Law and Constitutional Rights in Ireland* 3rd ed. (Dublin: Gill and Macmillan, 1994) xxvi + 308 pp. [1st ed. 1984].

Farrell, B. (ed.),   *De Valera's Constitution and Ours* (Dublin: Gill and Macmillan for RTE, 1988) iii + 209 pp.

Finlay, T.A.,   *The Constitution Fifty Years On* (Dublin: Round Hall Press, 1988) Address in pamphlet form distributed with *Irish Law Times*, February 1988.

Foley, J.A. and Lalor, S., *Gill and Macmillan Annotated Constitution of Ireland 1937-1994* (Dublin: Gill and Macmillan, 1995) xxi + 353 pp.

Forde, M.,   *Constitutional Law of Ireland* (Cork: The Mercier Press, 1987) lii + 801 pp.

Hanafin, P.,   *Constituting Identity: Political IdentityFormation and the Constitution in post-Independence Ireland* (Aldershot: Ashgate, 2001) vi + 127 pp.

Hannon, P.,   *Church, State, Morality and Law* (Dublin: Gill and Macmillan, 1992) 159 pp.

Kelly, J.,   *Fundamental Rights in the Irish Law and Constitution*
                                  2nd ed. (Dublin: Allen Figgis, 1967) xxxii + 355 pp. [1st
                                  ed. 1961].

Kelly, J., Hogan, G.   *The Irish Constitution* 3rd ed. (Dublin: Butterworths, 1994)
  & Whyte, G.,   cxxii + 1222 pp.

Kohn, L.,   *The Constitution of the Irish Free State* (London: George
                                  Allen and Unwin Ltd, 1932) xv + 432 pp.

Litton, F. (ed.),   *The Constitution of Ireland 1937-1987* (Dublin: I.P.A.,
                                  1988) 225 pp.

Lynch, P. and Meenan, J.,   *Essays in Memory of Alexis FitzGerald* (Dublin: ILSI,
                                  1987) 249 pp.

Mansergh, N.,   *The Irish Free State: Its Government and Politics* (Lon-
                                  don, 1934).

Millen, C.,   *The Right to Privacy and its Natural Law Foundations in
                                  the Constitutions of the United States and Ireland* (Dub-
                                  lin: Blackhall Publishing, 1999) xx + 164 pp. Bibliog.

Morgan, D.G.,   *Constitutional Law of Ireland: The Law of Executive, Leg-
                                  islature and Judiciary* 2nd ed. (Dublin: Round Hall Press,
                                  1990) 319 pp. [1st ed. 1985]

Morgan, D.G.,   *The Separation of Powers in the Irish Constitution* (Dub-
                                  lin: Round Hall Sweet and Maxwell, 1997) xxvi + 314
                                  pp.

Murphy, T. and   *Ireland's Evolving Constitution 1937-1997: Collected
  Twomey, P. (eds),   Essays* (Oxford: Hart Publishing, 1998) xiii + 346 pp.

Ó Briain, B.,   *The Irish Constitution* (Dublin: The Talbot Press, nd
                                  (1920s)) viii + 182 pp.

Ó Cearúil, M.,   *Bunreacht na hÉireann: A Study of the Irish Text*. Com-
                                  missioned by the All-Party Oireachtas Committee on the
                                  Constitution, and with original contributions by Professor
                                  Martin O Murchu (Dublin: Stationery Office, 1999) x +
                                  759 pp

O'Flaherty, H.,   *Justice, Liberty and the Courts: Talks and Reflections*
                                  (Dublin; Round Hall Sweet and Maxwell, 1999) xxii +
                                  180 pp. Bibliog.

Ó Rahilly, A.,   *Thoughts on the Constitution* (Dublin: Brown and Nolan,
                                  1937) 75 pp.

O'Reilly, J. (ed.),   *Human Rights and Constitutional Law: Essays in Hon-
                                  our of Brian Walsh* (Dublin: Round Hall Press, 1992) xx
                                  + 366 pp.

O'Reilly, J. & Redmond, M.,	*Cases and Materials on the Irish Constitution* (Dublin: ILSI, 1980) lv + 712 pp.
Reid, M.,	*The Impact of Community Law on the Irish Constitution* (Dublin: ICEL, 1990) v + 117pp. Bibliog.
Ryan, F.,	*Constitutional Law Essential Texts Series* (Dublin: Round Hall, 2001)
Sinnott, R.,	*Irish Voters Decide: Voting Behaviour in Elections and Referendums since 1918* (Manchester: Manchester UP, 1995) xiii + 331 pp. Bibliog. and maps.
Swift MacNeill, J.G.,	*Studies in the Constitution of the Irish Free State* (Dublin: The Talbot Press, 1925) xxiii + 244 pp
Ward, A.J.,	*The Irish Constitutional Tradition: Responsible Government and Modern Ireland 1782-1992* (Dublin: Irish Academic Press, 1994) viii + 412 pp. Bibliog.
Whelan, A. (ed.),	*Law and Liberty in Ireland* (Dublin: Oak Tree Press, 1993) 204 pp.

Consumer Law

Bird, T.C.,	*Consumer Credit Law* (Dublin: Round Hall Sweet and Maxwell, 1998) lv + 701pp.
Findlater, J.(ed.),	*Consumer Policy: The New EC Trading Environment* (Dublin: ICEL, 1991) 100 pp.
Grogan, V., King, T. and Donelan, E.J.,	*Sale of Goods and Supply of Services: A Guide to the Legislation* (Dublin: ILSI, 1983) xxii + 133 pp.
Linehan, D.,	*Irish Consumer Law* (Cork: Irish Legal Publishers 1980)
O'Reilly, P.F.,	*Commercial and Consumer Law* (Dublin: Butterworths, 2000) xix + 1070 pp.
Whinicup, M.H.,	*Consumer Legislation in the UK and the Republic of Ireland* (New York: Von Nostrand Rheinhold, 1980) viii + 209 pp.

Contract Law

Clark, R.,	*Contract Law in Ireland*, 4th ed. ((Dublin: Round Hall Sweet and Maxwell, 1998) lxiii + 540 pp.
Clark, R. and Clarke, B.,	*Contract Cases and Materials* (Dublin: Gill and Macmillan, 1994) xxvii + 1075 pp
Doolan, B.,	*A Casebook on Irish Contract Law* (Dublin: Gill and Macmillan, 1989) xxi + 330 pp.

Farry, M.,	*Cases on Contract* (Dublin: Phoenix Press, 1995) 297 pp.
Friel, R.,	*The Law of Contract* 2nd end (Dublin: Round Hall Sweet and Maxwell, 2000) lviii + 382 pp. [1st ed., 1995]
Haigh, S.,	*Contract law in the E-Commerce Age* (Dublin: Round Hall, 2001)
McLeod, N.,	*Early Irish Contract Law* (Sydney: Centre for Celtic Studies, University of Sydney, c. 1992) 340 pp. Bibliog.
Waldron, K.,	*Guidelines on the Law of Contract and Agency* (Dublin, 1971). Published by author.
Williams, G.L.,	*Joint Obligations: A Treatise on Joint and Joint and Several Liability in Contract, Quasi-Contract and Trusts in England, Ireland and the Commonwealth Dominions* (Holmes Beach, Florida: Gaunt, 1997) 179 pp. Reprint of work first published by Butterworths, 1949.

Conveyancing *(see also* **Land law** *and* **Landlord and Tenant***)*

Brennan, G and Casey, N. (eds.),	*Conveyancing* (London: Blackstone Press/Law Society of Ireland, 2000) xxxiii + 570 pp.
Farrell, J.,	*Irish Law of Specific Performance* (Dublin: Butterworths, 1994) xlv + 362 pp.
Laffoy, M. and Wheeler, D.,	*Irish Conveyancing Precedents* (Dublin: Butterworths, loose-leaf).
Linehan, D.M.,	*Irish Land and Conveyancing Law* (Cork: Legis Publications, 1989).
McAllister, D.L.,	*Registration of Title in Ireland* (Dublin: ILRCI, 1973) xxxi + 578 pp.
Wylie, J.C.W.,	*Irish Conveyancing Law* 2nd ed. (Dublin: Butterworths, 1996) cx + 914 pp. [1st ed. 1978].
Wylie, J.C.W.,	*Conveyancing Law* Butterworths Irish Annotated Statutes series (Dublin: Butterworths, 1999) 1 + 573 pp. [1st ed. *sub nom. Irish Conveyancing Statutes,* 1994]

Copyright. *See* **Intellectual Property.**

Coroners

Farrell, B.,	*Coroners: Practice and Procedure* (Dublin: Round Hall Sweet and Maxwell, 2000) xxxiii+ 561 pp.
O'Connor, P.,	*Handbook for Coroners in the Republic of Ireland* (Swinford: Old House Press, 1997) 197 pp. Bibliog.

Courts. See **Judiciary and Legal System**

Credit Unions

Quinn, A.P.,   *Credit Unions in Ireland* 2nd ed. (Dublin: Oak Tree Press, 1999) xxxv + 315pp. [1st ed., 1995]

Criminal Injuries

Kennedy, A. and   *The Law on Compensation for Criminal Injuries in the*
McWilliam, H.R.,   *Republic of Ireland* (Dublin: 1977) xxxi + 88 pp.

Criminal Justice. See also **Criminal Law, Juvenile Justice** and **Prisons Law.**

Report of the Committee of Inquiry into the Penal System Pl 3391 (The Whitaker Report) (Dublin: Stationery Office, 1985) iv + 360 pp. Bibliog.

Expert Group on the Probation and Welfare Service. First Report Pn 6152 (Dublin: Stationery Office, 1998) 31 pp.

Expert Group on the Probation and Welfare Service: Final Report Pn 7324 (Dublin: Stationery Office, 1999) 128 pp.

Bacik, I. and   *Crime and Poverty in Ireland* (Dublin: Round Hall Sweet
O'Connell, M. (eds.),   and Maxwell, 1998) viii + 98 pp.

Breen, R. and   *Crime Victimisation in the Republic of Ireland* (Dublin:
Rottman, D.B.,   ESRI, 1985) vii + 113 pp.

Brewer, J.D., Lockhart, B.   *Crime in Ireland 1945-1995. 'Here be Dragons'* (Oxford:
and Rodgers, P.,   Clarendon Press, 1997) xiv + 268 pp.

Crime Forum,   *Report of the National Crime Forum 1998* (Dublin: I.P.A., 1998) 194 pp.

Department of Justice,   *The Management of Offenders: A Five Year Plan* Pn 0789 (Dublin: Department of Justice, 1994) 163 pp.

Department of Justice,   *Tackling Crime: Discussion Paper* (Dublin: Stationery Office, 1997) 180 pp.

Dept of Justice, Equality   *Illegal and Harmful Use of the Internet: First Report of*
and Law Reform,   *the Working Group* Pn 5231 (Dublin: Stationery Office, 1998) iv + 95 pp.

Dept of Justice, Equality   *Strategy Statement 1998-2000: Community Security and*
and Law Reform,   *Equality* (Dublin: Stationery Office, 1998) ii + 108 pp.

Dublin Chamber of   *Crime and the Law: Toward a More Effective Criminal*
Commerce,   *Justice System* (Dublin: Chamber of Commerce, 1990).

Fennell, C.,   *Crime and Crisis in Ireland: Justice by Illusion?* (Cork, Cork UP, 1993) vi + 69 pp.

Glaser, D.,   *Towards More Rational Decisions on Criminals* 16th Geary Lecture (Dublin, ESRI, 1984) 18 pp.

IMPACT,   *Probation and Welfare in the 1990s* (Dublin: Probation and Welfare Officers' Branch of IMPACT, 1996) 23 pp.

IMPACT,   *The Management of the Drug Offender in Prison and on Probation* (Dublin: Probation and Welfare Officers' Branch of IMPACT, 1996) 56 pp. Bibliog.

Irish Penal Reform Trust,   *Is Penal Reform Possible?* (Dublin: Irish Penal Reform Trust, 1997) 50 pp.

Irish Penal Reform Trust   *The Treatment of Sex Offenders* Conference Proceedings (Dublin: Irish Penal Reform Trust, 1999) 3 + 48 pp.

Irish Penal Reform Trust,   *Restorative Justice: Examining the Issues* (Dublin: Irish Penal Reform Trust, c. 1999) 36 pp.

Irish Penal Reform Trust,   *The Restorative Justice Directory* (Dublin: Irish Penal Reform Trust, 1999) 50 pp.

Keane, M. *et al.,*   *Attrition in Sexual Assault Offence Cases in Ireland: A Qualitatative Analysis* (Dublin: Dept of Justice, Equality and Law Reform, 2001) vi + 166 pp.

Kelleher, P. and   *Safety and Sanctions: Domestic Violence and the Enforce-*
   O'Connor, M.,   *ment of Law in Ireland* (Dublin: Women's Aid, 1999) 187 pp.

Keogh, E.,   *Illicit Drug Use and Related Criminal Activity in the Dublin Metropolitan Area* (Dublin: An Garda Síochána, 1997) xi + 64 pp.

McBride, S. (ed.),   *Crime and Punishment* (Dublin: Ward River Press, 1982) 184 pp.

McCullagh, C.,   *Crime in Ireland: A Sociological Introduction* (Cork: Cork UP, 1996) xi + 244 pp.

McCutcheon, P. and   *The Confiscation of Criminal Assets: Law and Procedure*
   Walsh, D.P.J. (eds.),   (Dublin: Round Hall Sweet and Maxwell, 1999) 122 pp.

McLoone, J.,   *The Offender and the Community* (Galway: The Social Study Conference, 1981) ix + 102 pp.

Mulloy, E.,   *Emergency Legislation: Dynasties of Coercion* Field Day Pamphlet No 10 (Derry: Field Day Theatre Co. Ltd., 1986) 26 pp. Bibliog.

Murphy, T.,   *Rethinking the War on Drugs in Ireland* (Cork, Cork UP, 1996) vii + 92 pp.

NESC

The Criminal Justice System: Policy and Performance Report No 77 (Dublin: NESC, 1984)

O'Brien, M. and
Moran, R.,

Overview of Drugs Issues in Ireland 1997: A Resource Document (Dublin: The Health Research Board, 1997) xiv + 110 pp.

O'Donnell, I and
   O'Sullivan, E.,

Crime Control in Ireland: The Politics of Intolerance Undercurrents Series (Cork: Cork University Press, 2001) vii + 107 pp. Bibliog.

O'Mahony, P.,

Crime and Punishment in Ireland (Dublin: Round Hall Press, 1993) xvii + 252 pp. Bibliog.

O'Mahony, P.,

Criminal Chaos: Seven Crises in Irish Criminal Justice (Dublin: Round Hall Sweet and Maxwell, 1996) xi + 289 pp.

O'Mahony, P.,

Mountjoy Prisoners: A Sociological and Criminological Profile (Dublin: Stationery Office, 1997) 192 pp. Bibliog.

Probation and Welfare
Service,

Criminal Justice (Community Service) Act 1983. The Management of the Community Service Order (Dublin; Probation and Welfare Service, 1999) 78 pp.

Rottman, D.R.,

Crime in the Republic of Ireland: Statistical Trends and their Interpretation (Dublin: ESRI, 1980) vii + 158 pp.

Tomlinson, M., Varley, T.,
& McCullagh, C.,

Whose Law and Order? Aspects of Crime and Social Control in Irish Society (Sociological Association of Ireland, 1988) 192 pp. Bibliog.

Walsh, D. and Sexton, P.,

An Empirical Study of Community Service Orders in Ireland (Centre for Criminal Justice Studies, University of Limerick for Department of Justice, Equality and Law Reform, 1999) 118 pp. Bibliog.

Watson, D.,

Victims of Recorded Crime in Ireland. Results of the 1996 Survey (Dublin: Oak Tree Press and ESRI, 2000) 329 pp.

Criminal Law and Criminal Procedure. See also **Criminal Justice, Evidence, Practice and Procedure.**

Report of Committee to Enquire into Certain Aspects of Criminal Procedure (The Martin Report) (Dublin: Stationery Office, 1990) 49 pp.

Bacik, I., Maunsell, C.
& Gogan, S.,

The Legal Process and Victims of Rape (Dublin: Rape Crisis Centre, 1998) xx + 394 pp. Bibliog.

Byrne, R. *et al.*,

Innocent Till Proven Guilty? (Dublin: ICCL, 1983) 72 pp.

Casey, E. (ed.),   *Judgments of the Court of Criminal Appeal 1984-1989*
                            (Dublin: Round Hall Press, 1991) xxiv + 322 pp.

Charleton, P.,   *Controlled Drugs and the Criminal Law* (Dublin: An Cló
                            Liúir, 1986) xxiv + 240 pp.

Charleton, P.,   *Offences Against the Person* (Dublin: Round Hall Press,
                            1992) lxxiv + 415 pp.

Charleton, P.,   *Criminal Law: Cases and Materials* (Dublin: Butterworths
                            Ireland Ltd, 1992) xlvii + 637 pp.

Charleton, P., McDermott,   *Criminal Law* (Dublin: Butterworths, 1999) cv + 1224
  P.A. & Bolger, M.,   pp.

Cole, J.S.R.,   *Cases on Criminal Law* (Dublin and Cork: Golden Eagle
                            Books, 1975) xi + 240 pp.

Cooney, T. and   *Report of the ICCL Working Party on Child Sexual Abuse*
  Torode, R (eds.),   (Dublin: ICCL, 1988) 116 pp.

De Blacam, M.,   *Drunken Driving and the Law* 2nd ed. (Dublin: Round Hall
                            Press, 1995) xxiv + 148 pp.

Dept. of Justice, Equality *The Law on Sexual Offences: A Discussion Paper* (Dub-
  & Law Reform,   lin: Stationery Office, 1998) 124 pp.

Findlay, M. &   *A Casebook of Irish Criminal Law* (Dublin: Precedent,
  McAuley, F.,   1981) xi + 447 pp.

Frewen, G.L.,   *Judgments of the Court of Criminal Appeal 1924-1978*
                            (Dublin: ICRI, nd) xxxi + 619 pp.

Frewen, G.L.,   *Judgments of the Court of Criminal Appeal 1979-1983*
                            (Dublin: ICLRI, nd) xxxix + 226 pp.

Hanly, C.,   *An Introduction to Irish Criminal Law* (Dublin: Gill and
                            Macmillan, 1999) xxvii + 378 pp.

Hogan, G. and Walker, C.,   *Political Violence and the Law in Ireland* (Manchester:
                            Manchester UP, 1989) x + 342 pp. Bibliog.

ILSI,   *Garda Síochána Guide* 6th ed. (Dublin: ILSI, 1991) xxxii
                            + 1627 pp.

McAuley, F.,   *Insanity, Psychiatry and Criminal Responsibility* (Dub-
                            lin: Round Hall Press, 1993) xiv + 248 pp. Bibliog.

McAuley, F. and   *Criminal Liability: A Grammar* (Dublin: Round Hall
  McCutcheon, P.,   Sweet and Maxwell, 2000) lxxvi + 950 pp. Bibliog.

McCutcheon, J.P.,   *The Larceny Act 1916* (Dublin: Round Hall Press, c. 1988)
                            xix + 153 pp.

McCutcheon, J.P.,   *Legislation Affecting the Substantive Criminal Law 1996
                            and 1997* (Limerick: Centre for Criminal Justice, UL,
                            c.1998) 21 pp.

McIntyre, T.J.,	*Criminal Law* Essential Texts Series (Dublin: Round Hall, 2001)
O'Connor, J.,	*The Irish Justice of the Peace: A Treatise on the Powers and the Duties of the Justices of the Peace in Ireland* 2nd ed. (Abingdon, Professional Books, 1985) 2 Vols., lx + 587; cvii + 1346 pp. First published in Dublin in 1915.
O'Malley, T.,	*Sexual Offences: Law, Policy and Punishment* (Dublin: Round Hall Sweet and Maxwell, 1996) xxxix + 511 pp.
O'Malley, T.,	*Sentencing Law and Practice* (Dublin: Round Hall Sweet and Maxwell, 2000) l +535 pp.
Ó Síocháin, P.A.,	*The Criminal Law of Ireland* 8th ed. (Dublin: Foilsiuchain Dli, 1988) 344 pp.
Robinson, M.T.W.,	*The Special Criminal Court* (Dublin: Dublin UP, 1974) 48 pp.
Ryan, E.F. and Magee, P.P.,	*The Irish Criminal Process* (Dublin and Cork: Mercier Press, 1983) lxxi + 595 pp.
Sandes, R.L.,	*Criminal Law and Criminal Procedure in the Republic of Ireland* 3rd ed. (London; Sweet and Maxwell, 1951) xxxv + 212 pp [1st ed., 1930].
Waldron, K.,	*Guidelines on the Criminal Law* (Dublin, 1981) Published by author.

Data Protection

Clark, R.,	*Data Protection Law in Ireland* (Dublin: Round Hall Press, 1990) xix + 182 pp.

Dictionaries and Reference Books

Murdoch, H.,	*A Dictionary of Irish Law* Revised 3rd ed. (Dublin: Topaz Publications, 2000) xii + 896 pp. [1st ed. 1988]
Ó Catháin, L.,	*Focal sa Chúirt* (Dublin: Coiscéim, 2001) 242 pp.
Oifig an tSolathair,	*Tearmai Dlí: English/Irish and Irish/English* (Dublin: Stationery Office, nd).

Disability Law

Mooney, R.,	*Guide for the Disabled* (Dublin: Ward River Press, 1982) 255 pp.
Quinn, G., McDonagh, M. and Kimber, C.,	*Disability Discrimination Law in the United States, Australia and Canada* (Dublin: Oak Tree Press in association with NRB, 1993) viii + 224 pp.

Digests and Indexes

Aston, J and Doyle, M. (eds.),	*Index to Irish Superior Court Written Judgments 1976-1982* (Galway: IALT, 1984) 4+ 156 pp.
Aston, J., Doyle, M., Kerr, A. and McCutcheon, P. (eds.),	*Index to Unreported Judgments of the Irish Superior Courts 1 1966-1975* (Galway, IALT, 1990) 3 + 122 pp.
Aston, J. (ed.),	*Index to Irish Superior Court Written Judgments 1983-1989* (Dublin: General Council of the Bar of Ireland, 1991)iv + 275 pp.
Clancy, A.,	*The Irish Times Law Reports. Index for the Years 1989-1994 inclusive* (no publisher or date) 88 pp.
Clancy, J.,	*Index to the Irish Law Reports Monthly 1976-1990* (Dublin: Round Hall Press, 1992)
Clancy, J.,	*Index to the Irish Law Reports Monthly 1991-1995* (Dublin: Round Hall Sweet and Maxwell, 1996) 367 pp.
Clancy, J.M.	*Irish Digest 1994-1999* (Dublin: ICLRI, 2001).
Clancy, J.M.	*Digest of Cases 1989-1993* (Dublin: ICLRI, 1995) cci + 930 pp.
Clancy, J.M. and Ryan, E.F.,pp.	*Irish Digest 1984-1988* (Dublin: ICLR, 1991) cxvii + 608
Daly, B. and Murphy, Y.,	*Irish Times Law Reports Index 1989* (Dublin, 1990) 23 pp.
Daly, B., and Murphy, Y.,	*Irish Times Law Reports Index 1990* (Dublin 1991).
De Blaghd, E.,	*The Irish Digest 1971-1983* (Dublin: ICLRI, 1987) cxi + 512 pp.
Humphreys, R.,	*Index to Irish Statutory Instruments* 3 vols. (Dublin: Butterworths, 1988) xiii + 1952; xv + 1047; xiii + 314 pp.
Harrison,	*Irish Digest 1948-1958* (Dublin: ICLR, nd)
Harrison,	*Irish Digest 1939-1948* (Dublin: Falconer, 1952) cxxix + 533 pp.
Ryan, E.F.,	*Irish Digest 1959-1970* (Dublin: ICLR, nd)
Ryan, E.F.,	*Notes of Irish Cases 1949-1958* (Cork, Cork UP, 1960) 2+ 101 pp.
Ryan, E.F.,	*Notes of Irish Cases 1959-1968* (Cork, Cork UP, 1970) 2 + xv + 94 pp.
Ryan, E.F.,	*Notes of Irish Cases 1969-1973* (Cork, Cork UP, 1982) 1 + xxii + 77pp.

Stationery Office,	*Index to the Statutes 1922 to 1982 with Tables and Supplement for 1983 to 1985*. Separate Supplement for 1986 (Dublin Stationery Office).
Stationery Office,	*Index to the Statutory Instruments*. Separate volumes published for the periods 1948-1960; 1961-63; 1964-70; 1971-74; 1975-79; 1980-86 (Dublin: Stationery Office).
Stationery Office,	*Chronological Tables of the Statutes 1922-1995* (Dublin: Stationery Office, nd) xiv + 1038 pp.

Discrimination and Equality Law. See also **Constitutional Law** and **Labour Law.**

Bolger, M. and Kimber, C.,	*Sex Discrimination Law* (Dublin: Round Hall Sweet and Maxwell, 2000) xlv + 473 pp.
Byrne, R. and Duncan, W. (eds.),	*Developments in Discrimination Law in Ireland and Europe* (Dublin: ICEL, 1997) vii + 130 pp.
McEwen, M.,	*Tackling Discrimination in Europe: An Examination of Anti-Discrimination Law in Practice* (Oxford: Berg, 1995) vii + 232 pp. Contains chapter partly devoted to Ireland.
O'Connell, D.,	*Equality Now. The SIPTU Guide to the Employment Equality Act 1998* (Dublin: SIPTU, 1998) 125 pp.

Domestic Violence. See Criminal Justice,

Early Irish Law. See **Legal History.**

Elder Law

Costello, J.,	*Law and Finance in Retirement* (Dublin: Blackhall Publishing, 2000) 195 pp.
National Council on Ageing ,	*The Law and Older People: A Handbook for Service Providers* Report No 51 (Dublin: National Council on Ageing and Older People, 1998) xii + 276 pp.

Economic Law

McMahon, B.M.E.,	*Report on Irish Economic Law* EC Commission Approximation of Legislation Series (Brussels, 1977) 151 pp.

Education Law

Farry, M.,	*Education and the Constitution* (Dublin: Round Hall Sweet and Maxwell, 1996) xxvii + 179 pp.

Farry, M.,   *Vocational Teachers and the Law* (Dublin; Blackhall Pub-
                              lishing, 1998) xxxiv + 224 pp.

Glendenning, D.,   *Education and the Law* (Dublin: Butterworths, 1999) xliv
                              + 607 pp. Bibliog.

Mahon, O.,   *Negligence and the Teacher* (Ennis: Ennis Teachers'
                              Centre, 1995) vii + 97 pp. Bibliog.

Emergency Law

Campbell, C.,   *Emergency Law in Ireland 1918-1925* (Oxford: Clarendon
                              Press, 1994) xxiii + 429 pp. Bibliog.

Employment Law. See Labour Law.

Environmental Law and Planning Law

Comerford, H. and   *Environmental Law: A Glossary and Handbook* (Dublin:
    Fogarty, A.R.M.,   Round Hall Sweet and Maxwell, 2000) lxviii + 453 pp.

Drumgoole, S.,   *Legal Protection of Underwater Heritage: National and
                              International Perspectives* (The Hague: Kluwer Law In-
                              ternational, 1999) xx + 239 pp. Contains chapter by N.
                              O'Connor on Ireland.

Duggan, F.   *EEC Environmental Legislation: A Handbook for Irish
                              Local Authorities* 2nd ed. (Dublin: Environmental Research
                              Unit, 1992) vii + 148 pp. 1st ed. by Cabot published by An
                              Foras Forbartha in 1985.

E.F.I.L.W.C.,   *The Law Relating to Transport of Dangerous Wastes: Ire-
                              land* (Dublin: European Foundation for the Improvement
                              of Living and Working Conditions, 1987) 58 pp.

Fitzpatrick, H.M.,   *Trees and the Law* (Dublin: ILSI, 1985) 84 pp.

Galligan, E.,   *Irish Planning Law and Procedure* (Dublin: Round Hall
                              Sweet and Maxwell, 1997) lxii + 453 pp.

Grist, B.,   *An Introduction to Irish Planning Law* (Dublin: I.P.A.,
                              1999) xi + 98 pp.

Hallo, R.E. (ed.),   *Access to Environmental Information in Europe: The Im-
                              plementation and Implications of Directive 90/313/EEC*
                              (London: Kluwer Law International, 1996) xxxvi + 459
                              pp. Contains chapter on Ireland

ICEL,   *Environmental Protection and the Law of the European
                              Community* (Dublin: ICEL, 1990) iii + 142 pp.

Maguire, B., O'Reilly, M.   *Irish Environmental Legislation* (Dublin: Round Hall
    & Roche, M.S.,   Sweet and Maxwell, 1999) cvi + 982 pp.

Matheson Ormsby Prentice *A Guide for Business and Industry to Environmental Law*
   and IDA   *in Ireland* (Dublin: Matheson Ormsby Prentice and IDA,
                                        1991) 53 pp.

Nowlan, K.I.,   *A Guide to Planning Legislation in the Republic of Ire-*
                            land 2nd ed. (Dublin: Law Society of Ireland, 1999) xlvii +
                            587 pp.

O'Donnell, M.,   *Planning Law* (Dublin: Butterworths, 1999) xv + 393 pp.

O'Sullivan, P.,   *Irish Planning and Acquisition Law* (Dublin: I.P.A., 1978)
                            vii + 77 pp.

O'Sullivan, P. and   *A Sourcebook on Planning Law in Ireland* (Abingdon:
   Shepherd, K.,   Professional Books, 1984) xxxviii + 568 pp.

O'Sullivan, P. and   *A Sourcebook on Planning Law in Ireland: 1987 Supple-*
   Shepherd, K.,   *ment* (Abingdon: Professional Books, 1987) xxi + 217 pp.

O'Sullivan, P. and   *Irish Planning Law and Practice* 2 vols. (Dublin:
   Shepherd, K.,   Butterworths, loose-leaf).

Scannell, Y.,   *The Law and Practice Relating to Pollution Control in*
                            Ireland 2nd ed. (London: Graham and Trottman,

                            1982) xxix + 215 pp. [1st ed., 1976]

Scannell, Y.,   *Environmental and Planning Law in Ireland* (Dublin:
                            Round Hall Press, 1995) lxxxvii + 584 pp.

Scannell, Y, *et al,*   *The Habitats Directive in Ireland* (Dublin: Centre for En-
                            vironmental Law and Policy, Law School, TCD, 1999) iv
                            + 22 + 221 pp.

Equity and Trusts, and Charity Law

Brady, J.C.,   *Religion and the Law of Charities in Ireland* (Belfast:
                            NILQ, c. 1976) viii + 173 pp.

Courtney, T.B.,   *Mareva Injunctions and Related Interlocutory Orders*
                            (Dublin: Butterworths, 1999) lx + 569 pp.

Delany, V.T.H.,   *The Law Relating to Charities in Ireland* Revised ed.
                            (Dublin, c. 1962) xxxi + 253 pp.

Delany, H.,   *Equity and the Law of Trusts in Ireland* 2nd ed. (Dublin:
                            Round Hall Sweet and Maxwell, 1999) xci + 706 pp. [1st
                            ed., 1996]

Farrell, J.,   *Irish Law of Specific Performance* (Dublin: Butterworths,
                            1994) xlv + 362 pp.

Keane, R.,   *Equity and the Law of Trusts in the Republic of Ireland*
                            (London/Edinburgh: Butterworths, 1988) liii + 387 pp.

Keeton, G.W.,	*An Introduction to Equity* 5th ed. with Irish supplement by L. A. Sheridan (London, Pitman, 1961) xiv + 400 pp.. Some earlier editions also had Irish supplements.
Keeton, G.W.,	*The Law of Trusts* 9th ed. with Irish supplement by L. A. Sheridan (London: Pitman, 1968). Some earlier editions also had Irish supplements.
Keeton, G.W. and Sheridan, L.A.,	*The Comparative Law of Trusts in the Commonwealth and the Republic of Ireland* (Chichester: Rose, 1976)lvi + 370 pp. First Supplement published in 1981.
Kiely, T. O'N.,	*The Principles of Equity as Applied in Ireland* (Dublin: Fodhla Printing Co, 1936) vi + 398 pp.
O'Halloran, K.,	*Charity Law* (Dublin: Round Hall Sweet and Maxwell, 2000) xlvii + 471 pp.
Sheridan, L.A.,	*Fraud in Equity: A Study in English and Irish Law* (London: Pitman, 1957) xliii + 235 pp.
Sheridan, L.A. and Delany, V.T.H.,	*The Cy-Pres Doctrine* (London: Sweet and Maxwell, 1959; first supplement, 1961). Contains some Irish material.
Wylie, J.C.W.,	*A Casebook on Equity and Trusts in Ireland* 2nd ed. (Butterworths, 1998) lviii + 1262 pp.

European Law *see also* Human Rights Law

Barrington, R. & Cooney, J.,	*Inside the EEC: An Irish Guide* (Dublin: O'Brien Press, 1984) 192 pp.
Cahill, D., Kennedy, T.P & Power, V.,	*Applied European Law* (Dublin: Blackstone Press/Law Society of Ireland, 2000) xxxii + 327 pp.
Conlan, P. (ed.),	*EC/EU Legislation in Ireland* (Dublin: Gill and Macmillan, 1994) xxvi + 1427 pp.
Conlan, P. (ed.),	*EC Labour Legislation in Ireland* (Dublin: Gill and Macmillan, 1996) xvi + 719 pp.
Connolly, J.,	*Riding the Tiger: Ireland, European Security and Defence. An Examination of Issues in the Light of Maastricht and Beyond* (Dublin: Irish Commission for Justice and Peace, 1992) viii + 78 + 6 pp.
Curtin, D. and O'Keeffe, D.,	*Constitutional Adjudication in European Community and National Law. Essays for the Hon. Mr Justice T.F. O'Higgins* (Dublin: Butterworths (Ireland) Ltd, 1992) xxxi + 307 pp.
European Movement,	*A Guide to the Amsterdam Treaty* (Dublin: The European Movement, 1998) 47 pp.

European Parliament Office, *Documents on Political Union* (Dublin: European Parliament Office, 1992) 106 pp.

Heusel, W.,   *Community Law in Practice, including facets of consumer protection law* (Dublin: ICEL, 1997).

Hogan, G. and Whelan, A.,   *Ireland and the European Union: Constitutional and Statutory Texts and Commentary* (London: Sweet and Maxwell, 1995) xxxxiii + 483 pp.

ICEL,   *Legal Implications of 1992* (Dublin: ICEL, 1988) 97 pp.

ICEL,   *Mobility of People in the European Community* (Dublin: ICEL, 1990) 99 pp.

ICEL,   *Distribution and Franchising Agreements: Corporate Needs and Competition Rules* (Dublin: ICEL, 1990)

IEA.   *Agenda 2000: Implications for Ireland* (Dublin: IEA, 1999) xiii + 122 pp.

Keatinge, P. (ed.),   *Ireland and EC Membership Evaluated* (London: Pinter, 1991) 300 pp.

Keatinge, P. (ed.),   *Maastricht and Ireland: What the Treaty Means* (Dublin: IEA, 1992) x + 175 pp.

Laffan, B.,   *Constitution Building in the European Union* (Dublin: IEA, 1996) viii + 239 pp.

McMahon, B. & Murphy, F.,   *European Community Law in Ireland* (Dublin: Butterworths (Ireland) Ltd, 1989) lxviii + 529 pp.

Moloney, G. and Robinson, K.,   *The Brussels Convention on Jurisdiction and the Enforcement of Foreign Judgments* (Dublin: ICEL, 1989) 251pp.

Myles,   *EU Brief* (Lisburn: Locksley Press, ongoing) 4 vols., looseleaf.

O Caoimh, A.,   *Butterworths Ireland Guide to European Communities Law*, Irish edition (Dublin, Butterworths (Ireland) Ltd.,1989) xxiii + 205 pp.

Phelan, D.R.,   *Revolt or Revolution: The Constitutional Boundaries of the European Community* (Dublin: Round Hall Sweet and Maxwell, 1997) lxv + 475 pp. Bibliog.

Power, V.,   *EC Shipping Law* 2nd ed. (London: Lloyds of London Press, 1998) lxxxvi + 1024 pp.

Reid, M.,   *The Impact of Community Law on the Irish Constitution* (Dublin: ICEL, 1990) v + 117 pp. Bibliog.

Robinson M. & Findlater, J. (eds.), *Creating a European Economic Space: Legal Aspects of EC-EFTA Relations* (Dublin: ICEL, 1990) 287 pp.

Temple Lang, J.	*European Community Law, Irish Law and the Irish Legal Profession*. Frances E. Moran Lecture No 2 (Dublin: TCD, 1982) 28 pp.
Temple Lang, J.,	*The Common Market and the Common Law - Legal Aspects of Foreign Investment and Economic Integration in the European Community with Ireland as a Prototype* (London: University of Chicago Press, 1966) 573 pp.
Tonra, B.,	*Amsterdam: What the Treaty Means* (Dublin: IEA, 1997) viii + 224 pp.
Whyte, G. (ed.),	*Sex Equality, Community Rights and Irish Social Welfare Law: The Impact of the Third Equality Directive* (Dublin: ICEL, 1988) ix + 213 pp.

Evidence

Cole, J.S.R.,	*Irish Cases on Evidence* 2nd ed. (Dublin: ILSI, 1982) xxi + 264 pp. [1st ed., 1972).
Daly, B. (ed.),	*The Role of the Expert Witness* (Dublin: Inns Quay Ltd., 1999) viii + 152 pp.
Fennell, C.,	*The Law of Evidence in Ireland* (Dublin: Butterworths (Ireland) Ltd., 1992) xlv + 400 pp.
Ó Síocháin, P.,	*Outline of Evidence, Practice and Procedure in Ireland* (Dublin: Foilsiucháin Dlí, 1953) viii + 122 pp.
Ó Síocháin, P.	*Dlí na Fianaise in Éirinn* 2nd ed. (Dublin: Stationery Office, 1962). Irish translation by P Ua Maoileoin of *Outline of Evidence, Practice and Procedure in Ireland*.
Shroff, K.B. and Clarke, S.F.,	*Admissibility of Illegally Obtained Evidence: A Comparative Analysis of the Laws of England, Scotland, Ireland, Canada, Australia, and New Zealand* (Washington: Library of Congress, 1981) 73 pp.
Waldron, K.,	*Guidelines on the Law of Evidence* (Dublin, 1971). Published by Author.
Wolfe, R.,	*A Police Guide to the Law of Evidence* (Dun Laoghaire, nd, c.1955) 80 pp. Published by author.

Essays, Collections of

| | *The Future of the Common Law* (Cambridge, Mass.: Harvard UP, 1937). Contains essay by Judge Hanna on Ireland. |
| Breen, O., Casey, J. and Kerr. A., | *Liber Memorialis: Professor J.C. Brady* (Dublin: Round Hall, 2001) |

Duncan, W. (ed.),	*Law and Social Policy: Some Current Problems in Irish Law* (Dublin: Dublin University Law Journal, 1987)
Lynch, P. and Meenan, J. (eds.),	*Essays in Memory of Alexis Fitzgerald* (Dublin: ILSI, 1987) 249 pp.
McAuley, F. and O'Keeffe, D (eds.),	*Essays in Honour of Geoffrey G. Hand* (Dublin Round Hall Sweet and Maxwell in association with UCD, 1996) xii + 300. (Volume 31 of *Irish Jurist*).
O'Dell, E.,	*Leading Cases of the Twentieth Century* (Dublin: Round Hall Sweet and Maxwell, 2000) lviii + 519 pp.

Expert Witnesses. See Evidence.

Export Law

Coras Trachtála,	*Legal Aspects of Appointing an Export Agent/ Distributor with in the European Community* compiled by D. Curtin, (Dublin; Coras Trachtála, 1985) 27 pp.

Extradition

Farrell, M.,	*Sheltering the Fugitive? The Extradition of Irish Political Offenders* (Dublin & Cork: Mercier Press, 1985) 139 pp.
Forde, M.,	*Extradition Law* (Dublin: Round Hall Press, 1995) xxiv + 261 pp. [1st ed., *sub nom. Extradition Law in Ireland* 1988]
Forde, M.,	*The Law of Extradition in the United Kingdom* (Dublin: Round Hall Press, 1995) xxxvii + 370 pp.
Hogan, G. and Walker, C.,	*Political Violence and the Law in Ireland* (Manchester, Manchester UP, 1989) x + 342 pp. Bibliog. [Contains chapter on Extradition].

Family Law

	Report of the Joint Oireachtas Committee on Marriage Breakdown (Dublin: Stationery Office, 1985) *Marital Breakdown: A Review and Proposed Changes* Pl 9104 (Dublin: Stationery Office, 1992) 216 pp.
AIM,	*Modern Marriage: A Fresh Approach* Seminar Report (Dublin: AIM, 1983).
Attorney General,	*The Law of Nullity in Ireland* (Dublin: Stationery Office, 1976) 57 pp.
Binchy, W.,	*Is Divorce the Answer?* (Dublin: Irish Academic Press, 1984) 115 pp.

Binchy, W.,   *A Casebook on Irish Family Law* (Abingdon: Professional
                             Books, 1984) xl + 487 pp.

Brown, D.,   *Separation and Divorce Matters* (Dublin: Attic Press,
                             1991)

Cherish,   *Singled Out: Single Mothers in Ireland* (Dublin: Wom-
                             en's Community Press, 1983) 52 pp.

Dept of Justice,   *Wards of Court: An Information Booklet* (Dublin: Dept of
                             Justice, c. 1998) 23pp.

Donlon, Fennell, and   *Marriage and Family Law* (Dublin: AIM, c. 1991).
Mulcahy,

Duncan, W.R. and   *Marriage Breakdown in Ireland: Law and Practice* (Dub-
Scully, P.,   lin: Butterworths (Ireland) Ltd, 1990) lvii + 520 pp.

Ekeelaar, J. and Nhlap, T., *The Changing Family: International Perspectives on the
                             Family and Family Law* (Oxford: Hart Publishing, 1998)
                             xix + 634 pp. Contains chapter by K. O'Halloran on Irish
                             family law.

Fahey, T. and Lyons, M.,   *Marital Breakdown and Family Law in Ireland: A Socio-
                             logical Study* (Dublin: ESRI, 1995) xix + 160 pp. Bibliog.

Gavan Duffy, C.,   *The Married Women's Status Act 1957* (Dublin: ILSI,
                             1963) 39 pp.

Glendon, M.,   *Irish Family Law in Comparative Perspective* 4th Frances
                             E. Moran Lecture (Dublin: TCD, 1986) 23 pp.

Hamilton, C. and   *Family Law in Europe* (London: Butterworths, 1995) lv +
Standley, K.,   706 pp. Contains chapter by W. Duncan on Irish family
                             law.

Jackson, N. and   *Family Law (Divorce) Act 1996* (Dublin: Round Hall
Coggans, S.,   Sweet and Maxwell, 1998) 216 pp.

McAreavey, J.,   *The Canon Law of Marriage and the Family* (Dublin: Four
                             Courts Press, 1997) 254 pp

Mullally, M., Madigan, P   *Law and the Family. A Practical Guide* (Dublin: Blackhall
and Kearney S.,   Publishing, 1998) xiv + 145 pp.

Nestor, J.,   *An Introduction to Irish Family Law* (Dublin; Gill and
                             Macmillan, 2000) xxiv + 278 pp.

Power, C. (ed.),   *Family Legislation Service* (loose-leaf), (Dublin; Round
                             Hall Sweet and Maxwell, 2000).

O'Connor, P.A.,   *Key Issues in Irish Family Law* (Dublin: Round Hall Press,
                             1988) xxx + 236 pp.

Shannon, G. (ed.),   *The Divorce Act in Practice* (Dublin, Round Hall Ltd)
                             xxiii + 141pp.

Shannon, G. (ed),	*Family Law* (London: Blackstone Press/Law Society of Ireland, 2000) xxix + 303 pp.
Shannon, G. (ed.),	*Family Law Practitioner* (loose-leaf), (Dublin; Round Hall Sweet and Maxwell, 2000).
Shatter, A.J.,	*Family Law* 4th ed. (Dublin: Butterworths, 1997) xcix + 1097 pp.
Walls, M. and Bergin, D.,	*The Law of Divorce in Ireland* (Bristol: Jordans Publishing, 1997) xxxviii + 313 pp.
Walls, M. and Bergin, D.,	*Irish Family Legislation Handbook* (Bristol: Jordans Publishing, 1999) x + 510 pp.
Walpole, H.E.,	*Tax Implications of Marital Breakdown* 3rd ed. (Dublin: ITI, 1999) xiv + 222 pp.
Ward, Peter,	*Divorce in Ireland: Who Should Bear the Cost?* (Cork: Cork UP, 1993) vi + 65 pp.
Ward, Paul,	*The Child Care Act 1991* (Dublin: Round Hall Sweet and Maxwell, 1997) 112 pp.
Wood, K. and O'Shea, P.,	*Divorce in Ireland* (Dublin: O'Brien Press, 1997) 189 pp.

Financial Services and Capital Markets

ICEL,	*The Single European Market and Financial Services in Ireland* (Dublin: ICEL, 1988) 129 pp.

Fisheries Law

Keary, B.,	*Acquaculture Legislation in Ireland: An Examination and Critique of Section 54 of the Fisheries Act 1980* SSRC Research Report No 6 (Galway: NUI, Galway 1996) 33 pp.

Food Law

Food Safety Authority,	*Compendium of Food Law in Ireland 1998* (Dublin: Food Safety Authority, 1998) x + 89 pp.
Laing, C. (ed.),	*International Food and Beverage Law* (London: Kluwer Law International, 1996) viii + 465 pp. Contains chapter by P. O'Donovan on Ireland.

Freedom of Information

Doyle, M. and Donnelly, J. (eds.),	*Freedom of Information: Philosophy and Implementation* (Dublin: Blackhall Publishing, 1999) xii + 129 pp.

McDonagh, M.,   *Freedom of Information Law in Ireland* (Dublin: Round
                        Hall Sweet and Maxwell, 1998) lviii + 454 pp.

North, P.M.,   *Public or Private? A Paradox for 1984* Frances E Moran
                        Lecture No 3 (Dublin: TCD, 1984) 29 pp.

Gender and the Law

Commission on the   *Report to the Government by Second Commission for
  Status of Women,* ·   *the Status of Women* Pl 9557 (Dublin: Stationery Office,
                        1993) 535 pp.

Connelly, A.,   *Gender and the Law in Ireland* (Dublin: Oak Tree Press,
                        1993) x + 238 pp.

ICCL,   *Women's Rights in Ireland* (Dublin: Ward River Press,
                        1983) 52 pp.

ICCL,   *Equality Now for Lesbians and Gay Men* (Dublin: ICCL,
                        1990) vi + 71 pp.

Reilly, N. (ed.),   *Women's Rights as Human Rights.* Proceedings of ICCL
                        conference in 1997 (Dublin: Women's Human Rights
                        Campaign, 1997) 66 pp.

Health and Safety, and Medical Law

Barrington, R.,   **Health, Medicine and Politics in Ireland 1900-1970*
                        (Dublin: I.P.A., 1987) xi + 348 pp.

Brown, P.,   *The Health (Nursing Homes) Act 1990* Briefing Paper
                        (Dublin: IPA, 1991) 19 pp. Bibliog.

Byrne, R.,   *The Health, Safety and Welfare at Work Act, 1989: A Guide*
                        (Dublin: NIFAST, 1990) v + 66 pp.

Byrne, R.,   *A Guide to the Safety, Health and Welfare at Work Regu-
                        lations* (Dublin: NIFAST, 1995) xvii + 198 p

Casey, P. and Craven, C.,   *Psychiatry and the Law* (Dublin: Oak Tree Press, 1999)
                        lv + 603 pp. Bibliog.

Coliver, S. (ed.),   *The Right to Know: Human Rights and Access to Repro-
                        ductive Health Information* (London: Article 19, 1995)
                        xiv + 391 pp. Contains chapter by S. Coliver on Ireland.

Cooney, T and O'Neill, O.,   *Psychiatric Detention: Civil Commitment in Ireland*
                        (Wicklow: Baikonur , 1996) xviii + 350 pp.

---

*Books essentially about health policy but with some material on law.

Dept. of Health,	*Green Paper on Mental Health* (Dublin: Stationery Office, 1992).
Dept of Health,	*A New Mental Health Act* White Paper Pn 1824 (Dublin: Stationery Office, 1995) 133 pp.
Finnane, M.,	**Insanity and the Insane in Post-Famine Ireland* (London: Croom Helm, 1981) 241 pp.
Garavan, T,	*The Irish Health and Safety Handbook* (Dublin: Oak Tress Press, 1997) xxiv + 930 pp. Bibliog.
Hanafin, P.,	*Last Rites: Death, Dying and the Law in Ireland* (Cork: Cork UP, 1997) vi + 114 pp.
Haward , L. and McGann, B.,	*Psychiatry, Psychology and the Law Courts: A Symposium* (Dublin: Institute of Psychology, 1973) 23 pp.
Hensey, B.,	**The Health Services of Ireland* 4th ed. (Dublin: I.P.A., 1988) viii + 292 pp.
ICCL,	*Report on Mental Health Bill* (Dublin: ICCL, 1982)
Law Society of Ireland,	*Mental Health: The Case for Reform* Report by Law Society's Law Reform Committee (Dublin: LSI, 1999) 53 pp. Bibliog.
McAuley, F.,	*Insanity, Psychiatry and Criminal Responsibility* (Dublin, Round Hall Press, 1993) xiv + 248 pp. Bibliog.
O'Kelly, S. and Ronan, J.,	*Nursing Law* (Dublin; Butterworths, 1994) xxi + 208 pp.
Robins, J.,	**Fools and Mad: A History of the Insane in Ireland* (Dublin: I.P.A., 1986) 256 pp.
Shilliman,	*The Factory Legislation in Ireland* (Dublin: Falconer, 1956)
Stranks, J.,	*The Blackhall Guide to Health and Safety at Work in Ireland* (Dublin: Blackhall Publishing, 1998) x + 162 pp.
Tomkin, D. and Hanafin, P.,	*Irish Medical Law* (Dublin: Round Hall Press, 1995) xxx + 299 pp.
Weedle, P.B. and Cahill, M.J.,	*Medicines and Pharmacy Law in Ireland* (Dublin: Kenlis Publications, 1991) 602 pp.

Holiday Law

Buttimore, J.,	*Holiday Law in Ireland* (Dublin: Blackhall Publishing, 1999) xxv + 216 pp.

---

*Books essentially about health policy but with some material on law.

Hotel and Catering Law

Dempsey, F. J.,	*A Handbook of Essential Law for the Irish Hotel and Catering Industry* (Dublin: CERT, 1990) xv + 280 pp.
McDonald, M.,	*Hotel, Restaurant and Public House Law:, Registrations, Licenses and Names* (Dublin: Butterworths Ireland, 1992) xxix + 441 pp.

Human Rights

Berger, V.,	*Case Law of the European Court of Human Rights* Vol. 1 1960-1987 (Dublin: Round Hall Press, 1989) xviii + 478 pp.
Berger, V.,	*Case Law of the European Court of Human Rights* Vol. II, 1988-1990 (Dublin: Round Hall Press, 1992) xiv + 291 pp.
Berger, V.,	*Case Law of the European Court of Human Rights,* Vol. III, 1991-1993 (Dublin: Round Hall Press, 1995) xvi + 454 pp.
Coliver, S. (ed.),	*The Right to Know: Human Rights and Access to Reproductive Health Information* (London: Article 19, 1995) xiv + 391 pp. Contains chapter by S. Coliver on Ireland.
Department of Foreign Affairs,	*International Covenant on Civil and Political Rights: First Report by Ireland* (Dublin: Dept. of Foreign Affairs, 1992) vi + 137 pp.
Department of Foreign Affairs,	*International Covenant on Civil and Political Rights: Second Report by Ireland* (Dublin: Dept. of Foreign Affairs, 1998) v + 106 pp.
Department of Foreign Affairs,	*International Covenant on Civil and Political Rights: Second Report by Ireland* (Dublin: Dept. of Foreign Affairs, 2000) vii + 86 pp.
Dickson, B. (ed.),	*Human Rights and the European Convention: The Effects of the Convention on Britain and Ireland* (London: Sweet and Maxwell) xxxiv + 256 pp. Contains chapter on Ireland by Dr A. Connelly.
Driscoll, D. (ed.),	*Irish Human Rights Review* (Dublin: Round Hall Sweet and Maxwell, 2000)
Falconer, A.D.,	*Understanding Human Rights* (Dublin: Irish School of Ecumenics, 1980) xi + 242 pp.
Gearty, C. (ed.),	*European Civil Liberties and the European Convention on Human Rights: A Comparative Perspective* (The Hague: Martinus Nijhoff Publishers, 1997) xv + 420 pp. Contains chapter by L. Flynn on Ireland.

Heffernan, L. (with
Kingston, J.) (ed.),

Human Rights: A European Perspective (Dublin: Round Hall Press and ICEL, 1994) xxxii + 437 pp.

Irish Commission for
Justice and Peace,

UN Covenant on Civil and Political Rights: A Guide to Making an Independent Submission (Dublin: Irish Commission for Justice and Peace, 1991) 33pp.

O'Flaherty, M and
Heffernan, L.,

International Covenant on Civil and Political Rights: International Human Rights Law in Ireland (Dublin: Brehon, 1995) xxvii + 210 pp.

Quinn, G. (ed.),

Irish Human Rights Yearbook 1995 (Dublin: Round Hall Sweet and Maxwell, 1995) xxvii + 142 + 5 pp.

Reilly, N. (ed.),

Women's Rights as Human Rights. Proceedings of ICCL conference in 1997 (Dublin: Women's Human Rights Campaign, 1997) 66 pp.

Industrial Relations. See **Labour Law**

Information Technology

Kelleher, D. and
Murray K.,

Information Technology Law in Ireland (Dublin: Butterworths, 1997) xlii + 486 pp.

Insurance Law

Buckley, A.,

Insurance Law in Ireland (Dublin: Oak Tree Press, 1997) lxviii + 555 pp.

Corrigan, M. and
Campbell, J.A.,

A Casebook of Irish Insurance Law (Dublin: Oak Tree Press, 1995) xix + 612 pp.

Ellis, H. (ed.),

Regulation of Insurance in the United Kingdom and Ireland (London, Kluwer, 1983) loose-leaf.

O'Regan Cazabon, A.,

Insurance Law in Ireland (Dublin: Round Hall Sweet and Maxwell, 1999) xxxvii + 645 pp.

Schutte, J.,

Insurance Law in Ireland (Dublin, 1988)

Intellectual Property

Clark, R. and Smyth, S.,

Intellectual Property Law in Ireland (Dublin: Butterworths, 1997) xcvii + 837 pp.

Cotter, S. (ed.),

International Intellectual Property Law (Chicester: Wiley, 1995) xxv + 519 pp. Contains chapter on Ireland.

Hanna, P.,

Being Successful in Patents, Copyright and Trade Marks (Dublin: Blackhall Publishing, 1999) 155 pp.

Lavery, P.,   *Commercial Secrets: The Action for Breach of Confidence in Ireland* (Round Hall Sweet and Maxwell, 1996) xxx + 262 pp.

ICEL,   *Intellectual Property* (Dublin; ICEL, 1989) ii + 76 pp.

Tierney, M.,   *Irish Trade Marks Law and Practice* (Dublin: Gill and Macmillan, 1987) xxv + 178 pp.

International Law and International Relations

Carty, A.,   *Was Ireland Conquered? International Law and the Irish Question* (London: Pluto Press, 1996) vii + 203 pp.

Gageby, D.,   *The Last Secretary General: Sean Lester and the League of Nations* (Dublin: Town House and Country House, 1999) ix + 276 pp.

Kennedy, M.,   *Ireland and the League of Nations, 1919-1946: International Relations, Diplomacy and Politics* (Dublin: Irish Academic Press, c.1996) 285 pp. Bibliog.

Skelly, J.M.,   *Irish Diplomacy at the United Nations 1945-1965. National Interests and the International Order* (Dublin: Irish Academic Press, 1997) 314 pp. Bibliog.

Symmons, C.,   *Ireland and the Law of the Sea* 2nd ed. (Dublin: Round Hall Sweet and Maxwell, 2000) xlviii + 443 pp. [1st ed. 1993]

Treves, T.,   *The Law of the Sea: The European Union and its Member States* (The Hague: Martinus Nijhoff Publishers, 1997) xxiv + 590 pp. Contains chapter by Dr C Symmons on Ireland.

Irish Language

Andrews, J.A. and Henshaw, L.G.,   *The Welsh Language and the Courts* (Aberstwyth: University of Wales Press, 1984) x + 116 pp. Contains chapter on Irish language and the courts.

Fasach Report,   *An Ghaeilge agus an Dli – Tuarascail* (Baile Atha Cliath: Bord na Gaeilge, 1986)

Oifig an tSolathair,   *Tearmai Dli – English/Irish and Irish/English* (Dublin: Stationery office, nd).

O Cathain, L.,   *Focal sa Chuirt* (Dublin: Coisceim, 2001) 242 pp. [Dictionary]

Ó Cearúil, M.,   *Bunreacht na hEireann: A Study of the Irish Text*. Commissioned by the Oireachtas All-Party Committee on the

Constitution, and with original contribution by Professor Martin O Murchu (Dublin: Stationery Office, 1999) x + 759 pp.

Ó Maille, T.,   *The Status of the Irish Language: A Legal Perspective* (Dublin: Bord na Gaeilge, 1990) vi + 40 pp. Bilingual.

Ó Riain, S.,   *Pleanáil Teanga in Éirinn 1919-1985* (Baile Atha Cliath: Carbad agus Bord na Gaeilge, 1994) 245 pp. Maps.

Ó Tuathail, S. (ed.), *Tuairisci Éireann. The Irish Report, Special Reports, 1980-1988* (Dublin: ILCR, 2000)

Judicial Review, *see* **Administrative Law**.

Judiciary

Report of Committee on Judicial Conduct and Ethics Pn 9449 (Dublin: Stationery Office, 2000) vi + 114.

Bartolomew, P.C.   *The Irish Judiciary* (Dublin: I.P.A., 1971) x + 86 pp. Bibliog.

Juvenile Justice

Report of Committee on Reformatory and Industrial Schools. The Kennedy Report. Prl. 1342 (Dublin: Stationery Office, 1970) vii + 136 pp.

Barnes, J.,   *Irish Industrial Schools 1868-1908: Origins and Development* (Dublin: Irish Academic Press, 1989) 192 + 6 pp. Bibliog.

Burke, H., Carney,   *Youth and Justice: Young Offenders in Ireland* (Dublin:
  C. and Cook, G.,   Turoe Press, 1981) xi + 222 pp.

Cook, G. and   *Juvenile Justice at the Crossroads* (Dublin: UCD Dept of
  Richardson, V.,   Social Administration, 1982) 104 pp.

Farrelly, J.,   *Crime, Custody and Community: Juvenile Justice and Crime* (Dublin: Voluntary and Statutory Bodies, c. 1989) 152 pp

Hart, I,   *Factors Relating to Reconviction Rates among Young Dublin Probationers* (Dublin: ESRI, 1974) 124 pp.

Mitchell, D.,   *A Report on the Law and Procedures regarding the Prosecution and Disposal of Young Offenders* (Dublin: Office of the Director of Public Prosecutions, 1977) 103 + 4 pp. Bibliog.

National Youth Federation,	*Justice for Young People: National Youth Federation Policy for Juvenile Justice* (Dublin: Irish YouthWork Press, 1996) 50 pp.
Osborough, N.,	*Borstal in Ireland: Custodial Provision for the Young Adult Offender 1906-1974* (Dublin, IPA, 1975) xvi + 184 pp. Bibliog.
O'Gorman, N. and Barnes, J.,	*Survey of Dublin Juvenile Delinquents* (Dublin: St. Michael's Assessment Unit, 1991)

Jurisprudence, *see* **Legal Theory.**

Labour Law. See also **Discrimination and Equality Law.**

Bolger, M. and Kimber C.,	*Sex Discrimination Law* (Dublin: Round Hall Sweet and Maxwell, 2000) xlv + 473 pp.
Byrne, G.,	*Transfer of Undertakings: Employment Aspects of Business Transfers in Irish and European Law* (Dublin: Blackhall Publishing, 1999) xxxviii + 442 pp.
Calleder R. and Meenan, F.,	*Equality in Law between Men and Women in the European Community: Ireland* (Dondrecht: Martinus Nijhoff Publishers, 1994) 262 pp.
Coleman, J.V.,	*An Employer's Duties at Common Law in Ireland* (Dublin: Allen Figgis, 1961) 92 pp.
Coolock Community Law Centre/FLAC,	*Maternity Rights: Employment and Social Welfare Entitlements*(Dublin, 1997) 35 pp.
Curtin, D.,	*Employment Equality Law* (Dublin: Round Hall Press, 1989) xliv + 378 pp.
Fennell, C. and Lynch, I.,	*Labour Law in Ireland* (Dublin: Gill and Macmillan, 1993) xxiii + 295 pp.
FIE,	*A Guide to Employment Legislation* 5th ed. (Dublin: FIE, 1991) 201 pp.
Finlay, I.,	*The Labour Court: A History of Fifty Years of the Labour Court from 1946 to 1996* (Dublin: The Stationery Office, 1996) 116 pp.
Forde, M.,	*Industrial Relations Law* (Dublin: Round Hall Press, 1991) xxxviii + 326 pp.
Forde, M.,	*Employment Law* 2nd edn (Dublin: Round Hall Sweet & Maxwell, 2001) lvii + 416 pp.
Gunnigle, P, Garavan, T. and Fitzgerald, G,	*Employee Relations and Employment Law in Ireland* (Limerick, 1992) viii + 166 pp.

Harvey, N. and Twomey, A. F., — *Sexual Harassment in the Workplace: A Practical Guide for Employers and Employees in Ireland* (Dublin: Oak Tree Press, 1995) xii + 189 pp.

Hepple, B.A. et al. — *Labour Law in Great Britain and Ireland to 1978* (London: Sweet and Maxwell, 1981) xxii + 131 pp.

Higgins, E. and Keher, N., — *Your Rights at Work: A Comprehensive Guide to Rights at Work in Ireland* 2nd ed. (Dublin, IPA, 1996) vii + 240 pp.

I.C.T.U., — *Industrial Relations Act 1990* (Dublin: ICTU, 1990) 45 pp.

I.C.T.U., — *European Case Law and Equality: A Guide for Negotiators* (Dublin: ICTU, c.1995) 88 pp.

Kerr, A., — *The Trade Union and Industrial Relations Acts in Ireland: Commentary* (London: Sweet and Maxwell, 1991) xx + 250 pp.

Kerr, A., — *Termination of Employment Statutes: Commentary* (London: Sweet and Maxwell, 1995) xiv + 284 pp.

Kerr, A. (ed.), — *The Acquired Rights Directive* (Dublin: ICEL, 1996) 146 pp.

Kerr, A., — *Irish Employment Legislation* (Dublin: Round Hall Sweet and Maxwell, Loose-leaf).

Kerr, A. & Whyte, G., — *Irish Trade Union Law* (Abingdon: Professional Books, 1985) lxiv + 383 pp.

McCarthy, C., — *Trade Unions in Ireland 1894 –1960* (Dublin: I.P.A., 1977).

Madden, D. and Kerr, T., — *Unfair Dismissals: Cases and Commentary* 2nd ed. (Dublin: IBEC, 1996) xi + 497 pp.

Maguire, C., — *Trade Union Membership and the Law* (Dublin: Round Hall Sweet and Maxwell, 1999) xxiv + 185 pp.

Meenan, F., — *Working within the Law: A Practical Guide for Employers and Employees* 2nd ed. (Dublin: Oak Tress Press, 199?) xxxviii + 666 [1st ed., 1994]

O'Connell, D., — *Equality Now. The SIPTU Guide to the Employment Equality Act 1998* (Dublin: SIPTU, 1998) 125 pp.

O'Hara, B. J.,, — *The Evolution of Irish Industrial Relations Law and Practice* (Dublin: Folens, 1981) 146 pp.

O'Higgins, P., — *Irish Labour Law: Sword or Shield?* (Dublin: Irish Association for Industrial Relations, 1979)

Roche, W.K. and Redmond, M.,	*Legislation, Collective Bargaining and the Regulation of Working Time in Irish Industrial Relations* (Dublin: UCD Graduate School of Business, 1994) 77 pp. Bibliog.
Redmond, M.,	*Labour Law and Industrial Relations in Ireland* (Dublin: Bridgefoot Press, 1984) 188 pp.
Redmond, M.,	*Dismissal Law in Ireland* (Dublin: Butterworths, 1999) lxviii + 619 pp. Earlier book entitled *Dismissal Law in the Republic of Ireland* was published by ILSI, Dublin in 1984.
von Prondzynski, F.,	*Freedom of Association and Industrial Relations* (London: Mansell, 1987) x + 248 pp.
von Prondzynski, F. and McCarthy, C.,	*Employment Law in Ireland* 2nd ed. (London: Sweet and Maxwell, 1989) xxx+ 223 pp.
Wayne, N.,	*Equal Pay, Collective Bargaining and the Law* (Dublin: ICTU, 1979)
Wayne, N.,	*Labour Law in Ireland: A Guide to Workers' Rights* (Dublin: ICTU/Kincora Press, 1980) 286 pp.

Land Law (*see also* Conveyancing)

Bland, P.,	*The Law of Easements and Profits a Prendre* (Dublin: Round Hall Sweet and Maxwell, 1997) liv + 371 pp.
Cannon, R.,	*Land Laws*, Round Hall Nutshells (Dublin: Round Hall Sweet & Maxwell, 2001) xvi + 148 pp.
Carson,	*Real Property Statutes* Reissued in Butterworths Important Irish Reprint Series
Conway, H.,	*Co-Ownership of Land. Partition Rights and Remedies* (Dublin: Butterworths, 2001) lx + 368 pp.
Coughlan, P.,	*Property Law* 2nd ed. (Dublin: Gill and Macmillan, 1998) lxiv + 496 pp. [1st ed., 1995]
Fitzgerald, B.,	*Land Registry Practice* 2nd ed. (Dublin: Round Hall Press, 1995) xlviii + 382 pp. [1st ed. 1989]
Harrison,	*The Law and Practice Relating to Ejectments in Ireland* (1903). Reissued in Butterworths Important Irish Reprint Series
Key and Elphinstone,	*Compendium of Precedents in Conveyancing* 2 vols. (1923). Reissued in Butterworths Important Irish Reprint Series.
Jackson, P. and Wilde, D.C.,	*The Reform of Property Law* (Aldershot: Dartmouth, 1997) xiii + 400 pp. Contains chapter by Dr A. Lyall on Ireland.

Linehan, D.M.,	*Irish Land and Conveyancing Law* (Cork: Legis Publications, 1989) xxviii + 258 pp.
Linehan, D.M.	*Irish Land Law* (Cork: Legaline Series, 1984)
Lyall, A.,	*Land Law in Ireland* 2nd ed. (Dublin: Round Hall Sweet and Maxwell, 2000) clix + 1164 pp. [1st ed. published by Oak Tree Press, 1994]
McAllister, D.L.,	*Registration of Title in Ireland* (Dublin: ICLRI, 1973) xxxi + 578 pp.
Mee, J.,	*The Property Rights of Cohabitees: An Analysis of Equity's Response in Five Common Law Jurisdictions* (Oxford: Hart Publishing, 1999) xxxvii + 331 pp.
Pearce, R. and Mee, J.,	*Land Law* 2nd edn (Dublin: Round Hall Sweet and Maxwell, 2000) xxxv + 292 pp. [1st ed. by Pearce published by Sweet and Maxwell, London in 1985)
Scanlon, J.W.,	*Practice and Procedure in Administration and Mortgage Suits* (Dublin: ICLRI, 1963).
Sheridan, L.A.,	*Irish Supplement* (London, 1956) to C. Sweet, *Challis' Law of Real Property* 3rd ed. (London, 1911).
Waldron, K.,	*Guidelines on Real Property* (Dublin, 1971). Published by author.
Waldron, K.,	*Guidelines on Mortgages and Registration* (Dublin, 1971). Published by author.
Wolstenhome,	*Conveyancing and Settled Land Acts* 10th ed. (1913). Reissued in Butterworths Important Irish Reprint Series.
Wylie, J.C.W.,	*Irish Land Law* 3rd ed. (Dublin: Butterworths, 1997) ccxv + 1176 pp.
Wylie, J.C.W.	*A Casebook on Irish Land Law* (Abingdon: Professional Books, 1984)

Landlord and Tenant

Brennan, G. (ed.),	*Landlord and Tenant* (London: Blackstone Press/Law Society of Ireland, 2000) xix + 262 pp.
Coghlan, J.R.,	*The Law of Rent Restrictions in Ireland* 3rd ed. (Dublin: 1979) [1st ed. 1944]
Deale, K.E.L.,	*The Landlord and Tenant Acts 1931 and 1943 Annotated* (Dublin: Browne and Nolan Ltd, 1953) xxi + 214 pp.
Deale, K.E.L.,	*The Law of Landlord and Tenant in the Republic of Ireland*, xxxviii + 393 pp.

De Blacam, M.,   *The Control of Private Rented Dwellings* 2nd ed. (Dublin: Round Hall Press, 1992) 129 pp.

Dowling, J.A.   *Ejectment for Non-Payment of Rent* with supplement by G. McCormack on Republic of Ireland (Belfast: SLS Legal Publications, 1986) xvii + 84 pp.

Wylie, J.C.W.,   *Landlord and Tenant Law* 2nd ed. (Dublin: Butterworths, 1998) cxxii + 715 pp.

Law Officers. *See* Legal System

Law Reform

Deloitte Touche,   *Review of the Organisation and Management of the Law Reform Commission. Final Report* (Dublin, 1997) 67 pp.

Legal Aid

Committee on Legal Aid and Advice. Report to the Minister for Justice. The Pringle Report Prl 6862(Dublin: Stationery Office, 1977) 289 pp.

F.L.A.C.   *The Closed Door: A Report on Civil Legal Aid Services in Ireland* (Dublin: F.L.A.C. and Coolock Community Law Centre, c. 1987) 31 pp.

Legal History. *See also* Constitutional Law, International Law and International Relations, and Legislation, Collected.

Ball, F.E.,   *The Judges in Ireland 1221-1921* (Dublin: Round Hall Press, 1993) 2 Vols., xxii + 365 + 408 pp. [First published in 1926 by John Murray (London)]

Binchy, D.A.,   *Corpus Iuris Hibernici* 6 vols. (Dublin: Dublin Institute of Advanced Studies, 1978) xxviii + 2343 pp.

Bonsall, P.,   *The Irish RMs. The Resident Magistrates in the British Administration of Ireland* (Dublin: Four Courts Press, c. 1998) 224 pp.

Breathnach, L. (ed.),   *Uraiceacht na Riar* Early Irish Law Series Vol. II (Dublin: Dublin Institute of Advanced Studies, 1987) xxii + 189 pp.

Bryant,   *Liberty, Order and Law under Native Irish Rule* (Port Washington: Kennikat, 1970) /// Reprint of 1923 edition.

Burke, H.,   *The People and the Poor Law in Nineteenth Century Ireland* (Littlehampton: Women's Education Bureau, 1987) xiv + 369 pp.

Burton, D.H. (ed.),   *Holmes-Sheehan Correspondence: The Letters of Judge*
                              Oliver Wendell Holmes, Jr. and Canon Patrick Augustine
                              Sheehan Revised ed. (Bronx, NY: Fordham UP, ////) 96
                              pp.

Campbell, C.,   *Emergency Law in Ireland 1918-1925* (Oxford: Clarendon
                              Press, 1994) xxiii + 429 pp. Bibliog.

Carroll-Burke, P.   *Colonial Discipline. The Making of the Irish Convict Sys-*
                              tem (Dublin: Four Courts Press, 2000) 256 pp. Bibliog.

Charles-Edwards, T. and   *Becbretha: An Old Irish Law Tract on Bee-keeping* Early
Kelly, F. (eds.),   Irish Law Series, Vol. 1 (Dublin: Dublin Institute for Ad-
                              vanced Studies, 1983) xii + 212 pp.

Colbert C.F. and   *Land Reform in Ireland: A Legal History of the Irish Land*
O'Brien, T.,   *Problem and its Settlement* Occasional Paper No 3 of the
                              Department of Land Economy, University of Cambridge
                              (Cambridge, 1975) 76 pp. Bibliog.

Costello, C. (ed.),   *The Four Courts: 200 Years. Essays to Commemorate*
                              the Bicentenary of the Four Courts (Dublin: ICLRI, 1996)
                              265 pp.

Crawford, J.G.,   *Anglicising the Government of Ireland: The Irish Privy*
                              Council and the Expansion of Tudor Rule (1556-1578)
                              (Dublin: Irish Academic Press, 1993).

Crossman, V.,   *Local Government in Nineteenth Century Ireland* (Bel-
                              fast: QUB, The Institute of Irish Studies, 1994) 115 pp.
                              Bibliog.

Crossman, V.,   *Politics, Law and Order in 19th Century Ireland* (Dublin:
                              Gill and Macmillan, 1996) vii + 290 pp. Bibliog.

Dawson, N., Greer, D.   *One Hundred and Fifty Years of Irish Law* (Belfast: SLS
and Ingram, P.,   Legal Publications; Dublin: Round Hall Sweet and
                              Maxwell, 1996) xvi + 257 pp.

Farrell, B.,   *The Founding of Dáil Éireann: Parliament and Nation*
                              Building (Dublin: Gill and Macmillan, 1971) xx + 89 pp.

Farrell, B. (ed.),   *The Irish Parliamentary Tradition* (Dublin: Gill and
                              Macmillan, 1973) 286 pp. Bibliog.

Garnham, N.,   *The Courts, Crime and the Criminal Law in Ireland, 1692-*
                              1760 (Dublin: Irish Academic Press, 1996) viii + 309 pp.

Greer, D.S. and   *Mysteries and Solutions in Irish Legal History. Irish Le-*
Dawson, N.(eds.),   *gal History Discourses and other Papers 1996-1999*
                              (Dublin: Four Courts Press in association with Irish Le-
                              gal History Society, 2001) x + 252 pp.

Hand, G.J.,   *English Law in Ireland 1290-1324* (London: Cambridge
                              UP, 1967) xi + 280 pp. Bibliog.

Hanna, H.,

The Statute Law of the Irish Free State (Saorstát Éireann) 1922 to 1928 - reviewed and indexed by Mr Justice Hanna assisted by A. Denis Pringle (Holmes Beach, Florida: Gaunt, 1999). First published by Alex Thom, Dublin, 1929.

Hart, A.R.,

A History of the King's Sergeants at Law in Ireland: Honour rather than Advantage? (Dublin: Four Courts Press in association with ILHS, 2000) xvi + 213 pp.

Hickey, E.,

Irish Law and Lawyers in Modern Folk Tradition (Dublin: Four Courts Press in association with ILHS, 1999) xv + 240 pp.

Hogan, D.,

The Legal Profession in Ireland 1789-1922 (Dublin: ILSI, 1986) xii + 176 pp.

Hogan, D.,

The Honorable Society of King's Inns (Dublin: Council of the King's Inns, 1987) 23 pp.

Hogan, D and
Osborough, W.N.,

Brehons, Sergeants and Attorneys: Studies in the Irish Legal Profession (Dublin: Irish Academic Press and ILHS, 1990) 287 pp.

Henry, B.,

Dublin Hanged: Crime, Law Enforcement and Punishment in Late Eighteenth Century Dublin (Dublin: Irish Academic Press, 1994) 222 pp. Bibliog.

ILSI,

Incorporated Law Society of Ireland. Record of the Centenary of the Charter 1852-1952 (Dublin: ILSI, 1953).

Keane, E., Phair, P.B.
and Sadleir, T.U.,

King's Inns Admission Papers 1607-1867 (Dublin: Stationery Office for Irish Manuscripts Commission, 1982) xv + 542 pp.

Kelly, F.,

A Guide to Early Irish Law Early Irish Law Series Volume III (Dublin: Dublin Institute of Advanced Studies, 1988) xx + 358 pp.

Kenny, C.,

King's Inns and the Kingdom of Ireland: The Irish 'Inn of Court' 1541-1800 (Dublin: Irish Academic Press in association with Irish Legal History Society, 1992) xxiii + 352 pp. Bibliog.

Kenny, C.,

Tristam Kennedy and the Revival of Irish Legal Training 1835-1885 (Dublin: Irish Academic Press, 1996) xviii + 269 pp. Bibliog..

Kotsonouris, M.,

Retreat from Revolution: The Dáil Courts 1920-24 (Dublin: Irish Academic Press, 1994) 172 pp. Bibliog.

Lydon, J. (ed.),

Law and Disorder in Thirteenth Century Ireland: The Dublin Parliament of 1297 (Dublin: Four Courts Press, 1997) 171 pp.

McArdle, J.,   *Irish Legal Anecdotes* (Dublin: Gill and Macmillan, 1995) x + 230 pp.

McDowell, R.B.,   *The Irish Administration 1801-1914* (London: Routledge and Kegan Paul, 1964) xi + 329 pp.

McEldowney, J.F.,   *Irish Jury Trial: A Survey of some Eighteenth and Nineteenth Century Statutes* (Coventry: University of Warwick School of Law, 1979) 21 pp.

McEddowney, J.F.,   *Law Reform in 19th Century Ireland: The Work of the Statistical Society* (Coventry: University of Warwick School of Law, 1982) 13 + 4 pp.

McEldowney, J.F. and O'Higgins, P.,   *The Common Law Tradition: Essays in Irish Legal History* (Dublin: Irish Academic Press, 1990) 249 pp.

McLeod, N.,   *Early Irish Contract Law* (Sydney: Centre for Celtic Studies, University of Sydney, c. 1992) 340 pp. Bibliog.

Meyer, K.,   *Cain Adamnan; An Old Irish Treatise on the Law of Adamnan* edited and translated by Kuno Meyer (Oxford: Clarendon Press, 1905) viii + 56 pp.

Mitchell, A.,   *Revolutionary Government in Ireland. Dáil Éireann 1919-1922* (Dublin: Gill and Macmillan, 1995) xii + 423 pp. Bibliog.

Newark, F,H.,   *Notes on Irish Legal History* 2nd ed. (Belfast: Boyd, 1964) 29 pp. [1st ed. 1960]

Nichols, K.,   *Land, Law and Society in Sixteenth Century Ireland* O'Donnell Lecture (Dublin: NUI, 1976).

O'Callaghan, M.,   *British High Politics and a Nationalist Ireland: Criminality, Law and Order under Foster and Balfour* (Cork: Cork UP, 1994) xi + 223 pp.

Osborough, W.N.,   *Law in Ireland 1916-1926* (Banbridge: Banbridge Chronicle Press, 1972)

Osborough, W.N.,   *The Irish Legal History Society: Inaugural Addresses* (Dublin: ILHS in association with Irish Academic Press, 1989) 31pp.

Osborough, W.N. (ed.),   *Explorations in Law and History: Irish Legal History Society Discourses, 1988-1994* (Dublin: ILHS in association with Irish Academic Press, 1995)xiv + 191 pp.

Osborough, W.N.,   *Law and the Emergence of Modern Dublin: A Litigation Topography for a Capital City* (Dublin: Irish Academic Press in association with ILHS, 1996)xxii + 225 pp. illustrated.

Osborough, W.N.,   *Studies in Irish Legal History* (Dublin: Four Courts Press, 1999) ix + 340 pp.

O'Sullivan, D.,   *The Irish Constabularies 1822 –1922. A Century of Policing in Ireland* (Dingle, Co Kerry: Brandon, 1999) 410 pp. Bibliog.

Prawlish, H.S.,   *Sir John Davies and the Conquest of Ireland: A Study in Legal Imperialism* (Cambridge: Cambridge UP, 1985) x + 244 pp.

Richardson, H.G. and   *The Irish Parliament in the Middle Ages* (Philadelphia, Sayles, G.O.,   1952)

Sayles, G.O.,   *Documents on the Affairs of Ireland before the King's Council* (Dublin: Stationery Office, for Irish Manuscripts Commission, 1979) xxv + 336 pp.

Sexton, B.,   *Ireland and the Crown 1922-1936: the Governor Generalship of the Irish Free State* (Dublin: Irish Academic Press, 1989) 238 pp.

Shaw, A.G.L.,   *Convicts and Colonies: A study of Penal Transportation from Great Britain and Ireland to Australia and Other Parts of the British Empire* (Melbourne, Melbourne UP, 1977) 399 pp. Bibliog. First published in London by Faber and Faber, 1966.

Stacey, R.C.,   *The Road to Judgment: From Custom to Court in Medieval Ireland and Wales* (Philadelphia: University of Pennsylvania Press, 1994) xvi + 342 pp. Bibliog.

Townshend, C.,   *Political Violence in Ireland: Government and Resistance since 1848* (Oxford: Clarendon Press, 1983) x + 445 pp. Bibliog.

Legal Profession

Fair Trade Commission,   *Report of Study into Restrictive Practices in the Legal Profession* (Dublin: Stationery Office, 1990) ix + 334 pp.

ILSI,   *A Guide to Professional Conduct for Solicitors in Ireland* (Dublin: ILSI, 1988)

ILSI,   *Record of the Centenary of the Charter of the Incorporated Law Society of Ireland 1852-1952* (Dublin: ILSI, 1953)

Law Society of Ireland   *The Law Directory* published annually by Law Society of Ireland, Dublin.

National Prices   *Solicitors' Remuneration in Ireland* Prl 5946 (Dublin:
   Commission,   Stationery Office, 1976) 216 pp.

O'Callaghan, P.,   *The Law Relating to Solicitors in Ireland* (Dublin:
                        Butterworths, 2000) lv + 461 pp.

Tyrell, A. and   *The Legal Professions in the New Europe: A Handbook*
    Yaqub, Z.(eds.),   *for Practitioners* (Oxford: Blackwell, ////) xxii + 522 pp.
                        Contains chapter by B. Hartnett on Ireland.

Legal System

Bartolomew, P.C.   *The Irish Judiciary* (Dublin: I.P.A., 1971) x + 86 pp.
                        Bibliog.

Boyle, C.K. and   *The Legal Systems North and South.* A paper prepared
    Greer, D.S.,   for the New Ireland Forum (Dublin: Stationery Office,
                        1983) 63 pp.

Brennan, O.,   *Laying Down the Law: A Practical Guide* (Dublin and
                        Cork: Oak Tree Press, 1991) 146 pp.

Byrne, R. &   *The Irish Legal System* 3rd ed. (Dublin: Butterworths,
    McCutcheon, P.,   1996) lxxiv + 762 pp.

Casey, J.,   *The Irish Law Officers: Roles and Responsibilities of the*
                        Attorney General and the Director of Public Prosecutions
                        (Dublin: Round Hall Sweet and Maxwell, 1996) xxxv +
                        374p

Chubb, B.,   *Sourcebook of Irish Government* 2nd ed. (Dublin: I.P.A.,
                        1983) viii + 255 pp. Bibliog. Assisted by G. O'Dea.[1st
                        ed. 1964]

Chubb, B.,   *Cabinet Government in Ireland* (Dublin: I.P.A., 1974, repr.
                        1982) 98 pp.

Chubb, B.,   *The Government and Politics of Ireland* 3rd ed. (London:
                        Longman, 1993) xiii + 342 pp.

Coleman,   *How Law and Order Work in Ireland.* 16-page pamphlet
                        printed by McEvoy Press, Bray, Co, Wicklow. No date or
                        publisher given.

Delany, H.,   *The Courts Acts 1924-1997 including the Courts Service*
                        Act, 1998 2nd ed. (Dublin: Round Hall Sweet and Maxwell,
                        2000) lxxi + 538 pp.

Delany, V.T.H.,   *The Administration of Justice in Ireland* 4th ed. edited by
                        Charles Lysaght (Dublin: I.P.A., 1975) vi + 105 pp. [1st
                        ed. 1962]

Doolan, B.,   *Principles of Irish Law* 5th ed. (Dublin: Gill and
                        Macmillan, 1999) xxxviii + 491 pp. [1st ed. 1981].

Farrell, B.,   *The Founding of Dáil Éireann: Parliament and Nation*
                        Building (Dublin: Gill and Macmillan, 1971) xx + 89 pp.

Farrell, B. (ed.),	*The Irish Parliamentary Tradition* (Dublin: Gill and Macmillan, 1973) 286 pp. Bibliog.
Farrell, B.,	*Chairman or Chief?: The Role of the Taoiseach in Irish Government* (Dublin: Gill and Macmillan) xiii + 110 pp.
Faulkner, M., Kelly, G. and Turley, P.,	*Your Guide to Irish Law* (Dublin: Gill and Macmillan, 1993) 185 pp.
Forde, C.P.,	*You and the Law* (Dublin: Torc Books, 1972)
Garvin, T.,	*The Irish Senate* (Dublin: I.P.A., 1969) 8 + 100 pp.
Grimes and Horgan,	*Introduction to Law in the Republic of Ireland* (Dublin: Wolfhound Press, 1981) /// with 1988 supplement.
Kotsonouris, M.,	*Talking to Your Solicitor* (Dublin: Gill and Macmillan, 1992) 98 pp.
Lee, J.,	*Ireland: Towards a Sense of Place* (Cork: Cork UP, 1985). Contains Chapter by Professor B. McMahon on legal system.
Litton, F.,	*Unequal Achievement: The Irish Experience 1957-1982* (Dublin: I.P.A., 1982) x + 304 pp. [Contains chapter by Professor J Casey on 'Law and the Legal System 1957-1982']
McDunphy, M.,	*The President of Ireland: His Powers, Functions and Duties* (Dublin: Browne and Nolan, 1945) 120 pp.
Murphy, E.,	*Irish Legal Framework for Business Students* 2nd ed. (Dublin: Gill and Macmillan, 2000) xxx + 520 pp.
O'Donnell, J.,	*How Ireland is Governed* 6th ed. (Dublin: I.P.A., 1979, repr. 1985) vii + 152 pp.
Smyth, J. McG.,	*The Theory and Practice of the Irish Senate* (Dublin: I.P.A., 1972) vi + 100 pp.
Smyth, J. McG.,	*The Houses of the Oireachtas* 4th ed. (Dublin: I.P.A., 1979) 62 pp.

Legal Theory

Kelly, J.M.,	*A Short History of Western Legal Theory* (Oxford: Clarendon Press, 1992) xvi + 466 pp.
Quinn, G, Ingram, A. and Livingstone, S.,	*Justice and Legal Theory in Ireland* (Dublin: Oak Tree Press, 1995) 209 pp.
Ó Suilleabháin, M. (ed.),	*Legal Theory and Cases: Shifting Frontiers* (Munchen, Mering: Rainer Hampp Verlag, 1994) 71 pp.
Phelan, D.R.,	*It's God We Ought to Crucify. Validity and Authority in Law* (Dublin; Four Courts Press, 2000) 76 pp.

Legislation, Collected

	The Irish Statutes: Revised Edition. AD 1310-1800 with an introductory essay by W.N. Osborough (Dublin: Round Hall Press, 1995) 21+ lxiv + 848p
Forde, M. (ed.),	*Commercial Legislation* (Dublin, Round Hall Sweet and Maxwell, 1998) viii + 658p
Kennedy, D. and Maguire, E.,	*Irish Family Law Handbook* (Dublin: Butterworths, 1999) vii + 397 pp.
Kerr, A.,	*The Civil Liability Acts 1961and 1964* (Dublin: Round Hall Press, 1993) 150 pp.
Kerr, A.,	*The Civil Liability Acts* (Dublin: Round Hall Sweet and Maxwell, 1999) xiv + 106 pp.
Kerr, A.,	*Irish Employment Legislation* (Dublin: Round Hall Sweet and Maxwell, loose-leaf).
Nowlan, K.I.,	*A Guide to Irish Planning Legislation* (Dublin: Law Society of Ireland, 1999) xlvii + 587.
O'Donnell, M.,	*Planning Law* (Dublin: Butterworths, 1999) xv + 393 pp.
O'Reilly, P.F.,	*Commercial and Consumer Law* (Dublin: Butterworths, 2000) xix + 1070.
Walls, M. and Bergin, D.,	*Irish Family Legislation Handbook* (Bristol: Jordans Publishing, 1999) x + 510 pp.
Wylie, J.C.W.,	*Conveyancing Law* (Dublin: Butterworths, 1999) l + 573 pp. [1st ed. 1994 *sub nom. Irish Conveyancing Statutes*]

Licensing Law

Cassidy, C.,	*The Licensing Acts 1833-1995* (Dublin: Round Hall Sweet and Maxwell, 1996) li + 1001 pp.
Cassidy, C. (ed.),	*The Licensing Handbook* (Dublin: Round Hall Sweet and Maxwell, 1996) vii + 62 pp.
Woods, J.V.,	*Liquor Licensing Laws of Ireland* 2nd ed. (Limerick, 1992) xxxvii + 480 pp. Published by author.

Local Government Law

Canny, J.K.,	*The Law of Local Government* (Dublin: Round Hall Sweet and Maxwell, 2000) xliii + 370 pp.
Keane, R.,	*The law of Local Government in the Republic of Ireland* (Dublin: ILSI, 1982) xliv + 423 pp.

Roche, D.,   *Local Government in Ireland* (Dublin: I.P.A., 1982) x +
                                391 pp.

Street, H.A.,   *The Law Relating to Local Government* (Dublin: Station-
                                ery Office, 1955) xi + 1524 pp.

Media Law

Adams, M.,   *Censorship; The Irish Experience* (University of Alabama
                                Press, 1967; Dublin: Scepter, 1968) 265 pp.

Boyle, K. and   *A Report on Press Freedom and Libel* (Dublin: NNI, 1988)
   McGonagle, M.,   68 pp.

Boyle, K. and   *Media Accountability: The Readers' Representative in
   McGonagle, M.,   Irish Newspapers* (Dublin: NNI, 1995) vi + 60 pp.

McDonald, M.,   *Irish Law of Defamation* 2nd ed. (Dublin: Round Hall Press
                                in association with Irish Academic Press, 1989) xxx + 304
                                pp. [1st ed. 1987]

McGonagle, M.,   *A Textbook on Media Law* (Dublin: Gill and Macmillan,
                                1996) xxxvi + 314 pp.

McGonagle, M. (ed.),   *Law and the Media: The Views of Journalists and Law-
                                yers* (Round Hall Sweet and Maxwell, 199?) xxxvii +
                                319p.

McHugh, D.,   *Libel Law: A Journalist's Handbook* 2nd edn (Dublin: Four
                                Courts Press, 1989) 96 pp.

Murphy, Y,   *Journalists and the Law* 2nd edn (Dublin: Round Hall
                                Sweet and Maxwell, 2000) xxxvi + 226 pp.

Woodman, K.,   *Media Control in Ireland* (Carbondale: Southern Illinois
                                UP, 1985) viii + 248 pp.

Medical Law. See **Health, Safety and Medical Law.**

Medical Negligence. See **Tort.**

Meetings: Law of

Maloney, M. and   *The Law of Meetings* (Dublin: Round Hall Sweet and
   Spellman, J.,   Maxwell, 1999) xxx + 201 pp.

Military Law

Humphreys, G. and   *Military Law in Ireland* (Dublin: Round Hall Sweet and
   Craven, C.,   Maxwell, 1997) xl + 420 pp.

Non-Governmental Organisations

Cousins, M., *A Guide to Legal Structures for Voluntary and Community Organisations* (Dublin: Combat Poverty Agency, 1994) vi + 62 p

Nursing Law. See Health and Safety, and Medical Law.

Partnership Law

Twomey, M.J., *Partnership Law* (Dublin: Butterworths, 2000) xcii + 933 pp.

Pensions Law

Finucane, K. and
 Buggy, B., *Irish Pensions Law and Practice* (Dublin: Oak Tree Press, 1996) xlvi + 756 pp.

McLoughlin, A., *Pensions: Revenue Law and Practice* 3rd ed. (Dublin: ITI, 1999) xxii + 508 pp.

Personal Injuries. See Tort Law

Personal Property

Bell, A.P., *Modern Law of Personal Property in England and Ireland* (London: Butterworths, 1989) lxiv + 557 pp.

Planning Law. See Environmental and Planning Law

Policing

Report of the Steering Group on the Efficiency and Effectiveness of the Garda Síochána Pn 4630 (Dublin: Stationery Office, 1997) iv + 100 pp.

Allen, G., *The Garda Síochána. Policing Independent Ireland 1922-1982* (Dublin; Gill and Macmillan, 1999) xii + 306 pp. Bibliog.

Brady, C., *Guardians of the Peace* (Dublin: Gill and Macmillan, 1974)

Breathnach, *The Irish Police Force from the Earliest Times to the Present Day* (Dublin: Anvil Books, 1974).

Herlihy, J., *The Royal Irish Constabulary. A Complete Alphabetical List of Officers and Men 1816-1922* (Dublin: Four Courts Press, 1999) xxxi + 488 pp.

Herlihy, J.,	*The Royal Irish Constabulary. A Short History and Ge-nealogical Guide* (Dublin: Four Courts Press, 1997) 254 pp.
McNiffe, L.,	*A History of the Garda Síochána* (Dublin; Wolfhound Press, 1997) viii + 200 pp. Bibliog.
O'Sullivan, D.,	*The Irish Constabularies 1822 –1922. A Century of Po-licing in Ireland* (Dingle, Co Kerry: Brandon, 1999) 410 pp. Bibliog.
Palmer, S.H.,	*Police and Protest in England and Ireland 1780-1850* (Cambridge: Cambridge UP, 1984) xxiv + 824 pp. Bibliog.
Walsh, D.P.J.,	*The Irish Police: A Legal and Constitutional Perspective* (Dublin: Round Hall Sweet and Maxwell, 1998) lviii + 475 pp.

Practice and Procedure

Barron, J. and Ford, M.,	*Practice and Procedure in the Master's Court. Handbook for Barristers and Solicitors* (Dublin: Round Hall Press, 1994) xx + 106 pp.
Brady, J.C. & Kerr, A.,	*The Limitation of Actions* 2nd ed. (Dublin: ILSI, 1994) xxxv + 257 pp.
Buttimore, J.,	*Security for Costs* (Dublin: Blackhall Publishing, 1999) xxiii + 93 pp.
Byrne, P.,	*The EEC Convention on Jurisdiction and the Enforce-ment of Judgments* (Dublin: Round Hall Press, 1990) xvii + 246 pp.
Byrne, P.,	*The European Union and Lugano Conventions on Juris-diction and the Enforcement of Judgments* (Wicklow, Baikonour, 1994) xxxiv + 552 pp.
Cahill, E.,	*Discovery in Ireland* (Dublin; Round Hall Sweet and Maxwell, 1996) xxiv + 107 pp.
Collins, A.M. and O'Reilly, J.,	*Civil Proceedings and the State in Ireland: A Practition-er's Guide* (Dublin: Round Hall Press, 1990) li + 429 pp.
Crotty, J.F.,	*Practice and Procedure in the District Court* (Cork: Cork UP, c.1960) xxxv + 373 pp.
Daly, B.D.,	*The Irish Courts Guide. The Pocket Guide to the Irish Courts* (Dublin: Inns Quay Ltd., 1998) xii + 132 pp.
Deale, J.,	*Circuit Court Practice and Procedure* 2nd edn (Dublin: Fitzbaggot Publications, 1994) xxvi + 460 pp.

Finlay, T.A.,   *Advocacy: Has it a Future?* (Dublin: Round Hall Press, 1986) 20 pp.

Flynn, J.T. and Halpin, T., *Taxation of Costs* (Dublin: Blackhall Publishing, 1999) lxxv + 757 pp.

Frewen, G.,   *Handbook for Commissioners of Oaths* (Dublin, 1970)

Gill, S.,   *The Circuit Court: Draft Order Precedents* (1994) viii + 248 pp. Published by author.

Glanville, S.,   *The Enforcement of Judgments* (Dublin: Round Hall Sweet and Maxwell, 1999) xliv +201 pp.

Kay, P.,   *Methods of Executing Orders and Judgments in Europe* (Chicester: Wiley, 1995) xxxii + 334 pp. Contains chapter by P. Bradley on Ireland.

McDermott, P.A.,   *Res Judicata and Double Jeopardy* (Dublin: Butterworths, 1999) xxxix + 315 pp.

Montgomery, E.J.,   *Manual on the Practice of Notaries Public in Ireland* (Dublin, 1976) 29 pp.

O'Connor, E.R.,   *The Irish Notary* (Abingdon: Professional Books, 1987) xxvi + 263 pp.

Ó Floinn, B. (with   *Practice and Procedure in the Superior Courts* (Dublin: Gannon, S),   Butterworths, 1996) civ + 1381 pp.

Osborne,   *The Jurisdiction and Practice of the County Courts in Ireland in Equity and Probate Matters*, 2nd ed. revised by Babington (Dublin, 1910).

Peart (ed.),   *Peart's Practice Guide for Solicitor's and Law Clerks* (Dublin: Pearts Solicitors, 1983).

Peart, D.R.,   *Town Agency and General Practice* (Dublin: ILSI, 1968) 73 pp.

Wood, K.,   *The High Court: A User's Guide* (Dublin: Four Courts Press, 1998) xxvi + 180 pp.

Woods, J.V.,   *District Court Practice and Procedure in Civil, Licensing and Family Law Proceedings* (Limerick, 1997) lxxxiv + 1084 pp. Published by author.

Woods, J.V.,   *District Court Practice and Procedure in Criminal Cases* (Castletroy, Co. Limerick, 1994) lxxv + 790 pp. Published by author.

Woods, J.V.,   *District Court Practitioner: Remedies* (Limerick, 1987) xix + 514 pp. Published by author.

Woods, J.V.,   *District Court Practitioner: Forms* (Limerick, 1987) xix + 240 pp. Published by author.

Prisons

Report of the Committee of Inquiry into the Penal System Pl 3391 (Dublin: Stationery Office, 1985) iv + 360 pp. Bibliog.

Report of the Advisory Committee on Prison Deaths Pl 8389 (Dublin: Stationery Office, 1990) 111 pp.

Towards an Independent Prisons Agency: Report of Expert Group Pn 3694 (Dublin: Stationery Office, 1997) 110 pp.

Report of the Prison Service Operating Cost Review Group (Dublin: Stationery Office, 1997) 81 pp.

Byrne, R, Hogan, G. and McDermott, P., *Prisoners' Rights: A Study in Irish Prison Law* (Dublin: Co-Op Books, 1981) xvi + 145 pp.

Carey, T., *Mountjoy: The Study of a Prison* (Cork: The Collins Press, 2000) iii + 284 pp. Bibliog.

Council for Social Welfare, *The Prison System* (Dublin: Council for Social Welfare, 1983) 86 pp.

Heylin, G., *Evaluating Prisons, Prisoners and Others* (Dublin: The Policy Institute and Dept. of Justice, Equality and Law Reform, 2001) xii + 116 pp.

Irish Commission for Justice and Peace, *Towards an Irish Prison Inspectorate* (Dublin; Irish Commission for Justice and Peace, 1999) 31 pp.

McBride, S. (ed.), *Crime and Punishment* (Dublin: Ward River Press, 1982)

McDermott, P.A., *Prison Law* (Dublin: Round Hall Ltd, 2000) l + 591 pp.

O'Mahony, P., *Prison Policy in Ireland. Criminal Justice versus Social Justice* (Cork; Cork University Press, 2000) 128 pp. Bibliog.

O'Mahony, P. and Gilmore, T., *Drug Abusers in the Dublin Committal Prisons: A Survey* (Dublin: Stationery Office, 1983) 52 pp.

Prison Reform Group, *An Examination of the Irish Penal System* (Dublin, 1973).

Ruggiero, V. Ryan, M. and Sim, J., *Western European Penal Systems: A Critical Anatomy* (London: Sage, 1995) xi + 241 pp. Contains chapter by M. Tomlinson on imprisonment in Ireland.

Privacy Law. See **Constitutional Law**

Probate and Succession Law

Brady, J.C., *Succession Law in Ireland* 2nd ed. (Dublin: Butterworths, 1995) li + 364 pp.

ILSI,   *Administration of Estates: Simple Guidelines* (Dublin: ILSI, 1987)

Keating, A.,   *Probate Law and Practice* (Dublin: Round Hall Sweet and Maxwell, 1999) lxxii + 471 pp.

Keating, A.,   *Probate Law and Practice Casebook* (Dublin: Round Hall Sweet and Maxwell, 1999) lxxviii + 444 pp.

Keating, A., McGuire,   *The Succession Act 1965* with commentary by W.J.
   W.J. and Pearce, R.A.,   McGuire. 2nd ed. by R.A. Pearce (Dublin: ILSI, 1986) 152 pp. [1st ed. 1968]

Miller,   *Irish Probate Practice* revised ed. by Maxwell (Dublin: Falconer, 1907).

Mongey, E.G.,   *Probate Practice in a Nutshell* 2nd ed. (Dublin: 1998) 128 pp. Published by author.

Mongey, E.,   *The Weird and Wonderful World of Wills* (Dublin: Fort Publications, 1997) 140 pp.

O'Callaghan, J.M.,   *Taxation of Estates: The Law in Ireland* (Dublin: Butterworths (Ireland) 1993) 393 pp.

O'Connell, J.P.,   *Administration of Estates Act 1959* (Dublin: ILSI, 1959) 31 pp.

Spierin, B.E.,   *Wills: Irish Precedents and Drafting* (Dublin; 1999) xlii + 342 pp. Published by author.

Publishing, Law

Summers, D. (ed.),   *Where to Publish in Law in Great Britain and Ireland* (Cranbrook, Kent: Aestival Press, 1998) vi + 246 pp.

Refugee Law

Egan, S. and Costello, K.,   *Refugee Law. Comparative Study* (Dublin: Faculty of Law, UCD, 1999) 453 + 22 pp.

Restitution, Law of

Tettenborn, A.M.,   *Law of Restitution in England and Ireland* 2nd ed. (London: Cavendish, 1996) xxxv + 282 pp.

Road Traffic and Road Transport Law

Canny, J.K.,   *The Law of Road Transport and Haulage* (Dublin: Round Hall Sweet and Maxwell, 1999) xxvii + 179 pp.

De Blacam, M.,	*Drunken Driving and the Law* 2nd ed. (Dublin: Round Hall Press, 1995) xxiv + 637 pp.
O'Keeffe, G. and Hill, N.,	*Dangerous Driving Cases* (Dublin: Round Hall Sweet and Maxwell, 1999) xxxi + 618 pp.
Pierse, R.,	*Road Traffic Law* 2nd ed. (Dublin: Butterworths, 1995) xcii + 684 pp. [1st ed. *sub nom. Road Traffic Law in the Republic of Ireland,* 1989]
Wood, J.V.,	*Road Traffic Offences* 2nd ed. (Castletroy, Co. Limerick, 1990) xxx + 270 pp. Published by author. [1st ed. *sub nom. A Guide to Road Traffic Offences* published 1979]

Sentencing. See **Criminal Law.**

Social Welfare Law

Clark, R.,	*Annotated Guide to Social Welfare Law* (London: Sweet and Maxwell, 1995) xxi + 349 pp.
Council for Social Welfare,	*Emerging Trends in the Social Welfare System* (Dublin: Council for Social Welfare, 1992)
Cousins, M.,	*The Irish Social Welfare System: Law and Social Policy* (Dublin Round Hall Press, 1995) 175 pp. Bibliog.
Kaim-Caudle, P.R.	*Social Policy in the Irish Republic* (London: Routledge, 1967) 120 pp.
Kaim-Caudle, P.R.,	*Social Security in Ireland and Western Europe* (Dublin: ESRI, 1964) 48 pp.
O Cinneide, S.,	*A Law for the Poor: A Study of Home Assistance in Ireland* (Dublin: I.P.A., 1970)
Whyte, G.,	*Social Welfare Law in Ireland: A Guide to its Sources* (Dublin: Round Hall Press, 1987) 85 pp. A cumulative supplement covering the tears 1987 and 1988 was published by the author at Law School, TCD.
Whyte, G. (ed.),	*Sex Equality, Community Rights and Irish Social Welfare Law: The Impact of the Third Equality Directive* (Dublin: ICEL, 1988) ix + 213 pp.

Succession Law, see **Probate and Succession Law**

Tax Law (a selection of mainly recent texts)

Appleby, T. and Carr, F.,	*The Taxation of Capital Gains* 10th ed. (Dublin: ITI, 1998) xxviii + 902 pp.

Berg, T.F. and Moore, A.,   *Tax Law 99* 2 vols. (Dublin: Taxworld International, 1999).

Bohan, B.,   *Capital Acquisitions Tax* (Dublin: Butterworths, 1995) xvii + 858 pp.

Bohan, B. (ed.),   *Capital Acquisitions Tax Consolidation* (Dublin: LSI, 1996) xxv + 205 pp.

Burke, J and   *Case Law for the Tax Practitioner* 4th ed. (Dublin: ITI, O'Driscoll, T.,   2000) xxx + 646 pp.

Brennan, F. and   *Tax Acts: Commentary 2000-2001* (Dublin: Butterworths, Howley, S.,   2000) xli + 1090 pp.

Butterworths,   *Irish Tax Treaties* (Dublin: Butterworths, loose-leaf).

Cooney, T., McLaughlin,   *Taxation Summary: Republic of Ireland 1999/2000* (Dub- J. and Marytn, J.   lin: Institute of Taxation in Ireland, 1999) xxiv + 360.

Corrigan, K.,   *Revenue Law* 2 vols. (Dublin: Round Hall Sweet and Maxwell, 2000) xcii + 1266 pp; lviii + 924 pp.

Donegan, D. and Friel, R., *Irish Stamp Duty Law* (Dublin: Butterworths, 1998) xi + 526 pp.

Feeney, M.,   *The Taxation of Companies 1999-2000* (Dublin: Butterworths, 1999) xix + 2129 pp.

Fitzpatrick, T. (ed.),   *The Law on Capital Acquisitions Tax* (Dublin: ITI, 1999) 753 pp.

Frecknell, A. (ed.),   *Tax Acts 2000-2001* (Dublin: Butterworths, 2000) viii + 2565.

Haccius, C.,   *An Introduction to the Irish Death Duties* (Dublin: ITI, 1969) 153 pp plus indexes and tables.

Institute of Taxation,   *Case Law for the Tax Practitioner*, 2nd ed. edited by F. Carr (Dublin: ITI, 1998) x + 551 pp. (Previous ed. 1997).

O'Hara, J. et al.,   *Tax Guide 2000-2001* (Butterworths, 2000) xxxvii + 1483 pp.

Plunkett, E.A.,   *The Stamp Duty Legislation 1890-1962* (Dublin: ILSI,

Ward, J.,   *Judge Irish Income Tax Law 1999-2000* (Dublin: Butterworths, 2000) xi + 2320.

Telecommunications Law

Hall, E.,   *The Electronic Age: Telecommunication in Ireland* (Dublin: Oak Tree Press, 1993) xxii + 569 pp. Bibliog.

Tort Law

Daly, B. (ed.),   *Professional Negligence Law Reports: Previously Unre-*
                           ported Judgments 1968-1993 (Dublin: Brehon Publish-
                           ing, 1995) viii + 564 pp.

Dept. of Enterprise   *Report on the Economic Evaluation of Insurance Costs*
  & Employment,   *in Ireland* (Deloitte Touche Report) (Dublin: Stationery
                           Office, 1996) 91 + 10 pp.

Dept. of Enterprise   *First Report of Special Working Group on Personal Inju-*
  & Employment,   *ries Tribunal* (Dublin: Dept of Enterprise and Employ-
                           ment, 1997) 29 + 5 pp.

Healy, J.,   *Medical Negligence: Common Law Perspectives* (Lon-
                           don: Sweet and Maxwell, 1999) xviii + 302 pp. Bibliog.

Kerr, A.,   *The Civil Liability Acts 1961 and 1964* (Dublin: Round
                           Hall Press, 1993) 150 pp. (The Round Hall Press Irish
                           Statutes Annotated Series).

Kerr, A.,   *The Civil Liability Acts* (Dublin: Round Hall Sweet and
                           Maxwell, 1999) xiv + 106 pp. (The Round Hall Anno-
                           tated Legislation Series).

McMahon, B.M.E. and   *Irish Law of Torts* 3rd ed. (Dublin: Butterworths (Ireland)
  Binchy, W.,   Ltd, 2000) ccxxii + 1295 pp. [1st ed. 1981]

McMahon, B.M.E.   *A Casebook on the Irish Law of Torts* 2nd ed. (Dublin:
  Binchy, W.,   Butterworths (Ireland), 1992) xxvii + 761 pp.[1st ed. 1983)

McMahon, B.M.E.,   *Judge or Jury: The Jury Trial for Personal Injury Cases*
                           in Ireland (Cork: Cork UP, 1985)

Neville, R.M.   *Civil Liability Act 1961* (Dublin: ILSI, 1963) 27 pp.

Pierse, R.,   *Quantum of Damages for Personal Injuries 1999* (Dub-
                           lin: Round Hall Sweet and Maxwell, 1999) xlvii + 368
                           pp. [1st ed. 1997].

Quill, E.,   *Torts in Ireland* (Dublin: Gill and Macmillan, 1999) lii +
                           547 pp.

Schutte, J.,   *Personal Injuries and the Law* 5th ed. (Dublin, 1990)

Schutte, J.   *Accidents at Work* (Dublin, 1991)

Waldron, K.,   *Guidelines on Tort* (Dublin, 1971), published by author.

White, J.P.M.,   *Irish Law of Damages for Personal Injury and Death*
                           (Dublin: Butterworths (Ireland) Ltd, 1989) 2 vols., xlv +
                           xi + 771 pp.

White, J.P.M.,   *Civil Liability for Industrial Accidents* (Dublin: Oak Tree
                           Press, 1994) 2 vols., xcvi + 1538; xxxii + 1684 pp.

White, J.P.M.,   *Medical Negligence Actions* (Dublin: Oak Tree Press, 1996) xxxiv + 461 pp.

Travellers and the Law. See also Equality and Discrimination Law

Binchy, W. (ed.),   *Travellers, Society and the Law* Conference Proceedings (Dublin: TCD Law School, 1997) 117 pp.

D.T.E.D.G.   *Anti-Racist Law and the Travellers* (Dublin: Dublin Travellers Education and Development Group, ICCL and Irish Traveller Movement, 1993) 73 pp.

Trees and the Law

FitzPatrick, H.,   *Trees and the Law* (Dublin: ILSI, 1985).

Trials

Comyn, J.,   *Irish at Law* (London: Secker and Warburg, 1981; Sphere Books, 1983)

Crow, D.,   *Theresa: The Story of the Yelverton Case* (London: Rupert Hart Davis, 1966) 296 pp.

Deale, K.E.L.,   *Memorable Irish Trials* (London: Constable & Co., 1960) x + 190 pp.

Deale, K.E.L.,   *Beyond Any Reasonable Doubt? A Book of Irish Murder Trials* (Dublin: Gill and Macmillan, 1990) 225 pp. (Originally published in 1971).

McAree, N.,   *Murderous Justice: A Study in depth of the Infamous Connemara Murders* (limerick: Wildshaw Books, 1990) 232 pp.

McDonnell Bodkin, J.,   *Famous Irish Trials* reprint (Dublin: Ashfield Press, 1997).

Reddy, T.,   *Murder Will Out: A Book of Irish Murder Cases* (Dublin: Gill and Macmillan, 1990) 190 pp.

MacIntyre, T.,   *Through the Bridewell Gate: A Diary of the Dublin Arms Trial* (London: Faber and Faber, 1971) 219 pp.

Waldron, J.,   *Mammtrasna: The Murders and the Mystery* (Dublin: Burke Publications, 1992) 335 pp.

APPENDIX 5

List of Publications of the Law Reform Commission

In the following list, 'WP' stands for Working Paper, 'R' for Report and 'C' for Consultation Paper. For the correct citation of the Commission's documents, *see Para.4.6.1 above.*

First Program for Examination of Certain Branches of Law with a View to their Reform (December 1976) (Prl.5984)

WP 1-1977, *The Law Relating to the Liability of Builders, Vendors and Lessors for the Quality and Fitness of Premises*

WP 2-1977, *The Law Relating to the Age of Majority, the Age of Marriage and some Connected Subjects*

WP 3-1977, *Civil Liability for Animals*

WP 4-1978, *The Law Relating to Breach of Promise of Marriage*

WP 5-1978, *The Law Relating to Criminal Conversation and the Enticement and Harbouring of a Spouse*

WP 6-1979, *The Law Relating to Seduction and the Enticement and Harbouring of a Child*

WP7-1979, *The Law Relating to Loss of Consortium and Loss of Services of a Child*

WP 8-1979, *Judicial Review of Administrative Action: The Problem of Remedies*

WP 9-1980, *The Rule Against Hearsay*

R 1-1981, *First Report on Family Law—Criminal Conversation, Enticement and Harbouring of a Spouse or Child, Loss of Consortium, Personal Injury, to a Child, Seduction of a Child, Matrimonial Property, and Breach of Promise to Marry.*

WP 10-1981, *Domicile and Habitual Residence as Connecting Factors in the Conflict of Laws*

R 2-1982, *Report on Civil Liability for Anima/s*

R 3-1982, *Report on Defective Premises*

R 4-1982, *Report on Illegitimacy*

R 5-1983, *Report on the Age of Majority, the Age of Marriage and some connected subjects*

R 6-1983, *Report on Restitution of Conjugal Rights, Jactitation of Marriage and Related Matters*

R 7-1983, *Report on Domicile and Habitual Residence as Connecting Factors in the Conflict of Laws*

R 8-1983, *Report on Divorce a Mensa et Thoro and Related Matters*

R 9-1984, *Report on Nullity of Marriage*

WP 11-1984, *Recognition of Foreign Divorces and Legal Separations*

R 10-1985, *Report on Recognition of Foreign Divorces and Legal Separations*

R 11-1985, *Report on Vagrancy and Related Offences*

R 12-1985, *Report on the Hague Convention on the Civil Aspects of International Child Abduction and Some Related Matters*

R 13-1985, *Report on the Competence and Compellability of Spouses as Witnesses*

R 14- 1985, *Report on Offences under the Dublin Police Acts and Related Offences*

R 15-1985, *Report on Minors' Contracts*

R 16-1985, *Report on the Hague Convention on the Taking of Evidence Abroad in Civil or Commercial Matters*

R 17-1985, *Report on the Liability in Tort of Minors and the Liability of Parents for Damage Caused by Minors*

R 18-1985, *Report on the Liability in Tort of Mentally Disabled Persons*

R 19-1985, *Report on Private International Law Aspects of Capacity to Marry and Choice of Law in Proceedings f or Nullity of Marriage*

R 20-1985, *Report on Jurisdiction for Nullity of Marriage, Recognition of Foreign Nullity Decrees, and the Hague Convention on the Celebration and Recognition of the Validity of Marriages*

R 21-1985, *Report on the Statute of Limitations: Claims in respect of Latent Personal Injuries*

CI-1987, *Consultation Paper on Rape*

R 22-1987, *Report on the Service of Documents Abroad re Civil Proceedings—the Hague Convention.*

R 23-1987, *Report on Receiving Stolen Property*

R 24-1988, *Report on Rape and All led Offences*

R 25-1988, *Report on the Rule Against Hearsay in Civil Cases*

R 26-1988, *Report on Malicious Damage*

R 27-1988, *Report on Debt Collection: (I) The Law Relating to Sheriffs*

R 28-1989, *Report on Debt Collection: (2) Retention of Title*

R 29-1989, *Report on the Recognition of Foreign Adoption Decrees*

R 3-1989, *Report on Land Law and Conveyancing Law; (I) General Proposals*

C 2-1989, *Consultation Paper on Child Sexual Abuse*

R 31-1989, *Report on Land Law and Conveyancing: (2) Enduring Powers of Attorney*

R 32-1990, *Report on Child Sexual Abuse*

R 33-1990, *Report on Sexual Offences Against the Mentally Handicapped*

R 34-1990, *Report on Oaths and Affirmations*

R 35-1990, *Report on Confiscation of the Proceeds of Crime*

C 3-1991, *Consultation Paper on the Civil Law of Defamation*

R 36-1991, *Report of the Hague Convention on Succession to the Estates of Deceased* Persons

C 4-1991, *Consultation Paper on Contempt of Court*

C 5-1991, *Consultation Paper on the Crime of Libel*

R 37-1991, *Report on the Indexation of Fines*

R 38-1991, *Report on the Civil Law of Defamation*

R 39-1991, *Report on Land Law and Conveyancing Law: (3) The Passing of Risk fromVendor to Purchaser*

R 40-1991, *Report on Land Law and Conveyancing Law: (4) Service of Completion Notices*

R 41-1991, *Report on the Crime of Libel*

R 42-1992, *Report on the United Nations (Vienna) Convention on Contracts for the International Sale of Goods 1980*

R 43-1992, *Report on the Law Relating to Dishonesty*

R 44-1992, *Report on Land Law and Conveyancing Law: (5) Further General Proposals*

C 6-1993, *Consultation Paper on Sentencing*

C-1993, *Consultation Paper on Occupiers' Liability*

C-1994, *Consultation Paper on Family Courts*

R 45-1994, *Report on Non-Fatal Offences against the Person*

R 46-1994, *Report on Occupiers' Liability*

R 47-1994, *Report on Contempt of Court*

R 48-1995, *Report on the Hague Convention Abolishing the Requirements of Legalisation for Official Documents*

R 49-1995, *Report on the Interests of Vendor and Purchaser in Land during the Period between Contract and Completion*

C-1995, *Consultation Paper on Intoxication as a Defence to a Criminal Offence*

C-1995, *Consultation Paper on Privacy: Surveillance and Interception of Communications*

R 50-1995, *An Examination of the Law of Bail*

R 51-1995, *Report on Intoxication*

R 52-1996, *Report on Family Courts*

R 53-1996, *Report on Sentencing*

R 54- 1996, *Report on Personal Injuries.*

C-1997, *Consultation Paper on the Implementation of the Hague Convention on Protection of Children and Co-Operation in Respect of Inter Country Adoption.*

C-1998, *Consultation Paper on Aggravated, Exemplary and Restitutionary Damages.*

C-1998, *Consultation Paper on the Statutes of Limitation: Claims in Contract and Tort in respect of Latent Damage (other than Personal Injury).*

C 55- 1997, *Report on the Unidroit Convention on Stolen orIllegally Exported Cultural Objects*

C 56-1998, *Report on Land Law and Conveyancing Law; (6) Further General Proposals including the Execution of Deeds*

C 57-1998, *Report on Privacy: Surveillance and the Interception of Communications*

C 58 –1998, *Report on Hague Convention on Protection of Children and Co-Operation in Respect of Inter County Adoption*

C-1999, *Consultation Paper on Statutory Drafting and Interpretation: Plain Language and the Law*

C-1999, *Consultation Paper on Section 2 of the Civil Liability (Amendment) Act, 1964: The Deductability of Collateral Benefits from Awards of Damages*

C-2000, *Consultation Paper on the law of Limitations of Actions arising from non-sexual abuse of Children*

R 59 –2000, *Report on Gazumping*

R 60 – 2000, *Report on Aggravated, Exemplary and Restitutionary Damages*

R 61 –2000, *Report on Statutory Drafting and Interpretation: Plain Language and the Law*

R 62 – 2000, *Report on the Rules against Perpetuities and Cognate Rules.*

R 63-2000, *Report on the Variation of Trusts*

C-2001, *Consultation Paper on Homicide: The Mental Element*
R 64-2001, *Report on Statutes of Limitation: Claims in Contract and Tort in Respect
    of Latent Damage (other than Personal Injury)*

In addition, the Commission has published Annual Reports since 1977.

APENDIX 6

Interim Reports of the Committee on Court Practice and Procedure

1. *The Preliminary Examination of Indictable Offences Pr. 7164*

2. *Jury Service Pr. 8328 (c. 1965)*

3. *Jury Trial in Civil Actions Pr. 8577 (1965)*

4. *Jury Challenges (published in same volume as No. 3)*

5. *Increase of Jurisdiction of the District Court and the Circuit Court Pr. 8936 (c. 1966)*

6. *The Criminal Jurisdiction of the High Court Pr.9168 (1966)*

7. *Appeals from Conviction on Indictment Pr. 9196 (1966)*

8. *(i) Service of Documents by Post (ii) Fees of Professional Witnesses Prl. 218 (1968)*

9. *Proof of Previous Convictions Prl. 819 (1969)*

10. *Interest Rate on Judgment Debts Prl . 1118(1969)*

11. *The Jurisdiction and Practice of the Supreme Court Prl. 1835 (1970)*

12. *Courts Organization Prl. 2000 (1970)*

13. *The Solicitor's Right of Audience Prl. 2347 (1971)*

14. *Liability of Barristers and Solicitors for Professional Negligence Prl. 2348 (1971)*

15. *On the Spot Fines Prl. 2349 (1971)*

16. *The Jurisdiction of the Master of the High Court Prl. 2350 (1972)*

17. *Court Fees Prl. 2699 (1972)*

18. *Execution of Money Judgments, Orders and Decrees Prl. 1118 (1969)*

19. *Desertion and Maintenance Prl. 3666 (1974)*

20. *Increase of Jurisdiction of the District and Circuit Court Prl. 7459(1978)*

21. *Section 25(3) of the Criminal Justice Act 1984 (Majority Verdicts)*

22. *Prosecution Appeals*

23. *The Provision of a Procedure to enable representatives of the media to be heard by the court, where an application is being made in civil proceedings to have a case heard otherwise than in public.*

24. *Preliminary Examination of Indictable Offences*

25. *The Provision of Documentation to Juries in Serious Fraud Trials.*

(Reports 21 to 25 inclusive were published together in 1997).

The European Convention on Human Rights: A Practitioner's Guide to Sources

The European Convention on Human Rights will become incorporated into Irish law in the near future, although the manner of incorporation has yet to be fully specified. In any event, litigants will be able to invoke the Convention before the Irish courts and, in all probability, will be allowed to challenge existing legislation or state practice on the ground of incompatibility with the Convention. Lawyers practising in the fields of criminal law and constitutional law, in particular, must become familiar with the text of the Convention and the jurisprudence of the European Court of Human Rights and, indeed, of the former Commission on Human Rights. The workings of the Court and Commission have already been described in Chapter 10. It is anticipated that once the Convention is incorporated into Irish law, the articles most frequently invoked will be those dealing with personal liberty and security (Article 5), fair trial (Article 6), privacy (Article 8) and freedom of expression (Article 10).

Text of Convention

This may be found on the Internet at www.echr.coe.int/. A copy of the Convention may also be had by writing to the Council of Europe, but as it is important to have the various Protocols as well as the basic Convention itself, it is worth investing in the Council's own publication, *Human Rights Today. European Legal Texts,* which costs about 18 Euros and can be had from Council of Europe Publishing, F-67075 Strasbourg Cedex, France. The text is also provided on an article by article basis at the beginning of each chapter in the book by Harris, O'Boyle and Warbrick mentioned below under "Textbooks and Guides".

Textbooks and Guides

As with all legal research, it is best to begin with a good textbook when researching any aspect of the European Convention, and there are a few books that can be recommended without hesitation. Harris, O'Boyle and Warbrick, *Law of the European Convention on Human Rights* is a most respected and scholarly analysis of the Convention and its case law. The second edition is due for publication by Butterworths in October 2001. A companion volume, *Cases and Materials on the European Convention on Human Rights,* by Harris and O'Boyle was published by Butterworths in March 2001. Another major work, and one perhaps more designed for practitioners, is Clayton, Tomlinson and others, *The Law of Human Rights.* This is a large volume running to 1,800 pages and it costs £145. It is published by Oxford University Press, having been reissued in 2000. There will be annual updating supplements, the first of which is due to appear in September 2001. For those specializing in criminal law, a single chapter of this book has been published as a separate volume. This is entitled *Fair Trial Rights* and costs less than £30. It too is published by Oxford University Press. The great merit of Clayton and Tomlinson is that it covers not only European human rights law but also relevant law from Britain, Commonwealth countries and elsewhere. All prices mentioned here are in sterling.

Another book well worth having is *Blackstone's Human Rights Digest* by Starmer, Klug and Byrne. It was published by Blackstone Press in 2001. It is in digest form and includes key extracts (with analysis) of the judgments of the European Court of Human Rights, decisions of the Commission on Human Rights, and cases from the U.K. and Commonwealth jurisdictions. It is accompanied by a CD-ROM which contains the full texts of all the judgments of the European Court as well as key decisions of the Commission up to September 2000. It costs Stg£59.00.

Finally, there is another indispensable work already mentioned in Chapter 10, namely Clements, Mole and Simmons, *European Human Rights: Taking a Case under the Convention* 2nd edn (London: Sweet and Maxwell, 1999). This is primarily a practitioner's guide to preparing and conducting litigation before the European Court, but it is also a mine of information on the Convention itself, and would therefore be very useful for anyone raising Convention issues before domestic courts.

Law reports

Anyone seriously involved in human rights litigation will probably find it worth subscribing to the *European Human Rights Reports*, published by Sweet and Maxwell. These have the usual added value of formal law reports with headnotes and so forth, which means that they are particularly useful for practice and research. Otherwise, one can make do with the Internet (and perhaps the CD-ROM attached to *Blackstone's Human Rights Digest* mentioned above). The full texts of all the judgments of the European Court of Human Rights are available at www.echr.coe.int/hudoc/ . There is also an electronic digest where one may search for judgments by subject matter. This is at: www.beagle.org.uk/ which is described in more detail at 10.48 above. The many decisions made by the superior courts in the various jurisdictions of the U.K. since the European Convention on Human Rights was incorporated into their law will also be of considerable interest to Irish lawyers once the Convention is incorporated here. All of these decisions are, of course, recent which means that most, if not all, of them are on the Internet (and accessible through www.bailii.org/). Remember that the Scottish courts (accessible through the same web site) have also made interesting decisions in respect of the Convention, which was incorporated earlier in Scotland than in England and Wales. Most decisions of any significance by the English and Scottish courts touching on the Convention will, of course, be reported in the *Law Reports,* the *All England Law Reports* and other general series. Significant human rights cases of both the European and U.K. courts are often reported, in abbreviated form, in *The Times* (London) and are to be found on the Internet at www.thetimes.co.uk/. Click on "British news" for the recent reports.

Comments on European cases

There are many journals devoted to human rights law, although few of them will be found outside academic libraries. A particularly useful source, however, is the *Criminal Law Review*, published monthly by Sweet and Maxwell. It now regularly includes analyses of European Court decisions in relation to criminal law and criminal procedure, mainly under Articles 5 and 6 of the Convention. Most of the commentary is by Professor Andrew Ashworth, a leading expert in the area.

A Selection of Useful Web Sites

What follows is a short list of useful web sites for legal research. A few points should be borne in mind when using it. There is an enormous amount of overlap on the Internet. For example, the web sites of many university law schools and other legal institutions collect together a wide range of more particular web pages. The *Bailii* web site, for example, brings together most of the primary sources of Irish and British law. The University of Cambridge web site does much the same for British, European and international law, and for law reform agencies throughout the English-speaking world. Secondly, as explained in Chapter 2, it is seldom necessary to have the exact addresses (URLs) of these sites. There are now many excellent search engines such as Google and Yahoo which can easily be used to search for relevant documents by subject matter. For example, if having difficulty finding any of the Cambridge web sites mentioned below, just find the Faculty of Law, University of Cambridge, using a search engine. Once a good site is found, it can be bookmarked (see 2.11 above) and thereby stored for later use. The present list has deliberately been kept short, and confined to those web sites that will grant ready access to most of the material that lawyers or law students are likely to need on a regular basis.

American law	www.findlaw.com/ Click on "Laws: Cases and Codes" for federal and state constitutions, statutes and cases.
Australian law	www.austlii.uts.edu.au has an enormous range of Australian materials including judgements of the Australian High Court since 1947. Click on "Commonwealth" for High Court judgments. Another URL is: www.austlii.edu.au/ .If having difficulty with these URLs, look for the Australian Legal Research Institute using a search engine such as Google (www.google.com)
Bailii	www.bailii.org/ The best site for primary Irish and British legal materials.
British law	Most of the primary sources will be found in *Bailii* (above) and at www.venables.co.uk or www.infolaw.co.uk/ More specific sites are listed in Chapter 6 above. For direct access to law reports, the best site is the University of Cambridge web page at www.cam.ac.uk/urllists/law_rept.htm/ See also *Daily Law News* below.
Booksellers	www.amazon.co.uk/

www.barnesandnoble.com/

www.blackwell.co.uk

Canadian law

www.gahtan.com/cdnlaw/ Click on "Cases" for judgments of Supreme Court and many other courts.

Competition law (Irish)

www.tca.ie/ . Can also be accessed through *Bailii* (above)

Current Affairs

www.aldaily.ie/ (*Arts and Letters Daily* with links to many leading newspapers, journals and magazines).

Daily Law Notes **(U.K.)**

www.lawreports.co.uk/infodln.htm/

European Union law

www.europa.int/ Click on "The European Union on line" for the English language version. www.europa.int/eur-lex/en/

Employment law (Irish)

www.equality.ie/ (the Equality Authority).

www.odei.ie (Office of Director of Equality Investigations).

www.lrc.ie/ (Labour Relations Commission)

www.entemp.ie/erir/empl_appeal.htm/ (EAT).

Health and Safety Authority

www.hsa.ie/

Human rights law (European)

www.echr.coe.int/

www.beagle.org.uk/

Human Rights (United Nations)

www.un.org/Depts/dhl/resguide/spechr.htm

Information Commissioner (Ir.)

www.irlgov.ie/oic

Irish government

www.irlgov.ie/

Irish cases

Use *Bailii* (above).

Irish law

www.bailii.org/ has virtually all of the primary sources currently available on the Internet, including decisions of the Competition Authority and of the Information Commissioner. For other material, including recent statutes, see "Oireachtas" below.

Irish statutes

See *Bailii* (above) and Oireachtas (below).

Irish Times

www.ireland.com/

Law (general)

www.venables.co.uk

www.infolaw.co.uk

www.ucc.ie/ucc/depts/law/irishlaw/ All of these sites are excellent gateways to a wide range of Irish, British and international legal resources.

Law libraries (online catalogues) http://udtal.ucd.ie/ (University College Dublin)

www.tcd.ie/library/ (Trinity College, Dublin)

http://library.ox.ac.uk/ (Oxford; click on "Connect to OLIS)

www.lib.cam.ac.uk/ (Cambridge)

www.yale.edu/law/library/morris/ (Yale)

http://hollisnet.harvard.edu/ (Harvard)

http://catalog.loc.gov/ (Library of Congress)

www.lib.cam.ac.uk/Catalogues/ (Hosted by University of Cambridge, providing access to leading library catalogues throughout the world).

Law Reform Commissions <www.irlgov.ie/lawreform/index.htm> (Irish Law Reform Commission). This site also has links to other commissions. Better still is the Cambridge site at www.law.cam.ac.uk/urllists/reform.htm

Law reports www.law.cam.ac.uk/urllists/law_rept.htm/ This site, hosted by the University of Cambridge Faculty of Law is one of the best means of access to Irish, British, Commonwealth, American and international cases and law reports.

Northern Ireland law Use *Bailii* (above) and see Chapter 5 (above).

Oireachtas www.irlgov.ie/ Click on "Houses of the Oireachtas" and scroll down for parliamentary debates since 1919 and bills and statutes since 1997. For statutes since 1922 to 1998, see *Bailii* above.

Social science and law www.sosig.ac.uk/

Scottish law Use *Bailii* (above).

Search engines www.waikato.ac.nz/lawlib/search.html/ provides a good list of the leading search engines and direct access to them.

Solicitors' Firms Many Irish firms of solicitors now have web sites, and some of the larger Dublin firms have interesting material on various aspects of law, especially commercial law and related areas. The various sites are collected together by Delia Venables at www.venables.co.uk/

Index